Advance Praise for *Web of Deceit*

"How the U.S. came to invade Iraq and how that invasion became the great debacle of U.S. foreign policy has been told again and again. Lando tells a different story—how the U.S. helped make Saddam the tyrant he was and how the U.S. helped him win the war he started against Iran and how the U.S. helped keep him in power. You will be convinced that the U.S. was complicit in Saddam's crimes."

—Marvin Zonis, professor, Graduate School of Business,
The University of Chicago; author of *Majestic Failure:
The Fall of the Shah*

"In unraveling the threads of the Iraq fiasco, going back to the fall of the Ottomans, Barry Lando creates a tapestry that makes sense of today's events. *Web of Deceit* clarifies the precedents—nay, the warnings— that were available to the U.S. government in 2003, and that were consistently ignored in the stumble into war."

—Milton Viorst, author of *Storm from the East:
The Conflict between the Arab World
and the Christian West*

"A superb review of decades of institutionalized dishonesty, ignorance, and arrogance paid for by innocent people in Iraq and the United States."

—H.C. von Sponeck, U.N. Humanitarian Coordinator
for Iraq, 1998–2000

WEB OF DECEIT

The History of Western Complicity in Iraq,
from Churchill to Kennedy to
George W. Bush

BARRY M. LANDO

Other Press • New York

Copyright © 2007 Barry M. Lando

Production Editor: Robert D. Hack

Text design: Jeremy Diamond

This book was set in 11 pt. Janson Text by Alpha Graphics of Pittsfield, NH.

10 9 8 7 6 5 4 3

Library of Congress Cataloging-in-Publication Data

Lando, Barry.
  Web of deceit : the history of Western complicity in Iraq, from Churchill to Kennedy to George W. Bush / Barry M. Lando.
    p. cm.
  Includes bibliographical references and index.
  ISBN-13: 978-1-59051-238-8
  ISBN-10: 1-59051-238-3
    1. Iraq–Foreign relations. 2. Great Britain–Foreign relations–Iraq. 3. Iraq–Foreign relations–Great Britain. 4. United States–Foreign relations–Iraq. 5. Iraq–Foreign relations–United States. I. Title.
  DS70.95.L36 2007
  327.5670182'1–dc22

                                                        2006012511

For my mother,
Edith Mitchell Lando (1917–2003),
who introduced me to the world of journalism

CONTENTS

CHRONOLOGY OF EVENTS

1914   British troops occupy Basra after Turkey declares an alliance with Germany.

1916   British and French officials secretly agree that southern Mesopotamia, including Baghdad, will be handed to Great Britain.

1917   British forces occupy Baghdad.

1918   British troops occupy Mosul.

1920   *April*—San Remo conference grants British a mandate for governing Iraq.

        June–October—Widespread Iraqi revolt quelled by British troops and RAF.

1921   British officials in Cairo appoint Prince Faisal bin Hussain al-Hashemi of what is now Saudi Arabia to be king of Iraq.

1922   British High Commissioner creates Kuwait on the border of southern Iraq.

1925   *March*—The government of Iraq agrees to the Turkish Petroleum Company oil concession.

        December—At Britain's request, the League of Nations incorporates the Kurdish territory of Mosul into Iraq.

1930   A new Anglo-Iraq Treaty promises independence to Iraq.

1932   Iraq is granted formal autonomy from Britain. Britain continues to operate military bases in the country.

1933   King Faisal dies in September and is succeeded by his erratic son Ghazi.

1935   An oil pipeline from Kirkuk to the Mediterranean is opened.

1939   King Ghazi dies in April, succeeded by his infant son Faisal II. Pro-British Nuri al Said dominates the ruling regency.

1941   In an April coup, a group of nationalist Iraqi officers known as the Golden Square call for Arab independence. British troops retake Baghdad in May, execute coup leaders, and restore the regency.

1948   *January*—A new Anglo-Iraqi treaty that would grant greater influence to Britain is withdrawn after mounting protests in Baghdad.

   May—Iraq sends an expeditionary force to Palestine to battle the new State of Israel. The force withdraws again in February 1949, infuriating Arab nationalists.

1951   Mohammed Mossadegh takes power in Iran and declares the country will control its own oil.

1952   The Iraq Petroleum Company (IPC) and Iraq agree in February to split profits 50-50. Gamal Abdel Nasser and the "Free Officers" oust the monarchy in Egypt.

1953   CIA-supported plot overthrows Mossadegh and places Shah in power in Iran.

1954   *May*—King Faisal II takes the throne, ending the regency.

   October—Gamal Abdel Nasser takes power in Egypt.

1955   Iraq signs the Baghdad Pact, an alliance of Western powers against the Soviet Union and Nasser's Egypt.

1956   During the Suez crisis, Nasser issues a call for Arab independence. Pro-Nasser riots break out in major Iraqi centers.

1958 *February*—The United Arab Republic (UAR) is formed by Egypt and Syria, which pressure Iraq to join as well.

July—Free Officers' military coup executes King Faisal II. Abd al-assem Qasim, an increasingly vocal advocate of Arab nationalism, heads the new government.

1959 *October*—Qasim is wounded by would-be assassins with links to the CIA; Saddam Hussein, one of the conspirators, flees to Cairo.

December—Iraq withdraws from the Baghdad Pact.

1961 *June*—Qasim demands that newly independent Kuwait be incorporated into Iraq, but backs down when Britain sends troops.

December—Qasim nationalizes huge areas of IPC's petroleum concessions that have not been developed.

1963 *February*—Qasim is overthrown in a coup by the military and Baath party. Saddam Hussein participates in the torture and murder of supposed Communists and leftists, many of whose names are provided by the CIA.

October–November—After weeks of turbulence, General Abdel Salam Aref expels the Baathists from the ruling alliance.

1964 President Abdel Salam Aref enacts land reform and nationalizes insurance companies, banks, and large industrial firms.

1966 President Abdel Salam Aref dies in a helicopter crash in April and is succeeded by his brother, General Abdel Rahman Aref.

1967 To show support for the Arab fight against Israel, Iraq sends a small force to Jordan.

1968 A July coup by Arab nationalists and Baath military officers, with some aid from the CIA, installs Hasan al-Bakr as President and Chairman of the Revolutionary Command Council (RCC). President al-Bakr and Saddam Hussein eject non-Baathists from the government.

1969   *June*—Iraq and the Soviets sign an accord for Soviet assistance in developing Iraq's oil fields.

      November—Saddam Hussein becomes vice-chairman of the Revolutionary Command Council.

1971   Iran and Iraq break diplomatic relations in their dispute over control of the Shatt-al Arab waterway.

1972   *April*—Iraq and the Soviet Union sign a fifteen-year agreement of "Friendship and Co-operation."

      June—U.S. President Nixon and Henry Kissinger agree with the Shah of Iran and Israel to back Iraqi Kurds in revolt against Baghdad. Iraq nationalizes the IPC. The country is placed on the State Department's list of nations supporting terrorism.

1975   After Saddam Hussein and the Shah of Iran agree to joint control over the Shatt-al Arab in March, outside aid to the Kurds is halted, leaving thousands of Kurds subject to reprisals from Baghdad.

1979   *January–February*—Following the overthrow of the Shah, Ayatollah Khomeini takes power in Iran. He and Iraqi Shiite leaders launch ever more virulent attacks on Iraq's Baath government.

      July—President al-Bakr is forced out by Saddam Hussein, who initiates a bloody purge.

      November—Fifty-four American diplomats in Tehran are taken hostage. Tensions soar between the U.S. and Iran, as well as between Iran and Iraq. Forty thousand Iraqi Shiites are expelled to Iran.

1980   *January*—President Carter proclaims what becomes known as the "Carter Doctrine": The U.S. will intervene militarily to prevent any other power from gaining control of the strategically vital Gulf.

      September—Iraq invades Iran, launching the Iran-Iraq war.

1982   Massive weapons shipments from the Soviets and the West arm both Khomeini and Saddam. Iraq is removed from the U.S.'s terrorist nation list to facilitate aid and arms sales and the sharing of intelligence.

1983   President Reagan sends Donald Rumsfeld as a special envoy to Saddam to improve relations with Iraq.

1984   The U.S restores full diplomatic relations with Iraq. President Reagan authorizes increased support of Baghdad, though the U.S. is aware that Saddam is still using chemical weapons.

1985   The U.S. and Israel begin supplying American-made arms to Iran in what will become known as the Iran-Contra scandal when it is revealed in September 1986.

1986   After Iran captures the Al Faw peninsula, the U.S. again increases aid to Iraq.

1987   The U.S. attacks Iranian oil platforms.

1988   *February*—The al-Anfal campaign in Kurdistan begins.

March—Iraq launches a chemical attack on the Kurdish town of Halabja.

May—Despite efforts by Pentagon experts and others to restrict trade to Iraq, the U.S. Commerce Department opens the door to wider sales of sophisticated dual-use equipment to Baghdad. The Atlanta Branch of Italy's Banco Nazionale del Lavoro makes considerable loans to Iraq.

August—Iraq and Iran sign a cease-fire, ending their eight-year war. Despite this, Al-Anfal continues.

September—U.S. officials admit that Iraq is using chemical weapons against the Kurds. The Reagan administration continues to resist sanctions against Iraq.

1989   U.S. War Plan 1002, originally conceived to counter a Soviet threat, is modified by Norman Schwartzkopf to target Iraq as the main potential threat in the region.

October—U.S. President Bush signs a secret National Security Directive (NSD-26) declaring the intention to wean Saddam from his tyrannical ways by encouraging more U.S. trade and investment.

November—CIA Director William Webster and the head of Kuwaiti State Security meet and agree to pressure Saddam to recognize Kuwait's border.

December—Saddam's scientists test a three-stage rocket that could deliver a warhead over a distance of a thousand miles.

1990   *January*—George H. W. Bush overrides congressional objections and authorizes a new line of credit for Iraq from the U.S. Ex-Im Bank, worth nearly $200 million.

May—Saddam accuses other Gulf states of waging economic war against Iraq by increasing oil production and refusing to forgive Iraq's loans.

July—Iraqi troops mass near the Kuwaiti border. Various U.S. officials declare U.S. has no treaty ties to defend Kuwait.

August—Iraq invades Kuwait. President George H. W. Bush adopts a hard line, refusing any proposals other than an immediate and total withdrawal of Iraqi troops. U.N. Resolution 661 cuts off all trade with Iraq, which had been importing 70 percent of its food.

November—The U.N. Security Council authorizes the use of force if Iraq doesn't withdraw from Kuwait by January 15, 1991.

December—Infant mortality in Iraq has doubled due to sanctions. Standards of health and nutrition will plummet over the following years.

1991   *January*—The U.S. Congress authorizes the president to use force if Saddam doesn't withdraw by January 15. On January 17, Operation Desert Storm, a series of air assaults throughout Iraq and Kuwait that will last forty-two days, is launched.

February—President George H. W. Bush urges the Iraqi people to overthrow Saddam. Despite a promise by Iraq to withdraw from Kuwait, the U.S. launches a ground assault known as Operation Desert Sabre. As Saddam's forces are quickly beaten, uprisings among Shiites in southern Iraq begin.

March—The U.S. and Iraq sign a cease-fire allowing Iraq to continue to use military helicopters that will be deployed to suppress internal revolt. A Kurdish uprising begins.

April—The U.N. Security Council votes to keep sanctions against Iraq in place. The U.N. Special Commission (UNSCOM) is established to ensure Iraq is free of weapons of mass destruction and to establish a long-term monitoring program, along with inspectors from the International Atomic Energy Agency. President Bush establishes a safe zone for the Kurds in northern Iraq, but not for Shiites in the south.

1995   Saddam's son-in-law, General Hussein Kamel, flees to Jordan and tells U.N. inspectors that Iraq's weapons of mass destruction were destroyed four years earlier.

1996   *March*—The WHO reports that child mortality in Iraq is up 600 percent since sanctions were imposed.

May—Modifications to the sanctions, known as Oil for Food, allow Iraq to export $1 billion worth of petroleum every ninety days to purchase food and essentials. The funds generated equal thirty cents per Iraqi per day.

June—A plot to overthrow Saddam with the help of CIA agents planted with the U.N. weapons inspectors is discovered by Iraqi secret police. Eight hundred Iraqis are arrested. Another CIA-backed plot fails in Kurdistan.

September—On the eve of U.S. presidential elections, Bill Clinton launches forty-four cruises missiles against Iraqi military targets.

1998   *February*—Pressured by conservatives, Clinton signs the Iraq Liberation Action, allocating $97 million for training and equipping the Iraqi opposition.

December—Warned by the U.S. of imminent air attacks against Iraq, the head of UNSCOM inspectors orders his staff to leave Iraq. President Clinton unleashes Operation Desert Fox, four days of intensive American bombing and missile strikes.

1999   The U.N. Security Council expands the Oil for Food program. Increased petroleum sales now amount to about forty-seven cents per Iraqi per day. A UNICEF study concludes that half a million Iraqi children have died as a result of the sanctions.

2000   American neoconservatives issue their Project for a New American Century calling for, among other things, the overthrow of Saddam.

2001   *January*—At his first high-level National Security Council meeting, George W. Bush lists getting rid of Saddam Hussein as one of his key objectives.

September—In the wake of the 9/11 attacks by Al-Qaeda, President Bush instructs aides to search for links with Saddam Hussein. Over the following days, without evidence of such ties, Bush and other administration officials push for moves against the Iraqi dictator.

November—Donald Rumsfeld instructs General Tommy Franks to prepare plans to attack Saddam.

2002   *January*—President Bush declares Iraq, Iran, and North Korea an "Axis of Evil."

March—The president and top aides make clear in private remarks that Bush is determined to attack Iraq.

June—President Bush declares that the U.S. has the right to launch a preemptive attack to protect its national security.

July—A memo by the British intelligence chief reports that Bush seems resolved to take military action against Iraq, and that "the intelligence and facts were being fixed around the policy."

August—A series of speeches and leaks by administration officials to lay the groundwork for the invasion of Iraq begins with Vice President Cheney's warning that Saddam could subject the U.S. to nuclear blackmail.

September—President Bush declares, "You can't distinguish between Al-Qaeda and Saddam." Donald Rumsfeld claims "bulletproof" evidence of a connection between the two.

October—The CIA issues a classified National Intelligence Estimate on Iraq that makes alarming claims, downplaying the strong reservations of many in the intelligence community. On October 10, the U.S. House of Representatives empowers the president to use armed force in Iraq; the Senate follows the next day. The White House attempts to squelch a report that North Korea is insisting on its right to develop nuclear weapons.

November—Saddam agrees to accept Unmovic weapons inspectors into Iraq. On November 15, the U.N. Security Council resolves that if Saddam continues to violate his obligations to get rid of his WMD, he would face "serious consequences."

December—CIA Director George Tenet reassures the president and his top aides that the case against Saddam Hussein is "a slam dunk."

2003   *January*—Hans Blix, Chief U.N. Weapons Inspector, delivers a mildly optimistic interim report to the U.N., stating that Unmovic inspectors had uncovered no new WMD or production sites. Mohammed El Baradei of the International Atomic Energy Agency, in a similar tone, expresses the hope that the IAEA could wind up work within next few months. In his state of the union address, President Bush repeats the discredited charge that Saddam recently tried to buy uranium in Africa.

February—Secretary of State Colin Powell presents to the Security Council the U.S. case that Saddam's WMD pose a dangerous threat. Most charges cited by Powell later turn out to be false.

March—President Bush declares he has ordered military action against Iraq. On March 19 (March 20 in Iraq), the U.S.-led "Coalition of the Willing" attacks.

April—Baghdad falls to American troops on April 9. Looting is rampant. Jake Garner arrives in Baghdad to head the interim American administration. Secretary Rumsfeld's representative on the team, Larry Di Rita, announces that all but 25,000 American troops will have withdrawn by September 2003.

May—President Bush declares "mission accomplished." Garner is replaced by Paul Bremer, who takes charge of the Coalition Provisional Authority. As looting continues, Bremer disbands the Iraqi army and dismisses 35,000 government employees because of Baath party membership.

July—U.S.-selected twenty-five-member Governing Council of prominent Iraqis takes office.

August—Truck bomb explodes outside United Nations offices in Baghdad, killing twenty-two people, including Sergio Vieira de Mello, top U.N. envoy in Iraq. The frequency of insurgent attacks escalates.

December—Saddam Hussein is captured.

2004 *March*—The Iraqi Governing Council signs an interim constitution. Marines attempt to retake the Sunni city of Fallujah after angry mobs kill four American private security guards.

April—Pictures of the mistreatment of prisoners by American troops at the Abu Ghraib prison are broadcast around the world.

June—The CPA formally transfers sovereignty to the interim government of Ayad Allawi.

August—Ten months after Congress authorized $18.4 billion dollars for reconstruction in Iraq, only $400 million has been spent. Radical Shiite cleric Muqtada al-Sadr agrees to withdraw his militia from the holy city of Najaf after three weeks of heavy fighting with U.S. and Iraqi troops.

October—The top U.S. arms inspector finds no evidence that Saddam's regime produced any weapons of mass destruction after 1991.

December—Al-Qaeda leader Osama bin Laden urges Iraqis to boycott the coming election and names Abu Musab al-Zarqawi his deputy in Iraq. Thousands of Iraqis are fleeing the country to escape increasingly random violence.

2005 *January*—Iraqis elect a 275-seat National Assembly. A Shiite-dominated coalition wins 48 percent of the votes, a Kurdish alliance garners 26 percent. Most Sunni Arabs boycott voting.

February—A suicide car bomb explodes in a crowd of Iraqi police and army recruits in Hillah, killing 125 people in the bloodiest attack of the insurgency to date.

March—Iraq's National Assembly convenes.

April—Legislators elect Kurdish leader Jalal Talabani as president, with Shiite and a Sunni Arabs as vice presidents. Ibrahim al-Jaafari, a Shiite, is appointed prime minister. Reports charge that the Shiites are packing the interior ministry with their own militias.

July—First criminal case filed against Saddam Hussein for killing 148 Shiite villagers after a 1982 assassination attempt against the dictator.

August—Iraq's Constitutional Committee signs a draft charter after protracted negotiations and over the objections of many Sunni Arab leaders.

September—More than a dozen coordinated bombings rip Baghdad, killing at least 167 people and wounding 570 in the insurgency's deadliest day.

October—Iraqi voters approve a new constitution in a referendum. Saddam's trial opens.

December—Despite insurgents' threats, Iraqis elect a new parliament, with Shiite parties winning the biggest bloc but not enough to govern without support from other groups.

2006 *January*—Intense negotiations begin to form a ruling coalition including all main Shiite and Sunni Arab and Kurd parties.

February—Bombs damage the Shiite Askariya shrine in Samarra, touching off sectarian bloodshed that kills more than 500, injures hundreds more, and threatens to push Iraq into civil war. Ethnic cleansing is going on in Baghdad and Basra.

March—President Bush concedes that, though their levels might be lower, American troops would still be in Iraq in 2009, when a new American president will take office.

May—A report charges that U.S. marines killed 24 Iraqi civilians in the village of Haditha the previous November. Iraqi leaders demand their own investigation. Iraq's new prime minister, Nuri Kamal al-Maliki, takes office.

June—Abu Musab al-Zarqawi is killed by U.S. bombers. Prime Minister Maliki finally obtains parliamentary approval for new Ministers of the Interior and Defense, declaring they will purge the ministries of sectarian forces. George Bush makes a surprise six-hour visit to Baghdad to demonstrate U.S. support for the new government, but advises Iraqis that they are ultimately responsible for its success or failure. The first of the trials that Saddam Hussein is to face moves into its final phase.

July—United Nations estimates religious and sectarian violence in Iraq is now killing one hundred a day.

August—The second trial of Saddam convenes, charging him with committing genocide against the Kurds.

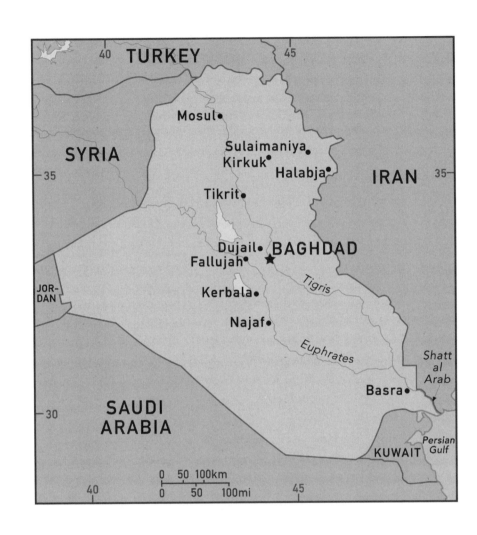

ACKNOWLEDGMENTS

This book would not have been written without the intercession of my agent, Ike Williams; the enthusiasm of my publisher, Judith Gurewich; the incisive comments and insights of my editor Danny Reid, constantly testing my judgments and tempering my occasional flights into purple prose; and the punctilious production process overseen by Bob Hack. I also owe much thanks to several who have written on various aspects of Iraq's history and its relations with the great powers, read portions of my manuscript, and provided me with their insights. They include Milton Viorst, John Randal, Richard Reeves, Richard Sale, and particularly historian Peter Sluglett, whose comments on the early history of Iraq were invaluable. Important contributions were also made by Michel Despratx, an investigative reporter from Canal + in France with whom I turned out a documentary on "The Trial of Saddam Hussein—the Trial You'll Never See." Whatever errors of fact and interpretation remain, however, are mine alone.

Finally, thanks to my wife, Elisabeth, whose loving counsel, support, and patience were key to this project; and to my children, Edward, Dominique, and Jeffery, for their help and encouragement.

.

WEB OF DECEIT

Introduction : The Trial of Saddam

When United States troops pulled Saddam Hussein from the cramped "spider hole" where he had been hiding on December 13, 2003, I wrote an article in which I speculated that, although they exulted at having finally captured the former Iraqi tyrant alive, a lot of very important people around the world might well have preferred the disheveled fallen dictator to have been riddled by a hail of bullets, blown up by a grenade, or self-dispatched by a cyanide capsule when all seemed lost. That would have provided a nice, neat end to the tale. There would have been no need for a trial.

Hypothetically, the trial of the former dictator could have been a ghastly global media circus in which many of the world's great leaders, past and present, would have found themselves pilloried as codefendants— charged with complicity in many of the crimes against humanity that occurred during Saddam's bloody reign. It wouldn't take unusual skill for Saddam's defense team to make such a case. Those leaders would include, but certainly not be limited to, American presidents Jimmy Carter, Bill Clinton, and George Bush *pere* and *fils*; other world leaders such as Margaret Thatcher, Jacques Chirac, Leonid Brezhnev, Mikhail Gorbachev, King Hussein of Jordan, and Prince Fahd of Saudi Arabia; Israel's Menachem Begin; and many of the men and women who guided their foreign policy, ran their military, and oversaw their intelligence agencies. Outside the political sphere, the accused might include hundreds of American and foreign businessmen, leaders of agrobusiness, oil tycoons, and arms merchants from across the globe who profited handsomely from doing business with Saddam Hussein while closing their eyes to what he was up to—or, in some cases, despite knowing full well.

It's not that such foreign involvement in any way alleviates Saddam's guilt; it's just that these and other foreign notables, through Saddam and on their own, were also responsible for much of the suffering of the Iraqi people. And without their sophisticated arms and massive financing, their intelligence information and diplomatic support—their sins of omission and commission—Saddam would never have wreaked the horrors that he did.

In the months following Saddam's capture, I wondered how the Americans and their Iraqi allies would deal with the judicial problem: How to put Saddam and his lieutenants on trial for the crimes against humanity committed during his rule, without implicating these others who were either directly complicit in his crimes or turned their back on them when they occurred? How to avoid transforming the trial of Saddam Hussein into an explosive chronicle of the foreign cynicism and greed that helped shape the history of modern Iraq, including the crimes of Saddam?

The Americans and their Iraqi allies handled the problem quietly. To avoid the jurisdiction of any international court or group of independent jurists, they established their own special Iraqi tribunal. According to the regulations of that tribunal, only Iraqi citizens could be charged or subpoenaed. This meant, for instance, that if Saddam's attorneys sought to summon George H. W. Bush to ask why, in February 1991, he had first called for the Iraqi people to rise up against Saddam and then ordered American soldiers to refuse all aid to the rebels while enabling Saddam to crush them, that embarrassing line of questioning wouldn't be admitted by the tribunal.

The same logic would apply to Saddam's gassing of thousands of Kurds at Halabja in 1988. There is no way his attorneys could point out that Saddam's chemical weapons were supplied primarily by French, Belgian, and German firms, or that the U.S. State Department refused even to meet with Kurdish leaders who had proof of the attacks, or that the U.S. and its allies had steadfastly blocked international moves to condemn Saddam for his use of mustard and nerve gasses.

The period considered by the tribunal is also strictly limited to the time when Saddam ran the country, from 1978 to 2003, so that his attorneys also could not refer to historical deeds that might have cast his foreign accusers as something more sinister than liberators of the Iraqi people. They could not point out the fact that the first to use aircraft, machine guns, and bombs to put down unruly Iraqis were the British, in 1920, when Winston Churchill was British Secretary of State for War. Or the fact that the 1963 coup that brought Saddam's Baath party to power was supported by John F. Kennedy's Central Intelligence Agency, which also provided lists of hundreds of supposed Iraqi Communists, who were duly arrested, tortured, and executed—Saddam at the time was not yet a prominent political figure, just one of the principal torturers. Nor could Saddam's lawyers recount the ruthless fashion in which Iran, Israel, and the United States under Richard Nixon made use of the Kurds to undermine the central government in Iraq by encouraging, arming, and training them—and then left them to be massacred by Saddam in 1975 when they no longer served their sponsors' purposes.

After all, as former secretary of state Henry Kissinger pointed out when a congressional committee later queried him about abandoning the Kurds, "One should not confuse undercover action with social work." Kissinger should not be singled out; over the years, American officials became renowned for pithy quotes demonstrating their keen, hardheaded *realpolitik*.

In 1991, for instance, Ronald Reagan's first secretary of state, Alexander Haig, chided an investigative journalist for appearing surprised that Israel's Ariel Sharon had denied that Israel illegally transferred U.S. arms to the Iranians during the Iran-Iraq War, though that was precisely what Israel had done. "Come on. Jesus! God!" Haig exploded, disgusted at the reporter's naïveté. "You'd better get out and read Machiavelli or somebody else, because I think you're living in a dream world! People do what their national interest tells them to do, and if it means lying to a friendly nation, they're going to lie through their teeth."[1] Ten years later, I received a similar reply from Thomas

Pickering, George H. W. Bush's former ambassador to the United Nations. I asked him how he could justify President Bush's first calling on the Iraqis to rise up in 1991, then leaving them to be slaughtered by the Iraqi dictator. "In war and love, all's fair," Pickering confided with a knowing smile.

That same flinty attitude—the world is a tough place, and you've got to get your hands dirty to survive—has been the proud hallmark of U.S. Secretary of Defense Donald Rumsfeld. As he put it when questioned about the rampant looting after the U.S. takeover in Baghdad that was to presage the nightmarish years of violence and death that were to follow, "Stuff happens." Iraq has the misfortune of being a case study of how "stuff happened" over almost a century as gimlet-eyed foreign leaders ignored considerations of morality and justice in the name of greater causes, like fighting Communism or Islamic terrorism—while ensuring access to the region's vast petroleum resources.

In the latest episode, in 2003, the United States under George W. Bush first illegally invaded and occupied Iraq, and then helped set up, train, and finance a special tribunal to bring Saddam Hussein to justice for his crimes against humanity. Though they brought preliminary charges against Saddam Hussein for seven different atrocities involving altogether the deaths of hundreds of thousands of Iraqis, the men running the tribunal decided to begin by focusing on one discrete crime that took place in July 1982 in the Shiite town of Dujail.[2] After an abortive attempt to assassinate him, the Iraqi tyrant, it was charged, ordered the torture and subsequent execution of some 148 Shiite men and boys from Dujail, some as young as eleven years old. Dujail was a good case for the inexperienced judges and lawyers of the tribunal to begin with. There would be lots of moving testimony and no question about who ordered the killings: they had the execution decree signed by Saddam Hussein himself: slam dunk convictions. There would, of course, be no mention of the fact that even as the torture and executions were going on, Donald Rumsfeld, fully apprised of Saddam's brutal methods, arrived in Baghdad as special envoy of Ronald Reagan to strengthen relations with the Iraqi dictator and begin a process that culminated with the U.S. and Saddam as virtual allies.

And thus it was that in October 2005, millions of television viewers in Iraq and across the globe watched the opening of what was planned to be the first of several trials that, one after the other, would reveal the horrific reign of Saddam Hussein—a process that in fact was a charade, a classic case of victors' justice: rewriting history by ignoring it. As George Orwell put it, "Those who control the present, control the past." And when it was all over, they would take Saddam Hussein and a few of his lieutenants out and hang them. And George W. Bush would solemnly declare that justice has been done.

It was not the first time this happened. The same thing occurred in the Tokyo trials following World War II, where the crimes of Japanese officials were documented in gruesome detail (except for the biological warfare programs, which Washington wanted to explore further itself, and except for the involvement of the emperor, who was to serve U.S. purposes during the occupation), while the crimes of the victors, such as the horrific fire-bombing raids of Tokyo and the destruction of Hiroshima and Nagasaki, were disregarded. In fact, when Japanese lawyers attempted to bring up the U.S. nuclear strikes against Japan, the American prosecution interrupted and ordered their remarks stricken from the record.[3]

The procedures at the Nuremburg trials of top Nazi officials after World War II have been similarly criticized. Though the crimes of Hitler and his generals were horrendous, the U.S. and its allies did not come to the court with clean hands. For instance, the Soviet Union, one of the sponsors of the tribunal, were allied with the Nazis when they invaded and occupied Poland. There would also be no talk of the Soviet slaughter of at least 1,000 Polish officers in the Katyn forest— nor of the allied bombing of cities like Dresden. Likewise, the U.S. trial of Panamanian fallen ruler Manuel Noriega was carefully scripted to avoid revealing the long-time ties between Noriega and the U.S. government, particularly between Noriega and former CIA director George H. W. Bush.

In the year following Saddam's capture, I worked with Michel Despratx, a French investigative reporter with Canal + in Paris, to produce a documentary on some of the matters discussed above.[4] The more I learned, the more difficult it was to understand why so few commentators were making an issue of the hypocrisy and cynicism behind the whole carefully staged affair. Such apathy paralleled the puzzling lack of outrage among Americans, first to the mounting evidence of lies and distortions that the Bush administration used to justify the 2003 invasion of Iraq, and then to the woeful mismanagement of the occupation that followed.

Of course, Saddam Hussein was a monster and deserved whatever punishment the tribunal meted out. But to stage-manage a trial to make it appear that Saddam and his lieutenants were solely to blame for the blood-drenched history of Iraq, to excuse prominent world leaders and businessmen from their role in crimes that resulted in the deaths of more than a million people in Iraq and neighboring countries, and to get away with it—that was outrageous.

It is the cumulative impact of each cynical episode of foreign intervention in Iraq, year after tawdry year, that I find so shocking. That is the story I set out to tell here.

Barry M. Lando
Paris, September 2006
http://barrylando.com

CHAPTER ONE

Beginnings : Setting the Stage for Saddam
1914–1959

The people of England have been led in Mesopotamia [Iraq] into a trap from which it will be hard to escape with dignity and honour. They have been tricked into it by a steady withholding of information. The Baghdad communiqués are belated, insincere, incomplete. We are today not far from disaster.

—Colonel T. E. Lawrence, *London Sunday Times*, August 1920[1]

Turmoil in Iraq unleashed by invasion; a spreading insurgency against an occupying Western power and its local allies; allegations of atrocities on both sides; calls for withdrawal from critics back home, alarmed by wasteful expenditures and woeful incompetence; loud declarations that revelations by the press are somehow traitorous and encourage the rebels—this familiar scenario has been played out before in Iraq, by the British, more than eighty years ago. Only the uniforms were different.

The British Mandate

In a sense, Iraq and its people may have been doomed to this recurring history from the moment their country was formed in 1921. The modern nation of Iraq, an artificial creation of foreigners preoccupied with empire and oil, was from the beginning a tenuous mixture of ethnic groups, tribes, and religions.

The roots of internal discord in the Middle East, of course, go back further, to the time when men first began growing crops and building mud brick villages on the land between the Tigris and Euphrates rivers. Ancient Mesopotamia—"the land between the rivers"—was one of the great cradles of Western civilization, beginning with the Sumerians' development of cuneiform writing and tentative plotting of the stars and planets. The great conquerors of the ancient world—Hammurabi, Sargon, Nebuchadnezzar, Cyrus, Alexander—swept through or ruled from the region; over thousands of years, kingdoms and empires rose and flourished, then withered and decayed, some vanishing with scarcely a trace.

In 638 A.D., Mesopotamia was invaded and taken over from the Persian Sasanian Empire by conquerors from the Arabian peninsula, newly converted to Islam. In 750 the Arabs established the Abbasid caliphate and constructed their celebrated capital, Baghdad. The city was a sort of Babylon, reborn with marvelous treasure houses, mosques, markets, and grand gates that led to all corners of a vast empire that stretched from Central Asia to southern Spain. But even as poets and scientists thrived in this realm, so did political intrigue and violence. More than eighty of its ninety-two caliphs were killed in disputes over power and wealth.[2] Their empire came to a violent end in 1258, when Baghdad was sacked by the Mongols under Hulagu, the grandson of Genghis Khan, who destroyed the dikes on the Tigris and drowned most of the population. In June 1401, Tamerlane, another descendant of the great Khan, conquered Baghdad and massacred 20,000 of its citizens. He ordered that every soldier should return with at least two severed human heads to show for his troubles.

In 1534, almost a century after capturing Constantinople and defeating the Byzantine Empire, the Ottoman Turks seized Baghdad and gained control of Mesopotamia. For the next three hundred years, the region remained a battleground as the Ottomans repeatedly clashed with the Safavid Empire to the east.

In what they regarded as a last-ditch attempt to counter the reverses they had suffered at the hands of the British and French in the latter half of the nineteenth century, the Ottomans sided with the

Germans and the Hapsburgs in World War I. Thus, in 1914, Britain sent an expeditionary force to the region, and eventually became the new ruler of Mesopotamia. When British forces marched into Baghdad in 1917, they announced they had come not as "conquerors but liberators,"[3] as the U.S.-led coalition would also proclaim eighty-six years later.

In fact, the British were no more interested in liberating the local inhabitants and their lands than were any of the conquerors who had preceded them, but their real concern was a new one. The British were already developing the enormous oil reserves of southwestern Iran, and preliminary surveys indicated that the potential of Mesopotamia itself might be just as vast. Indeed, spontaneous blazes due to oil seepage from underground deposits had always featured in travelers' accounts and intelligence reports in the region.

With naval power the key to empire and the Royal Navy in turn now fueled increasingly by oil rather than coal, there was no question in the minds of many British officials that the possession of Mesopotamia was vital. As Rear Admiral Sir Edmond Slade wrote in a report to the British admiralty in 1918, "It is evident that the Power that controls the oil lands of Persia and Mesopotamia will control the source of supply of the majority of the liquid fuel of the future." Britain must therefore "at all costs retain [its] hold on the Persian and Mesopotamian oil fields."[4] Sir Maurice Hankey, influential secretary of the imperial war cabinet, vehemently agreed, sending a memo to Foreign Secretary Arthur Balfour that "oil in the next war will occupy the place of coal in the present war. The only big potential supply that we can get under British control is the Persian and Mesopotamian supply."[5] In August 1918, Balfour told the prime ministers of the dominions, "I do not care under what system we keep this oil, but I am quite clear it is all-important for us that this oil should be available."[6]

Even before the end of the First World War, the British and French held secret negotiations to determine how they would split up the remnants of the Ottoman Empire. But after the United States entered the conflict in 1917, the European governments had to contend with America's troublesome views. U.S. President Woodrow Wilson had condemned colonialism, promised a new era of self-determination, and declared that the age of empires was over. That was not quite what the British and French had in mind.

To assuage Wilson's anti-imperialist stance, Hankey suggested Britain should explain that the reason it was advancing so aggressively in Mesopotamia was "to secure a proper water supply." By a happy coincidence, the path to fresh water led across most of the oil-bearing regions.[7] On October 30, 1918, when the Armistice was signed with Turkey, British troops had occupied two of the Ottoman provinces, Basra and Baghdad. Three days later, ignoring the Armistice, British troops seized the town and province of Mosul, which was reputed to have huge oil reserves. The Turks later protested, but to no avail.

Since Britain first started building its globe-spanning Empire, the country's political and mercantile elite had veiled their desire for conquest—for new lands and resources and compliant new markets—with talk of Britain's civilizing mission and the White Man's Burden. They would introduce the obvious benefits of Western rule to peoples steeped in tyranny and darkness.

That was certainly the view of Arnold Wilson, the distinguished administrator and scholar whom the British government appointed "Acting Civil Commissioner" to oversee its new holdings in Mesopotamia. A punctilious supervisor, Wilson was not interested in listening to the views of his native subjects, nor would he brook any opposition from them. Their duty was to consent while British officials skilled in the arts of statecraft brought them into the modern world. Wilson wrote to London in November 1918 that the majority of the natives were more than content with this arrangement: "The average [Iraqi] Arab, as opposed to the handful of amateur politicians of Baghdad, sees the future as one of fair dealing and material and moral progress under the aegis of Britain. . . . The Arabs are content with our occupation."[8]

Others in the British administration in Baghdad, such as Gertrude Bell, flatly disagreed with Wilson's rosy assessment. The desire for Arab independence, they concluded, threatened to become an unstoppable force. Bell advised that the Arabs be granted self-rule under British tutelage.[9]

Indeed, the Arabs, it turned out, were not at all content when they understood that Britain had no intention of liberating the conquered territories. At the first signs of native protest, Wilson dropped all pretenses to benevolence. When native dissidents demanded to meet with him to present their complaints, Wilson first packed the assembly with selected supporters, and then, for good measure, dispatched a British warship in the Tigris River to train its guns on the meeting place.[10]

Since the tradition of transforming conquered lands into colonies was no longer politically correct, the Great Powers concocted a facade called a mandate to be granted by the League of Nations. As Jawaharlal Nehru wryly commented, the League's mandates were the equivalent "of appointing a tiger to look after the interests of a number of cows or horses."[11] In 1920, Britain was given the Mandate for Iraq (and Palestine and Transjordan), to be exercised until they "had prepared the peoples for Democracy." The British also continued to control Mosul.

The inhabitants of Britain's new territories were predominately Muslim Arabs: Sunnis and Shiites in the province of Baghdad and Shiites in Basra, each group representing one of the great branches of Islam with a long history of tension and bitterness between them.[12] Half the population of the northern province of Mosul was inhabited by another people, the Kurds, who had their own language (linguistically related to Persian) and culture and a fervent if ill-focused desire for self-rule.

To tighten their hold on Baghdad and Basra, the British attempted to govern through local tribal leaders, giving them privilege and power over their countrymen. Rather than calming the situation, that tactic only fueled growing anti-British resentment. Sporadic insurrections were repressed with ever more brutal force. For a while, however, the British succeeded in uniting the mutually hostile Sunnis and Shiites. But even the Kurds, usually anti-Arab, were seething at their Western governors. On June 30, 1920, uprisings against the British exploded across the country.

The British then had 133,000 troops in the area—roughly the same number as the U.S. had after the invasion of 2003. They fought back with armored cars and planes that could strike with impunity, bombing and machine-gunning the terrorized natives. In six months of bloody fighting, thousands of Sunnis, Shiites, and Kurds were killed, many of them lined up and executed by firing squads. The British themselves lost more than 1,600 men.[13]

Shocked by the human and material cost, many British political leaders and editorialists were up in arms. The embattled government attempted to turn the tables and accused the press of inflaming the situation. Winston Churchill, then England's Secretary of State for the Colonies, declared the newspaper reports were "a factor which provoked and promoted the rebellion."[14] British officials assured the press and public that victory was just around the corner and that the uprising was weak, composed of disaffected "remnants" who were being incited by outside forces.

Imminent or not, victory for the empire was proving expensive, and not just in Iraq. Insurrection was also sweeping Egypt and Ireland. The cost of battling another revolt in far-off Iraq and maintaining other garrisons scattered around the globe was draining the Exchequer. No one was more concerned about those costs than Churchill.

The most effective, as well as the cheapest way of dealing with the restless tribes of Mesopotamia, he came to argue, was not with more stationary military garrisons but with more resources for the Royal Air Force. The RAF had already shown how its planes could petrify insurgents with bombs and machine-gun fire. Chemical weapons, Churchill instructed the RAF, should also be explored. "I think you should certainly proceed with the experimental work on gas bombs, especially mustard gas, which would inflict punishment on recalcitrant natives without inflicting grave injury upon them."[15]

Ultimately, it appears that—perhaps because they were impractical dropped from the air—the RAF never employed chemicals against the rebellious Iraqis. They had equally devastating weapons at hand: phosphorous bombs, rockets, shrapnel, liquid fire, delay-action bombs, and metal crowsfeet (to maim livestock and lay thousands of acres of crops to waste). Many of these weapons were specifically designed by the Air Ministry for use against tribal villages and were the antecedents of napalm and air-to-ground missiles. Indeed, Iraq turned out to be a valuable laboratory and training ground for the RAF.[16]

But Churchill had also concluded that Britain eventually had to extricate itself from the Mesopotamia quagmire. As he saw it, the huge costs of holding Iraq far outweighed any potential benefits. His communiqués to British Prime Minister Lloyd George could be memos to President George W. Bush arguing against current U.S. policies in Iraq. "Evidently we are in for a long, costly campaign in Mesopotamia which will strain to the uttermost our military resources," Churchill warned. "I hope that may be the worst. . . . There is something very sinister to my mind in this Mesopotamian entanglement, coming as it does when Ireland is so great a menace. It seems to me so gratuitous that after all the struggles of war, just when we want to get together our slender military resources and re-establish our finances and have a little in hand in case of danger here or there, we should be compelled to go on pouring armies and treasure into these thankless deserts."

Churchill continued, "We have not got a single friend in the press on the subject, and there is no point of which they make more effective use to injure the Government. Week after week and month after month for a long time we shall have a continuance of this miserable, wasteful, sporadic warfare marked from time to time certainly by minor disasters and cuttings off of troops and agents, and very possibly attended by some very grave occurrence."[17]

Churchill argued that Britain should give up its attempts to control Kurdish Mosul and Sunni-dominated Baghdad and retain only the Shiite province of Basra in the south, which was a strategic link to British possessions in Persia. If the British cabinet had followed his advice, each of the principal peoples of Iraq—Shiites, Sunnis, and Kurds—would have had its own government; the groups who were bound together as Iraqis might have had a much less tragic history. Churchill, however, was overruled by Lloyd George, and as a loyal cabinet member he was obliged to continue publicly to make the case for a policy he privately argued was disastrous—that Britain should continue to rule Mesopotamia.

As another veil for their imperial power, the British established in late 1920 a provisional council of state with strictly limited powers and filled it with handpicked Iraqis, who were instructed to accept the advice of British officials. The country continued to seethe with rebellion. The insurgent Shiites were a majority in the new territory, but the British opted instead to rule through the more educated, urbanized Sunnis.

King Faisal I

In March 1921, Winston Churchill summoned a group of British Middle East experts to the elegant Semiramis Hotel in Cairo to redraw the map of the British Middle East. This was necessarily accomplished without consulting most of the people of the region themselves, as Churchill didn't approve of Arabs coming into the hotel, or even into the garden.[18]

A major problem confronting the British was how to hold on to the new lands of Mesopotamia, particularly oil-rich Mosul, and at the same time radically reduce the cost of governing the territory. The solution was what could be called empire lite. Rather than control the new lands directly as a British colony, they created a new Arab state, which they named Iraq after the name for the region used by the Arabs since the sixth century. To rule over it, the British imported the Hashemite King Faisal, son of the Sharif of Mecca and a friend of Colonel T. E. Lawrence (of Arabia). Since they were handing him the crown, they presumed he would be compliant with the directives of a British high commissioner. The fact that Faisal had never been to Iraq was considered an inconvenience, but not an insurmountable one.

The British organized elections to make it appear as if Faisal was the choice of Iraq's leaders, but the vote was not left to chance. As Churchill dismissively put it, elections were "scarcely worthy of the name in so scattered and primitive a community."[19] Blatant vote rigging and ballot buying were the order of the day and became regular features of all subsequent Iraqi elections. When one of the Iraqis who had been appointed by the British to the provisional government in Baghad protested, he was exiled to the far-off British colony of Ceylon.[20] Finally, on July 11, 1921, the thirty-six-year-old king, resplendent in khaki uniform and spiked helmet, was proclaimed Faisal I of Iraq. The throne he ascended, a far cry from the model in Westminster, had been hastily cobbled together from packing cases, still bearing the imprint *Asahi Beer*.[21]

Since everyone, including the king, understood he was a creation of the British, his immediate concern was to convince his new subjects that he could rule in Iraq's, not just Britain's, interest. Obsessed by their own imperial designs, however, London neither understood nor sympathized with Faisal's predicament. His first attempts at establishing a modicum of independence provoked the sort of reprimand one might send to an unruly child. He should be grateful to the British government, Faisal was warned, for continuing to spend so many millions to support his government; he should thus have the good manners to follow the "advice" bestowed by the British high commissioner. Or, as Churchill put it in a succinct directive to the new monarch, "while we have to pay the piper we must be effectively consulted as to the tune."[22]

To man the government, the British relied on the minority Sunnis, ceding to them a virtual monopoly of top posts in the military ranks and civilian bureaucracy. Under the terms of the Anglo-Iraqi treaty of 1922, the British retained control of foreign affairs, the army, and finances, and maintained several large military bases of their own. The majority Shiites naturally continued to view the Sunnis as an army of occupation.

The British were well aware of the continued potential for religious and tribal discontent. Gertrude Bell had been warned by an American missionary, "You are flying in the face of four millenniums of history if you try to draw a line around Iraq and call it a 'political entity'! They have never been an independent unity. You've got to take time to get them integrated, it must be done gradually. They have no conception of nationhood yet."[23] Indeed, with the minority Sunni maintained in power by the British, violent unrest continued to grow.

Hard pressed to contain the uprisings, the Royal Air Force queried Churchill about using chemical weapons against the insurgents. Churchill's military aide recommended against: "If the people against whom we use it consider it a barbarous method of warfare, doubtless they will retaliate with equally barbarous methods. . . . Say what we may, the gas is lethal. It may permanently damage eyesight, and even kill children and sickly persons, more especially as the people against whom we intend to use it have no medical knowledge with which to supply antidotes."[24]

Fully aware that chemical weapons had killed or crippled thousands of British soldiers during World War I, Churchill nevertheless ignored this advice. On December 16, 1921, he replied to the RAF, "I am ready to authorize the construction of such bombs at once; the question of their use to be decided when the occasion arises. In my view they are a scientific experiment for sparing lives which should not be prevented by the prejudices of those who do not think clearly. The fullest details of the recent American experiments [should] be supplied."[25]

At the same time, Churchill continued to push for Britain to pull out of Iraq. Prime Minister Lloyd George would hear nothing of it. "If we leave," he wrote in 1922, "we may find in a year or two that we have handed over to the French and the Americans some of the richest oilfields in the world."[26]

In fact, the British decided that very year to *expand* the artificial nation by incorporating the Kurdish province of Mosul into Iraq, though Sir Arnold Wilson had earlier warned London that the Kurds would "never accept an Arab ruler."[27] Indeed, in 1920, the Treaty of Sèvres between the victorious allies and the defeated Ottomans had promised the non-Arab Kurds an autonomous state, but the treaty was rejected by the emerging Republic of Turkey with the result that the promise was never fulfilled. The British did not especially want to rule the Kurds, but they were intent on exploiting the area's huge reserves of oil. They concluded that the only way to do that was to make the province of Mosul part of the new Iraq. Also, it was thought that the future oil revenues from Mosul would help to pay the bills for the rest of the ungainly country.

In return for a cut of the take, the other great powers—including the United States—acquiesced in the arrangement. An oil consortium, the Iraq Petroleum Company, was set up to exploit Mosul's oil riches; the ownership of the consortium was divvied up between British, Dutch, French, and American companies. As for the promises of self-determination that had been made to the Kurds, they were quietly abandoned. The isolationists who now ruled in America wanted as little as possible to do with any entanglements in far-off lands like Iraq. There would be no assistance or sympathy for nationalist politicians, however moderate or amenable to American influence, when, as Washington put it, such assistance threatened regional order.

Thus, the hapless Kurds found themselves part of a volatile ethnic jumble, a minority ruled over by an Arab government in Baghdad.

In 1923, their resentment exploded in uprisings that were brutally repressed by the Royal Air Force.

As Wing Commander Sir Arthur Harris (who later became renowned as "Bomber Harris," head of Britain's WWII Bomber Command that carried out the firebombing of Dresden) declared with obvious satisfaction in 1924, "[T]he Arab and Kurd . . . now know what real bombing means, in casualties and damage; they now know that within 45 minutes a full sized village . . . can be practically wiped out and a third of its inhabitants killed or injured by four or five machines which offer them no real target, no opportunity for glory as warriors, no effective means of escape."[28]

In 1925, the League of Nations, bowing to the British, decided to make the Kurds formally a part of Iraq, and Kurdish resentment smoldered. Uprisings continued in other parts of Iraq, and the RAF continued its devastating raids. The "recalcitrant" tribes targeted were not just those attacking British installations and personnel, but also those accused of sheltering rebel leaders or refusing to pay taxes. British officials reassured the British public and Parliament that despite continued reports of RAF excesses, such actions were entirely "legitimate and proper."

"The natives of a lot of these tribes love fighting for fighting's sake," Chief of Air Staff Hugh Trenchard assured Parliament. "They have no objection to being killed." The military's argument was that, though the often indiscriminate air attacks might perturb some civilized folks back in London, such acts were viewed differently by the Arabs. As one British commander observed, "[Sheikhs] . . . do not seem to resent . . . that women and children are accidentally killed by bombs." In other words, as Lawrence himself explained: to Arabs, women and children were "negligible" casualties compared to those of "really important men." He assured the British public that this was "too oriental a mood for us to feel very clearly."[29]

It was also clear to King Faisal and the men around him that the presence of the RAF, despite its often ruthless tactics, was vital to the survival of the fragile new government. Indeed—as was to be the case some eighty years later with American forces in Iraq—the overwhelming British military presence was the main force holding together the fractious, tinkertoy nation that Britain had constructed.[30] As Leo Amery, the Secretary of State for the Colonies, wrote in May 1925, "If the writ of King Faisal runs effectively throughout his kingdom, it is entirely due to British aeroplanes. If the aeroplanes were removed tomorrow, the whole structure would inevitably fall to pieces.[31]

In 1932, the last British high commissioner in Iraq was still warning against clipping the "claws" of the RAF because "the term 'civilian population' has a very different meaning in Iraq than what it has in Europe . . . the whole of its male population are potential fighters as the tribes are heavily armed."[32]

After his installation in 1921, protected by the British and the RAF, King Faisal grew in his role as a monarch far beyond what the British had expected—or wished. Through the army and schools, he attempted to forge a sentiment of nationhood among the hodgepodge of peoples and tribes that made up his kingdom. But he was constantly stymied by bitter internecine feuds and bickering, and especially by the corruption and penchant for intrigue that permeated Iraq's political elite.

His efforts to unify the country were also often subverted by the British. Ignoring the king and the central government, they frequently dealt directly with tribal leaders, doling out privileges and honors. Their objective was not to build a viable state, but to preserve their sway over the region and its huge oil resources.

Though Britain formally granted Iraq independence in 1932, the agreement still left the country subservient to London. The British retained sovereign rights over two major military bases and unlimited use of Iraqi airfields, ports, railroads, and roads in case of war. Iraq was also obliged to promise "full and frank consultations" in all questions of foreign policy.[33] The upshot was that Iraq and its monarch remained submissive to a foreign power despised by most Iraqis.

Fifteen Iraqi prime ministers came and went during Faisal's twelve-year reign. Elections were rigged to make sure there were no challenges to the cozy political merry-go-round, the same faces reappearing in each new government. The chasm between social classes widened; wealth, land, and power were increasingly concentrated in the hands of a tiny minority of privileged Sunnis and a few Shiite sheikhs.

In a confidential memo a dispirited Faisal wrote, "There is still—and I say this with a heart full of sorrow—no Iraqi people, but an unimaginable mass of human beings devoid of any patriotic ideas, imbued with religious traditions and absurdities, connected by no common tie, giving ear to evil, prone to anarchy, and perpetually ready to rise against any government whatsoever. Out of these masses we want to fashion a people which we would train, educate and refine. . . . The circumstances being what they are, the immenseness of the efforts needed for this [cannot be imagined]."[34] Disconsolate in his final years, Faisal died of coronary thrombosis in Switzerland in September 1933.

The British transported his body back to Iraq, where huge crowds wailed in mourning as the funeral cortege wound through the streets of Baghdad. It was an acclaim he had never achieved in life. What counted for the British was that Faisal had served their interests well: safeguarded their imperial air route to India, their local military bases, and their monopoly of Iraqi trade. Most important of all, despite the mounting protests of Iraqi nationalists, the king had never challenged the British-managed Iraq Petroleum Company's monopoly of the Mosul oil deposits. Under the original agreement, Iraqis were to have received a 20 percent share of the potentially huge concession. That was another promise never fulfilled.[35]

Ghazi, Victorious Son of Faisal

Faisal's crown was inherited by his twenty-one-year-old son, Ghazi, whose name meant "victorious"—which, unfortunately, was to prove highly inappropriate. He was, in fact, an incompetent, feckless playboy, lacking the intelligence or dedication of his father. Nonetheless, he was also fervidly anti-British, and that was to win him the widespread popularity his father never enjoyed.

What ignited Ghazi's hatred of the British was the fact that they had humiliated his grandfather, the Bedouin leader Hussein I, by reneging on their promise to make him king of the Arabs after World War I in return for his help against the Germans. Ghazi's dislike of the British was confirmed when, as a young man, he was packed off to Harrow to receive a proper British education. Boorish and virtually illiterate, he was miserable during his stay there. When he slept, he wore a fur-lined aviator's cap tightly over his head so that malevolent spirits would not be able to enter his ears.[36] At one point, he threatened to take his revenge for a perceived transgression by his housemaster by summoning the Iraqi army to burn down the residence hall. He left England without finishing his studies and enrolled in the Military Academy in Baghdad, where he spent most of his time at nightclubs and parties.

This unlikely young ruler, however, would become a national hero. The process began even before he took power. While his father, King Faisal, was out of the country on a trip, the Assyrian Christians in the north of Iraq rose in rebellion. There were suspicions that the British were behind the revolt, using the Assyrians to pressure the central government. Taking charge, Ghazi dispatched the Iraqi Army and Air Force to smash the uprising and teach the Assyrians a lesson they would never forget. And so the military did, killing thousands of Assyrian men, women, and children.

Overnight, Ghazi became a hero to Iraqi nationalists. He basked in the role. When he finally ascended the throne, he strutted about in sunglasses and military uniform with revolvers strapped to both thighs, glorying in the company of nationalist military officers. Though he spent most of his days and nights amusing himself with fast cars, horses, aircraft, and the scum of Iraqi society, he became an increasingly irritating thorn in London's side.

It was a curious power arrangement: an anti-British monarch, supported by nationalist officers, reigning over a country administered by a cabal of pro-British politicians. Foremost among these last was Nuri al-Said, who shrewdly managed the political game by playing one interest and tribe against another. Other top government officials came and went in a blur of intrigue. Power became increasingly centralized among the Sunnis of Baghdad, and corruption flourished at all levels of the administration. To keep pressure on the hostile king, the British and their civilian allies encouraged a series of tribal uprisings.

When the Shiite tribes of the south rebelled in 1935, the Sunni-led army reacted with a vengeance, destroying Shiite fields and villages and executing hundreds of tribesmen. The following year, Ghazi supported a bloody military coup against the civilian government. Pro-British Iraqi politicians fled the country. London was now decidedly alarmed by this upstart young ruler.

In 1937, Ghazi ratcheted his anti-British campaign up a notch further by setting up a radio station in the royal palace. Then, with himself and his army officers as announcers, he transmitted virulent attacks against the British and launched a cry for Arab independence. His broadcasts were heard in much of the Middle East. Outraged, the British ambassador demanded the station immediately go off the air. Ghazi refused.

Glorying in the uproar, he used his broadcasts to challenge the independence of the tiny oil-rich Sheikhdom of Kuwait. He maintained—as did most Iraqis—that Kuwait had been artificially carved by the British out of territories that should legally be part of Iraq. As a gesture to drive home his claims, Ghazi dispatched a small unit of Iraqi police and military in the dead of night to pull up the old border boundary markers, placed by the British, and move them southward into Kuwait. London was not amused. A British cabinet minister warned darkly that "the king [was] playing with fire." Official British communications between London and Baghdad talked in half-veiled terms of controlling or doing away with the monarch.[37] Nuri al-Said and other pro-British Iraqi politicians joined the ranks of plotters, as did some members of the king's own family.

On the night of April 3, 1939, Ghazi was seriously injured in an automobile accident, while he himself was supposedly at the wheel. He died a few hours later. No autopsy was ever carried out. The two members of the palace staff who were in the car with him disappeared. The communiqué from the British embassy to the foreign office in London on the day of the king's death is missing from the files. The following day, the *Guardian* newspaper disclosed that "Ghazi's death solved a problem for the British, who were thinking of removing him."[38]

Whether the British organized his murder or not, overnight Ghazi became a martyr to the cause of Arab independence across the Middle East, the kind of leader the people of Iraq desperately wanted:

someone who would be more than just a figurehead, who could unite their country, regain control over its resources, and become the leader of the Arab world.

The Golden Square and the Free Officers

Instead, they got Ghazi's almost equally corrupt and incompetent brother-in-law, who was to serve as regent for Ghazi's three-year-old son, Faisal II. In 1941, a small group of Iraqi army officers, who became known as the "Golden Square," overthrew the Baghdad government and called for Arab independence. Since they were anti-British, there was talk of allying themselves with the Germans. Refusing to recognize the new government, the British invaded Iraq for the second time, easily defeating the out-gunned Iraqis. They swiftly tried and executed three of the coup leaders, dismissed several hundred other army officers, and, in effect, reoccupied the country. That act destroyed any remaining credibility of the restored Iraqi monarchy and the Iraqi politicians who served the British cause. A new set of nationalist martyrs had been created. Saddam Hussein was only one of many young Iraqis who grew up determined to avenge the deaths of King Ghazi and the colonels of the Golden Square.

Anti-British sentiment was further inflamed over the following years, first by British efforts to retain the two large RAF bases they had established in Iraq, and then by the humiliating defeat of Arab armies in 1948 by the new state of Israel, which England had helped to create. Then in 1952, Arabs everywhere were electrified by the arrival of Gamal Abdel Nasser in Egypt, with his stirring call for Arab unity. At last, it seemed here was an Arab leader who could stand up to the West.

In 1955, as if oblivious to the mounting nationalist threat, the Americans and British pressured a reluctant Iraqi government to join the Baghdad Pact, an anti-Communist alliance. It included Iraq, Turkey and Iran, and Great Britain, the country most Iraqis held responsible for their plight. It was an attempt to weaken the Soviet Union and Nasser, but it only further undermined Iraq's British-backed monarchy. Another humiliation followed in 1956, when Nasser nationalized the Suez Canal, and the Iraqi government stood by as Britain,

France, and Israel joined forces in an effort to retake it. Iraqis swarmed into the streets to protest.

Finally, on July 14, 1958, the monarchy came to a bloody end. Iraqi soldiers calling themselves the "Free Officers" stormed the palace and executed the royal family. Not a single military unit fought to defend them. The hated pro-British politician Nuri al-Said was murdered when he was discovered attempting to flee, disguised as a woman. "They killed him," according to one lurid description, "then ran their cars back and forth over his body, buried him, then disinterred him and tore what remained into small scraps. His fingers and other parts of his body were paraded by people in the manner of a football trophy, and there were reports that some people drank his blood and ate his flesh."[39]

The virulent anti-British declarations of the Free Officers, with their implicit threat to Western oil interests, sent alarms clanging in London and Washington. The West made it very clear they would not allow the revolutionary contagion to spread. A few days later, British marines landed in Jordan to support King Hussein's fragile rule, while American marines were dispatched to Lebanon to prop up the pro-Western regime of President Camille Chamoun, who was already confronting pro-Nasser insurgents.

From the start, Brigadier Abdel Karim Qasim, the leader of the Free Officers, had attempted to reassure the West. Within twenty-four hours of the coup, he met with the British ambassador and declared that he had no intention of joining Nasser's United Arab Republic—the union of Egypt and Syria—or of restricting the supply of Iraqi oil to the world. According to one knowledgeable reporter, those assurances saved Iraq from a Western military attack,[40] though not from continued concern in London and Washington for their interests in the region.

Over the next few weeks, however, Qasim's regime launched a series of measures that were viewed as decidedly hostile in the West. Declaring Iraq neutral in the Cold War, he pulled out of the Baghdad Pact, closed British military bases, and tossed out Western advisors and contractors. Top British officials were so concerned about the threat to their oil interests that they even discussed preemptively occupying Kuwait.[41] In Washington, President Eisenhower, after assuring the

British he was equally concerned about the problem, ordered Joint Chiefs Chairman General Nathan F. Twining to "be prepared to employ, subject to [Eisenhower's] approval, *whatever* means might become necessary to prevent any unfriendly forces from moving into Kuwait."[42]

Meanwhile, in Baghdad, some pan-Arab nationalists expected that the next step would be union with the United Arab Republic and Nasser. But Qasim, it turned out, had no intention of deferring to Nasser. His goal was to develop the potential of his own country: Iraq first.

That policy provoked immediate hostility from pan-Arab officers in the army, who wanted to join with Nasser. Engaging in a dangerous political balancing act, Qasim purged hundreds of Nasserite officers and turned for support to the Communists, the best organized party in the country. To replace the British who had been his sole suppliers, Qasim signed an arms purchase agreement with the Soviets. Two Communists were given ministerial positions. He proclaimed a major, if over-hasty and ill-thought-out, land reform, which was extremely popular. His moves, however, provoked growing opposition in the army, increased fears in Washington and London, and pressured for regime change in Iraq.

Among the small groups that decried Qasim's policies was a party known as the Baath, which counted as a member the young Saddam Hussein. In October 1959, he joined a small hit squad charged with killing Qasim with the assistance of Egypt's intelligence service—and the CIA.

CHAPTER TWO

A Presentable Young Man : *Saddam's Rise to Power*
1959–1979

George W. Bush was not the first American president to attempt to overthrow the government of Iraq: Eisenhower, Kennedy, and Johnson led the way. Ironically, the result of their interventions was to give the Baath Party control of Iraq, thereby launching the political career of Saddam Hussein. Over the following years, most of the world's leaders looked on benignly as the brutal dictator-to-be took charge of his country and set about buying the components of a world-class military—including the means to construct a nuclear bomb—from governments and businesses around the globe. In fact, despite his crude methods of enforcing domestic order, Saddam would come to be regarded as one of America and Europe's most important strategic allies—and customers—in the Middle East.

The Hit

The story of the Baath Party's rise to power is one of imperial arrogance and unintended consequences, told in three parts. On October 7, 1959, on Al Rashid Street in Baghdad, a group of six or seven Baathists intercepted a car driving President Abdel Karim Qasim, intending to kill him. Saddam Hussein, then twenty-three, was supposed to cover their escape. The would-be assassins had been trained in Syria by Nasser's police; the CIA was also very much involved.[1]

Americans had long realized the importance of Iraq's huge oil reserves. In 1945, a State Department memo described them as "a stupendous source of strategic power and one of the greatest material prizes in world history."[2] But before 1956 Washington had never paid special attention to Iraq, which was considered Britain's area of interest. Britain's power, however, was waning, and the Eisenhower administration chose to intervene to keep oil in the Gulf in Western hands and out of those of the Soviets.

Cold-War Washington refused to recognize Iraq President Qasim's drive for Arab independence and increased control over the region's petroleum resources. They saw only a leader who claimed neutrality in a conflict in which the United States firmly believed there could be no neutrality—and who dealt with the local Communist Party, even naming Communists to key government posts and making arms deals with the Soviets.

In 1952, when Iranian Premier Mohammad Mossadegh's nationalist oil policies threatened American and British interests, the CIA had organized a coup to oust him. They had disposed similarly of left-leaning President Jacobo Arbenz in Guatemala in 1956. By April 29, 1959, CIA Director Allen Dulles was warning the U.S. Congress that Iraqi communists were close to a "complete takeover" and that the situation in the country was "the most dangerous in the world today."[3] In this context, eliminating Qasim must have seemed a logical move, and this is exactly what the CIA, along with Egyptian intelligence and members of the Iraqi Baath Party, attempted to do.[4]

According to some reports, the CIA helped set up and train a hit team, even installing Saddam in an apartment across the street from Qasim's office to observe his movements,[5] but the attempt to assassinate the Iraqi leader turned into farce. On the assigned day, Qasim's car showed up later than planned; his attackers lost their nerve and started firing too early. One of the would-be killers found the bullets he had been given didn't fit his gun; another was armed with a hand grenade that got stuck in the lining of his coat. Qasim's driver was killed by the attackers, but Qasim himself, though wounded, survived. One of the attackers was also killed, and Saddam was hit in the leg, probably by a shot fired by one of his fellow conspirators.[6] Saddam managed to escape, first to his native village of Tikrit, then to Damascus. Though Saddam was later decried as a cold-blooded killer by U.S. leaders, his ruthlessness was the very thing that had attracted the plot organizers to him in 1958 and led them to continue training him when the coup failed. According to Richard Sale, from Damascus Saddam went to Beirut where he spent two weeks in a basic CIA intelligence course, learning about codes and dead drops. After that he was taken to Cairo and established in a well-to-do neighborhood under the watchful eyes of Egyptian intelligence.[7] He played backgammon in Cairo's cafés and became caught up in exile politics. He also made regular visits to the U.S. embassy in Cairo, meeting with one of the CIA's most experienced operatives, Miles Copeland.

The Agency was still determined to overthrow Qasim. Saddam was one of many CIA "assets," young, ambitious, brutal, and a member of the Baath Party at a time that the CIA was interested in developing ties with that group. It was secular and fervidly anti-Communist. Many American officials came to view the Baath as their hope for the Arab world.

The Most Perfect Coup

The CIA would not succeed in toppling Qasim for another four years. In the meantime, he continued to challenge the West and the international oil companies. The Iraq Petroleum Company (IPC) had outraged Iraqis by leaving most of the country's oil fields undeveloped while the consortium's members exploited reserves they held elsewhere. In 1961, Qasim reacted, taking back into government control all the unexploited IPC concessions. He announced plans to create an Iraqi national oil company to develop those fields. His moves delighted Iraqis, but they were a dangerous challenge to the international oil cartel and its control of world markets. Any attempts by Iraq to market its own petroleum, the British and American governments warned, would be blocked by the cartel.

In June 1961, Qasim—as Saddam would do much more forcefully almost three decades later—sent a few Iraqi soldiers south in a quixotic gesture to challenge the newly declared independence of Kuwait, whose oil wealth was still controlled by the British. Confronted by Britain, who immediately dispatched troops to Kuwait, Qasim backed off.[8]

Despite his popular moves against the West, when it came to running the country, Qasim had little political sense. The regime that had begun with great revolutionary hopes disintegrated into shambles, largely dependent on the army and the secret police. The Kurds again rose in revolt in 1961, this time backed by the U.S., Britain, and Israel, as well as Iran, all of whom were eager to see Qasim overthrown. To meet the Kurdish threat, Qasim continued to purchase arms from the Soviets, which only confirmed the U.S. view that the Iraqi leader had to go.

With the approval of President Kennedy, the CIA took decisive action. American agents across the region helped organize a coup. From their base in Kuwait, they intercepted Iraqi communications and transmitted commands to the Iraqi plotters. A secret CIA unit known as the Health Alteration Committee sent Qasim a monogrammed, poisoned handkerchief, which may be ranked along with the poisoned cigars reputedly sent to Fidel Castro as among the more preposterous failed CIA assassination plots.[9]

What seems to have irked the U.S. and London the most was Qasim's refusal to drop Iraq's claims to its oil rich neighbor. At the beginning of February 1963, Qasim told a journalist from Le Monde that he had received a note from Washington "scarcely veiled, calling upon me to change my attitude under threat of sanctions against Iraq. . . . All our trouble with the imperialists began the day we claimed our legitimate right to Kuwait."[10] A few days later several army units, supported by the Baath and the CIA, rose in revolt, and by February 9 the unpopular president was a prisoner in his own palace, deserted by most of his former allies. Qasim was summarily tried and condemned to death. He and a few of his top officers were then taken immediately to the music studio of the government television station, where they were shot at point blank range. A TV camera was turned on, and one of his executioners held Qasim's head up by the hair to make it clear that his reign was at an end.[11]

The new revolutionary government was made up of army officers who were either Nasserites or members of the small Baath Party—one of whose low-ranking members was Saddam Hussein, treated to his first taste of power. There is no question that the CIA had played a major role in organizing and financing the affair. As Ali Sa'di al-Saleh, one of the key plotters, later said, "We came to power on a CIA train."[12]

"Almost certainly a gain for our side," Robert Komer, a National Security Council aide, wrote to Kennedy the day of the takeover. Former CIA Middle East expert James Crichtfield boasted for years after, "It was the CIA's most perfect coup. We really had the t's crossed on what was happening. It was regarded as a great victory."[13]

Immediately after the coup, the new government announced it was revoking the takeover of the IPC deposits and renouncing any claims to Kuwait. The U.S. State Department declared it was pleased with the new regime, avoiding any comment on another policy of the new rulers: a bloody reign of terror that the Baath Party unleashed in Iraq after the coup. Thousands of supposed Communists and leftists—army officers, doctors, teachers, lawyers, students—were arrested and tortured, sometimes shot on the spot or executed thirty at a time. The savagery went on for months and stripped Iraq of its most educated classes.[14]

In fact, far from protesting against these actions, the U.S. had enabled them. According to several sources, among them King Hussein of Jordan, who maintained strong links with the CIA, lists of "Communists" to be dealt with were relayed by radio to Baghdad from Kuwait on the day of the coup.[15] The butchery began as soon as the lists reached Baghdad. According to Said Aburish, one of the main sources for the list was William McHale, a CIA agent operating under the cover of a *Time* magazine correspondent.[16]

Among the torturer-executioners was Saddam Hussein. Thanks to his tribal connections with one of the principal coup leaders, Ahmad Hasan al Bakr, Saddam was appointed to the ill-defined president's bureau. He visited detention centers to oversee the disposal of suspected Communists and plunged into the bloody process himself. He had long admired the vicious tactics of Joseph Stalin and frequently repeated the Soviet dictator's grim maxim, "If there is a person, then there is a problem; if there is no person, then there is no problem."[17] "We had one simple order: exterminate the Communists," said Hatef Abdallah, who played a leading role in the 1963 massacres. "Saddam was in charge of torturing workers by pumping water into their bodies, breaking their bones, and electrocuting them."[18]

Estimates of the number killed in the 1963 bloodbath range from several hundred to several thousand. No one really knows; nor did the U.S. really care. A former senior U.S. State Department official admitted, "We were frankly glad to be rid of them. You ask that they get a fair trial? You have to be kidding. This was serious business."[19]

At the time, the overthrow of regimes judged pro-Soviet by the CIA was frequently followed by similar bloodbaths. The CIA's coup against Arbenz in Guatemala in 1956 led to the slaughter of thousands of peasants and workers by military death squads. Similar massacres followed the anti-Communist coup of Suharto in Indonesia. A few years later, military regimes in Chile and Argentina also tortured and disappeared thousands of young leftists, with the veiled approval of U.S. Secretary of State Henry Kissinger. Rather than protest the violence, Kissinger secretly advised the Argentinean generals to speed up their work lest a pesky U.S. Congress bestir itself to react.[20]

In the same spirit, after the 1963 coup in Iraq, U.S. and Baath officials met in Baghdad to formalize their ongoing relationship.[21] One of the points agreed upon was the common desire to contain Communism throughout the region.

Following the coup, doors that had been closed to the West, and particularly the Americans, suddenly reopened. Robert Anderson, a former U.S. treasury secretary under President Eisenhower who later developed close ties to the CIA, became a key intermediary for Americans wanting to do business with Iraq. Major American corporations like Parsons, Bechtel, and Mobil landed lucrative contracts and concessions. Iraq's new leaders performed another very useful service to the CIA, handing over Russian-built Mig-21's, T-54 tanks, and Sam missiles for United States experts to examine.[22]

A Final Putsch

The 1963 coup, however, was to give the Baath only the briefest shot at ruling the country. Within a few months, party members were feuding among themselves over everything from land reform to policy toward Kuwait to union with Nasser's Egypt and Syria. Saddam offered to help his faction by liquidating opposition leaders.[23] However, on November 18, 1963, President Abd al-Salam Aref, one of the army officers who had helped lead the coup, took advantage of the turmoil among his former Baath allies. Backed by several army units, he purged the Baath from power and arrested many of their leaders. Others, like Saddam, were driven underground, where they resolved to transform the Baath into a more potent, tightly knit clandestine party.

Meanwhile, Abd al-Salam Aref continued the nationalist oil policies that had been launched by Qasim. He formed the Iraqi National Oil Company (INOC), and announced that Iraq would start selling its own oil from non-IPC fields. Feeling their hold over the market threatened, the international oil companies declared they would refuse to supply oil to countries that dealt directly with the Iraqi government.[24]

In April 1966, Abd al-Salam Aref died in a helicopter crash during a sandstorm. He was replaced by his brother, General Abd al-Rahman Aref, an ineffectual leader intent on continuing his brother's nationalist policies. To counter the Americans and British, Aref invited the French oil consortium ERAP and the USSR to help develop the vast Rumaila oil field in southern Iraq and market its oil. He also refused to recognize the independence of Kuwait. Then he dealt Washington another stinging blow: he would grant a huge sulfur mining concession the Americans had been seeking to a French company.[25]

Fearful of losing its grip on Iraq and its resources, the U.S was irate, and the Baath Party had its opening. Secret negotiations between the Americans and the Baath resulted in an agreement that, if the party took power, the oil and sulfur concessions would be granted to American companies.[26]

President Aref attempted to gain support by playing the nationalists, but the incompetence and corruption of his government won him mostly hatred from his people. That contempt increased with the humiliating defeat of the Arab armies by Israel in the Six-Day War of 1967. Iraq's military contribution had been halfhearted and next to useless. Despite Aref's grand declarations, Iraqi troops never left Jordan. The Baath sent swarms of protestors into the streets to express their scorn.

Aref was finally overthrown on July 17, 1968, in an almost blood-less coup. At three A.M. a top Baath army officer simply telephoned the president and announced that troops were on their way to the palace. Aref agreed to leave peacefully for London to join his ailing wife, but only after he and the officer who came to depose him first took tea together.[27]

With this third attempt, the Baath took control of Iraq for good. Once again, the U.S. was involved. Already in 1966 Saddam had contacted the U.S. consulate in Basra asking for their help in overthrowing Aref.[28] According to Robert Morris, who served on the White House National Security Council, the U.S. helped organize the 1968 coup.[29] That charge was confirmed by one of the key Iraqi participants in the plot, the former Iraqi intelligence chief, Abd al-Razzaq al-Nayyif, who explicitly stated in his memoirs, "For the 1968 coup, you must look to Washington."[30]

When the Baath seized power along with the military in 1963, they were weak, bickering, and speedily purged from government. This time they were determined they would never be forced out again. However, their position, with only about 5,000 full-fledged members, was tenuous. They had convinced key military commanders to join the coup by promising that, once in power, the Baath would be content with a secondary role. Thus, though the new interim president, General Ahmed Hasan al-Bakr, was a Baathist, the party received only six of twenty-four ministries in the cabinet.

Saddam was picked to head the government's new security agency, innocuously called the Office of General Relations. His enforcement credentials were excellent: prior to the final takeover, he had worked underground in Iraq, establishing a burly, tightly knit paramilitary force for the Baath that was crucial to the 1968 coup.

With Saddam providing much of the muscle, the Baath lost no time in ousting its military partners. Within a few weeks President Bakr had seized sole control. In the background Saddam was consolidating his own power through the Mukhabarat, the ruthless new intelligence service run by officials who were personally loyal to Saddam. Soon, just the sight of one of their white Toyota Land Cruisers prowling the streets was enough to strike terror into the heart of any Iraqi. Even the mildest expression of dissatisfaction with the new regime could result in the most horrific forms of torture, prison, disappearance, or death.[31]

In November 1969, in classic Stalinist fashion, Saddam announced that his intelligence services had uncovered a plot by the CIA and Israeli spies to destroy the new regime. After a speedy show trial, fourteen of the accused—nine of them Iraqi Jews—were publicly hanged. Over the following months, there were more drumhead trials of other groups, abject confessions, and executions. Saddam also greatly expanded the Baath Party, tightening its control over the entire country, including the military. By the end of 1969, he was already considered the most powerful man in Iraq, and President Bakr's obvious heir apparent.

The British embassy in Baghdad took a keen interest in the ruthless young leader. On November 15, 1969, Paul Balfour, the ambassador, dispatched a brief, confidential biography to London, describing Saddam as "a presentable young man. Initially regarded as a Party extremist, but," he added hopefully, "responsibility may mellow him."[32]

On December 20, after finally meeting with Saddam, the ambassador sent another chatty report to London. Saddam, he said, "struck me as a much more 'serious character' than the other Baath leaders; and his engaging smile, when he deployed it, seemed part and parcel of his absorption of the subject in hand, and not, as with so many of the others, a matter of superficial affability. I should judge him, young as he is, to be a formidable, single-minded, and hard-headed member of the Baath hierarchy, but one with whom, if only one could see more of him, it would be possible to do business. It may have been an 'act'; but if so, it was a skillful performance for someone with so little experience of the outside world."[33]

There was no mention in either of those communications from the British embassy of Saddam's already notorious despotic penchants. This was, after all, a region of despots. Saddam was just a bit more tyrannical and blood spattered than others. What counted for Britain at the time were the tense, ongoing negotiations over the fate of the British-controlled Iraq Petroleum Company and its huge holdings in Iraq. British ears had perked up when, to balance the power of the British and Americans, Saddam had turned to the Soviets for help. The Soviets were already developing the huge Rumaila oil field, but Saddam still gave the British the impression he might be willing to make a deal.[34]

Instead, on June 1, 1972, Iraq finally nationalized the IPC and most of its holdings in Iraq. "Our wealth has returned to us," Saddam proclaimed.[35] Iraq's leaders, however, also wanted increased military aid from the USSR to deal with the Kurds. The tribesmen were once again engaged in guerrilla warfare in northern Iraq, with military backing from the Shah, the U.S., and the Israelis. The upshot was that Iraq and the USSR had signed a fifteen-year treaty of "friendship and cooperation." The Soviet Air Force was also granted access to Iraqi airfields, and their warships were given visiting rights at Umm Qasr, a small but strategically important Iraqi port on the Gulf—the same waters that U.S. ships were patrolling from Iranian harbors. In addition, two members of the Iraqi Communist Party were invited to join the government. To worried Cold Warriors in Washington, it looked as if Iraq might slide into total dependence on the Soviet Union.

Boom Times

But then came the Arab oil boycott of 1973, in the wake of Egypt's invasion of Israel, and everything changed. Oil prices shot skyward. The result was a bonanza to the oil-producing countries of the Gulf, including Iraq, which floated on 10 percent of the world's known petroleum reserves. Between 1972 and 1978, income from petroleum expanded from $575 million to $23.6 billion.[36]

Saddam had been raised in an impoverished village, in a region of semifeudal traditions and banditry, where a pair of shoes was considered a luxury. Now he was determined to use his power and the country's vast new wealth to transport Iraq into the twentieth century—whatever the human cost. He launched one of the most ambitious programs of economic and social development the world had ever seen. Billions of dollars were spent, and of course much of it wasted, on huge new industrial projects. In the once-impoverished countryside there were sprawling new dairy farms and irrigation projects. The most remote villages suddenly found themselves linked with Baghdad by electrical grids and networks of roads and broad highways. Baghdad's hotel lobbies and government ministries teemed with perspiring businessmen bearing the calling cards of the world's major corporations—Bechtel, Morrison Knudson, ITT, International Systems Controls, Caterpillar.

There were vast new hospitals and clinics with the best equipment money could buy—service free of charge for people who had known only poverty and disease. There were new universities and schools and literacy campaigns, programs to send thousands of young Iraqis for specialized training all over the globe. It was a magical era: Iraq was on an escalator heading up with no end in sight—its oil wealth seemed limitless.[37] As one journalist described the scene in the mid-1970s, "On the streets, double-decker buses imported from London traversed al-Rashid street; hawkers sold black-velvet paintings of Elvis Presley in a white sequined suit; and women from the villages, clutching plastic pocketbooks stuffed with dinars, pushed their way into the crowded gold souks."[38]

Saddam's ambitions went far beyond Iraq. He was determined to be the new leader of the Arab world, a modern Nebuchadnezzar who would avenge the repeated, shameful losses to Israel. Before he could found a new Babylonian Empire, however, he had to transform Iraq's military from a third-rate backwater force to a modern juggernaut, capable of holding its own against Israel.

It also had to be mighty enough to take on any other potential foe, such as the Shah of Iran, who had his own fantasies of restoring imperial grandeur. The Shah's visions were encouraged by the United States, who became much more involved in the region after the British withdrew in the late 1960s, exhausted by the cost of maintaining the Empire. America, however, was mired in Vietnam and needed a proxy to handle the Gulf. So, in 1972, President Richard Nixon and Secretary of State Henry Kissinger met with the Shah and, in effect, anointed him as America's policeman in the region. Over the following years, they trained his military and intelligence services and sold him billions of dollars in arms to block any further attempts at expansion into the oil-rich region by the USSR. They were already concerned about the Soviets' influence in Iraq.[39]

As Baghdad saw it, however, a resurgent Iran hell-bent on restoring past splendor represented a dangerous threat. The countries were uncomfortable neighbors, the Iraqis sometimes concerned about the large number of Persian nationals permanently resident in Iraq. They had nearly come to blows recently over the Shatt al-Arab, the broad, muddy channel at the mouth of the delta of the Tigris and Euphrates that connects to the Gulf. Since 1937, the whole waterway had been considered under Iraqi control, but the Shah now challenged that status.

Rather than confront each other directly, the two sides chose to battle through surrogates. Saddam expelled thousands of Iraqis supposedly of Iranian origin and promoted a rebellion among the predominately Arab population of the Iranian state of Khuzistan. For his part, the Shah launched a much more serious challenge, encouraging the Iraqi Kurds to renew their guerilla struggle against Baghdad.

The Kurds also received military support from Israel and the United States, who saw the rebellion as a way of weakening a country they considered a Soviet ally and a "terrorist state," which Washington had declared Iraq to be after it took in the notorious Palestinian Abu Nidal.

By 1975, Kurdish guerrillas controlled thousands of square kilometers of northern Iraq, threatening the vital petroleum center of Kirkuk and crippling the government's programs for building a new Iraq. Despite increasingly desperate requests from Saddam, for reasons best known to Moscow, military supplies from the Soviets ground to a halt. Saddam later revealed that by the time a truce with Iran was reached, "there were only three heavy missiles left in the air force and very few artillery shells."[40] He was obliged to make a humiliating deal with the Shah. In Algiers, in March 1975, the two men signed an agreement that gave Iran sovereignty over its side of the Shatt. In return, the Shah ended his support of the Kurds.

Saddam now appeared to be mending fences with his other neighbors in the region, talking about settling border disputes with Kuwait and Saudi Arabia and moving closer to Egypt and Jordan—which gave the Americans second thoughts about the Iraqi tyrant. He may have been a brutal dictator and the patron of some nasty people, but he also seemed to be a very down-to-earth leader who had brought a measure of stability to a traditionally chaotic land. Though his fulminations against Israel continued full blast, they could be easily dismissed as empty rhetoric.

On April 28, 1975, at his regular *tour d'horizon* with his assistants, Secretary of State Henry Kissinger listened as Roy Atherton gave his assessment that Iraq was "suddenly projecting the image of a country that wants to play a very dynamic and accurate [*sic*] role in the Arab world. . . . Hussein is a rather remarkable person. . . . He's the Vice President of the Command Council, but he is running the show; and he's a very ruthless and recently, obviously—pragmatic, intelligent power. I think we're going to see Iraq playing more of a role in the area than it has for many years."[41]

That certainly seemed to be the case. On July 17, at the residence of the Iraqi ambassador in Paris, Kissinger sat down for a secret meeting with Sa'dun Hammadi, Iraq's minister of foreign affairs. It was the first such top-level meeting between the two countries in several years. Kissinger first told the minister that one of the reasons for the U.S.'s unyielding support of Israel was that "until 1973 the Jewish community had enormous influence. It is only in the last two years, as a result of the policy we are pursuing, that it has changed." Though the U.S. would never cease its support of Israel, Kissinger continued, there was no reason why the U.S. and Iraq should not be able to normalize relations. He admitted that the U.S. had been backing the Kurdish rebellion in Iraq "because we thought you were a Soviet satellite." But the U.S.'s views had now changed. "We think you are a friend of the Soviet Union but you act on your own principles."

After recommending further exchanges between the U.S. and Iraq, Kissinger concluded optimistically, "Things will evolve."[42]

Arming Saddam

The humiliating agreement Saddam was obliged to sign with the Shah in 1975 made him even more determined to turn Iraq into a major military power. He also vowed never again to be at the mercy of a single weapons supplier, as he had been with the Soviet Union. He later revealed very frankly in a Machiavellian declaration to his official biographer, "The states that supply us with arms are friendly, but we cannot guarantee that the present will continue indefinitely. The states that supply us do not agree with us in all of our aims, for the boundaries of our aims and ambitions do not lie in Iraq but extend throughout the whole Arab homeland."[43]

With that principle in mind and Iraq's enormous oil wealth as a bankroll, Saddam and his agents went hunting for the most sophisticated weapons money could buy. The first stop on his shopping spree was Paris. Saddam had traveled there in 1972 to enlist French interest in developing Iraq's petroleum resources. At the time he had also purchased eighteen French helicopters, which proved valuable in battling the Kurds. In anticipation of his repeat visit, French officials gave anonymous background interviews to the press, talking excitedly of potential multibillion-franc weapons sales to Iraq.

By selling arms to Iraq, the French hoped to break the stranglehold that the United States and the Soviets had on the vast international arms trade. At the same time, they would provide a service to the West, weaning Saddam from his dependence on the USSR. From Saddam's point of view, France would be a useful partner: the country boasted a powerful military-industrial complex hungry for business. It wasn't by chance that Iraq opened a new cultural center in Paris in a building owned by the family of one of the most influential French arms merchants, Marcel Dassault.

Dassault was a Jew who fought in the resistance against the Germans during World War II, then converted to Christianity. His drive and brilliance had created one of Europe's greatest aerospace companies, Dassault Aviation. It turned out a stunning array of ingenious weaponry, the star of which was the Mirage fighter, marketed around the globe. Saddam's shopping spree represented a mind-boggling opportunity for the company. And Dassault had the clout to make things happen: he was a prominent member of the French Parliament and a close friend of France's most influential political leaders.

Dassault wasn't alone. Almost one thousand French companies in the arms business would sign lucrative deals with Iraq—including the French government, which was deeply involved in arms production and exports itself. Without large foreign sales, France would not have been able to afford the massive development costs of modern weapons.

France's powerful labor confederations also joined the weapons lobby, since more exports meant more high-paying jobs. In short, the government, the military-industrial complex, and the unions joined forces to supply Saddam in 1972. This meant that the French and Iraqis were soon talking about more and bigger deals. In 1974, Premier Jacques Chirac was greeted in Baghdad by a glowing Saddam. Iraq was now spectacularly on a roll. There were detailed discussions of mammoth infrastructure projects and arms deals. The French told Saddam they could not only sell him the same Mirage 3 fighters that Israel had so devastatingly used against the Arabs in 1973, but they could go one step further: they could provide Iraq with the Mirage F1, a much better-performing aircraft that was just completing flight tests. The Iraqis were delighted, and talked about ordering thirty-six of the new aircraft straight away, with an option on thirty-six more. The U.S. did not comment, in effect giving its tacit approval. There was no question those sales would weaken the Soviets' hold on Iraq.

On September 5, 1975, Saddam landed at Orly Airport in Paris, where he was embraced by Chirac, who welcomed the Iraqi tyrant as his "personal friend" and continued, "I assure you of my esteem, my consideration, and my affection." Over the following days Saddam was treated like visiting royalty, housed in the ornate Marigny Palace in Paris, feted at Versailles, invited to state lunches at the Elysee.[44] With Chirac in attendance, Saddam and his entourage—with a brief detour for a French bullfight—made the rounds of the best and most expensive weapons France had to offer. At a French Air Force testing site at Istre in southern France, they gawked as a French pilot put the Mirage through its paces.

At the end of the trip, Chirac bade his guest farewell. "French policy," he solemnly declared, "is dictated not merely by interest, but also by the heart."[45] Interests alone would probably have been enough—by then they included sales of giant petrochemical and desalination plants, telecommunications systems, broadcast networks, a new subway system, and an airport. As for weapons systems, the French under Chirac and subsequent administrations would sell the Iraqis the gamut: sea-skimming Exocet missiles, attack helicopters, tanks, rockets, howitzers, and a vast state-of-the-art ground defense radar system that would ultimately confound the U.S.-led coalition preparing to attack Saddam in 1990.

On July 16, 1977, in Baghdad, Raymond Barre, who had replaced Chirac as French Premier, settled the contract for thirty-two Mirage jet fighters. France would train the Iraqi pilots and maintenance crews and—in a clause that particularly infuriated the Soviets—French technicians would also maintain some Soviet weapons systems in Iraq.[46]

The French were walking a fine line. They refused to equip Saddam's fighters with the same sophisticated machines that Dassault was producing for the French Air Force itself—the equivalent of front-line NATO aircraft. Saddam reluctantly agreed to this restriction, but only on the condition that the French would provide him with the most advanced model in the future. So eager for sales were the French that they sweetened the deal by offering to set up an engine maintenance facility for the new Mirage F1 in Iraq. This was of particular interest to Saddam, since his ultimate goal was to make Iraq the center of a massive Arab arms industry. The Soviets had refused to give the Iraqis the skills to overhaul the engines of their high-performance jet fighters; the French had no such qualms.

Saddam may have captured Chirac's heart, but he was determined to play the field, to diversify his suppliers of weapons, military infrastructure, and training. Britain was only one of many nations happy to oblige. British firms constructed highly reinforced military airports and bomb-proof subterranean command posts for Saddam—the same targets that the Americans, British, and their allies would have such difficulty destroying in 1990.[47] In 1976 they also began training Iraqi Air Force officers along with other foreign military personnel at Cambridge, according to rigorous RAF standards.[48]

West German arms manufacturers had an obstacle to surmount. In the flush of pacifist sentiment following World War II, the German parliament had drafted a law making it illegal for Germans to export arms. Despite that prohibition, one of Germany's major arms companies, Messerschmitt-Bolkow-Blowm (MBB) was able to export thousands of antitank and antiaircraft missiles to Iraq by selling them through a consortium with Aerospatiale in France. As long as Germans weren't the ones actually doing the selling, there was no problem. The Italians found their niche by providing Saddam with a modern navy. For $2.6 billion they agreed to furnish the Iraqis a nine-ship, ready-made fleet, complete with docks, maintenance facilities, weapons systems, and training for several hundred Iraqi naval officers in Italy.

Brazil also played a key role. In return for rights to develop oil in Iraq, the Brazilians equipped Saddam with armored cars and trucks. Thanks to those sales, the Brazilians were able to vastly expand their own growing weapons industry.[49]

These massive deals with the West—particularly with France—and the defeat of the Kurds emboldened Saddam to distance himself from the Soviets by cracking down on the Iraqi Communist Party, whose support he felt he no longer needed. In 1976 he executed twenty-one Iraqi soldiers for the crime of belonging to the Party. A new law had decreed that the military could only belong to the Baath; Saddam gladly applied it ex post facto. In the same year he also demanded that the Soviets move their embassy from its spot adjacent to the presidential palace, where they could presumably eavesdrop electronically on the most sensitive government matters. When the Soviets demurred, Saddam cut off their water and electricity until they relented. He also announced he would no longer align Iraq's foreign policy with that of Moscow.[50]

Despite that defiance, the Soviets were still eager to sell Saddam billions of dollars worth of the most sophisticated equipment they had to offer—including their high performance MIG-23 fighter. The USSR also provided training for Iraqi Air Force officers and mechanics.

But the most advanced jet fighters and missiles were not enough for Saddam. He wanted a first-class military—with more than just conventional weapons. For starters, Saddam wanted chemical weapons and the facilities to produce them. Chemical weapons were cheap and could be devastating on the battlefield, and all the great powers had them. The Egyptians had used them in the mid-60s to put down a rebellion in Yemen. Saddam wanted the full range, from asphyxiating mustard gas to the nerve agents Tabun and Sarin, of which a single drop on the skin kills instantly.

Chemical weapons are the perfect dual-use weapon—the same plant that produces fertilizers or insecticides one day can turn out deadly nerve and mustard gas the next. Saddam dispatched agents abroad to shop for production facilities, working behind front companies that apparently had nothing to do with the military. They first contacted the Soviets, but Moscow was leery of Saddam's objectives and turned him down. In 1974, an Iraqi agent paid a call to the Pfaulder Chemical Company in Rochester, New York, which specialized in constructing chemical plants. Pfaulder provided a detailed plan of the kind of pesticide facility he said he wanted, and a few months later, Pfaulder technicians came to Iraq ready to deal. But they were surprised at the highly toxic chemicals the Iraqis said they needed, the huge volumes involved, and the Iraqis' impatient disregard for normal safety procedures. Pfaulder backed out of the deal, but the Iraqis held on to the plans.[51]

In late 1976, the Iraqis visited two British companies about building a modern pesticide plant for Iraq. Immediately wary of the specifications, both companies turned down the request, and one of them, Imperial Chemical Industries, promptly informed British intelligence, which passed on the information to their American counterparts. The other company turned the Iraqis down.[52]

Saddam's procurement teams had much better luck in East Germany. Over the following years many East German specialists actively worked on a joint chemical weapon production program between their government and Iraq's.[53] They finally assembled a plant with components purchased in East and West Germany and Italy, probably based on the original plan furnished by Pfaulder. The chemicals produced by this plant would be used with lethal effect against Iranian troops and Iraq's own people. One East German expert on chemical weapons later reported that the Iraqis had confided in one of their first meetings, "You Germans have great expertise in the killing of Jews with gas. This interests us in the same way. . . . How [can] this knowledge . . . be used to destroy Israel?"[54]

One of the most massive projects was overseen by the Belgian firm Sybetra. They used more than fifty subcontractors from around the world to build the giant al-Qaim fertilizer complex along the Euphrates between 1980 and 1983. Years later, in 1991, U.N. inspectors found that the complex also housed a chemical weapons plant.[55] The companies involved claimed to have been innocent dupes of the Iraqis, despite the extremely toxic chemicals the Iraqis were after and the substantial military fortifications around those supposedly civilian sites.

As Saddam saw it, these chemical weapons, though useful, were small change. If he was going to be the new leader of the Arab world, the new Saladin who would confront the Imperialists and the Zionist state, he had to have nuclear weapons. They were Israel's ace in the hole. China had them; India was working on them. There was talk that the Shah was, too. Even Qadaffi was said to be interested. In 1973 Saddam secretly declared himself the head of Iraq's nuclear program and told his scientists to build him an arsenal.[56]

Again, the Iraqis first approached the Soviets, who had already furnished Iraq with a couple of small research reactors. But they insisted that any deal would have to be accompanied by strict controls to ensure there was no diversion of reactor by-products for weapons purposes. The Iraqis weren't interested. Canada also turned down an Iraqi approach.

France was a different matter. Like the conventional arms business, the nuclear trade was dominated by the United States and the Soviet Union. The French, who had always followed an independent nuclear policy, wanted a piece of the action. In the 1950s, the French socialists had sold a reactor to Israel that helped launch its nuclear weapons program. Why shouldn't the French under Chirac sell a reactor to Saddam Hussein?

During his visit to France in September 1975, the Iraqi leader and his entourage toured the Cardache nuclear research center in southern France, one of the most advanced in Europe. The Iraqis were interested in a fast breeder reactor to produce nuclear fuel—for purely civilian purposes, they claimed. It was obvious that France's attitude on nuclear sales to Iraq would have a direct bearing on winning other huge projects that were currently being negotiated. They finally agreed to furnish the Iraqis with two research reactors: one full-sized, which became known as Osirak, the other a smaller-scale model. Though not as large as the

Iraqis desired, the deal would still enable them to obtain bomb-grade plutonium. The French also agreed to train six hundred Iraqi nuclear technicians in some of France's leading institutions. The deal, the French loftily declared, was an outstanding example of how rich nations of the north could transfer technology to aid the developing world.

That remained the official French position despite the fact that the day Saddam ended his visit to France, a major Lebanese weekly published an interview with the Iraqi leader in which he declared, "The agreement with France is the first step toward the production of the Arab atomic weapon."[57] It is clear that French officials knew they were engaged in questionable business. Major international accords usually receive full public scrutiny. However, official publication of the Franco-Iraqi Nuclear Cooperation Treaty was handled in a much more devious fashion: the full text was not revealed until eight months after the signing, buried in the French public register, *Le Journal Officiel*, of June 18, 1976. This helped keep under wraps the embarrassing stipulation that "all persons of the Jewish race or the Mosaic religion" be excluded from participating in the program, either in Iraq or in France."[58]

As criticism of the French-Iraqi deal mounted, the French attempted to modify the terms so that they would furnish the reactors with a much lower grade, "clean" fuel that would be unusable for weapon production. Saddam refused the change, and spoke darkly of canceling other lucrative commercial deals with France. The French finally relented, attempting to save face by insisting that the fuel be delivered in smaller consignments—a change that would not have prevented the Iraqis from producing a nuclear weapon. By October 1979, French exports to Iraq were up a staggering 53 percent over the previous year, mainly from weapons systems. Iraq now supplied France with 25 percent of its petroleum needs.

The French government curtly rebuffed requests from Israel and the U.S. that they call off their deal with Iraq. That infuriated Israeli Prime Minister Menachem Begin, who viewed Saddam as another Adolf Hitler; he opted for direct action. On April 6, 1979, a group of seven Israeli commandos slipped into a warehouse at La Seyne-sur-Mer near Toulon in southern France. They placed specially shaped charges on eight crates containing elements for the core of the Osirak reactor, ready to be shipped to Iraq. At 3:15 A.M. explosions shattered the early morning silence. The core components were totally destroyed. An unknown organization called the French Ecological Group claimed credit for the blast. The French SDECE intelligence agency concluded that the Israeli Mossad was almost certainly responsible. Then in June 1980, Dr. Yahya al-Meshad, an Egyptian metallurgist working for Iraq's nuclear program who was in France to arrange for French nuclear fuels to be shipped to Iraq, was stabbed to death in a Paris hotel. Since nothing was taken from his room, the police ruled out robbery as a motive. Mossad watchers were quick to credit Israel. The Israelis probably expected such actions would persuade the French to end their nuclear dealings with Iraq. They were wrong.[59]

France was not the only country to assist Saddam's quest for the bomb over the protests of its allies. In 1978, an Italian subsidiary of Fiat agreed to provide Iraq with four nuclear laboratories and three "hot cells," needed to handle nuclear fuel. When the U.S. tried to block the sale, the Italians protested that if they didn't complete the deal, the Iraqis would cancel the huge naval contract they had signed.[60]

Iraq's nuclear program ultimately involved a tangled web of secret agreements and scientific collaboration that spanned the globe. They signed a clandestine accord, for instance, with the Brazilians, who had begun their own secret nuclear development program. The Iraqis calculated that, via the Brazilians, they would get access to West German nuclear expertise as well, since the West Germans had an accord with the Brazilians. Meanwhile, under Saddam's instructions, the Iraqis penetrated a delegation from the International Atomic Energy Agency that was supposed to be inspecting Iraq's civilian nuclear program at al-Tuwaitha, north of Baghdad. Over the following years, almost under the eyes of those inspectors, Saddam's scientists built a huge secret annex, where they planned to produce Iraq's own nuclear weapons.[61]

End Game

Saddam was now the unquestioned power in Iraq. His security services were everywhere, alert to even a whisper of opposition. Yet it wasn't just fear of the Mukhabarat that muffled popular discontent. For the first time ever, Iraqis finally had a sense of stability—ruthlessly enforced, certainly, but still a novelty. Thanks to oil, for Iraqis who stayed clear of politics, life was good and getting better.

President Bakr, supposedly weakened with heart problems, had faded into the background, a pale father figure for the country. In July 1979, Saddam finally ended the charade. Bakr had supported the idea of a union between Iraq and Syria—a move that would have undercut Saddam's ambitions to take power formally and completely in Iraq. To prevent this, Saddam confronted Bakr, forced him to resign, and undertook a massive, brutal purge of his government.

On July 22, at the large Al-Khuld conference center in Baghdad, Saddam, who had been inaugurated as president five days earlier, summoned an extraordinary conference of more than one thousand top Baath Party members from across the country. The event was filmed as a warning to anyone even thinking of conspiring against the new leader. After an official declared that a plot against the regime had been discovered, Saddam solemnly announced to the transfixed audience that the guilty were present. As their names were called one after another, sixty-six people, including some of Saddam's oldest colleagues, rose to be led away by his security forces. Iraq was transformed from a military dictatorship to a totalitarian state.

Within a few weeks, fifty-five Baathists were convicted of being party to the supposed conspiracy; twenty-two of them sentenced to death through "democratic executions." Regional Baath associations across the country were each ordered to provide one delegate to participate in the firing squads, implicating the entire Baath Party in the killings; the fate of the executioners would be tied to Saddam's.

Again, Saddam ordered the entire proceedings filmed. The condemned kneeled, blindfolded, their hands bound behind their back. Saddam handed a pistol to each of the executioners, then he himself fired the first shot to initiate the massacre. Some of the shots missed their mark; the executioners were inexperienced or nervous. The wounded lay writhing on the ground. They were finally dispatched by a more professional executioner: a single pistol shot to the head.[62]

Over the following months and years, Saddam's hit men would continue to hunt down and assassinate any Iraqis who had earned the tyrant's fear or displeasure. Former President Bakr himself was killed three years later, in 1982, when the disastrous war with Iran prompted talk of restoring him to power. One report has it that he was murdered by a team of Saddam's security agents, posing as doctors who had been sent to treat Bakr for health problems. They injected the ex-president with a large dose of insulin, provoking a coma from which he never recovered.[63]

According to one report, Saddam could not have undertaken this brazen coup without first lining up support from his pro-West neighbors—as well as the CIA. Early in July 1979, he traveled to Jordan to brief King Hussein (and, through him, the Saudis) on his plans to block a proposed union of Syria and Iraq and get rid of Bakr. Saddam also notified the CIA station in Amman. Since the Americans and their allies in the region feared a possible union of Syria and Iraq, they let the dictator know they would do nothing to oppose his move.[64]

After July 1979, Saddam's control was supreme. He ruled Iraq like a tribal sheikh. He and his relatives and old associates from Tikrit held almost every key position. Saddam, of course, also had ambitions that extended far beyond the borders of Iraq. And thanks to arms merchants from around the world, he now had at his command one of the most powerful military forces in the region. Even after the bloody 1979 purges and Saddam's extraordinary display of ruthlessness, governments from the West and East tripped over each other in their desire to provide the tyrant with ever more deadly weapons.

The stage was set for the next tragedy—the invasion of Iran, which launched the longest war of the twentieth century.

CHAPTER THREE

The Tilting Game: The Iran-Iraq War 1980–1988

I hope they kill each other . . . too bad they both can't lose.

—Henry Kissinger, Nobel laureate and former
secretary of state, on the Iran-Iraq War

When speculation first began about the trial of Saddam Hussein and the crimes for which he would be charged, high on the list was his illegal invasion of Iran in September 1980. It precipitated a bloody conflict that lasted for eight horrific years and resulted in the deaths of more than one million soldiers and civilians; at least another two million were wounded.

But as preparations for the trial proceeded, the invasion of Iran and the ensuing war were dropped as charges. One reason may be that Iran was still considered a major threat by the United States; there was little sympathy for that battered country among the Americans who played the key role in organizing the tribunal. Another possible reason is that the United States, through its allies, had encouraged Saddam to launch his aggression, giving him a green light for the crime. They did not want that kind of dirty political linen to be washed in public.

Over the eight years of the war, Washington, while claiming to be neutral, tilted back and forth between the two belligerents, funneling arms and intelligence first to one side, then to the other; at one point to both sides at once. The tilting reflected conflicting views within the Reagan and Bush administrations themselves—and a short-sighted conception of American interests in the region. By the end, American forces were clandestinely engaged in the conflict themselves.

The Green Light

First, there was a strengthening of relations between the U.S. and Iraq. The Cold War largely determined Washington's view of the Middle East in 1979. As the Carter White House saw it, they were confronting a multipronged Soviet offensive in the region. The Soviets had invaded Afghanistan, they were behind an attempt to take over North Yemen, and now came the radical Islamic upheaval in Iran, which toppled one of the U.S.'s key allies in the Gulf.

On January 16, 1979, the Shah of Iran, who, along with the Saudis, had been viewed as one of the two pillars of American policy in the region, was overthrown by a wide-ranging popular revolt and driven into permanent exile. He was replaced by a fire-breathing Shiite leader, Ayatollah Ruhollah Khomeini, preaching a revolutionary form of Islamic fundamentalism and hatred of the U.S.

As popular demonstrations against the Shah had flared, the Carter administration had encouraged the monarch to cede power, hoping for a more moderate civilian administration. Instead, they watched helplessly as Khomeini's revolution became increasingly radicalized, and the new Iranian leader rebuffed overtures for dialogue. With the storming of the American embassy on November 4, 1979, and the taking of fifty-five hostages, the radicals were unquestionably in control of the country. Khomeini escalated his verbal attacks against the United States, whom he accused—correctly—of having supported the Shah and continuing to back the monarchies of the Gulf.

The U.S. was also becoming radicalized in its views of Khomeini. There was fear among some in Washington that the Soviets were attempting to manipulate his revolution. Domestic politics also drove White House concern. Each day that the hostages remained in Iranian custody was another blow to the flagging reelection campaign of President Jimmy Carter, already humiliated by a failed attempt to rescue the fifty-five Americans. Khomeini was now America's foreign enemy number one. He had to go, or at least enough pressure had to be applied to force him to temper his policies, and particularly release the hostages.

It was an ideal opening for Saddam Hussein, whom Khomeini threatened much more directly than he did the United States. Hussein and other Middle Eastern rulers were explicitly in the Iranian revolution's cross-hairs. "Other tyrants," Khomeini darkly warned, "have yet to see their day of reckoning." His radical message spread like wildfire outside the borders of Iran, provoking riots and political unrest among the Shiite populations of the Gulf—and nowhere more so than in Iraq, where the Shiites had always been a restive majority unhappily dominated by the Sunnis.[1] One charismatic cleric, Mohammed Baqr al-Sadr, inspired by Khomeini's rants against the non-Islamic Baath, formed the Al Dawa Party to unite all Muslims of Iraq—Shiites, Kurds, and Sunnis—against Saddam's secular government.[2]

On April 1, 1979, young members of Sadr's party, which had already been implicated in the murder of several Iraqi government officials, tried to assassinate Saddam's deputy prime minister, Tariq Aziz. Four days later, a Dawa hit squad attacked the funeral of the Baath loyalists who had been killed in the attack on Aziz and murdered more people.

Saddam's response was characteristically swift and savage. Membership in the Dawa Party became punishable by death. Thousands of Shiites were detained and tortured; hundreds were killed. Riots broke out in southern Iraq. More people were executed or disappeared, and thousands more were arrested. Tens of thousands of impoverished Shiites, unable to prove their Iraqi identity, were forcibly deported to Iran without their belongings. Along the border with Iran, bloody skirmishes became a daily affair.

Saddam called for the destruction of Khomeini's regime to ensure stability in Iraq. But there was another motive: With the Shah no longer the U.S. gendarme in the Gulf, why shouldn't Saddam take his place? Indeed, why shouldn't Saddam truly become the leader of the Arab world? Though the U.S. and Iraq had had no formal diplomatic relations since the Arab-Israeli Six-Day War of 1967, Washington and Baghdad realized they now needed each other.

So began a delicate political ballet that would lead to a green light from the United States for Saddam's invasion of Iran. In 1979 the Iraqi dictator began toning down his anti-West rhetoric. He condemned the Soviet invasion of Afghanistan and signed an alliance with Saudi Arabia to block the Soviet-backed attempt to take over North Yemen. In 1979 he also allowed the CIA, which he had once so virulently attacked, to open an office in Baghdad.[3]

In Washington, meanwhile, on January 23, 1980, concerned by the Soviet invasion of Afghanistan and reported Soviet inroads in revolutionary Iran, President Jimmy Carter, enunciating what would become known as the "Carter Doctrine," issued a clear warning to Moscow. Declaring that Soviet troops in Afghanistan posed "a grave threat to the free movement of Middle East oil," Carter proclaimed: "Let our position be absolutely clear: an attempt by any outside force to gain control of the Persian Gulf region will be regarded as an assault on the vital interests of the United States of America, and such an assault will be repelled by any means necessary, including military force."[4]

President Carter's national security advisor, Zbigniew Brzezinski, who had drafted the president's speech, had also been proposing behind the scenes that the U.S. reconsider its "nonrelationship" with Iraq. This was just a few months after Saddam had seized total power through a bloody nationwide purge, at a time when he was torturing and executing many Iraqi Shiites and forcibly evicting tens of thousands of others. Brzezinski went public in April 1980, writing in the *New York Times*, "We see no fundamental incompatibility of interests between the United States and Iraq. We feel that American-Iraqi relations need not be frozen in antagonism." America and Iraq, he assured his readers, wanted the same thing: "a secure Persian Gulf."[5]

Washington showed a new willingness to aid the Iraqi dictator. As part of Iraq's $2.6 billion contract to purchase a navy from the Italians, Saddam's Ministry of Defense insisted that the Italian frigates be equipped with General Electric gas turbine engines from the United States. The U.S. Department of Commerce approved the deal, but outraged U.S. senators, pointing out that Iraq was still branded a terrorist state by the U.S., moved to block the sale as "contrary to common sense." Undaunted, in the summer of 1980, the Carter administration maneuvered behind the scenes to defeat the Senate objections. Saddam was quick to interpret the move as a sign of U.S. encouragement to move against Iran.[6] He wasn't wrong—the White House was interested in any move that could bring pressure on the regime in Tehran.

As it became increasingly clear that the dispute between Saddam and Khomeini could lead to war, Saddam also began looking for allies among his neighbors. He portrayed himself as the new standard-bearer of the Arabs. He and his envoys received sympathetic hearings in Jordan, the Gulf States, and Egypt. Their leaders were thoroughly shaken by the febrile response of their own Shiite populations to Khomeini's diatribes against the "corrupt and impure" rulers of the region. The most important of these meetings was with Saudi Prince Fahd. As if contracting a mafia hit team, Fahd promised Saddam billions of dollars of support for any move to eliminate Khomeini.[7]

The United States followed all this with obvious approval. Though Jimmy Carter later denied in his memoirs that the U.S. was behind Iraq's invasion of Iran, in fact the U.S. sent a nuanced but explicit signal via America's major ally in the region, the Saudis. A confidential two-page "talking points" memo drawn up by Alexander Haig, Ronald Reagan's first secretary of state, and uncovered by reporter Robert Perry in 1993, offers an account of Haig's first tour through the Middle East in April 1981. Haig writes of his meetings with Saudi Prince Fahd and Egypt's Anwar Sadat, "It was also interesting to confirm that President Carter gave the Iraqis a green light to launch the war against Iran through Fahd." When Perry later attempted to ask Haig about the memo, he refused to discuss it.[8]

The Carter White House had played a delicate game, inducing Saddam to move against Khomeini without leaving American fingerprints on the operation. As one insider put it, "Brzezinski was letting Saddam assume there was a U.S. green light for his invasion of Iran, because there was no explicit red light." James Aikens, former U.S. ambassador to Saudi Arabia (1973–1975), also believes there was a U.S. green light given to Saddam via the Saudis.[9]

To encourage Saddam to attack, the United States passed on intelligence reports exaggerating the political turmoil in Iran. All Saddam had to do, it seemed, was to dispatch his troops across the border and the regime would collapse. According to Howard Teicher, who served on the White House National Security Council, "the reports passed on to Baghdad depicted Iran's military in chaos, riven by purges and lack of replacement parts for its American-made weapons. The inference was that Iran could be speedily overcome."[10]

"We were clearly stuffing Saddam's head with nonsense, to make conditions look better than they were," commented Richard Sale, who covered the intelligence community for United Press International at the time. "The information was deliberately fabricated, to encourage him to go in."[11]

There is convincing evidence that the U.S. played an even more direct role in convincing Saddam to invade. In July 1980, the Iraqi leader was in Amman, Jordan, at the same time as three top CIA operatives. According to the best informed of Saddam's biographers, the timing of those visits was more than coincidental. Either directly or indirectly via Jordan's King Hussein, Saddam exchanged views with the Americans about his plans to invade Iraq.[12]

There are some who charge that the United States not only prodded Saddam to invade Iran, but that Americans, along with dissident Iranian generals, were also involved in planning the attack. Aboholsom Bani Sadr, the president of Iran in 1980, has made that charge from his exile in France. He claims that his spies obtained the war plan drawn up in Paris by Iranian exiles and their Israeli and American advisors. He became convinced of the authenticity of the document, he says, "because the war was made exactly according to the plan. Fortunately, we bought it before the war, because it was that plan that saved Iran."[13] Richard Sale confirms that U.S. officials did have access to Iraqi plans prior to the attack.

Whether one accepts Bani Sadr's claim or not, the conclusion remains that the United States made certain that Saddam Hussein understood that an attack on Khomeini would be welcomed by Washington and supported by its allies in the Gulf. Indeed, when Iraqi forces swept into Iran on September 22, 1980, there were no indignant speeches from Western leaders or calls for a U.N. embargo, as there were when Saddam invaded Kuwait ten years later. The reason is obvious: in 1980, the man who would later be decried as the "Beast of Baghdad" was serving Western interests.

The United Nations Security Council delayed four days before holding a meeting. When it finally passed a resolution calling for an end to hostilities, there was no condemnation—or even mention—of the Iraqi aggression, nor did it demand a return to internationally recognized borders. As one expert concluded, "The Council more or less deliberately ignored Iraq's actions in September 1980."[14] The U.S. delegate to the U.N. scoffed at Iranian protests. He declared that since Iran had regularly ignored Security Council resolutions on the U.S. embassy hostages, it had no right to complain about the Council's lack of action in this case.

There was another sign that Saddam's invasion of Iran had been well coordinated with others. When the war broke out, both sides began attacking each other's oil production facilities. The damage could have brought chaos to the sensitive international oil market, but Saudi Arabia, the world's largest oil exporter, immediately acted to increase its oil production by 900,000 barrels a day. That quick action and the lack of panic by oil companies also indicated that tactics had been synchronized with Washington.[15]

The Standoff

From the beginning, however, the war did not go as Saddam had hoped. He planned a Blitzkrieg attack, like Israel's Six-Day War victory over the Arabs in 1967. But despite a few successful initial thrusts in September and October 1980, the invasion of Iran quickly became a bloody quagmire, an extended war with a country three times the population of Iraq and three times the oil revenues. The information Saddam had been given about Iran—that the population, fed up with Khomeini's radical revolution, would rise and greet the Iraqi leader as their liberator—turned out to be dead wrong. Instead of revolting against Khomeini, Iranians united under the banner of Islam and nationalism to defeat the Arab invaders.

As the *New York Times* reported, "The Iranian front lines tend to be scenes of chaos and dedication, with turbaned mullahs, rifles slung on their backs, rushing about on brightly colored motorcycles encour-

aging the troops. Religious slogans are posted everywhere, and sometimes reinforcements arrive cheerfully carrying their own coffins as a
sign of their willingness to be 'martyred.'"[16]

Within the first few months of the conflict, Saddam was searching for a face-saving way out of the mess, but the Ayatollah Khomeini
would hear nothing of it. He demanded reparations before any peace
treaty; he was determined to destroy the infidel who dared challenge
his Islamic revolution.

Saddam expected the great powers to intervene, but the great
powers—particularly the U.S.—were not particularly interested in
ending the conflict. When the war began, President Carter declared
that the U.S. would remain neutral. Publicly, he banned the sales of
weapons to either side. In fact, though, what Carter had been hoping
was that Saddam's attack would oblige Iran to release the hostages in
return for American arms to fight off Iraq. The Iranians were desperately in need of replacement parts for their many U.S.-made weapons,
like the Phantom A-4 jet fighters. The White House hoped they could
make a deal with the Iranians before the coming November elections
in the U.S. The Iranians were not interested. They were already buying huge stocks of U.S.-made military equipment from the Israelis, as
well as from other countries, such as Vietnam, where the U.S. had left
behind large caches of weapons in 1975.[17]

The Reagan administration, which took office on January 20, 1981,
also didn't want either side to win decisively. They hoped that Saddam's
attack would provide the impetus to topple Khomeini but not destroy
Iran. Indeed, there were many in Washington and other world capi-
tals who were content to look on over the following horrific years and
profit from the raging conflict. It was very similar to the American view
of the Nazis and the Soviets in World War II: it would be good to have
these two very unpleasant parties bleed themselves white. Or as Henry
Kissinger said a few years into the bloody conflagration, "Too bad they
both can't lose . . . I hope they all just kill each other."[18]

Kissinger's lofty detachment, however, obscured the fact that those
being blown apart were not Saddam Hussein and Khomeini, but hundreds of thousands of Iraqi and Iranian soldiers and civilians. As the
Iranians slowly pushed back the Iraqi lines, appalling numbers of

untrained and often unarmed young Iranian soldiers continued to be mowed down in massive assaults. After two desperate attacks in the Basra region in the summer of 1982, tens of thousands of Iranian soldiers lay dead on the field.

Saddam had no plan to terminate the war, nor did he have the marshal skills to win it.[19] Though he had never been in the military, he insisted on controlling every detail of the far-flung conflict himself. Experienced Iraqi generals were too terrified of the dictator's fury to offer contrary advice. They were timid in the field, afraid of being second-guessed by their leader, who often executed losing commanders himself.

Saddam, however, did have one success: he was able to mobilize the country behind the war effort. The Iraqi Shiites, rather than rising up to join their Iranian coreligionists, proved instead that they were willing to die for Iraq. But what held Iraqis together as much as Saddam's jingoism was the omnipresent terror of Saddam's spies and secret police—and the bloody retribution he would exact at any sign of resistance.

That was the fate of Dujail, a quiet farming village on a branch of the Tigris River about forty miles north of Baghdad. Its fathers and sons, predominately Shiites, were being decimated in the disastrous war. On July 8, 1982, Saddam Hussein visited Dujail to try to whip up patriotic fervor. Unknown to most of the villagers, a group of seventeen young men from Dujail planned to assassinate the tyrant as his convoy arrived. In the firefight that ensued, several of Saddam's bodyguards were wounded or killed. Saddam and his remaining escort were pinned down by the would-be assassins' fire, but the young men lacked weapons powerful enough to penetrate the armor of the dictator's car. A shaken Saddam was finally plucked from danger by a military helicopter. Eight of the attackers were killed; the rest fled the town.

It was the second assassination attempt on Saddam in four months, and he gave the order for a dreadful vengeance. Fifteen people were summarily executed; another 1,500 men, women, and children from the village were seized and trucked to the notorious Al-Hakimiyah prison, a remote desert internment camp, where they were brutally interrogated.[20]

"The sound of footsteps that stops by the door was enough for everyone to freeze," recounted Firas Mahmood Ya'koob. "The cell door would be opened, a name of one of the men would be announced, and he would be dragged to the interrogation room to return a few hours later, unconscious, covered by blood, wrapped in a blanket, and would be thrown on us. The women and children had their share, and this is what we saw: extraction of nails and teeth, electric shocks, whipping with lashes, using razors to tear the skin into shreds, my aunt was left hanging from the roof after her clothes had been ripped off her in front of her brothers to force them to talk."[21]

After a month, the villagers were transferred to the already infamous Abu Ghraib prison near Baghdad. There, 148 men and boys—the youngest eleven years of age—were taken away and never seen again. Some had not even been in Dujail at the time of the assassination attempt. The survivors were dispatched to a barren camp in the desert near the Iraqi-Saudi border, where they were confined for the next four years. When they were finally permitted to return to Dujail, all their property had been confiscated, their houses, fruit trees, and fields laid to waste.

The tragedy of Dujail would find a special place in Iraq's modern history: out of all the hundreds of thousands of people killed and tortured by Saddam's regime, their case would be the first to be heard by the special Iraqi tribunal. Of course, in the summer of 1982, as the boys and men of Dujail were led away to slaughter, none of the great powers—least of all the United States—was in the least concerned about Saddam's record on human rights. What counted for the West was that Saddam had become their proxy against Khomeini.

By mid-1982, Saddam's forces held only a few small enclaves in Iran. If the two sides had been deprived of arms and money, the exhausted combatants might have had no option but to negotiate peace. But as long as Saddam was willing to sacrifice a generation of young Iraqis, as long as Iranian soldiers were willing to march to their deaths, the rest of the world was willing to continue fueling the conflagration.

In fact, governments and arms dealers from around the globe were eager to provide the mountains of arms and ammunition that the war consumed. And, with the encouragement of the United States, Saddam's neighbors in the Gulf were ready to ante up the billions of dollars Iraq needed to pay for those weapons.[22]

As for Iran, Reagan's secretary of state, Alexander Haig, had appeared adamant against aiding the fundamentalist regime of Khomeini: "Let me state categorically today, there will be no military equipment provided to the government of Iran," he declared. In 1981, however, when Israeli Prime Minister Menachem Begin asked for permission to transfer additional U.S.-made weapons to Iran, Haig agreed that "in principle" it was all right, but only for certain crucial spare parts for Iran's F-4 fighter planes. Anything else, he said, would have to be specifically approved by the U.S.—though this caveat came to have little meaning. "The Americans needed us to save Iran," said General Avraham Tamir, who was national security advisor to the Israeli minister of defense. "They approved everything we sent—spare parts for airplanes, antitank missiles, and ammunition for the artillery. Israel was a U.S. proxy." There were even reports in Israel that Saddam offered to recognize Israel if it would stop supporting Iran.[23]

Khomeini routinely denounced Israel as "a viper state" and a puppet of "the Great Satan," but Israel had traditionally sold arms to Iran and received petroleum in return; they still hoped for a possible rapprochement with the new regime.[24] They also had large stocks of U.S.-made weapons and savvy arms dealers looking for markets. In any case, they were not at all adverse to seeing two of their enemies in the region engaged in bloody mutual destruction.

Israel's secret arrangement with the United States ended in 1982 when Haig, angered that the Israelis had breached their agreement, declared the U.S. would approve no further shipments. Over the following years, however, huge transfers of U.S.-made weapons to Iran continued via Israel, often handled by private arms dealers. Though top American officials were aware of what was going on, they did nothing to stop the flow.[25]

On December 8, 1991, the *New York Times* reported that "Israeli and American intelligence officials acknowledged that weapons, ammunition, and spare parts worth several billion dollars flowed to Iran each year during the early 1980s."[26] "We were getting literally daily reports of Israeli sales to Iran," a former high-level Reagan administration intelligence official told the *New York Times*. "It was so routine I didn't think twice about it. It was pretty clear that all the key players knew."

According to the *Times*, "The Reagan Administration continued to replenish Israel's stockpile of American-made weapons, despite clear evidence that Israel was shipping them to Iran." Indeed, some of the special flights transporting American weapons for Iran took off from a secret CIA air base near Tucson, Arizona. Israel also set up a clandestine office in New York City to direct the purchases of American-made military equipment for resale to Iran. Those weapons included some of the most sophisticated arms in the American arsenal, from Hawk anti-aircraft missiles and Lance surface-to-surface missiles to TOW anti-tank missiles and armor-piercing shells.[27]

Israel was shipping not just weapons but an unbelievable gamut of products. For instance, hundreds of thousands of young Iranian boy-soldiers were sent charging ahead of regular Iranian troops to absorb the brunt of Iraqi artillery bombardments or blow a path through enemy mine fields with their own bodies. They were glorified as martyrs to Islam and issued a small plastic key that, they were assured, would open the gates of Paradise. Those keys were manufactured on an Israeli kibbutz.[28]

Tilting to Baghdad

As it became obvious Saddam was in serious trouble on the battlefield, it also became clear there was no way the United States and its European allies would countenance a victory for Khomeini—even though the threat Khomeini now represented was partly due to the Reagan administration's secretly having allowed Israel to sell weapons to the Ayatollah. Among the major proponents for increasing aid to Iraq were Secretary of Defense Caspar Weinberger and Assistant Secretary of State Richard Murphy.[29] They were obsessed by the fear that Iran's Islamic fundamentalism would spread throughout the Gulf, threatening the moderate governments of Saudi Arabia and Kuwait and endangering the West's vital oil supplies. According to a report written later by the Senate Foreign Relations Committee, the administration felt that the only choice it had was "between permitting Iran to dominate the West's oil supply in the Persian Gulf and direct U.S. military intervention." "Many of us thought it would be better if Iraq won," Weinberger later said.[30]

It was time, they argued, for the United States to increase its tilt to Iraq—despite Saddam Hussein's atrocious record on human rights and his country's label as a terrorist state. A tilt to Iraq was also advocated by major American corporations with interests in the region. Exxon-Mobil, for instance, with its eyes on Iraq's vast oil reserves, had long been calling for support for the Iraqi dictator.[31] Its views were mirrored in the *Wall Street Journal*. In years to come, the paper would thunder righteously against Saddam Hussein. But as early as February 1981, the *Journal*'s editorialists were on another tack: "The [anti-American] rhetoric shouldn't obscure the fact that Iraq, probably more than any other Mid East nation except Israel, is embracing Western values and technology." Indeed, it was becoming an advanced secular society "with a car in every garage, a television set in every living room, universal education, and chic French fashions for emancipated Iraqi women. Such a society should eventually become congenial to the West."[32]

On the other side of the White House debate were figures like Reagan's National Security Advisor Robert McFarlane and Richard Perle, who was then assistant secretary of defense. "It is foolish to think," Perle said, "that a pro-Marxist, pro-Soviet Baath regime, the leader of Arab radicalism and rejectionism, is about to become an American ally or even a tacit partner without exacting an enormous price." It was dangerous, he concluded, to encourage Iraq's "imperial ambitions."[33]

President Reagan himself seemed to have opted out of the Gulf War debate. As Howard Teicher recalled, "there was substantially no leadership. Reagan was sleeping through it all."[34] In 1981, for instance, Secretary of State Alexander Haig tentatively praised Saddam Hussein for showing "a greater sense of concern about the behavior of Soviet imperialism in the Middle East." But unknown to Haig, CIA director William Casey had already quietly begun aiding the Iraqi effort.

There were clandestine contacts arranged or monitored by the CIA between shadowy international arms dealers and Iraqi arms procurement officials. Egypt, for instance, transferred hundreds of millions of dollars of Russian-made arms to Iraq with U.S. approval in 1981. That same year, one of Saddam's sons-in-law came to New York shopping for weapons, disguised as an Iraqi lieutenant.[35]

One of the most notorious international arms dealers was Sarkis Saghanalian, who claimed to have worked with the CIA to provide arms to various countries and causes over the years. In 1982 he began selling Austrian artillery to Saddam Hussein's Republican Guard. As he told ABC's *Nightline*, "The 155mm gun that went from Austria, you think the U.S. didn't know about it? I informed them. I told them what was happening. They said, 'Sure, go ahead and help them as much as you can.'"[36] The Iraqis also began to receive battlefield intelligence from American AWACs planes operating out of Saudi Arabia.[37]

By December 1981, with the death toll in the conflict now having passed one hundred thousand, the CIA was making use of front companies and fake end-user certificates that enabled foreign arms manufacturers from Brazil to South Africa to disguise the true destination of the huge stocks of weapons they were shipping to Baghdad. King Hussein's Jordan was a major transshipment point, a ready source of end-user certificates, as was Saudi Arabia. Jordan supplied U.S.-made helicopters to Iraq, even though such diversions were expressly prohibited by U.S. law. Eventually, traveling on Jordanian passports, Iraqi helicopter pilots were trained in the United States. "The Reagan administration looked the other way," wrote reporter Alan Friedman, one of the most informed students of this period.[38]

The government ministries and hotels of Baghdad were crawling with foreigners—many of them obviously intelligence agents or military officers in civilian dress. Their mission was to sell arms or to keep an eye on such sales and provide advice. The ongoing carnage represented a multibillion-dollar bonanza. During the first half of the 1980s, Iraq was the largest importer of major weapons systems in the world. In 1984 alone, Saddam Hussein spent $35 billion buying arms. This was all going on despite a U.S. ban on shipping arms to either side and a U.N. resolution calling for a worldwide embargo of weapons to the two belligerents.

Almost half of the weapons shipped to Saddam came from the Soviets, Iraq's traditional suppliers. They furnished the Iraqi dictator with everything from tanks, artillery, and helicopters to advanced MIG aircraft and missiles. The French came second, accounting for 28 percent of Iraq's weapons. Saddam continued to be a major customer for some of France's most sophisticated weapons systems, including advanced 155mm howitzers, Roland and Exocet Missiles, and the Mirages.[39]

The world's arms dealers and governments had no qualms about working both sides of the street. A 1987 report identified twenty-six countries that had purveyed weapons *both* to Iraq and to Iran, among them Israel.[40] Shortly after the beginning of the Iran-Iraq war, the U.S. embassy in Ankara reported on "Israeli acumen" in selling to both Iran and Iraq.

Iraq's being on the list of terrorist countries had been an irksome impediment to open American support for Saddam. But in February 1982, after the Iraqi dictator expelled notorious terrorist Abu Nidal, the State Department removed Saddam from the list. That meant he could now purchase so-called dual-use equipment from the United States and also be eligible for export credits to help pay for those purchases. Many in the U.S. government, however, were appalled. Abu Nidal's associates and other terrorists continued to operate openly out of Baghdad. As the leading Defense Department counterterrorism official later conceded, "No one had doubts about Saddam's continued involvement with terrorism. . . . The real reason [for taking Iraq off the list] was to help them succeed in the war against Iran."[41]

There was another reason as well. In his quest for U.S. support, Saddam in July 1982 also declared himself in favor of a negotiated settlement between Israel and the Palestinians.[42] It was a momentous about-face for a country that had been one of the most vociferous of the Arab hard-line states, and for the next few years, Iraq continued to court the U.S. and outrage radical Arabs by his support of U.S. peace initiatives.

Officially, however, in 1992, the U.S. was still supposedly neutral in the conflict, which meant that American companies were not allowed to sell arms to either side. That was the fiction; the fact was that U.S. military supplies, from ammunition to sophisticated defense electronics, computers, and weapons of all kinds, continued to be sent to Iraq via third parties, much of it under the direction of White House officials. When one junior White House aide, Howard Teicher, who was supposed to monitor arms transactions in the Middle East, asked what was going on, he was told not to concern himself with the problem. "The government," Teicher later said, "found third parties and private channels for our shipments. I call this our 'dirty policy.'" It was all being done, according to Teicher, "off the books," without even a secret authorization by the president. "That," he said, "would make it illegal."

One of the White House officials most active in that secret program, according to Teicher, was Vice President George H. W. Bush. "Bush's door," said Teicher "was always open to the Iraqis. If they wanted a meeting with Bush, they would get it."[43]

As the Iranian threat grew, so did clandestine American aid to Iraq. In June 1982, U.S. intelligence discovered that the Iranians were massing troops south of Basra for a breakthrough attack that would have been fatal to Iraq. The White House panicked. President Reagan issued a secret national security directive, decreeing that the United States would do whatever was necessary and legal to prevent Iraq from losing the war with Iran. The clandestine U.S. program was headed by CIA director William Casey. His mission was to ensure that Iraq had "sufficient military weapons, ammunition and vehicles to avoid losing the Iran-Iraq war."[44]

The U.S., however, provided far more to Saddam. American officials also began sending Iraq satellite intelligence displaying the precise location of Iranian troops. Because of its extremely confidential nature, the information was hand-carried to Baghdad by Jordan's King Hussein. Later, around the time that the villagers of Dujail were being tortured and executed, American intelligence agents were dispatched to Iraq to interpret the satellite images for Saddam's commanders.[45] Finally, the U.S. installed a sophisticated facility at the U.S. embassy in Baghdad to download the highly classified information directly to Iraq.

Meanwhile, CIA Director Casey and his deputy Robert Gates secretly made sure that Saddam also got the weapons he needed. In

1982, U.S.-owned Hughes Aircraft was given clearance to ship sixty Defender helicopters to Iraq. They were supposedly to be used for non-military purposes; when it was later discovered they were being flown by the Iraqi military, there was not a hint of American protest. Other clandestine shipments of American-made arms continued via Jordan, Saudi Arabia, Egypt, and Kuwait—in violation of the U.S.'s Arms Export Control Act.[46]

The French also were becoming increasingly concerned about Saddam's fate. As France's socialist President Francois Mitterand bluntly declared in public in November 1982, "We do not want Iraq to lose the war. The age-old balance between the Arab and the Persian worlds must absolutely be maintained." That sentiment, added to the pressure of France's powerful arms industry, transformed saving Saddam Hussein into a national cause.[47]

Officially, the U.S. claimed to be keeping its hands clean by refusing to license or sell U.S.-origin weapons to Iraq. In fact, the ammunition and spare parts that Saddam needed most urgently were not of American or NATO origin, but Soviet, since most of Iraq's major weapons had traditionally been supplied by Moscow. Once again, however, the CIA made sure that Saddam got those weapons, either directly from the U.S. stocks—in a program known as "Bear Spares"—or indirectly from other countries, like Egypt, who either manufactured Soviet-style weapons or had large quantities on hand.[48]

France agreed to supply Saddam with their Super Etendard fighter-bomber, capable of delivering the ship-killing Exocet missile that had proved so effective in the Falklands War. By the end of 1983, Saddam's pilots were firing the Exocet against Iranian petroleum shipping in the Gulf. The idea, pushed by the United States with the Iraqis and the French, was that with his oil revenues sharply reduced, Khomeini would be forced to negotiate a settlement. That's not the way things worked out, but it was certainly lucrative for France's Aerospatiale. By 1984, three out of every four Exocets that came off the company's production line were destined for Saddam Hussein. To cover all bases, however, France at one point also approached the Iranians, with the idea of quietly furnishing Iran weapons as well, the idea supposedly being to keep lines of diplomatic communication open with Tehran.[49]

Early in 1982, William Casey and Robert Gates decided that cluster bombs would be just the thing to blunt Iran's human-wave attacks—a perfect "force multiplier," as Casey called them.[50] Cluster bombs were one of the more horrific weapons created by the United States during the Vietnam War. Though not banned internationally, they were almost as random and devastating as chemical weapons. They consisted of a canister filled with hundreds of small bomblets packed in turn with razor-like metal shards. When they exploded, they could shred anything in an area the size of ten football fields.[51]

With CIA help and guidance, a Chilean businessman, Carlos Cardoen, became virtually overnight one of the globe's major producers of cluster bombs. The CIA not only supplied him the technology, they even arranged for the Chilean entrepreneur to import a special factory from the U.S. to make the weapon. Cardoen added his own lethal twist—bomblets that would explode hours after they were dropped. This meant they would shred not just soldiers but would-be rescuers as well, indeed anyone who strayed into their lethal path. Cardoen's prime customer—also thanks to the CIA—was Saddam Hussein.[52] Cardoen also furnished Saddam with thousands of fuses for the chemical weapons that were used against Iran. With the Chilean's assistance, Iraq was also developing cluster bombs to dispense chemical and biological weapons.[53]

Everyone wanted to cash in on the Gulf War bonanza. When the Iraqis encountered problems obtaining American-made night-vision equipment, U.S. officials secretly arranged with a Lebanese arms dealer to export the devices to Britain. There, a company formed by Margaret Thatcher's son, Mark Thatcher, reexported the devices to Iraq. Richard Nixon's discredited vice president, Spiro Agnew, and former attorney general John Mitchell put together a convoluted deal to sell Saddam $280 million worth of uniforms for the Iraqi Army. They enlisted Nixon to provide them with letters of introduction.[54]

Governments across Europe, such as Germany and Belgium, pretended they didn't realize what their arms dealers and weapon manufacturers were up to. Such huge sums and powerful interests were involved that they just didn't want to know. Export control officials accepted obviously false end-user certificates and phony front companies at face value, and in enormous quantities. It was later revealed that more than one hundred German companies violated restrictions on arms exports to Baghdad.[55]

Saddam, however, was increasingly strapped for money to finance his ravenous consumption of weapons. Because of the conflict, Iraq's oil revenues had plummeted. Here also the Reagan administration lent a hand. In February 1983, reluctant U.S. Treasury officials quietly approved $230 million worth of agricultural credit guarantees to Iraq. Despite the huge financial risk, American taxpayers would now be insuring payment for massive quantities of grain that Saddam purchased from the United States. If Iraq was ultimately unable to pay—as turned out to be the case—American taxpayers would be stuck with the tab. That first deal was only the beginning; between 1983 and 1990, some $4.7 billion in agricultural credit guarantees were extended to Iraq.[56]

The credit program had two effects. First, it made the U.S. farm lobby very happy. Those rock-ribbed Republicans and their congressional representatives became fans of Saddam Hussein overnight. Second, it allowed Saddam to divert billions of dollars that would have gone toward buying agricultural products to purchasing weapons, conventional and otherwise. Saddam's agents hugely inflated their shipping costs—also covered by those U.S. guarantees—and skimmed off the surplus to purchase even more arms. In fact, as U.S. officials well knew, much of that American grain never made it to Iraq. It was bartered for arms long before. In at least one case it was swapped for Soviet weapons.[57]

A small bank in Atlanta, Georgia, a branch of the Italian-government-owned Banca Nazionale del Lavora (BNL), soon came to play a key role in financing trade with Iraq. The tangled tale reads like a Robert Ludlum novel. In the beginning the deals the BNL arranged were backed by the U.S. government guarantees. Over the following years, however, the bank and its naive and ambitious manager, Christopher Drogoul, were financing Saddam's purchases without any U.S. government guarantees at all. They became Saddam's private bankers. Even European firms that wanted to do business with Iraq were directed to the Atlanta Branch of the BNL. Finally, Drogoul was underwriting billion-dollar purchases by Saddam completely off the books, supposedly without authorization by the bank's directors in Rome. By 1989 the Atlanta branch had underwritten a colossal $5 billion of Saddam's purchases, most of which the Iraqi dictator could never repay.

More than $1 billion of those BNL loans went to the government ministry in Baghdad that was coordinating the country's huge imports of sophisticated machine tools and military equipment—in short, to some of the very weapons projects that the U.S. would later use as an excuse to invade Iraq.[58] Later it would turn out that U.S. and Italian authorities and their intelligence agencies were aware of what was going on.[59]

The BNL also helped finance Saddam's ambition to build a long-range missile, called the Condor, capable of transporting a nuclear warhead. The project was a consortium with Argentina and Egypt, aided by West German engineers, and bankrolled by Saddam. Using front companies, they were able to purchase vital components and technology from around the world. According to Howard Teicher, the U.S. was well aware of all these doings. "We knew Mubarak was a middle man for arms sales to Iraq, for the Condor missile and other stuff. He was actually our covert agent."[60]

What WMD?

Saddam also made it clear early on that he would make full use of his weapons of mass destruction (WMD). In the summer of 1983, Iran began reporting that Iraq had deployed chemical weapons against Iranian troops. The Geneva Convention calls upon the nations of the world to react when any power uses these illegal weapons. Iran, however, was an international pariah. Its calls for a U.N. investigation received only faint support—even though the U.S. State Department had solid intelligence to substantiate the Iranian claims. The U.S. knew that Iraq was using them "on almost a daily basis," as one internal memo to Secretary of State Shultz declared. The memo warned that, in the face of continued human wave attacks, Iraq could be expected to persist in using the illegal weapons. And it added, "We also know that Iraq has acquired a CW [chemical weapon] production capability, presumably from Western firms, including possibly a U.S. foreign subsidiary."[61]

The State Department argued that, if the U.S. was to maintain its credibility as a signatory to the Geneva Protocol prohibiting the use of chemical weapons, it had, at the very least, to issue a strong public condemnation. The White House, however, opted not to act. A top-secret policy review, issued as a national security directive by Ronald Reagan on November 26, 1983, made no mention of chemical weapons.[62] America's priority was to prevent an Iranian victory. The U.S. would do whatever was necessary to make sure that nothing impeded the flow of oil from the Gulf.

That same month, Saddam's deputies signaled that the Iraqi tyrant would be open to a visit from a top Reagan envoy to discuss formally renewing diplomatic relations with Baghdad. Concerned about the continued threat from Iran—and also interested in enlisting Saddam's support to end the growing chaos in Lebanon—the Reagan administration seized the opening.

The mission was given to Donald Rumsfeld, who had served as secretary of defense for President Gerald Ford and was now in private industry, heading the multinational pharmaceutical company G. D. Searle. Rumsfeld flew to Baghdad on December 20, 1983, bearing a cordial handwritten note for Saddam from President Reagan. The American president offered to renew diplomatic ties with Iraq and to increase commercial and military links. As Howard Teicher, who accompanied Rumsfeld on that trip, put it, "Here is the U.S. president saying, 'We respect you, we respect you. How can we help you? Let us help you.'"[63]

Rumsfeld first met for two and a half hours with Saddam's foreign minister, Tariq Aziz. According to notes from the meeting, Rumsfeld affirmed the Reagan administration's "willingness to do more" regarding the Iran-Iraq war, but "made clear that our efforts to assist were inhibited by certain things that made it difficult for us, citing the use of chemical weapons, possible escalation in the Gulf, and human rights. He then moved on to other concerns."[64]

Rumsfeld's ninety-minute meeting with Saddam himself, however, would not be ruffled by any mention of chemical weapons and human rights.[65] It began with a photo-op: Saddam in military uniform, a revolver strapped to his waist, shaking hands warmly with a beaming

Donald Rumsfeld—a picture that would return to haunt Rumsfeld in years to come. In December 1983, Rumsfeld first "conveyed the president's greetings and expressed his pleasure at being in Baghdad." He went on to talk glowingly about great opportunities for the future—like a new petroleum pipeline to the Red Sea that the mammoth and well-connected U.S. construction firm Bechtel was eagerly proposing.[66] They also talked about Turkey, the Soviet Union, terrorism, Lebanon, Syria, Iran, and Israel. Instead of cautioning Saddam about such things as chemical weapons, torture, or death squads, however, Rumsfeld assured the Iraqi tyrant that America's "understanding of the importance of balance in the world and in the region was similar to Iraq's."

When Saddam asked that the Americans take action to block the flow of arms to Iran, the U.S. agreed to help and went further. It initiated a new series of U.S. government-backed loan guarantees to Iraq through the U.S.'s Export-Import Bank. Later, the U.S. interests section in Baghdad—a diplomatic step down from a formal embassy—cabled Rumsfeld that Iraq's leadership was "extremely pleased" with the visit. "Tariq Aziz had gone out of his way to praise Rumsfeld as a person."[67]

Despite those warm sentiments, after a brief pause, Saddam Hussein continued to use his chemical weapons. On February 4, 1984, with some five hundred thousand Iranians amassed for what was billed as the final offensive, Iraq's military commanders warned that "the invaders should know that for every harmful insect there is an insecticide capable of annihilating it, whatever the number, and Iraq possesses this annihilation insecticide." When the attack did occur, the Iraqis made good on their threat. Journalists described incredible scenes of carnage; they spoke of "carpets of bodies" and "hell on earth."[68]

Reporter Joe Trento flew into Iraq that month to prepare a documentary. The Iraqis allowed him to visit the front by helicopter. "We flew very low over the battlefield," Trento said later, "and we started seeing bodies, but the bodies weren't injured and there was body after body, just lying in position." His Iraqi military escort told him the deaths had been caused by mustard gas. Back in Baghdad, Trento talked with William Eagleton, who headed the U.S. interests section. "Eagleton knew exactly what Saddam was about," said Trento. "They knew all about the poison gas. They knew he was engaging in the production of illegal poison gases like mustard gas and that the by-products to make the gas were being brought in from Germany. The U.S. was well aware of how he was using it. Eagleton had a map that showed where all the chemical weapons facilities were."[69]

Eagleton confirmed Trento's account, but pointed out that the U.S. was at least making quiet diplomatic efforts to convince the Germans to stop their chemical weapons aid to Saddam. "They really didn't listen to us," he said, "but we were the only ones talking about it."[70]

Finally, Saddam's use of chemical weapons became too flagrant for the U.S. to avoid going public on the issue. On March 3, 1984, the State Department intervened to prevent an American company from shipping Iraq 22,000 pounds of phosphorous fluoride, which is used in chemical weapons production. Two days later—after first advising Saddam Hussein what it was about to do—the U.S. publicly condemned Iraq's use of chemical weapons, which Washington had known about for at least half a year.

"The denouncing was for public consumption," said Peter Galbraith, former staff director of the Senate Foreign Relations Committee. "It was a complete act of hypocrisy by the Reagan administration. Denounce the use of chemical weapons and at the same time back Saddam with military aid."[71]

Nevertheless, when Rumsfeld returned to Baghdad in late March 1984, the reception was frosty. The Iraqis were annoyed by the State Department condemnation. To make matters worse, Iraq had recently experienced more reverses on the battlefield. Secretary of State Shultz instructed Rumsfeld to reassure Tariq Aziz that the recent U.S. public criticism of Iraq "was made strictly out of our strong opposition to the use of lethal and incapacitating CW." It did not change U.S. determination to continue supporting Iraq and further improve relations between the two countries.[72] Rumsfeld's meeting with Aziz was also sweetened with more promises of U.S. Export-Import Bank–backed credits for Iraq, and a campaign—"Operation Staunch"—led by the United States for an international embargo on weapons sales to Iran.

There was another extraordinary offer of aid personally transmitted by Rumsfeld. It came from Israel, a nation despised by Saddam.

Three years earlier the Israelis had sent their planes to destroy Saddam's French-built nuclear reactor; they had also supplied billions of dollars in U.S.-made arms to Iran. By the spring of 1984, however, Israel concluded that, because of Iran's growing influence in Lebanon, it had become a more dangerous threat to the Zionist state than Iraq. Israeli Foreign Minister Yitzhak Shamir asked Rumsfeld to deliver a secret offer of Israeli assistance to Iraq and Rumsfeld agreed. But when he attempted to hand the letter for Saddam to Aziz, the foreign minister refused to accept it. As he explained to Rumsfeld's delegation, "he would be executed on the spot by Hussein if he did so."[73]

Saddam had no need to worry about the U.S.'s condemnation of his chemical weapons. In March 1984, when asked whether it would have any effect on recent U.S. initiatives to expand commercial relations and restore diplomatic ties, a State Department's spokesperson replied, "No, I'm not aware of any change in our position. We're interested in being involved in a closer dialogue with Iraq."[74]

On March 29, determined not to ruffle the Iraqi dictator's sensitivities, the State Department cautiously asked the Iraqi government's help "in avoiding . . . embarrassing situations." But they assured Saddam's representative in Washington that the U.S. "did not want this issue to dominate our bilateral relationship." Indeed, thanks to U.S. intervention, a U.N. Security Council statement generally condemning the use of chemical weapons did not cite Iraq as the guilty party.

"The use of gas on the battlefield by the Iraqis was not a matter of deep strategic concern," a former senior U.S. Defense Intelligence officer said later. "We were desperate to make sure that Iraq did not lose."[75] To that end the CIA continued providing Iraq with satellite intelligence that it needed to calibrate their mustard gas attacks on Iranian troops.[76]

The toll in human life in the ongoing war was enormous, not just from chemical weapons and cluster bombs but because of the religious and nationalist passions that fired the conflict. An Iranian doctor told the *Sunday Times* on February 26, 1984, "I have seen young boys burned alive. I have seen Iranian and Iraqi boys tearing each other literally with their nails and teeth. It is raging hate against raging hate."[77]

"I have never seen carnage on such a scale," said a seasoned TV reporter.[78]

In November 1984, Iraq and the United States finally restored formal diplomatic relations. The door was open for U.S. manufacturers to invade Baghdad. David Newton, who had been *charge d'affaires* in Baghdad, became the new American ambassador. Like many American experts on the Middle East—and many in the White House—he felt that the potential in Iraq for the U.S. was enormous. Expanded trade was the best way to nudge Saddam to more civilized behavior, he declared. He recommended U.S. companies concentrate particularly on high-tech products, and that the U.S. government step in with more credits to finance that trade. Those views were just fine with Saddam—many of those dual-use American-made products would wind up as components in Saddam's rocket and WMD programs.[79]

Pressured by the White House, the Commerce Department continued overruling Pentagon objections to the export of sophisticated dual-use equipment to Iraq. When Iraqi jets attacked Iran's key oil terminal at Karg Island, they used the latest laser-guided weapons obtained from Thompson of France. Some of the most advanced components for those weapons came from the United States and required U.S. approval—which Thompson never obtained—before being shipped to Iraq. Though Thompson was also a major supplier to the Pentagon, not a word of disapproval was ever uttered by the U.S., though the U.S. was closely monitoring shipments of French arms to Iraq.[80] In some cases the U.S. Commerce Department simply lied about the nature of the equipment it okayed for shipment to Iraq. It frequently simply stopped referring sensitive Iraqi license requests to other government agencies. As one State Department official had put it, "We don't give a damn as long as the Iran-Iraq carnage does not affect our allies or alter the balance of power."[81]

Though Newton fully recognized the thuggish nature of Saddam's regime, he felt that the Iraqi tyrant was maturing. Once the war was over, things would loosen up, he told a visiting reporter. "This is a regime that does not need to terrorize people on a daily level to prove it is in charge," he said. "Everybody knows who is in charge."[82] This last claim was true—Saddam had destroyed all internal opposition. Spies were everywhere, people simply disappeared, and no one dared ask what had become of them.[83]

Amnesty International was one of the few independent organizations attempting to monitor what was going on in Iraq, though its reports were generally ignored by the rest of the world. On April 15, 1985, it issued a special study called "Torture in Iraq," presenting a chilling catalogue of the sadistic methods employed by Iraqi interrogators. Aside from some of the more common techniques, like beatings with whips and iron bars, extracting fingers and toe nails, torturing children in front of their parents, and performing mock executions, there were other procedures:

"Suspending the victim by the wrists or ankles from a rotating fan in the ceiling, and beating him/her as he/she rotates; applying electricity to sensitive parts of the body, including the nostrils, ears, temples, nipples, kidney region, fingers, toes and genitals; burning parts of the body with cigarettes, hot domestic irons, electric hot plates or gas flames; tying the victim by the wrists and ankles to a cross bar which is then turned over flames (like a roasting spit); fixing the head of the victim in a cabin with intense ultraviolet rays, which burn the eyes; ... sexual abuse or assaults, including forcing the victim to sit on bottle necks or inserting a bottle or wire in the rectum; and mutilation of the body, including gouging out the eyes, cutting off the nose, ears, breasts, penis, axing the limbs, peeling the skin or cutting it open with a sharp instrument, hammering nails into the body."

At first, parents were summoned by the authorities to pick up the horribly mutilated corpses of their children. Later, the authorities stopped returning the bodies, issuing only paper receipts.[84]

In May 1985, just a month after that Amnesty report was issued, the U.S.-Iraq Business Forum was established in Washington to foster commercial relations with Saddam Hussein's Iraq. It was headed by Marshall Wiley, a retired American ambassador; its members included many of America's largest corporations, some of whom joined after Nizar Hamdoon, Iraq's canny ambassador to the U.S., wrote a letter advising that "any United States company interested in doing business with Iraq ... would do well to join the Forum."[85] It became a powerful lobby in Washington, essentially running a P.R. campaign for Saddam Hussein free of charge and successfully campaigning to further ease restrictions on the sales of sophisticated American equipment to the Iraqi dictator. Indeed, by 1985, it appeared as if the U.S. tilt to Saddam Hussein was heading toward an open embrace, a full marriage of convenience.

Arms for Hostages: The Countertilt

In the Reagan White House, however, a faction of senior advisors, who had long been arguing that the U.S. had drifted too close to Iraq, was pushing for a change of partners. As one of them wrote in a memo to CIA Director William Casey, "Our tilt to Iraq was timely when Iraq was against the ropes and the Islamic revolution was on a roll. The time may now have to come to tilt back."[86]

At the heart of the matter was the plight of seven Americans being held hostage in Lebanon by the radical Hezbollah group, which was supported by Iran. In 1980, the Republicans had excoriated Jimmy Carter as a liberal wimp because of his inability to free the American hostages in Tehran. Five years later, the Reagan White House found itself facing the same dilemma, and congressional elections were fast approaching. Publicly, Reagan refused to bargain. On July 8, 1985, he heatedly declared that Iran was a member of a "confederation of terrorist states . . . a new, international version of Murder Incorporated," and he vowed, "America will never make concessions to terrorists."[87]

The Israelis, however, had approached the U.S. with a secret proposal that ran directly counter to the intentions Reagan would state. Israel would once again ship U.S.-made arms to Iran; in return, the Iranians would release the Lebanon hostages. The Israeli proposal was pushed by the White House faction arguing for a new opening to Iran, headed by Robert McFarlane, Reagan's national security advisor, two members of his staff, Howard Teicher and Oliver North, and CIA Director Casey. They argued that—apart from the question of the American hostages—there was also now an urgent need to improve relations with Tehran in order to counter growing Soviet influence there.[88] Those alarmist views ran completely counter to the consensus of the CIA's Soviet analysts at the time, but they won the day. On June 11, 1985, two days after another American was kidnapped in Lebanon, President Reagan signed a secret directive ordering that the United States help Iran obtain selected weapons. The faction opposing a tilt to Iran was outraged. Secretary of State George Shultz objected heatedly; he felt the deal undermined the basic U.S. principle of not negotiating with terrorists. Secretary of Defense Caspar Weinberger—who also worried that the scheme could leave the U.S. wide open to blackmail down the road—wrote, "This is almost too absurd to comment on. It's like asking Qadaffi to Washington for a cozy lunch."[89]

Nevertheless, the U.S. government now set about contravening its own declared embargo. On August 30, Israel sold more than five hundred U.S.-made TOW missiles to Iran. Two weeks later one of the American hostages in Lebanon, the Reverend Benjamin Weir, was released. But in the following months, no more hostages were freed. By the end of May 1986, negotiations with Iran had stalled.[90]

It was at that point that CIA Director Casey dreamt up a profoundly treacherous gambit. For the Iranians to budge on the hostage question, Casey reasoned, they would have to become even more desperate for sophisticated American-made weapons. Thus, what was needed was for Saddam Hussein to escalate the war, to hit more vital Iranian economic targets. Saddam and his generals had been loath to risk Iraq's sophisticated jet bombers in long-range missions; that situation had to change.

The man Casey chose to carry his message to Saddam was Reagan's vice president, George H. W. Bush. "Bush was very much the diplomat," said Howard Teicher, who worked closely with Bush on the White House's covert initiatives. "Regarding Iraq, he and Casey both had great naïveté, thinking you could be friends with Saddam Hussein, which was not unlike a lot of government officials at that time. And he saw the geostrategic logic in a new relationship with Iran. Bush's goals were contradictory because our policy was full of contradictions. He thought rapprochement with Iran was good. He thought talking to both sides was good."[91]

On August 4, 1986, during a supposedly routine trip to the Middle East, Bush met with Egyptian President Hosni Mubarak and asked him to transmit to Saddam the inflammatory advice from the Reagan White House: "Escalate the air war and escalate the bombing deep inside

Iran."[92] The CIA in Baghdad was also providing the Iraqis with highly classified intelligence data on Iranian targets, and satellite images to assess the damage inflicted. Within forty-eight hours, the Iraqis greatly increased the number of bombing missions, striking several targets, including oil refineries deep inside Iran.[93]

The Iran-tilters' scheme seemed to be working: reeling from the new Iraqi attacks, on September 19, 1986, a high-ranking Iranian officer arrived in Washington with a list of weapons his country needed urgently to repel Saddam's air offensive. There was, however, one predictable hitch to the arms-for-hostages scheme: as U.S. hostages were liberated in Lebanon, new ones were kidnapped to take their place. The Iranians, after all, would need more arms. In October 1986, when the Iranians balked once more about releasing hostages, CIA Director Casey again strongly suggested to Tariq Aziz that Saddam make use of the American intelligence he was getting to launch even more devastating strikes on Iran.

But even as the CIA was supplying satellite intelligence information to Saddam, the deputy director of the CIA, John McMahon— in order to further encourage the Iranians to deal—was also passing on satellite intelligence on some of the Iraqi troop positions to the Iranians.[94] To make sure that neither side gained too much advantage, however, some of the intelligence given to each side was inaccurate or deliberately distorted. The CIA, in effect, was prolonging an incredibly bloody stalemate with the goal of preventing either side from winning.[95]

On November 3, 1986, the operation came to a sudden halt when a Beirut newspaper broke the whole sordid tale. By then, Iran had been reequipped with between $500 million and $1 billion worth of new U.S.-made weapons. On January 9, 1987, the Iranian army launched one of the most massive and sanguinary offensives of the war in the area around Basra, Iraq's second-largest city. Iraq hit back with wide-ranging aerial attacks against Iranian cities, including Tehran and the holy city of Qum. In response, the Iranians shelled Basra. The War of the Cities was launched. From Washington, it again appeared that an American-armed Khomeini might win the war outright; it was time to recalibrate the tilt.

Tilting Back to Saddam

In the following months, Saddam was to receive more overt and clandestine aid from Washington and its allies than ever before. U.S. officials went all out to blunt the new Iranian offensive, which covert White House policies had helped to create. In March 1987, Vice President Bush urged the reluctant head of the U.S. Export-Import Bank to issue hundreds of millions of dollars of new trade guarantees to Iraq—even though the bank's expert staff presumed there was no way Saddam would ever be able to repay the loan. Bush also informed the Iraqi ambassador in Washington that the U.S. Department of Commerce had finally issued export licenses for high-tech dual-use equipment that had been held up for approval. The Pentagon's fears that many of those items would be used for Saddam's WMD programs were swept aside.

At this point the U.S. was also secretly shipping American-made weapons directly to Iraq from the sprawling U.S. Rhein-Mein airbase at Frankfurt, which housed both a military and a civilian airfield. The weapons to be shipped were simply moved from the military side of the base to the civilian side, where Iraqi Airways cargo jets would land to load and pick them up, without any American personnel in sight.[96]

American military officers and intelligence agents were now engaged in activities that were not only controversial and secret, but also contrary to U.S. law, because they were not reported to Congress.[97] But the Americans weren't alone. The government of British Prime Minister Margaret Thatcher—coordinating their policy with Washington—either encouraged or turned a blind eye to shipments of hundreds of millions of dollars of British equipment sold to the Iraqi dictator. In 1990, Thatcher would demand of George H. W. Bush that he stand up to Saddam Hussein after the invasion of Kuwait. But in 1987, the Thatcher government's guidelines on arm exports to Iraq were secretly relaxed. In January 1988, her trade minister, Alan Clark, went even further, quietly advising British arms manufacturers to "downgrade" the descriptions of dual-use equipment in order to make it appear as if the products were suited only for civilian ends. In fact, sophisticated equipment supplied by British firms contributed to Saddam's nuclear and rocket projects as well as the dictator's ambitious but ill-fated "super gun," that would have been capable of firing nuclear or biological shells four hundred miles.[98]

Years later, called before a government inquiry, Clark admitted that he had encouraged British firms exporting sophisticated equipment to Iraq with a "nod and a wink" and was "economical with the *actualité*" (truth) when outlining government policy in public.[99] A former official of the British Foreign Office described the system more frankly as a "culture of lying."[100]

Other European companies continued making money from the conflict. An Italian firm 50 percent owned by Gianni Agnelli's Fiat shipped millions of land mines to Iraq by way of Singapore. Top Italian officials approved the transactions, knowing full well where the mines were headed. Another Fiat subsidiary provided parts for Saddam's long-range nuclear missile project.[101]

France was in a more precarious spot. Iraq was now in hock to the country for more than $5 billion worth of government credits extended for the weapons Saddam had purchased over the years. Yet he was still shopping for more, and the French found they had little choice: their intelligence services estimated that if France suspended its shipments of arms to Saddam, Iraq would collapse. Many transfers to Saddam continued in the shadowy world of false end-user certificates and phantom companies; government agencies responsible for controlling exports of weapons and dual-use equipment knew by now to look the other way.[102]

There were hundreds or thousands of personnel from around the world, Soviets, French, German, British—a small army of soldiers and spooks—operating out of Baghdad or assigned to Iraqi military bases. They were there to sell arms, maintain them, or show the Iraqis how to use them with even more deadly effect. French pilots stationed at Iraqi Air Force bases may even have flown combat missions against Iran.[103] Iraqi pilots were also being trained in France, England, and the Soviet Union, and some, using Jordanian passports, were learning how to fly Bell helicopters in the United States. Hundreds of Iraqi naval officers were also being taught in Italy. Meanwhile, some of Saddam's elite troops were sent to the United States for instruction in unconventional warfare by U.S. Special Forces at Fort Bragg.[104] The idea was that, in the event of an Iranian victory, the Iraqi soldiers would be able to wage a guerrilla struggle against the occupying Iranian force. Some day we may know whether any of those Iraqis turned their skills against American troops after the U.S. invasion in 2003.

The Reagan administration itself was about to embark on an even more active, though clandestine, role in the war against Iran. Encouraged by the U.S., Saddam had intensified his attacks against vital Iranian economic targets, including neutral tankers in the Gulf. The plan was to force Khomeini to negotiate a settlement, but Iran of course retaliated. Concerned about the safety of their own ships, the Kuwaitis asked for protection. Otherwise, they threatened, they would have to accept assistance that was being offered by the Soviets. Some U.S. officials worried that by venturing into the narrow confines of the Gulf, the U.S. risked becoming even more involved in the conflict. Despite such concerns, American warships were dispatched.

On May 17, 1987, however, it became dramatically clear how dangerous that policy was. An Iraqi Air Force plane mistakenly attacked an American frigate, the U.S.S. Stark, killing thirty-seven of the crew. The White House immediately accepted Iraqi apologies. Then, to counter mounting congressional opposition, the Reagan administration decided to go one step further. They would justify a continued U.S. naval presence in the Gulf by permitting Kuwaiti ships to operate under the American flag. That fiction would give the Kuwaitis the right to American protection.

A U.S. liaison officer was stationed in Baghdad to avoid a repeat of the Stark incident. That, at least, was the cover story; in fact, over the following months, American officers would help Iraq carry out long-range strikes against key Iranian targets, using U.S. ships as navigational aids. "We became," as one senior U.S. officer told ABC's *Nightline*, "forward air controllers for the Iraqi Air Force."[105]

The Reagan administration, in effect, decided to undertake a secret war, not bothering with congressional authorization.[106] Heavily armed U.S. Special Operations helicopters, stealthy, sophisticated killing machines that could operate by day or night, were ordered to the

Persian Gulf. Their mission was to destroy any Iranian gunboats they could find. Other small, swift American vessels, posing as commercial ships, lured Iranian naval vessels into international waters to attack them. The Americans often claimed they attacked the Iranian ships only after the Iranians first menaced neutral ships plying the Gulf. In some cases, however, the neutral ships which the Americans claimed to be defending didn't even exist.[107]

Beginning in July 1987, the CIA also began sending covert spy planes and helicopters over Iranian bases. Several engaged in secret bombing runs, at one point destroying an Iranian warehouse full of mines. In September 1987, a special operations helicopter team attacked an Iranian mine-laying ship with a hail of rockets and machine-gun fire, killing three Iranian sailors. Official authorization for these clandestine attacks was purposely restricted to a low level in the Reagan administration so that top government officials could deny all knowledge of the illegal operations.[108]

Early in 1988, the U.S. feared that Iran was preparing a massive spring offensive that could cut off Basra from Baghdad. The Pentagon's Defense Intelligence Agency dispatched additional officers to Baghdad. They were no longer just interpreting U.S. satellite information for the Iraqis. Now they were planning day-by-day strategic bombing strikes for the Iraqi Air Force.[109] In April 1988, the Iraqi army began its own offensive to retake the Faw Peninsula. It was one of the most crucial operations of the entire war. The day before the offensive began, in a twenty-four hour period, U.S. forces sank or demolished a destroyer and a couple of frigates, which represented half the Iranian navy.[110]

If Saddam had not ultimately prevailed, the Pentagon had prepared an even more ambitious strategy: to launch an attack against the Iranian mainland. "The real plans were for a secret war, with the U.S. on the side of Iraq against Iran, on a daily basis," said retired Lieutenant Colonel Roger Charles, who was serving in the office of the secretary of defense at the time.[111] This was confirmed by Admiral James A. "Ace" Lyons, who was commander in chief of the U.S. Pacific Fleet. As he put it, "We were prepared, I would say at the time, to drill them back to the fourth century."

Relatively cooler heads prevailed. According to Richard L. Armitage, who at the time was assistant secretary of defense, "The decision was made not to completely obliterate Iran. We didn't want a naked Iran. We wanted a calm, quiet, peaceful Iran. However, had things not gone well in the Gulf, I've no doubt that we would have put those plans into effect."[112]

CHAPTER FOUR

Halabja: The Tragedy of the Kurds
1980–1988

Who is going to say anything? The international community? Fuck them! The international community and those who listen to them.
—Ali Hassan al-Majid, known as Chemical Ali, 1987[1]

Halabja was an Iraqi town of about 80,000 people near the Iranian border, its population predominately Kurdish. In March 1988, Kurdish *pesh merga* fighters aided Iranian Revolutionary Guards in capturing the town, much to the distress of the many local inhabitants who actually supported the Iraqi government. But when avenging Iraqi forces counterattacked on March 16, they were bent on annihilating not just the *pesh merga* but the entire Kurdish population. Iraqi bombers hit the village repeatedly with chemical weapons. Many of the residents had taken shelter in primitive air-raid shelters in their basements, and they were trapped there by a gas heavier than air, smelling like old apples, some said, or burnt sulfur. Terrified, gagging, their eyes streaming, those who could still move raced back onto the streets where they found their fellow citizens already dead, or blind, or twitching uncontrollably, or laughing hysterically before falling suddenly to the ground.

Experts later declared that such quick deaths and clinical symptoms were associated not with mustard gas but with sarin, a nerve agent developed but never deployed by Nazi Germany. Some five thousand people are estimated to have died in the attack. Thousands more were injured, some permanently—mustard gas mutates DNA to cause cancer, and nerve agents, when they don't kill outright, can paralyze or cause lasting neuropsychiatric damage.

Over the following months and years, the name of this obscure Kurdish town would come to embody all the horrors of the regime of Saddam Hussein. Though he would later be accused of slaughtering hundreds of thousands of Iraqis during his reign, the murder of four to five thousand Kurdish men, women, and children in Halabja would be one of the few specific crimes for which the dictator would one day be formally charged.

Fifteen years later, justifying an approaching invasion of Iraq, President George W. Bush described the atrocity in his weekly radio address to the nation. "The chemical attack on Halabja—just one of forty targeted at Iraq's own people—provided a glimpse of the crimes Saddam Hussein is willing to commit, and the kind of threat he now presents to the entire world. He is among history's cruelest dictators, and he is arming himself with the world's most terrible weapons. . . . As the Nobel laureate and Holocaust survivor Elie Wiesel said, 'we have a moral obligation to intervene where evil is in control.' Today, that place is Iraq."[2]

Yet beginning in March 1988, as news of Halabja crystallized from unsubstantiated rumor to undeniable fact, first the Reagan and then the George H. W. Bush administrations did everything possible to squelch American outrage and block congressional sanctions against Iraq. It was the latest in a long string of cynical power plays at the Kurds' expense.

Revolt and Repression

The Kurds' tragic struggle was the all too predictable outcome of the ham-fisted attempts by British and French to divide up the remains of the Ottoman Empire after World War I. The Kurds, who are a non-Arabic, predominantly Sunni Muslim people with their own language, customs, and traditions, had at first been promised an independent state by the U.S. and its allies. That promise was forgotten when the British opted instead to incorporate the Kurdish territories—rich in oil—into their new mandate state of Iraq. To rule the state, the British tapped the Kurd's traditional enemies, the Arab Sunnis. The Kurds have strained to escape that bind ever since.

Over the following decades, the Kurds' quixotic struggle for some form of independence won admiration from journalists and diplomats who came to know them, but it doomed them to a seemingly endless cycle of rebellion followed by incredibly vicious repression. Those uprisings were usually encouraged by enemies of Iraq's rulers who made use of the Kurds to destabilize the regime in Baghdad. It was a ruthless, deceitful process, which resulted in hundreds of thousands of Kurds being slaughtered and displaced over the years. And it was practiced by some of the most unlikely partners, including the United States.

In 1963, when the Baath Party first came to power in Iraq with help from the CIA, the U.S. came down on the side of repression. When the Baathists requested assistance in quashing the then-raging Kurdish uprising, the U.S. military attaché in Baghdad readily obliged, delivering five thousand bombs, one thousand of them containing napalm. The U.S. hid its hand well: to this day, most Kurds assume that the napalm that devastated their villages back then had been supplied by the Soviet Union.[3]

A decade later, the U.S. would be playing the other side of the game. For years, the Shah of Iran had been secretly supporting the Iraqi Kurds to put pressure on Baghdad. So were the Israelis, who hoped to distract Iraq's increasingly virulent leader from joining an Arab attack on the Jewish state. In 1972, Henry Kissinger and Richard Nixon, motivated by fear that Iraq was becoming too cosy with the Soviet Union, agreed to a request from the Shah to help back the Kurds.

For the sake of deniability, the U.S. supplied the Kurds with Soviet arms seized in Vietnam, while Israel provided Soviet weapons they had captured from the Arabs. The clandestine operation was kept secret even from the U.S. State Department, which had argued against any such support.[4] The Kurds' new friends, however, did not want their protégés to win their struggle. An independent Kurdish state would be much too disruptive for the region, they felt. Their support was carefully doled out—enough to keep the revolt going, but not enough to take it to victory.

The Kurdish leader, Mustafa Barzani, was hard-headed enough to understand his people were being used by Iran, but not worldly enough to comprehend that his American backers could be equally duplicitous. "We do not trust the Shah," Barzani told reporter Jon Randal in 1973. "I trust America. America is too great a power to betray a small people like the Kurds."[5]

It was to be a fatal error of judgment. In 1975 the Shah and the leaders of Iraq abruptly agreed to settle their disputes and signed a treaty of friendship. A key part of the agreement was that Iran would immediately cease its support of the Iraqi Kurds. Overnight, Iranian army units that had been supporting the Kurds—with artillery, missiles, ammunition, and even food—retreated back across the border into Iran. The U.S. and the Israelis similarly called a sudden halt to their support. At the same time, Iraqi troops began a massive offensive against the hapless Kurds.

Thus, without any warning, the Kurds were abandoned; not just their fighting men, the *pesh merga*, but their villages, wives, and children, were exposed to a ferocious Iraqi onslaught. Barzani sent a desperate plea to Kissinger for aid. "Our movement and people are being destroyed in an unbelievable way with silence from everyone. We feel, Your Excellency, that the United States has a moral and political responsibility towards our people, who have committed themselves to your country's policy. Mr. Secretary, we are anxiously awaiting your quick response."[6]

Twelve days later, a U.S. diplomat in Tehran cabled CIA director William Colby, noting that Kissinger had not replied and warning that if Washington "intends to take steps to avert a massacre it must intercede with Iran promptly."

Meanwhile, a quarter of a million Kurds fled for their lives to Iran. Turkey closed its borders to thousands of others seeking refuge. Many of the militants left behind—especially students and teachers—were rounded up by the Iraqis, imprisoned, tortured, and executed. Some 1,500 villages were dynamited and bulldozed.

Over the following weeks and months, as the killing continued, Barzani issued more desperate appeals to the CIA, to President Gerald Ford, to Henry Kissinger. No one answered. Kissinger not only refused to intervene but also turned down repeated Kurdish requests for humanitarian aid for their thousands of refugees.

This duplicity of American officials might never have surfaced but for an investigation in 1975 by the U.S. Congress's Select Committee on Intelligence headed by New York Democrat Otis Pike. The Pike report concluded that for Tehran and Washington the Kurds were never more than "a card to play," a uniquely useful tool for weakening Iraq's "potential for international adventurism."[7] From the beginning, said the report, "The President, Dr. Kissinger, and the Shah hoped that our clients [Barzani's Kurds] would not prevail." The Kurds were encouraged to fight solely in order to undermine Iraq. "Even in the context of covert operations, ours was a cynical enterprise."

The report's damning conclusions continued: Had the U.S. not encouraged the Kurds to go along with the Shah and renew hostilities with Iraq, "the Kurds might have reached an accommodation with [Iraq's] central government, thus gaining at least a measure of autonomy while avoiding further bloodshed. Instead the Kurds fought on, sustaining thousands of casualties and 200,000 refugees."

One of the officials who testified before the committee in secret session was Henry Kissinger. When questioned by an appalled congressman about the U.S.'s decision to abandon the Kurds to their bloody fate, Kissinger chided the committee, "One should not confuse undercover action with social work."

Chemical Ali

In 1980 the tragic cycle started over again. This time a faction of the Kurds was backed by Iran's new leader, the Ayatollah Khomeini. In fact, Khomeini's arming of the Kurds helped precipitate Saddam's invasion of Iran. Over the following years, while Saddam's forces were taking enormous losses on the Iranian front, the Iraqi dictator had to contend with a sputtering guerrilla campaign by the Kurdish *pesh merga*. By 1987, the Kurds were threatening key petroleum and power supplies and tying down thousands of Iraqi troops. Saddam lashed out with characteristic fury.

In April 1987, to handle the mission, Saddam made his first cousin, Ali Hassan al-Majid, supreme commander in the Kurdish region.

Al-Majid set out on a massive campaign of ethnic cleansing.[8] All villages in the areas of *pesh merga* control were to be destroyed, their inhabitants dispatched to so-called victory cities. The armed forces, al-Majid decreed, "must kill any human being or animal present within these areas." This free-fire zone encompassed more than one thousand villages. Kurds captured there, al-Majid instructed, "shall be interrogated by the security services, and those between the ages of 15 and 70 must be executed after any useful information has been obtained."[9]

In February 1988, the drive began in full force, an all-out campaign code-named Al Anfal—"the spoils of war." Writes Jon Randal,

> Families were targeted and women and children arrested in a giant search and destroy effort designed to exterminate a people. Kurds were funneled into forts, the men separated from their women folk and children. Beaten, stripped to their undershorts, and ill fed, [the men] never stayed long before disappearing, handcuffed, in convoys of filthy vehicles to killing fields hundreds of miles from the theater of operations. Their families went to the same fate at a more leisurely pace. A handful of survivors told the same basic tale: daylong drives without food or water to southern desert sites, where at dusk or in early evening they were forced out of their windowless vehicles, handcuffs removed for future use, wrists tied with string, then ordered to the brink of shallow trenches, where, under the headlights of bulldozers, they were shoved in and shot by troops firing automatic weapons.[10]

Some groups of prisoners were lined up, shot from the front and dragged into pre-dug mass graves; others were shoved roughly into trenches and machine-gunned where they stood; some were made to lie down in pairs, sardine-style, next to mounds of fresh corpses, before being killed; still others were tied together, made to stand on the lip of the pit, and shot in the back so that they would fall forward into it. Bulldozers pushed earth or sand loosely over the heaps of corpses.[11] Age made no difference. Investigators later excavating the graves found babies shot point blank in the backs of their heads, and "the withered body of a 3- or 4-year-old boy, still clutching a red and white ball."[12]

To add further horror to his ethnic cleansing, Ali al-Majid turned to Iraq's stockpile of WMD, which is how he became Saddam's most infamous commander, Chemical Ali. He boasted to members of Iraq's ruling Baath Party how he would deal with the Kurds. "I will kill them all with chemical weapons!" he exulted. "Who is going to say anything? The international community? Fuck them! The international community and those who listen to them."[13]

Chemical Ali knew well that since 1983 the Iraqis had been using chemical weapons against Iranian troops, and that some of those attacks were guided with intelligence furnished by the CIA.[14] Though an American spokesman occasionally felt compelled to issue a public rebuke to Iraq, the issue was never considered serious enough to impede Washington's burgeoning support of Saddam. It was thus only a natural progression for Saddam's commander to target domestic troublemakers like the people of Halabja with the same kinds of weapons Iraq had used so successfully against the Iranian forces.

The effects were horrible. Skin turned black or blistered and began to bubble. One mother tried to prevent her infant child from breathing in the deadly fumes by holding her tightly to her breast. She died still holding the child. One survivor from Halabja later told Human Rights Watch, "People were running through the streets, coughing desperately. I too kept my eyes and mouth covered with a wet cloth and ran. . . . A little further on, we saw an old woman who already lay dead, past help. There was no sign of blood or any injury on her. Her face was waxen and white foam bubbled from the side of her mouth."[15]

Halabja, despite its subsequent notoriety, was just one of sixty towns hit by chemical attacks by Chemical Ali between April 1987 and August 1988. The attack there might well also have passed unnoticed but for the fact that the Iranian military, which controlled the village at the time, flew in several international journalists to bear witness. The Iranians left the bodies unburied as grisly evidence to back up the claims they had been making for years that Saddam was using chemical weapons.

David Hirt, Middle East correspondent of *The Guardian*, would write,

No wounds, no blood, no traces of explosions can be found on the bodies—scores of men, women, and children, livestock and pet animals—that litter the flat-topped dwellings and crude earthen streets in this remote and neglected Kurdish town. . . .

The skin of the bodies is strangely discoloured, with their eyes open and staring where they have not disappeared into their sockets, a greyish slime oozing from their mouths and their fingers still grotesquely twisted.

Death seemingly caught them almost unawares in the midst of their household chores. They had just the strength, some of them, to make it to the doorways of their homes, only to collapse there a few feet beyond. Here a mother seems to clasp her children in a last embrace, there an old man shields an infant from he cannot have known what.[16]

The *Washington Post* and the *Los Angeles Times* ran front page stories on March 24, 1988, and U.S. television networks broadcast appalling scenes of frozen, bloated bodies.[17] These nightmarish scenes confirmed the tales of horror that had been filtering out of Kurdistan for months. As the *Financial Times* editorialized on March 23, "What has been happening in the last year, especially the last week, in a remote corner of north-east Iraq, reveals unplumbed depths of savagery."[18]

Faced with the grisly evidence, Iraq claimed it was the Iranians who had attacked with chemical weapons.[19] U.S. officials deplored the attacks, but, alleging they had no idea which side was actually responsible, refused to condemn Iraq. Washington, it seemed, had no hard evidence about Iraq's use of chemical weapons, nor about the Anfal campaign. They also didn't seem too eager to investigate: the U.S. blocked an attempt to have the United Nations Security Council determine who was responsible for Halabja.[20]

Despite its protests of ignorance, however, the Reagan administration knew all about Halabja—and the ongoing atrocities against the Kurds that only gradually came to light in the Western media. According to Larry Pope, then State Department office director for Iran and

Iraq, "There was a lag of a couple of weeks at most [in State Department knowledge of events in Iraq]. We knew that something dreadful was going on. We knew al-Majid was running the show. We had the satellite overhead that showed the villages razed."[21] The State Department's 1987 human rights report described "widespread destruction and bulldozing of Kurdish villages, mass forced movement of Kurds, and exile of Kurdish families into non-Kurdish parts of Iraq."[22] Another report sent to Washington by the U.S. Embassy in Iraq in August 1987 stated that al-Majid was coordinating "ruthless repression, which also includes the use of chemical agents."[23]

The U.S. had other witnesses to Saddam's chemical weapons. Rick Francona was an Air Force captain with the U.S. Defense Intelligence Agency, assigned to Baghdad in March 1988. His job was to continue furnishing satellite information pinpointing the position of Iranian troops and to assist in planning Iraq's strategic bombing attacks.[24] The following month, as news of the massacre at Halabja was breaking internationally, he discovered that Saddam's forces had begun using a much more deadly form of nerve gas against Iran than the U.S. previously knew. Francona and his team were recalled to the U.S. while officials in Washington debated their options: ignore the chemical attacks and continue supplying intelligence to Saddam, or end the relationship on moral grounds and risk an Iranian victory in the Gulf. After two weeks, according to Francona, "the decision was made that we would restart our relationship with the Iraqis. We went back to Baghdad and continued on as before. This was not a friendly relationship with the Iraqis, this was cooperation." He and his team were back in Baghdad by May 9.[25]

The media coverage of Halabja, however, had its impact. On June 24, 1988, the U.S. Congress finally passed a unanimous resolution condemning Iraq's use of chemical weapons, but, thanks to White House lobbying, no tough sanctions were attached. Saddam Hussein could be reassured that the Reagan administration was still behind him. His soldiers could continue their deadly attacks.[26]

Margaret Thatcher's government also played down reports of Halabja. British companies, after all, were also doing a booming business with Saddam. Within a month of the Halabja attack, Thatcher's trade secretary, Tony Newton, was in Baghdad to offer Saddam 340 million pounds of British export credits.[27]

After the War

The fear that Saddam might also start targeting Iranian cities, as opposed to the Iranian army, with chemical warheads was a major reason Khomeini finally agreed to sue for peace and, as he put it, "swallow the poison of defeat." On August 20, 1988, Iran and Iraq signed an armistice agreement. It is estimated that one million soldiers and civilians on both sides had been killed—in a war that achieved nothing for either side.

Some in Washington naively assumed the end of the Iran-Iraq war would also mean the end of the Al Anfal campaign. The Kurds, after all, could not be considered a serious menace to Baghdad on their own. Saddam, however, was intent on annihilating the Kurdish mountain tribes once and for all. He ordered additional troops north for one final onslaught. Thousands more Kurdish men, women, and children were killed in mass executions, by bullets in the back of the neck—or by further chemical attacks.

Days after Saddam launched this offensive, the U.S. intercepted Iraqi military communications in which the Iraqis themselves confirmed they were using chemical weapons against the Kurds.[28] Morton Abramowitz, assistant secretary of state for intelligence and research, sent a memo to Secretary of State George Shultz, entitled "Swan Song for Iraq's Kurds." He warned, "Now with cease fire [with Iran], government forces appear ready to settle Kurdish dissidence once and for all. . . . Baghdad is likely to feel little restraint in using chemical weapons against the rebels and against villages that continue to support them." Saddam Hussein's forces, he pointed out, would consider Kurdish civilians and soldiers alike fair game.[29]

Instead of issuing a tough warning to Saddam, the State Department sent a cable to its embassy in Baghdad, urging the embassy to stress to Hussein's regime that the U.S. understood the Kurds had joined with Saddam's enemy Iran. U.S. diplomats were told to explain that they had "reserved comment" until they had been able to take

Baghdad's views fully into account. American Ambassador April Glaspie warned the Iraqi government that they had what she called "a major public relations problem." She asked permission to visit the Kurdish territories, but the Iraqis, though denying that chemical weapons were being used, turned down her request. The embassy's comment back to Washington was that "it has been clear for many days that Saddam has taken the decision to do whatever the army believes necessary to fully pacify the North."[30] Shortly afterward, two U.S. embassy officials managed to interview Kurdish refugees at the Turkish border and obtained what they considered convincing evidence of chemical weapons attacks. Washington kept this information to itself.[31]

Some of the survivors of this new round of chemical warfare managed to escape to eastern Turkey. The Turkish government, wary of its own restless Kurdish population and anxious not to offend Saddam Hussein, played down the issue. Turkish doctors who treated the refugees were told to change their diagnoses of injuries from chemical weapons to something more benign. The Turks also tried to prevent outside reporters and nongovernmental organizations (NGOs) from meeting survivors. Nevertheless, horrific tales gradually began to trickle out, only slowly overcoming the skepticism and lack of interest in the Western media. Even Amnesty International doubted the enormity of the atrocities the refugees reported.[32] (In fact, a later U.N. report confirmed these stories, and asserted that "Saddam Hussein's atrocities against the Kurds were so grave . . . that since the Second World War, few parallels can be found."[33])

Some Kurdish leaders with detailed accounts of the attacks attempted to contact Western officials. They were repeatedly stymied by the policy of many Western governments of avoiding official contact with the Kurds out of deference to the Turkish government. That is what happened when Kurdish leader Jalal Talabani came to Washington with chapter and verse on the Al Anfal campaign. He contacted the staff director of the Senate Foreign Relations Committee, Peter Galbraith, who was able to convince a mid-level State Department employee, Larry Pope, to meet with Talabani. Unfortunately, the president of Turkey, who happened to be in Washington at the time, found out about the appointment and issued an angry protest; Iraqi Foreign

Minister Tariq Aziz canceled a planned meeting with Secretary of State George Shultz and accused the United States of interfering in Iraq's internal affairs. Shultz, who had known nothing of the Kurdish meeting, exploded: "Who the hell had this bright idea?"[34]

The episode ended with Larry Pope's being reprimanded and the State Department issuing a groveling apology. A furious Shultz issued what was taken by the State Department as an injunction against any meetings between U.S. officials and Iraqi Kurds. According to Galbraith, that grew into a ban on contacts "with other members of the Iraqi opposition—because nobody wanted to upset Saddam Hussein. And if Kurds getting gassed was something that caused trouble in that relationship, neither the Reagan nor the Bush administration wanted to hear a word about it."[35]

Larry Pope's bitter conclusion was that his attempts had done more harm than good. "Rather than send a message of disapproval to Iraq, we sent the message that our relations with Iraq and Turkey were more important than anything Hussein did internally."[36]

The Kurds, however, slowly managed to get their message out, often through old friends in the Western press. In the late summer of 1988, mounting media reports of Saddam's vicious attacks against the Kurds and editorials criticizing U.S. inaction became too blatant for the administration to ignore. On September 5, for instance, in his *New York Times* column, William Safire wrote, "A classic example of genocide is under way and the world does not give a damn."[37] The *New York Times*, in a separate editorial, wrote, "Not just a whiff but the stench of genocide drifts from Kurdish territory. Sovereignty cannot legitimize genocide. . . . Enough silence."[38]

That same day, State Department Spokesman Phyllis Oakley blandly continued to reassure journalists that the U.S. government had nothing to substantiate the reports of Iraq's atrocities against the Kurds. Her colleague Charles Redman said on September 6 that he could not confirm the news stories. "If they were true, of course we would strongly condemn the use of chemical weapons, as we have in the past," he said. "The use of chemical weapons is deplorable. It's barbaric."[39]

These public professions of ignorance masked a well-informed Administration determined to maintain relations with Iraq. Though some in the White House felt it was time to end an increasingly cozy relationship with the ruthless Iraqi tyrant, the dominant faction believed that, despite Saddam's brutality, Iraq was still a valuable ally and a huge potential market for American products. Attacking Saddam or clamping sanctions on his country, they argued, would not cause Saddam to change his policies but would turn him into an enemy. In addition, there was still the specter of the Soviet Union making headway in Iraq if the U.S. left the field open to them.

As Peter Galbraith recalled, "It's hard to imagine now, but there was a real euphoria about Iraq as the next powerhouse in the region and unlimited amounts of money that could become an important American partner—and customer. There was also the hope that Iraq would cooperate in keeping stable oil prices—in short, that Iraq could be a moderating influence in the Persian Gulf and in the Mideast."[40]

Finally, on September 8, 1988, Charles Redman, speaking for Secretary of State George Shultz, was obliged to declare, "The United States government is convinced that Iraq has used chemical weapons in its military campaign against Kurdish guerillas." The State Department also revealed that, in a meeting with Iraqi Minister of State for Foreign Affairs Saadoun Hammadi, Shultz denounced the "unjustifiable and abhorrent" use of poison gas against the Kurds. That declaration sidestepped the fact that Saddam was using mustard and nerve gas not just against Kurdish fighting men but against a wide range of innocent civilians. Nor was any mention made of the fact that chemical weapons were just one part of the Iraqi dictator's campaign to annihilate the entire civilian population of the region.[41] The message seemed to be that if his forces would just stick to conventional methods of ethnic cleansing—destruction of villages, forced population transfers, and mass executions—there would be no problem.

Peter Galbraith, however, had been deeply affected by the reports from the Kurdish areas, and was determined to investigate further. The year before, traveling through the region, he had witnessed the devastation of hundreds of Kurdish villages. At the time, he had no idea what had been the fate of their inhabitants; in any case, there was a war going on, and the Kurds had backed the wrong side. But by late August 1988, the war had ended. As Galbraith saw it, Saddam's continued attacks were genocide, as legally defined: attempting to wipe out a group of people in whole, or in part.

He took his argument to Senator Claiborne Pell, the chairman of the Senate Foreign Relations Committee, who agreed. In a flurry, Galbraith drafted the Prevention of Genocide Act, which would cut off all U.S. oil imports from Iraq and all trade subsidies to the Iraqi government and require the U.S. to oppose all international loans to Iraq. To counter White House attempts to obfuscate what was going on, the Prevention of Genocide Act put the burden of proof on the Reagan administration to certify that genocide was *not* occurring. The bill swept through the Senate on September 9 by a unanimous voice vote.

The Senate bill, coming on the heels of the statement a day earlier by Secretary of State Shultz, got Baghdad's attention. Iraqi newspapers denounced the U.S. criticism as part of a Zionist plot; anti-American crowds took to the streets on the government's cue. Iraqi officials, meanwhile, continued to deny the charges. Tariq Aziz made the Al Anfal campaign sound like enlightened city planning: "This is not a deportation of people," he said, "this is a reorganization of the urban situation."[42]

But the unanimous passage by the Senate of the Prevention of Genocide Act was just the first round in the legislative battle. Though it had reluctantly condemned Saddam's use of chemical weapons, the Reagan administration was still determined to gut the act as it worked its way through Congress. Lobbyists for U.S. businesses and agricultural interests joined the fight, applying considerable pressure on Senator Pell to retreat.

To bolster his case for tough sanctions Peter Galbraith and another Senate staffer flew to Turkey in mid-September to gather more first-hand evidence of chemical attacks. It was a curious situation: Galbraith scrambling to come up with physical and medical evidence, even though U.S. officials already knew, through intelligence intercepts and their own first-hand interviews, that what Galbraith and his colleague were hoping to prove was true. The survivors he interviewed confirmed the charges that Saddam's forces had directed chemical attacks at Kurdish villages.

Their report was released immediately on their return, but public, first-hand evidence seemed to make little difference to the Reagan administration. Though Secretary Shultz had denounced the chemical attacks, the State Department still opposed doing anything about them. Said Galbraith, "In fact, the State Department spokesman described the sanctions as 'premature,' which of course raises in my mind the question when it would have been 'mature' to have taken action. I mean how many thousands of Kurds needed to die before a response was appropriate?"[43] The toughest position the State Department was willing to take was to warn Iraq that additional attacks would cause the department "to reconsider" its opposition to sanctions—this after more than four thousand Kurdish villages had been leveled and anywhere from fifty to one hundred thousand people killed.

Meanwhile there was another embarrassing revelation for Washington to deal with—the fact that the Iraqis were using U.S.-made helicopters in their bloody campaign against the Kurds. In September 1985, the U.S. government had approved the sale of forty-five Bell helicopters to Iraq for $200 million. It was stipulated that they could only be used for civilian purposes. But in September 1988, Western reporters flown into Kurdistan by the Iraqi military found themselves on one of those very helicopters, painted in military colors and piloted by Iraqi military officers. The reporters spotted another six to ten U.S.-made Bell helicopters parked on the aprons of the military airfields. Yet the U.S. government filed no protest with the Iraqis, nor did it seek to investigate the affair.[44] This time, ignoring the story actually did make it go away.

Despite these setbacks, the White House, State Department, and powerful business lobbyists were succeeding in their campaign to convince Congress not to impose tough sanctions via the Prevention of Genocide Act. Many of the senators who had supported the bill backed away from it; others actively worked to kill it. One Senate staffer representing Senator John Breaux of Louisiana reportedly confronted Peter Galbraith in tears and charged him with "committing genocide" against Louisiana rice growers.[45]

Several chemical companies also called to inquire how their products might be adversely affected if sanctions were imposed to punish chemical weapons use.[46] Other U.S. companies were preparing fall-back strategies that would render the bill ineffective, if it managed to pass.

April Glaspie, in a confidential State Department cable, reported that representatives of the U.S. construction company Bechtel confided that, in case of a U.S. embargo on trade with Iraq, Bechtel planned to employ "non-U.S. suppliers of technology and continue to do business in Iraq."[47]

It is unclear what would have happened to the economic relationship between the U.S. and Iraq if the U.S. had taken a hard stance on the Kurdish genocide. American diplomats in Baghdad warned, "If Hussein perceives a choice between correct relations with the USA and public humiliation, he will not hesitate to let the relationship fall completely by the wayside."[48] But others argued that Iraq was vulnerable— its economy had been devastated by the long war with Iran, and it needed to roll over some $70 billion in debt. In short, Saddam Hussein was in no position to turn his back on the U.S., which was also one of Iraq's major oil importers. However, the point is moot: under White House and commercial pressure, the Prevention of Genocide Act died, with congressmen from agricultural states exporting to Iraq delivering the legislative *coup de grace*.[49] Strengthening political and economic ties with Saddam Hussein—while ignoring his human rights abuses and drive for WMD—would be the goal of the Reagan and Bush administrations until the invasion of Kuwait.

General Colin Powell, then National Security Advisor to Reagan, was one of the officials who helped implement that policy. Many years later, on September 14, 2003, Powell made an emotional visit to Halabja to light candles at a memorial for Saddam's victims, declaring— incorrectly—that the U.S. government at the time had "roundly condemned" the attacks. "There was no effort on the part of the Reagan administration," said Powell, "to either ignore [the massacre] or not take note of it."[50]

To give the appearance of concern while avoiding taking a firm stand, President Reagan called for a major international conference with lots of experts to mull over the issue. In a speech to the U.N. General Assembly in September 1988, he decried the use of chemical weapons in general—without referring to Iraq. The conference was held a few months later. It could have been scripted by Kafka.

It was hosted by France, the same country that had sold several billion dollars worth of its most sophisticated weapons to Saddam. The delegates had problems defining the crime: U.N. investigators were never able to officially document attacks by Iraq against its Kurds because both Turkey and Iraq refused to allow a U.N. team to interview Kurdish survivors. In any case, the Kurds were denied entrance to the conference because one of the ground rules laid down by the French— at the insistence of the Iraqis and the acquiescence of America—was that only countries could attend. Several prominent jurists had declared that the Geneva Protocol against chemical weapons only pertained to states attacking other states; the treaty had never envisaged a state turning such hellish weapons on its own people. In theory, then, the Kurds had no case. When Human Rights Watch sent a letter to Secretary of State Shultz suggesting that the U.S. raise this key issue at the conference, the letter went unanswered.[51] French police also made sure Kurdish demonstrators could get nowhere near the delegates.

Instead of condemning Iraq, on January 11, 1989, the delegates issued a toothless declaration simply restating the original 1925 protocol making chemical weapons illegal, and reaffirming the intention of participating states to eliminate them. In the wake of the Halabja affair and the Paris conference, the U.S. government actually increased the number of licenses for the export of sensitive dual-use technology to Iraq by more than 50 percent. This huge jump occurred in spite of the fact that the U.S. Customs Service had "detected a marked increase in the activity levels of Iraq's procurement networks. These increased levels of activity were particularly noticeable in the areas of missile technology, chemical-biological warfare, and fuse technology."[52]

The White House line was that the government needed to be realistic and pragmatic. They had to understand the importance of Iraq— the bigger picture. They could not afford to allow emotional issues, like human rights or the gassing of Kurds, to get in the way. Yet a few months later, in August 1990, after Saddam invaded Kuwait, the same set of facts that the Bush administration considered immaterial prior to the invasion all of a sudden became the basis for an indictment of Saddam Hussein by George H. W. Bush as the "Adolf Hitler" of the Middle East.

CHAPTER FIVE

Signals: The Invasion of Kuwait 1988–1990

The American policy was clear. I spent too much time in Washington to make a mistake and received a constant stream of American visitors here. We knew the United States would not let us be overrun.[1]
—Sheikh Ali al-Khalifa of Kuwait, 1991

Congressman Lee Hamilton: *"If, for example, Iraq crossed the Kuwaiti border, for whatever reason, what would our position be regarding the use of American forces?"*
Assistant Secretary of State John Kelly: *"That's the kind of hypothetical question I cannot enter into . . ."*
Hamilton: *"If such a thing should happen, though, is it correct to say that we have no treaty, no commitment, which would oblige us to use American forces?"*
Kelly: *"That's exactly right."*[2]
—Hearings before the House Foreign Affairs Committee, July 31, 1990

On August 2, 1990, Saddam Hussein invaded Kuwait. That attack was listed as one of the seven preliminary charges for which the former dictator might ultimately be tried by the special Iraqi tribunal.[3] It seemed to be an open-and-shut case: brutal, unprovoked aggression against a neighboring country, an example of Saddam's Hitler-like tendencies, as President George H. W. Bush declared at the time.

However, for years before the invasion, President Bush and his top aides had refused to heed the warnings of Saddam's growing menace. They continued to help the Iraqi dictator construct the impressive military machine that ultimately swept into Kuwait. In fact, Saddam's invasion of Kuwait and its catastrophic aftermath was not simply due to the lust for power and wealth of a ruthless megalomaniac. It was also the result of fatally misleading signals sent by the United States to both Iraq *and* Kuwait—the product of woeful incompetence and a healthy dose of duplicity. American officials fueled the conflict, assuring the Kuwaitis of U.S. support and thereby encouraged them to reject attempts by Saddam Hussein to negotiate the serious issues between their two countries. At the same time, Washington, still determined to reform Saddam, avoided every opportunity to warn the Iraqi tyrant that invading Kuwait would bring immediate U.S. retaliation.

An Empty Victory

When the war with Iran ended in August 1988, Saddam Hussein claimed victory. He was now the dominant military power in the Gulf, with an army of 1.2 million men—the fourth largest in the world. He had at his disposal some of the most sophisticated weapons the world's arm dealers had been able to provide. But Iraq had paid a staggering price in lives and funds and had gained precious little from the eight-year conflict. Between 100,000 and 200,000 Iraqis were killed, and another 400,000 to 800,000 were injured. (Iraq's population numbered only 17 million; a proportionate number of American casualties today would be 10 million.[4]) The financial losses to Iraq from lower oil revenues, physical destruction, and money spent on weapons totaled more than $200 billion, driving up food prices and inflation and leaving the economy in tatters.

Iraq was also in hock to the world. Before the war, Baghdad had reserves of more than $30 billion. Now it owed $40 billion to its Gulf neighbors, who had helped finance its war effort, and another $46 billion to the non-Arab world. Just servicing that debt would cost the country $8 billion a year. The Japanese, who were due $3 billion, cut off Iraq's credit; so did the Soviets, who were owed $9 billion. Even Lufthansa and Swissair, which the country owed over $150 million for maintenance of Iraq's national airline, now refused to pay the government tax on tickets booked in Iraq.[5]

Saddam, in short, had sacrificed his people's lives and resources to win the war, but then, once victorious, the dictator and his nation found themselves worse off than before he invaded Iran. The fighting over, it would have seemed logical to temper his grandiose military ambitions, slash the army's rolls, get his disastrous financial situation back in shape, and return to rebuilding the country.[6] Unfortunately, Saddam could not afford to release his soldiers from duty. There were not enough jobs for civilians as it was; dismissing 350,000 men from uniform had already resulted in local riots. Besides, Saddam was still determined to increase Iraq's military might, develop long-range missiles and nuclear arms, and build the capacity to manufacture his own sophisticated weapons. By the spring of 1989, 88 percent of the revenues from Iraq's oil exports were being poured into the armed forces and expanded military industries.[7]

His attempts to create new civilian employment via an ambitious public works programs—a new subway for Baghdad, a new national rail system—quickly foundered for lack of funding. Cutting the wartime food subsidies to save money resulted in inflation of 25 percent in 1989, while per capita income tumbled to half the level of 1980. As unrest mounted, Saddam could no longer call for national unity in the face of Iran. He also no longer had a tightly structured, ideologically united party behind him. The Baath Party had been taken over by the Tikritis, Saddam's clan. They ruled by fear and repression, not ideology. The degree of savagery and corruption of those closest to Saddam, particularly his eldest son Uday, outdid anything Iraqis had experienced in the past. In the months following the ceasefire with Iran, Saddam executed several of his most respected military officers after his secret police uncovered a series of real or imagined plots.[8]

The basic problem was that Iraq's oil revenues were in desperate shape. The day after the Iran-Iraq war ended, Kuwait greatly increased its oil production, contravening quotas set by the other members of

OPEC; the United Arab Emirates followed suit. They were trying to get a larger share of the market, but the result was a glut in the world's supply of crude and a precipitous decline in the price of oil from $21 to $11 a barrel. Kuwait, whose finances were in much better shape, could afford the decreased price, but it spelled disaster for Iraq: a loss of $14 billion a year.[9] On July 17, 1989, without identifying the states involved, Saddam talked darkly of a foreign plot against Iraq: "We have warned them. It is a conspiracy to make us live in famine."[10]

Wooing Saddam

Meanwhile, the U.S. government's internal debate about how to deal with Saddam continued. On one side were those officials who warned of the Iraqi dictator's ongoing support for terrorism, his determination to build an arsenal of nonconventional weapons, and his atrocious record of human rights. They were the dissenters, however. Policy was being run by a small group of the most powerful figures in the Reagan and then the Bush administrations. They insisted that, despite Saddam's excesses, the United States could still tame the Iraqi dictator by offering the carrot of more U.S. trade and investment. They mistakenly believed that Saddam was as rational as they were. After all, Iraq was exhausted from eight years of war. Saddam certainly couldn't be ready to launch another bloody adventure. In the end, the argument went, pragmatism would prevail. A study by the Strategic Studies Institute of the U.S. Army War College, issued in early 1990, found that "Baghdad should not be expected to deliberately provoke military confrontations with anyone. Its interests are best served now and in the immediate future by peace. . . . Force is only likely if the Iraqis feel seriously threatened. It is our belief that Iraq is basically committed to a nonaggressive strategy, and that it will, over the course of the next few years, considerably reduce the size of its military. Economic conditions practically mandate such action."[11]

There were also powerful Cold War considerations in Saddam's favor. As Reagan's Deputy Secretary of State John Whitehead wrote in a highly classified memo, "The Soviets have strong cards to play: their border with Iran and their arms supply relationship with Iraq. They will continue to be major players and we should engage them as fully as possible."[12] Whitehead argued that, because of the disastrous arms-for-hostage dealings with Iran, the United States would have to put considerably more effort into winning back Saddam's trust.

Those concerns merged conveniently with the commercial interests of many of America's most powerful corporations, who coveted a share of what they hoped would be mammoth reconstruction projects in Iraq. The giants of U.S. agro-business were eager to expand already huge American sales of rice and grain to Iraq. American's oil barons were also solid supporters of Saddam, who sold petroleum to the United States at a discount off the world market price. By 1989 the U.S. had become the largest purchaser of Iraqi crude. Total trade with Iraq was worth more than $3 billion a year.[13] All these American corporations made their pressure felt in Washington through the U.S.-Iraq Business Forum.[14] They had enormous clout in the White House and on Capitol Hill and played a key role in blocking trade sanctions proposed by Congress.

When President George H. W. Bush took office in January 1989, his transition team could have changed U.S. policy toward Saddam Hussein. As one of his advisors wrote, the choice was "to decide whether to treat Iraq as a distasteful dictatorship to be shunned where possible, or to recognize Iraq's present and potential power in the region and accord it relatively high priority. We strongly urge the latter view."[15]

The memo continued, "The lessons of war may have changed Iraq from a radical state challenging the system to a more responsible, status-quo state working within the system, and promoting stability in the region." However, President Bush's advisors were under no illusions about the man they were dealing with: "Saddam Hussein will continue to eliminate those he regards as a threat, torture those he believes have secrets to reveal, and rule without any real concessions to democracy. He has announced a few cosmetic improvements, but few expect a humane regime will come to Iraq any time soon." It was also clear that Saddam would continue developing sophisticated chemical weapons and attempt to divert U.S. exports to Iraq's weapons programs. Nevertheless, the transition team concluded that the United States should continue playing ball with the Iraqi dictator.

Bush's advisors recommended that the U.S. government liberalize exports of dual-use equipment to Saddam. The fact that those licenses were being blocked by Pentagon experts wary of diversion to Saddam's nonconventional weapons programs was of secondary importance. The main thing was to get that trade and investment rolling. As the memo noted, Iraq had "vast oil reserves promising a lucrative market for U.S. goods."[16]

Bush's secretary of state, James Baker, had decisive power within the new administration and was critical in pushing the pro-Iraq line. As he admitted in his memoirs, "Our administration's review of the previous Iraq policy was not immune from domestic economic considerations. . . . Had we attempted to isolate Iraq we would have also isolated American businesses, particularly agricultural interests, from significant commercial opportunities."[17] At the time, Iraq was buying one quarter of America's rice exports; altogether, it was the ninth largest purchaser of U.S. food products in the world.

The incoming Bush administration's guidelines on Iraq could not ignore Saddam's atrocious record on human rights. But they seemed to regard it mainly as a P.R. problem. The last thing they wanted to do was convey any serious concern to the touchy dictator about his decimation of the Kurds. "In no way should we associate ourselves with the 60-year-old Kurdish rebellion in Iraq or oppose Iraq's legitimate attempts to suppress it," the guidelines admonished.[18]

Investigators for the human rights organization Middle East Watch wrote in a 1989 report that, "One senior [U.S.] state department official described the Iraqi government as 'possibly the worst violator of human rights anywhere in the world today.'"[19] The State Department, in fact, had been very clear about the horrors of Saddam Hussein in its most recent country report, describing the murders, extralegal detentions, torture, and disappearances of political opponents and government critics. The Bush administration, however, raised none of those findings in direct talks with Iraqi authorities.[20] In March 1989, at a meeting of the United Nations Human Rights Commission in Geneva, when twelve Western states cosponsored a tough resolution calling for the appointment of a special U.N. rapporteur to "make a thorough study of the human rights situation in Iraq," the United States declined to join.[21]

In his first State of the Union address, President Bush proclaimed that "our diplomacy must work every day against the proliferation of nuclear weapons." In the next few weeks, Bryan Siebert, an official at the U.S. Department of Energy, became convinced that Saddam was no more than three years away from achieving nuclear capability. He attempted to get his superiors and other departments to impose more rigid restrictions on U.S. exports to Iraq. At the time, however, Secretary of State Baker was intent on reducing restrictions. Department of Commerce publications now actually exhorted American companies interested in getting an edge in the Iraq market to sell "oil field and refinery equipment, computers, and other high-technology goods and services." Increasingly troubled, Siebert wrote a memo warning that Saddam could get the components he needed for his nuclear program from the United States under the current lax enforcement of export laws. His views were dismissed as overly alarmist by higher ups in his department. His concern, they said, was premature.[22]

Siebert was later astonished to learn that his own Department of Energy, along with the U.S. armed forces and U.S. nuclear laboratories, had actually invited two Iraqi nuclear scientists to the U.S. for a symposium on nuclear detonations. A senior Energy Department official later observed, "In a nutshell, the conference was the place to be . . . if you were a potential nuclear weapon proliferant."[23]

In May 1989, the Department of Commerce opened the door even wider to U.S. dual-use sales to Iraq. It notified the Pentagon, which had been most alarmed about such exports, that Pentagon experts would no longer be asked to review those transactions. The reason given for cutting out the Pentagon was mind blowing: "the development of biological and chemical weapons, as well as the missile technology regime, are part of the foreign policy controls and are beyond the preview [sic] of the Department of Defense."[24]

In June 1989, the Defense Intelligence Agency cautioned top U.S. officials that a clandestine procurement network for Saddam's military was operating around the world, including in the United States.[25] Meanwhile, the CIA joined with other U.S. intelligence agencies to produce a secret National Intelligence Estimate on Iraq. It warned of Saddam's program to develop long-range missiles and chemical and biological capacities, and estimated that Iraq would obtain nuclear weapons within five to ten years.[26]

Many of Saddam's purchases abroad were still being guaranteed by huge loans to Iraq by the Atlanta branch of Italy's Banca Nazionale del Lavoro (BNL). On April 8, 1989, Christopher Droghul, the branch manager, agreed to another whopping loan request for more than $1.1 billion, enough to finance one quarter of Iraq's industrial purchases for all of 1989.[27] The loan was unsecured and never listed on the bank's books. All pretenses had been cast aside: the branch bank was now doing business directly with Iraq's Ministry of Industry and Military Industrialization.[28] There was no attempt by the bank to see how the money was actually spent.[29]

Finally in August 1989, after a tip from a worried bank employee, the FBI and U.S. banking authorities began investigating the activities of this formerly obscure regional branch bank. They were to find billions of dollars in loans that the BNL had made to Iraq over the past few years—most of them similarly unsecured and off the books. They would also find that many of those loans had gone to finance sales from companies in the U.S. and Europe that went directly to Saddam's nonconventional weapons programs.

Investigators later learned from Droghul that while being escorted through an Iraqi military facility, his hosts proudly produced a drawing of a scud missile that had been upgraded, thanks to financing from BNL Atlanta.[30] BNL bankers also claimed that some of the companies looking to do business with Iraq were referred to the Atlanta branch by Vice President Dan Quayle. One of those companies was owned by a man with close business and personal links to the Quayle family; he ultimately constructed a brass refinery that recycled spent Iraqi artillery shells.

Much of the evidence indicated that U.S., British, and Italian authorities had known what was going on and had done nothing about it.[31] "It is becoming increasmgly clear," a somber Ted Koppel declared on ABC News Nightline, June 9, 1992, "that George [H. W.] Bush, operating largely behind the scenes throughout the 1980s, initiated and supported much of the financing, intelligence, and military help that built Saddam's Iraq into the aggressive power that the United States ultimately had to destroy."

From the start, however, the White House had been doing its best to keep the scandal from spreading further.[32] In February 1990, for instance—with the Bush administration still courting Saddam—Attorney General Dick Thornburgh blocked U.S. investigators from traveling to Rome and Istanbul to interview key Italian officials. Bureaucrats in the Commerce Department were ordered to alter Iraqi export licenses to obscure the exported materials' military function before transmitting the documents to Congress, which was investigating the affair. The CIA also withheld from Congress—and possibly from prosecutors—key documents showing what the government knew about BNL.[33]

"That Bush is tolerating a cover-up on Iraq conducted by others on his behalf can no longer be seriously doubted," *Washington Post* columnist Jim Hoagland wrote in October 1992. "That Bush has lied about his knowledge of shipments of U.S. arms to Iraq can no longer be seriously disputed."[34]

U.S. federal prosecutors—first under Bush and finally under Clinton—shied away from any aggressive investigation, provoking the outrage not only of journalists and congressmen but of the federal judge Marvin Shoob who presided over the legal proceedings in Atlanta, Georgia. On August 23, 1993, with the government insisting on limiting charges to a handful of mid-level employees of the Atlanta branch, Judge Shoob exploded, refusing to sentence them. He characterized those local employees as mere "pawns and bit players in a far more wide-ranging conspiracy."

"It is apparent," he wrote, "that decisions were made at the top levels of the United States Justice Department, State Department, Agriculture Department, and within the intelligence community to shape this case and that information may have been withheld from local prosecutors seeking to investigate the case or used to steer the prosecution."[35]

Earlier, he had commented, "I think the government entered into an effort early on to support Iraq as a matter of national policy. They used the CIA and Italy to effectuate that purpose. Many of the things that were done were in violation of acts of Congress and U.S. arms export laws. They were aware of the law, and they skirted it. It was an effort to arm Iraq, and then, when things got out of hand, they didn't want that information to come out."[36]

Finding a New Banker

With the BNL no longer available to play the role of Saddam's banker, Iraq and the companies wanting to sell to Iraq urgently needed to find another source of financing with similarly generous or nonexistent standards. The members of the U.S.-Iraq Business Forum directed their high-powered lobbying fire on the United States Export-Import Bank. The Ex-Im Bank was wary of Iraq for the very sensible reason that the country was a financial deadbeat; it had long ago stopped repaying its creditors. Cold banking logic, however, gave way before a parade of five-star executives from America's largest corporations—Bechtel, G.M., Halliburton—with powerful allies in Congress and the White House, most particularly Secretary of State James Baker. In reality, the lobbying companies were doing so at no risk to themselves—when Iraq was ultimately unable to pay, U.S. taxpayers would pick up the tab. The skeptical folks at the Ex-Im Bank were ultimately persuaded to change their views on Iraq, and, predictably, many of the deals made possible by the U.S. government guarantees the bank offered wound up benefiting Saddam's nonconventional weapons programs.[37]

And so it went through the fall and into the winter of 1989. Despite continued warnings from the intelligence community that Saddam Hussein was up to no good, the people at the top of the government—Bush and Baker in particular—continued to put their faith in trade and diplomacy. As trade accelerated, so did the amount of alarming information about Saddam's quest for sophisticated equipment for his WMD program. On September 3, 1989, for instance, the CIA reported to Secretary of State Baker that the Iraqi dictator had a program to build nuclear weapons and had "made use of covert techniques" to obtain the sophisticated technology he needed to build a bomb. The report listed some of the advanced dual-use technology Iraq was after, which included many products available in the United States.[38] That same month, the Department of Defense discovered that an Iraqi front company in Cleveland, Matrix Churchill, was funneling U.S. equipment to Iraq's nuclear-weapons program, but, in the name of continued trade, the Bush administration allowed the company to continue operations.[39]

In September 1989, President Bush, after a discussion of Saddam Hussein's brutal regime and military ambitions, asked Richard Kerr, the deputy director of the CIA, if it was possible that Saddam Hussein could really change. "The leopard does not change his spots," was the reply.[40] Nevertheless, the Bush administration continued its attempts to woo and reform. On October 2, the president signed a secret National Security Directive (NSD-26) that would guide United States policy toward Iraq over the following fateful months. The directive mentioned Saddam's brutal regime and his ongoing search for weapons of mass destruction, and talked vaguely about calling the dictator's attention to these concerns. But the bottom line remained: the only thing that would wean the Iraqi tyrant from his nefarious ways was more U.S. trade and investment. It was even decided that the United States would consider extending military assistance to Iraq on a case-by-case basis.

The next day, officials from several government agencies convened to discuss a new proposal to offer a $1 billion loan guarantee for Iraq to be backed by the same agricultural credit program that had been part of the BNL loans that were now being unraveled by the FBI and other government investigators. Many at the meeting were leery of risking any more financial ties with Iraq. Though Saddam was billions of dollars in debt, he was still pouring his oil revenues into military procurement. As one U.S. Treasury official warned, "Iraq's attitude toward its foreign debt is special. Once the Iraqis suck you in, they only service the debt if you give them ever-increasing amounts of credit."[41]

Those considerations did not faze Secretary of State Baker. On October 6, he met with Tariq Aziz, Saddam's foreign minister, and assured him the U.S. would come up with increased agricultural credits and push to liberalize dual-use exports to Iraq. Baker also expressed a vague—very vague—disquiet about Saddam's continued nuclear ambitions. According to the State Department's minutes of the meeting, "the Secretary admitted that the U.S. does have concerns about proliferation, but they are worldwide concerns."[42] One reason Baker was so intent on improving relations with Iraq was that he hoped Saddam Hussein would use his influence with other radical Arab states and the Palastine Liberation Organization (PLO) to support Baker's new Middle East peace initiative. Indeed, in order to gain points with the Bush administration, Saddam did play a key role in convincing Yasser Arafat to adopt a new, moderate position and to start talks with the U.S.[43]

On November 9, 1989, Iraq was allotted the $1 billion worth of new agricultural credits. At the same time the State Department refused to tighten restrictions on export licenses, even though much of the equipment was now being sent directly to Iraqi installations engaged in nuclear-capable missile development.[44]

On December 5, Saddam's scientists test launched a three-stage rocket that could deliver a warhead over a distance of a thousand miles. In response, some officials in the Pentagon and Commerce Department again pushed for stiff measures. As one of them said, "We made it very clear that we had to tighten up the controls—but we were met with indifference."[45] A month later, on January 17, 1990, President Bush overrode congressional objections to Saddam's human rights violations and authorized a new Ex-Im Bank line of credit for Iraq worth nearly $200 million.[46]

In 1989 alone, despite all the warnings, the United States had sold Saddam helicopter engines, vacuum pumps for a nuclear plant, sophisticated communications equipment, computers, and strains of the most deadly bacteria.[47] Later, Sam Gejdenson, a Democratic congressman investigating U.S. relations with Iraq, concluded that "it was the [Bush] Administration's sole desire and policy to aid and abet Saddam Hussein." Or, as he remarked, "The cop was put in the intersection, and he was waving the sellers on."[48]

The View from Baghdad

Ironically, even as the administration of George H. W. Bush was doing its best to keep credit and trade flowing to Saddam Hussein, the Iraqi dictator was increasingly convinced that the U.S. was conspiring to overthrow him. Saddam could never really comprehend the United States. The only Western country he had ever visited was

France. He could never understand how democracies functioned—that there could be a real separation of powers between the executive and legislative, that the head of state would be unable to control the press and television.

A paranoid dictator with plenty of domestic and foreign enemies, Saddam needed no encouragement to find plots and conspiracies everywhere. The Soviet Union, once his forceful backer, was disintegrating, as were dictatorial regimes across Eastern Europe. Saddam was vulnerable. From his own early experiences with the CIA in Iraq—the U.S.'s arming and subsequent betrayal of the Kurds, the secret American shipments of arms to Iran—Saddam knew how duplicitous the U.S. could be. How could the U.S. Congress attempt to impose an embargo on Saddam Hussein at the same time that the White House claimed it wanted more American trade and investment with Iraq? As Saddam saw it, this was all just shadow play. The U.S. must be plotting with his Arab neighbors to force him to his knees.

Saddam could be forgiven for being unable to decipher American policy toward Iraq. It is not clear, in fact, if there really was a coherent policy. On February 12, 1990, Assistant Secretary of State John Kelly visited Saddam Hussein. Kelly told the Iraqi leader of U.S. concerns about human rights and weapons of mass destruction, but then told Saddam, "You are a force for moderation in the region, and the United States wishes to broaden her relations with Iraq."[49]

Yet three days later, on February 15, the Voice of America (VOA), which purported to represent the views of the U.S. government, broadcast an editorial worldwide citing several countries, among them Iraq, where the rulers "hold power by force and fear, not the consent of the governed. But as East Europeans demonstrated so dramatically in 1989," the editorial continued, "the tide of history is against such rulers. The 1990s should belong not to the dictators and the secret police, but to the people."[50] Saddam, who had been shaken by the swift, bloody executions of Romanian strongman Nikolai Ceauşescu and his wife, was outraged by the VOA broadcast. His deputy foreign minister protested the "flagrant interference in the internal affairs of Iraq." He demanded an immediate apology from the United States.

Ambassador April Glaspie was instructed by the State Department's top officials to express regret for the VOA editorial. The cable read, "It is in no way USG [U.S. government] policy to suggest that the Government of Iraq is illegitimate or that the people of Iraq should or will revolt against the Government of Iraq." Relaying the State Department's message to Iraqi officials, Ambassador Glaspie concluded, "I am sorry that the Government of Iraq did not inform me of its concern about the editorial earlier, so that I could have provided you with the official assurance of our regret without delay."[51]

The most pressing source of anxiety for Saddam, though, was still his economic dispute with Kuwait over the massive debt he owed that country and its aggressive oil production policies. The Kuwaitis rebuffed Saddam's first, relatively diplomatic requests that they reconsider those policies. The Iraqi dictator had hoped he could convince the Gulf states to forgive his debts, which would help restore Iraq's credit rating, and instead lend financial support to his ambitious new projects. After all, Iraq had waged a proxy battle for the Gulf states, protecting their huge oil wealth from the radical threat of the Ayatollah Khomeini. In addition, the money they "loaned" Saddam Hussein was more than compensated by the windfall profits they reaped because of the catastrophic drop in Iraq's oil production due to the war; Iraq had even arranged for its neighbors to increase their production to replace the petroleum that Iraq would have sold. The Kuwaitis, however, refused to back down.

Saddam was increasingly suspicious that the U.S. was behind Kuwait's intransigence. Indeed, there is evidence of an effort between the U.S. and Kuwait at this early stage to weaken Saddam. Iraqi security forces, ransacking the files of Kuwaiti Intelligence after the invasion, found a memorandum describing a meeting in November 1989 between the head of Kuwaiti state security and CIA Director William Webster. One of the summary paragraphs released by the Iraqis to the press read: "We agreed with the American side that it was important to take advantage of the deteriorating economic situation in Iraq in order to put pressure on that country's government to delineate our common border. The Central Intelligence Agency gave us its view of appropriate means of pressure, saying that broad cooperation should be initiated between us on condition that such activities be coordinated at a high level."

The CIA's spokesman dismissed the document as a "total fabrication." But, according to the *Los Angeles Times*, which published it, "The memo is not an obvious forgery, particularly since if Iraqi officials had written it themselves, they almost certainly would have made it far more damaging to U.S. and Kuwaiti credibility." In fact, the CIA conceded that William Webster had received "a routine courtesy call" from senior Kuwaiti officials at that time. Since 1987, when the U.S. had allowed Kuwaiti ships in the Gulf to fly the American flag, American and Kuwaiti intelligence officers had forged an increasingly close relationship.[52] But the CIA insisted that there was no discussion of Kuwait's relations with Iraq.[53]

There were other documents released by court order in 1992, as Milton Viorst, who covered the Middle East for the *New Yorker*, has observed, that "revealed that the Reagan and Bush administrations, at a time of soaring trade deficits, had routinely urged the Saudis and the Kuwaitis to overproduce to force oil prices down. The documents revealed no explicit animus toward Iraq, but they did not have to. It was enough that in the spring of 1990, Washington and Baghdad had categorically opposite objectives in the oil market. Whatever America's role, Kuwait's oil policy severely weakened Iraq."[54]

Saddam decided to confront the U.S. directly and publicly. It would distract his people from their economic misery and, more important, would be another way to win financial support and respect from his neighbors. He still aspired to be the new Nasser, the first Arab leader to really back the PLO, to challenge the State of Israel, and defy its American sponsor. On February 19, 1990, on Jordanian television, he attacked the continued U.S. naval presence in the region and called for Arab control of the Gulf and its petroleum resources. For this cause he volunteered his own leadership.[55] Iraqi Air Force Mirages would now operate out of Jordan with Jordanian planes as part of a new "All Arab Air Squadron." Quick to react, on February 20, 1990, Israeli Prime Minister Yitzhak Rabin warned that Israel "would not be able to sit idly by if Iraqi military forces are deployed in Jordan, where they are only a four minute flight from Tel-Aviv."[56]

The next day in Washington, the powerful pro-Israel lobby swung into action. The House Foreign Relations subcommittee condemned Saddam's human rights record and proposed sanctions against Iraq. Though the Bush administration distanced itself from the subcommittee's actions, to Saddam it was just one more proof of "an imperialist-Zionist conspiracy."[57]

Saddam's drive for nuclear weapons was at least partially intended to balance Israel's nuclear strength. Since the end of the war with Iran, Iraqi military planners had viewed Israel and its nuclear arsenal as Iraq's most serious enemy in the region. For its part, Israel made no secret of its determination to prevent the Iraqi dictator from acquiring nonconventional weapons. In 1981, Israeli planes had destroyed Saddam's French-built nuclear reactor with scarcely a whimper from the rest of the world. Now Israelis were openly debating in their press when and where they should again strike Iraq.[58] In February 1990, an obvious new target presented itself, when Iraq opened its first clandestine uranium enrichment site at Tarmiyah.

Fearing another Israeli strike and also angered by the huge new flow of Soviet Jews to Israel, Saddam escalated his shrill attacks against Israel and the U.S. On February 23, at a meeting of Arab heads of state, the Iraqi dictator warned that with the Soviet Union in decline, America would try to govern the world.[59] "Isn't Washington helping Soviet Jews emigrate to Israel?" he said. "Aren't American ships still patrolling the Gulf, even though the war between Iran and Iraq is over?" Referring to the current political turmoil in Israel, Saddam warned that Israel might embark on "new stupidities."[60] The moderate Arab leaders with strong links to Washington were taken aback by the Iraqi leader's vitriolic anti-American statements, which, by implication, charged them with being America's lackeys. Egypt's Hosni Mubarak, who was receiving $2 billion a year from the United States, stalked out of the conference.

The next day, in a meeting with Mubarak and Jordan's King Hussein, Saddam railed against his intransigent debtors in the Gulf, whom he believed were supported by the United States. He declared, "If they don't cancel the debt and give me another $30 billion, I shall take steps to retaliate."[61] Not only did most of the Gulf states again refuse Saddam's requests, the Emir of Kuwait made it clear that the time had come for Iraq's debt to be repaid. Furthermore, Kuwait would refuse any negotiations, officials said, until Iraq officially recognized Kuwait's sovereignty.

This had long been a sticking point. Saddam, like almost all previous rulers of Iraq, maintained as an article of national faith that Kuwait was an integral part of Iraq, ripped away when it was set up as a separate state by the British imperialists. One day, every Iraqi schoolchild learned, that despicable act would be undone. In reaction to Kuwait's refusal to deal, Saddam ordered his commanders to immediately draw up plans for a massive deployment of troops on the shared border.[62]

His aides would later explain this as a show of force to convince the Kuwaitis to bargain, asserting that Saddam had not yet made any decision to actually invade his neighbor. His actions, however, predictably sent tensions soaring. The Iraqi dictator was often obtuse to the signals he was sending, but aides dared not contradict the tyrant. On March 15, for example, he ordered the execution of an Iranian-born British journalist, Farzad Bazoft. Bazoft had been discovered snooping around the test sites of a new Super Gun that Saddam was planning to build. He was charged with being an Israeli spy, which he probably was.[63] But instead of following the traditional process of trying the spy, denouncing Israel, and then quietly releasing him, Saddam hanged Bazoft publicly, despite—or perhaps because of—the West's appeals for clemency. It seems likely that his brazenness in doing this despite his dependence on Western credit arose at least in part from the obvious disconnect between the grand diplomatic pronouncements of the U.S. and their allies and the policies they actually implemented.[64]

The next week, Gerald Bull, a Canadian ballistics expert, who had been developing the giant Super Gun for Saddam, was shot to death as he entered his apartment in Brussels. His executioners were almost certainly the Israeli Mossad. Then, on March 28, five people were arrested in Heathrow Airport attempting to smuggle triggers for a nuclear weapon from the U.S. to Iraq via Britain. The worldwide outrage following the execution of Bazoft, the flagrant assassination of Bull, and the seized nuclear triggers all merged together in Saddam's mind as part of the ongoing Israeli-American plot against him.[65]

He feared that a new Israeli strike was imminent. Israel was the means by which he imagined the U.S. would derail his attempts to become a world-class military power that could challenge America's control of the Gulf. On April 2, 1990, the Iraqi dictator defiantly declared that Iraq didn't need an atomic bomb, because it possessed sophisticated binary chemical weapons. "I swear to God," thundered Saddam, "that we shall burn half of Israel if it tries to wage anything against Iraq. May God's curse fall upon the big powers."[66]

Most of the Western press headlined just the first part of the threat, a bloodcurdling vow to destroy the Zionist state, leaving out the conditional: that Iraq would strike back only if Israel were first to attack. Saddam was so concerned about outraged reaction to his speech that he asked King Fahd of Saudi Arabia to dispatch Prince Bandar, the Saudi ambassador to Washington and a close confidant of President Bush, immediately to Baghdad. Saddam assured Bandar that he would not initiate any strikes against Israel, and asked him to get similar assurances from the U.S. that Israel would not attack Iraq—which President Bush ultimately gave.[67] Saddam emphasized that he wanted to maintain good relations with the U.S. Why had he made the threats? One reason, he told Bandar, was to distract the Iraqi people from their huge economic problems. As Saddam put it, "I must whip them into a sort of frenzy of emotional mobilization, so they will be ready for whatever may happen."[68]

Careening toward Disaster

After Saddam's "burn half of Israel" speech, one of James Baker's closest aides, Dennis Ross, thought it was time to transmit a clear warning to the Iraqi dictator by enacting retaliatory trade sanctions.[69] Other government agencies, however, warned that such measures would hit American businessmen and cereal growers. Despite Saddam's rhetoric, President Bush still held grimly to hopes that U.S. policy could somehow transform the Iraqi leader. Reacting to Saddam's speech, the American president observed mournfully, "I think these statements are very bad. I'm asking Iraq very strongly to immediately reject the use of chemical weapons. I don't think it'll help the Middle East or Iraq's security; I would say that it'll have the opposite effect." Yet rather than issue any clear warning to Saddam, the president blandly concluded, "I suggest that such statements about chemical or biological weapons be forgotten."[70]

As relations between Iraq and the United States careened toward disaster, the attention of the real decision makers in the administration—particularly the key player, Secretary of State Baker—was elsewhere. These were momentous times. The Soviet Union was coming apart; there was a summit with Soviet leader Mikhail Gorbachev to be planned; German reunification was at hand. Iraq was a relatively small show in a far-off desert. It could wait. As one of Baker's closest associates put it, "the Iraqi missile hadn't yet been picked up by the radar in Washington."[71] In any case, except for the peace process with Israel, Baker had never shown much sustained interest in the Middle East.[72] Day-to-day policy was being overseen by Assistant Secretary of State John Kelly, who headed the Bureau of Near Eastern and South Asian Affairs (NEA). Kelly, with limited experience in the Middle East, was described by one experienced reporter as "abrasive, arrogant, and thoroughly detested by his peers in the field as well as by his Washington staff."[73]

Meanwhile, via back channels, the Bush administration was sending messages to reassure the Iraqi dictator of continued White House support. One of those messages was delivered on April 12, 1990, by a delegation of visiting American senators from agricultural states intent on bolstering U.S. grain sales to Iraq. Saddam first listened to their formal written message. They were concerned, they wrote, about his drive for chemical weapons and recent threats against Israel. "It would be a good thing for you and for peace in the Middle East," they mildly advised, "if you reconsidered such dangerous projects and such provocative statements and acts."[74]

Much more time, however, was spent attempting to soothe the Iraqi dictator. Senator Robert Dole of Kansas, who led the delegation, relayed President Bush's message that he wanted better relations with Iraq. Dole added his personal promise that Bush would oppose sanctions legislation currently before the U.S. Congress, "unless any provocative act should occur." The senator also apologized once again to Saddam for the Voice of America broadcast in February. He assured Saddam—incorrectly—that the person responsible had been fired.

After listening to Saddam complain of his problems with Congress and the American media, Senator Alan K. Simpson of Wyoming agreed that the foreign press was out to get him. "I believe that your problems lie with the Western media, and not the U.S. government," the senator intoned. "The press is spoiled and conceited. . . . My advice is that you allow those bastards to come here and see things for themselves."[75] After Saddam promised to destroy all his weapons of mass destruction if Israel did the same, Ohio Senator Howard Metzenbaum declared, "I am now aware that you are a strong and intelligent man and that you want peace." On his return to Washington, Senator Dole reported that Saddam Hussein was "the kind of leader the United States can easily be in a position to influence."

Just a week after the senators' visit, however, on April 19, Saddam Hussein repeated his promises to help liberate the Palestinians and warned that any attack against him would be met by a counterattack "to sweep away U.S. influence in the region." If there were hostilities, he declared, he would destroy British and American warships in the Gulf and unleash terrorists against the United States.[76] Saddam was now playing to the Arab public throughout the region. He was being celebrated as the first Arab leader in years to stand up to the West and to Israel; he relished the acclaim. He was coming to believe his own rhetoric.

Meanwhile, the Bush administration seemed paralyzed. On April 26, after listening to John Kelly explain why the administration refused to change its hopeful views on Saddam, California Congressman Tom Lantos exploded, branding the government policies "Alice in Wonderland." Rhetoric like Saddam's, he said, had not been heard since Adolf Hitler. When was the Bush administration going to realize that sanctions were necessary? Unfazed, John Kelly responded, "We believe there is still a potentiality for positive alterations in Iraqi behavior."[77]

In the spring of 1990, however, at the same time as the U.S. officials in Washington continued to issue such bland public protests of optimism, Saddam Hussein was informed by his own intelligence agencies that the U.S. Central Command, which was responsible for American security in the Gulf, was now conducting war games with its supposed enemy no longer the Soviet Union, but Iraq. Saddam was also receiving reports that CIA Director William Webster was a frequent visitor to Kuwait. After each visit, the Kuwaitis increased their oil production, which ensured that world petroleum prices stayed low and that Saddam Hussein became even more strapped for revenues.[78]

Then, on May 21, just a month after the senators' visit with Saddam, the U.S. Congress passed a bill suspending loans to Iraq. That measure put even more financial pressure on Saddam; he was desperate to resolve the impasse with Kuwait, which had now added insult to injury by attempting to sell Iraq's debt on the world market at deep discounts, further damaging the country's credit rating. When the Arab League heads of state convened in Baghdad at the end of May 1990, Saddam accused some "Arab brothers" of trying to destroy Iraq. "Every time the price of a barrel drops by one dollar, Iraq loses one billion dollars a year," he stormed. "You're virtually waging an economic war against my country."[79]

He demanded again the immediate cancellation of Iraq's debts and an additional $10 billion to keep his economy going. "We have reached a point," he warned, "when we can no longer withstand pressure." He also repeated his accusation that Kuwait was stealing crude from the Rumaila oil fields, and insisted that, to compensate Iraq for its misdeeds, Kuwait must give up the two tiny islands that controlled the entrance to Iraq's one usable port on the Gulf.[80] Afterward, a small, worried group of Arab leaders arranged a private meeting with Saddam and Javer Al-Sabah, the Emir of Kuwait, to work out a "brotherly solution" to the dispute. The Emir, however, still refused to compromise. Instead, he repeated his own demand that the Iraqi debt be repaid immediately. Over the following days, he continued to rebuff Saddam.[81]

At one point a Kuwaiti official, replying to Iraq's continued demands, suggested that if Iraq needed money, it should do what it had always done—"put its women on the streets."

"This was an unspeakable insult to the proud Iraqis," wrote former U.S. Ambassador Joseph Wilson.[82]

According to Foreign Minister Tariq Aziz, "We saw a conspiracy to bring about the economic collapse of Iraq . . . and a change of regime. But Kuwait was too small to do this without backing from a superpower. Weren't the Kuwaitis supported and encouraged by some other country? This was more threatening to us than an attack by Israel, to which we could retaliate. We had to challenge this conspiracy."[83]

Aziz had solid grounds for suspecting conspiracy, and the Kuwaitis made no effort to conceal them. At one point, Sheikh Sa'ad of Kuwait warned the Iraqis, "Don't threaten us. Kuwait has important friends." The Kuwaitis said the same thing to Jordan's King Hussein when he attempted to mediate the dispute.[84]

Where was Kuwait getting such assurance? From General Norman Schwarzkopf, the head of the U.S. Central Command, for one, who had initiated the change in U.S. military strategy in the region, identifying Iraq as the most likely threat. He had taken over the command in 1988 and was soon making repeated high-profile visits to Kuwait, hobnobbing with the country's rulers, sitting down to a lavish official dinner garbed in Arab robes as if he were Lawrence of Arabia, and making no secret of his contempt for Saddam. He saw his mission as convincing the Kuwaitis and the other Gulf Arabs that Iraq was now their major threat, as well.[85]

As an official in the U.S. embassy in Kuwait at the time said, "The Kuwaitis feared that when they called, we wouldn't come. Schwarzkopf insisted—explicitly or not—that we would. . . . I think Schwarzkopf finally convinced most Kuwaitis that if Iraq came in, we'd be there."[86] The Kuwaitis received such reassurances from other American officials, too. According to a senior American diplomat in Kuwait, "The embassy had repeatedly assured Kuwaiti officials that the United States would stand up for Kuwait's sovereignty and territorial integrity, as it had at the time of the reflagging."[87]

Nathaniel Howell, who was U.S. ambassador to Kuwait at the time, told me there was never any formal commitment made to the Kuwaitis prior to the invasion. But, after interviewing several top American and Kuwaiti officials shortly after the invasion, Milton Viorst, reporting for the *New Yorker*, wrote, "I was convinced that in the spring of 1990, the Kuwaiti government felt itself free to take a dangerous position in confronting Iraq. . . . The Kuwaitis played their tricks because Washington, deliberately or not, had conveyed the message to them that they could."[88]

As Sheikh Ali al-Khalifa of Kuwait confided to Viorst, "The American policy was clear. I spent too much time in Washington to make a mistake and received a constant stream of American visitors here. We knew the United States would not let us be overrun."[89] Another Kuwaiti official added, "No explicit commitments were ever made, but it was like a marriage. Sometimes you don't say to your wife, 'I love you,' but you know the relationship will lead to certain things."

Nor was Washington willing to respond to Iraq's several requests to help resolve the dispute. Indeed, rather than helping to defuse the crisis, American and British leaders actually urged the Kuwaitis to refuse any concessions to Saddam.[90]

Incredibly, while U.S. officials were blandly advising the Kuwaitis not to worry about Saddam's threats, not once during the spring and early summer of 1990 did CIA Director William Webster and Secretary of Defense Dick Cheney discuss the possibility of an Iraqi attack on Kuwait.[91] But one was on the way. On July 16, analysts at the U.S. Defense Intelligence Agency spotted Saddam's elite Hammurabi division on the Kuwaiti border. The next morning another division was seen moving in the same direction, and Saddam blasted certain unidentified Gulf Arab countries for plotting against Iraq with "imperialist and Zionist forces." For the first time, he issued a military threat: "If words fail to protect us, we will have no choice other than to go into action to reestablish the correct state of affairs and restore our rights."[92] By that date, said a senior Pentagon planner, "You could tell it wasn't a training exercise."[93]

The Bush White House, however, ignored its own experts who urged that an unmistakable warning be sent to Saddam Hussein not to move against Kuwait. The administration still didn't understand that an attack would take place; they hadn't even considered what America's response would be. Egypt's President Hosni Mubarak added to the confusion. On July 24, he flew to Baghdad, still attempting to negotiate a compromise. "As long as discussions last between Iraq and Kuwait," Saddam reportedly told Mubarak, "I won't intervene with force before I have exhausted all the possibilities for negotiation. But don't tell that to the Kuwaitis, Brother Mubarak." Immediately after, the Egyptian president informed the Emir of Kuwait—inaccurately—that there was no longer any urgent reason to worry. "I've had it from the mouth of Saddam Hussein himself," said Mubarak, "that he won't send troops and that he has no intention of attacking Kuwait." He transmitted the same message to Washington. What he forgot to include was Saddam's proviso: that he would abstain from military action *as long as* he could see a possibility for peaceful settlement.[94]

Meanwhile, Saddam's troops continued moving in force toward the Kuwaiti border. On July 25, a top analyst at the Pentagon's Defense Intelligence Agency (DIA) issued a "warning of war." There was a 60 percent chance, he judged, that hostilities would break out. Despite that alarm, he was still unable to get the attention of any key decision makers in the government. Those few U.S. officials who were paying attention remained convinced that Saddam's threats were not to be taken seriously. In fact, the Bush administration was still fighting to renew agricultural trade credits for Iraq and refusing efforts to restrict high-tech exports until the very eve of the invasion. In June 1990, dual-use equipment for Iraq's nuclear program was still being shipped from the United States.[95]

Eleven years earlier, in June 1979, a team under then-Pentagon analyst Paul Wolfowitz prepared a study for the U.S. secretary of defense entitled "Capabilities for Limited Contingencies in the Persian Gulf." The report pinpointed Iraq as a menace to the states of the Gulf and warned that in the case of any Iraqi threats, it would have to be made brutally clear to Iraq that the U.S. would react with military force to any aggression against his neighbors. America should be ready to send forces to the region at the first sign of trouble "before hostilities began, and while escalation might still be avoided."[96]

In July 1990, watching the ominous Iraqi troop buildup, planners in the Central Command proposed that the Bush White House take just such measures to let Saddam know, in no uncertain terms, that the U.S. was determined to defend Kuwait. They dispatched their urgent recommendations to the Joint Chiefs of Staff—and never heard about them again. No strong signal was ever sent.

Instead, on July 25, 1991, April Glaspie was instructed to convey to Baghdad a much blander U.S. concern about the threats against

Kuwait and the United Arab Emirates (UAE). She delivered the message to Iraq's foreign minister: "The implications of having oil production and pricing policy in the Gulf determined and enforced by Iraq guns [are] disturbing."[97] At the request of the UAE, which was concerned about Saddam's mobilization, the United States also announced a small joint air-naval maneuver with the Emirates. It was not the forceful action that others in the administration, such as Wolfowitz and Schwarzkopf, had been advocating, but it caught Saddam's attention. The U.S. had also suggested a similar symbolic gesture, like the visit of an American warship to Kuwait, but the Kuwaitis turned the offer down. They still thought Saddam would never attack and feared that such a move would only provoke the Iraqi leader. Ironically, Saddam thought they had accepted and would join in the U.S.-UAE maneuver.[98]

As if he were still attempting to decipher U.S. policy, Saddam became personally involved. Glaspie was summoned again to the Foreign Ministry, then driven to another office to find herself face to face with the dictator. Saddam launched into an account of his financial problems with Kuwait and his suspicions that the U.S. was encouraging Kuwait and the UAE to refuse to negotiate. He warned that America should not force Iraq into a position where in order to survive it would have to launch a new Gulf War. And he hinted at the possibility of terrorist retaliation: "We cannot come all the way to you in the United States, but individual Arabs may reach you."

When the American ambassador finally had a chance to talk, she told Saddam that the U.S. sympathized with his economic problems. As for his conflict with the Gulf states, she said "we have no opinion on Arab-Arab conflicts, like your border disagreement with Kuwait." It was the standard diplomatic reply, designed to stay clear of messy entanglements—delivered as though hundreds of thousands of Iraqi troops were not even then poised to entangle themselves in Kuwait.

Instead she said, "I have received an instruction to ask you, in the spirit of friendship, not in the spirit of confrontation, about your intentions." Saddam abruptly was called from the room to take a phone call from President Mubarak. When he returned he told the ambassador that the Egyptian president had informed him that the Kuwaitis had agreed to new talks at the end of the month in Jeddah, Saudi Arabia, to resolve the crisis. Saddam said he had told Mubarak to "assure the Kuwaitis and give them our word that we are not going to do anything until we meet with them." If all went well, said Saddam, nothing would happen. "But if we are unable to find a solution, then it will be natural that Iraq will not accept death. . . . There you have good news," he told the ambassador.[99]

Reassured by Saddam that an attack was no longer imminent, Glaspie cheerily parted, telling the dictator that she was off for a long-planned holiday. She immediately dispatched a cable to Washington—subtitled "Saddam's Message of Peace"—advising that the meeting was "cordial, reasonable, and even warm." She concluded, "His emphasis that he wants peaceful settlement is surely sincere; Iraqis are sick of war. But the terms are difficult to achieve." She played down Saddam's threats and wound up advising that relations would be better if criticism of Iraq in the U.S. could be "eased off for a while."[100]

Despite the optimistic tone of Glaspie's cable, the top U.S. diplomats at the embassy in Kuwait, already apprehensive of Saddam's intentions, were only further alarmed by her report. U.S. Ambassador Nathaniel Howell and his assistant clearly remembered the leadup to Saddam's invasion of Iran ten years earlier. "We both had the same reaction," said Howell. "It was déjà vu all over again. The sort of things Saddam was saying was the same as he did before going into Iran. It immediately rang bells with us, and we sent a cable to Washington saying, 'We think he is going to come across the border.'" Howell thought that some frank, forceful talk with Saddam might still have had some effect. But the State Department never answered his cable. "I don't think they were focusing much on it," he said. "We had very weak leadership in the Middle East Bureau with little Middle East experience."[101]

Long after the U.S. had counterattacked, Saddam gave an interview explaining his interpretation of Ambassador Glaspie's message. "I asked her to persuade [President Bush] to pressure Kuwait if necessary. . . . They said they would not interfere. In so saying they washed their hands. What response should I have waited for?"[102]

After Saddam Hussein invaded Kuwait, the Iraqis released the transcript of the Saddam-Glaspie meeting.[103] The American ambassador became the focus of a firestorm. Ultimately, she was made the scapegoat for the inaction and errors of much more powerful officials. For instance, several days before Glaspie's meeting with Saddam, on July 19, 1990, Secretary of Defense Dick Cheney declared at a morning breakfast with reporters that the American commitment, made during the Iran-Iraq war, to come to Kuwait's defense if it were attacked was still valid. But shortly afterward, Cheney's remarks were undercut by his own spokesman, Pete Williams, who explained that the secretary had spoken with "some degree of liberty." Cheney was then admonished by the White House: "You're committing us to war we might not want to fight," and advised pointedly that from then on, statements on Iraq would be made by the White House and State Department.[104] On July 24, the day before Glaspie met with Saddam Hussein, State Department spokesperson Margaret Tutweiler, when asked about U.S. defense ties with Kuwait, was very clear: "We do not have any . . . special defense or security commitments to Kuwait." The State Department also prevented the Voice of America from declaring that the United States was "strongly committed to supporting its friends in the Gulf."[105]

In Washington, Glaspie's optimistic report of her meeting with Saddam, added to the reassurances of Mubarak and the Saudis, led many to conclude that, despite the massive buildup, no invasion was in the offing. But a few officials, like Wolfowitz, after reading the bland message delivered by Ambassador Glaspie to Saddam, pushed for a much tougher follow-up letter from the president: a distinct red light to Saddam Hussein. Once again, however, the attention of the American president and his top foreign policy planners was riveted on the dramatic changes in the former Soviet bloc, not on the gathering crisis in the Gulf. The consensus was that the Iraqi problem was only "a passing summer cloud."[106] Rather than take a tough tone, the officials who drafted the letter in the president's name emphasized the faint hope that moderation might still prevail: "We believe that differences are best resolved by peaceful means and not by threats involving military force or conflict."

Nowhere in the bland three paragraph communication was there any indication that the United States would react with force to aggression in the region. When Wolfowitz saw the letter, he attempted to have it canceled. It would be better to send no message at all, but it had already been cabled to Baghdad. On April 28, Glaspie delivered it to the Iraqi Foreign Ministry—not in writing but orally, so it could always be disowned if it somehow leaked to the press.

According to Nizar Hamdun, then the Iraqi foreign ministry undersecretary and a key aide of Tariq Aziz, it was the letter from Bush—rather than the meeting with April Glaspie (where Hamdun had been present)—that gave Saddam the fatal impression that he could invade Kuwait with no fear of U.S. military response. "The letter was far too conciliatory," Hamdun recalled in New York, on April 2, 2003, during lunch with Joseph Wilson, who had been Glaspie's deputy in Baghdad at the time of the Kuwait invasion.[107] The Iraqis, in fact, "had been startled by the positive tone of the communication from the Bush letter." "That note," said Hamdun, "had sent the wrong signal to Saddam by not explicitly warning him against taking any military action, and not threatening harsh retaliation if he did. Saddam had concluded from the letter that the U.S. would not react militarily and that he could survive the political criticism that the invasion would provoke. This letter, much more than any other United States statement, appears to have influenced Saddam's thinking." Adds Wilson, "Nizar's memory in this regard was vivid and unflinchingly critical of the letter."

"We were reluctant to draw a line in the sand," a senior administration official later said. "I can't see the American public supporting the deployment of troops over a dispute over twenty miles of desert territory and it is not clear that the local countries would have supported that kind of commitment. The basic principle is not to make threats you can't deliver on. That was one reason there was a certain degree of hedging on what was said."[108]

Meanwhile, officials in the U.S. and Britain were secretly continuing to encourage the Kuwaitis to resist Saddam's pressure. The Emir of Kuwait instructed his brother, who was to represent Kuwait at the showdown meeting with Saddam, that neither the demands of Iraq nor the demands of the Saudis for compromise "will bear fruit . . . that is also the position of our friends in Egypt, Washington, and London."[109] Those "friends" were playing an extremely dangerous diplomatic game, with Iraqi troops posed on Kuwait's border.

When Jordan's King Hussein attempted to mediate the conflict, the Kuwaitis flatly refused. "If Saddam comes across the border, let him come," they said. "The Americans will get him out."[110] On July 29 the king advised the U.S. and British embassies in Amman to warn Washington and London that he foresaw serious trouble ahead.[111]

The DIA, meanwhile, was continuing to monitor the buildup of Iraqi troops near the Kuwaiti border. On July 30, 1990, DIA analyst Pat Lang advised his superiors that Saddam's huge military buildup made no sense if the dictator's aim was simply to intimidate Kuwait. Saddam, he said, "doesn't know how to bluff. It is not in his past pattern of behavior." There was only one reason for the dictator's moving such a sizable force, said Lang. "He intends to use it."[112]

The final act played out on July 31, 1990, at the meeting in Jeddah, Saudi Arabia. It was a disaster. The Iraqis refused to modify their demands. The Kuwaitis refused to back down. In response to Iraqi insinuations, the Kuwaitis replied once again, "Don't threaten us. Kuwait has important friends."[113]

Behind this fatal impasse stood months of feckless American policy: encouraging the Kuwaitis to hold firm with vague assurances that the U.S. and Britain stood with them and at the same time missing every opportunity to send an unmistakable signal to Saddam Hussein that invading Kuwait would be fatal. The U.S. was actually stoking the flames, while giving neither side any reason to put out the fire.

Indeed, the same day as the Jeddah conference collapsed, Assistant Secretary of State John Kelly continued indirectly to flash a green light to the Iraqi dictator. Appearing before an open session of the House Foreign Affairs Committee, Kelly was repeatedly asked by Chairman Lee Hamilton how the U.S. would respond if Saddam attacked Kuwait: "We don't have any defense treaty with the Gulf states. That's clear," said Kelly. "We support the independence and security of all friendly states in the region. . . . We call for a peaceful solution to all disputes, and we think that the sovereignty of every state in the Gulf must be respected."

Hamilton asked, "If, for example, Iraq crossed the Kuwaiti border, for whatever reason, what would our position be regarding the use of American forces?"

"That's the kind of hypothetical question I cannot enter into," replied Kelly. "Suffice it to say that we would be extremely concerned, but I cannot venture into the realms of hypothesis."

Hamilton persisted: "If such a thing should happen, though, is it correct to say that we have no treaty, no commitment, which would oblige us to use American forces?"

"That's exactly right."[114] Kelly's testimony was broadcast that same day over the BBC World Service.[115]

"For me, sitting it out in Iraq, that was the defining moment," said Joseph Wilson, who—in the absence of the vacationing April Glaspie—was then the top U.S. diplomat in Baghdad. "Within minutes, Kelly's testimony was transmitted to Iraq. Despite the qualifiers that Kelly put into place about America's preference for peaceful solutions to disputes, the only thing the Iraqi regime heard was that we had no legal obligation or even any mechanism to react to an invasion."[116]

Later, when the United States was mobilizing hundreds of thousands of soldiers to repulse the invasion, another American congressman, Tom Lantos, delivered a devastating critique of John Kelly and the U.S. government for having so long refused to recognize the true nature of Saddam Hussein. "This obsequious treatment of him by a large variety of high-ranking officials encouraged him to take this action, and there is no way of escaping this responsibility."[117]

On August 1, Pat Lang, viewing the latest moves of the Iraqi army, predicted Saddam would invade that evening. The CIA was now making the same assessment. But other officials still thought Saddam might be bluffing. There was some talk of President Bush issuing an urgent warning to Saddam. But nothing was done. Nobody high enough up was paying attention.[118]

Early on August 2, Iraqi forces rolled into Kuwait—and kept on going until they had occupied the entire country. At 11:20 P.M. in Washington, President Bush put out a strong statement condemning the invasion and demanding "the immediate and unconditional withdrawal of all Iraqi forces."[119] It was a forceful message, and it was much too late. As one study of the events noted, "The Bush administration drew a line in the sand in firm, deep strokes, but not until the Iraqis had already crossed it."[120]

More to the point, on August 3, 1990 the Bush administration still didn't know what its response to the Iraqi aggression would be.

CHAPTER SIX

No Exit : The Gulf War
August 1990–March 1991

Saddam Hussein may have been a shrewd if ruthless leader domestically, but by seizing all of Kuwait in August 1990, he made a fatal miscalculation—just as he did when he invaded Iran. In the months following the Kuwaiti invasion, Saddam's continuing blunders played into the hands of President George H. W. Bush, who—despite his rhetoric of searching for a peaceful solution—was determined to block any face-saving exit for the Iraqi tyrant. It was a stunning reversal of the policy of "constructive engagement" that the White House had pursued before the invasion, hoping to tame the Saddam's excesses with the carrot of trade and credits.[1] Now, Bush's much more resolute aim was to use Saddam's aggression as an excuse to destroy the tyrant and his military machine.

The Confrontation
If Saddam had contented himself with a small incursion into Kuwait to seize just the Rumaila oil field and the two tiny offshore islands that he had long coveted, he probably would have gotten away with it.[2] The United States and Britain would have condemned the act; there would have been threats of U.N. sanctions, the temporary suspension of U.S. loan programs, and probably not much else. There was no way the United States could have assembled the massive task force it ulti-

mately did to fight for two uninhabited specks of land in the Gulf and a few miles of disputed desert sand. In the end, Saddam Hussein might even have been able to withdraw his troops after negotiating with Kuwait and the other Gulf states for forgiveness of Iraq's huge debts—which is what he was really after. He might have emerged a heroic leader to his nation and the predominant power in the Arab world.[3]

The reason why Saddam chose instead to occupy all of Kuwait is still not clear. It was a last-minute decision that took many of his own advisors and generals by surprise. There were certainly obvious financial motives—seizing Kuwait was the equivalent of a massive bank heist. Apart from Kuwait's impressive oil production, there were supposedly huge stores of gold and other assets—billions of dollars' worth—sitting in the Kuwaiti treasury. The invasion would finesse the problem of Iraq's colossal debt to Kuwait.[4]

Like President George W. Bush prior to the invasion of Iraq in 2003, Saddam also had vague, unrealistic hopes that he would be greeted as a liberator by both the Kuwaitis and foreign residents, who had been chafing under the autocratic rule of the Al-Sabah family. Saddam's U.N. ambassador made the fatuous claim that the Iraqi invasion was prompted by a call for help from "young Kuwaiti revolutionaries."[5] Indeed, Saddam attempted to form a provisional government to give the invasion some cloak of legitimacy, but the small group of dissident Kuwaitis he had hoped to form the government turned him down; he had never consulted them before the attack.

Militarily, Saddam calculated that seizing all of Kuwait would leave the U.S. with no space to deploy the large force that would be necessary to expel the Iraqi troops. This, too, turned out to be an error. Saddam never suspected that the Saudis would agree to accept a massive presence of American troops on their territory. He also had not understood that he could no longer count on his traditional Soviet allies to dissuade any major American military thrust into the region or veto any tough sanctions against his regime. Further, Saddam Hussein did not expect the United States would be willing or able to assemble the large force necessary to expel Iraq's huge army from Kuwait. As the Iraqi dictator told U.S. Ambassador April Glaspie just prior to the

invasion, he was certain that, with the ghosts of Vietnam still lingering, the American people would never be willing to sacrifice thousands
of young men for the sake of a small emirate on the Persian Gulf.

Curiously, Saddam also failed to appreciate the great importance
that the U.S. attached to the petroleum resources of the Gulf.[6] In his
State of the Union address in 1980, President Carter, wary of a Soviet
threat in the region, had declared that "an attempt by any outside force
to gain control of the Persian Gulf region will be regarded as an assault on the vital interests of the United States of America. And such
an assault will be repelled by any means necessary, including military
force."[7] Now that the threat was coming from a state in the Gulf itself,
the reaction of President George H. W. Bush would ultimately be just
as forceful.

On the other hand, despite their massive intelligence resources,
President Bush and his advisors had also completely misread Saddam
Hussein's intentions—and the American president himself had no clear
idea at first of what his own reaction would be. True, on August 2, 1990,
after learning of the invasion, President Bush declared, "Let me tell
you that the United States strongly condemns the invasion and calls
for an immediate withdrawal. There is no place for this kind of brutal
aggression in today's world."[8] But what kind of muscle was Bush willing to put behind this condemnation? The president and his aides were
still trying to decide. When questioned by a reporter on August 2, the
president merely said, "We're not discussing intervention."[9]

Indeed, Saddam Hussein may have felt his gamble had paid off.
The U.N. Security Council, after an all-night meeting, condemned the
invasion on August 3. But the delegates also called for Kuwait and Iraq
"to begin immediately intensive negotiations for the resolution of their
differences."[10] Meanwhile, Bush and his aides continued mulling over
what the United States should do—and could do—to counter Saddam
Hussein.[11]

President Bush's family had made its fortune in the oil business
and had long had close ties with the Saudi royal family. They had also
done profitable business with Kuwait. The president was horrified at
the thought of Saddam Hussein adding the oil wealth of the Emirate
to the huge resources of Iraq. With 20 percent of the globe's oil re-

serves, Bush told his advisors, Saddam Hussein would be able to manipulate international oil prices and hold the world hostage to his political goals.[12] That economic clout, plus a million-man army, would transform the capricious tyrant into by far the most powerful figure in the Gulf, and a major contender around the globe.

On August 2, the president flew to Aspen, Colorado, to deliver a speech. British Prime Minister Margaret Thatcher took Bush's arm when they met there and said, "You must know, George, he's not going to stop."[13] She was referring to the possibility that Saudi Arabia could be the Iraqi dictator's next target. It wasn't just a question of containing Saddam Hussein, she insisted; he had to be expelled from Kuwait, his threat permanently destroyed.[14] President Bush seemed to be edging closer to military action. "We are not ruling any options in," he declared later that afternoon. "But we're not ruling any options out."[15]

Aside from his own uncertainty about how to proceed, Bush's noncommittal response was due in part to the hope of an intra-Arab resolution of the crisis. Jordan's King Hussein had immediately attempted to arrange a peaceful compromise. He was afraid that the turmoil would destabilize his own precarious monarchy, and he also realized that, if the invasion were not rolled back, it would mean that no one in the region would be safe from Saddam's ambitions. On the other hand, a military confrontation would open the way to a Western occupation of the Gulf.[16]

When King Hussein phoned Saddam on the day of the invasion, the Iraqi dictator told him, "We had to go in. We were driven to that," but he reassured the Jordanian monarch that his goal was not to take over Kuwait but to force the Kuwaitis to do some serious negotiating over their financial disputes. Once that took place, said Saddam, he would withdraw. In the meanwhile, he warned, public condemnation or threats from the Arab states or other powers would torpedo any peaceful settlement. "We may end up with Kuwait being part of Iraq," declared Saddam. The Iraqi ruler was unwilling to give the impression that he was caving in to external pressure.[17]

King Hussein was now optimistic that negotiations among the Arab states themselves could produce a settlement; war was not inevitable.[18]

He phoned Egyptian President Hosni Mubarak, told him of his conversation with Saddam, and said he planned to convene a mini-summit of Arab heads of state to resolve the crisis. But, worried about a meeting of Arab leaders that was due to convene in Cairo in just a few hours to discuss Iraq's invasion, King Hussein insisted that the attendees refrain from any hostile declarations against Saddam. Otherwise, the mini-summit would be jeopardized. According to King Hussein, Mubarak agreed. The Jordanian monarch then flew to Egypt and, together with Mubarak, on August 2, spoke by phone with President Bush. The king outlined his plan for a summit to resolve the crisis and warned the American president that it was critical that no leaders denounce Saddam Hussein until there had been a chance for negotiations. The United States, he particularly insisted, should refrain from pressuring Arab leaders to attack the Iraqi dictator. "We can settle the crisis, George," said the Jordanian leader. "We just need a little time." President Bush agreed to give the Arab leaders forty-eight hours. "You've got it," he promised, "I'll leave it to you."[19] Mubarak passed on the request for restraint to the other Arab leaders.

On August 3, in Baghdad, Saddam promised King Hussein he would attend the mini-summit in Saudi Arabia on August 5. The only moment that Saddam expressed any anger was when he warned again that any condemnation of his invasion by the Arab League would destroy any possibility of a peaceful solution. "I'll just say that Kuwait is part of Iraq and annex it." He also denied any intention of attacking Saudi Arabia.[20] A few hours later, Saddam issued a statement that he would begin withdrawing troops on August 5—the date of the mini-summit—but, possibly to add another bargaining point, he said that the Kuwait royal family would not be restored to power.[21]

Meanwhile, U.S. spy satellites had spotted Saddam's troops continuing to move south toward the frontier of Saudi Arabia. If Saddam was planning a further invasion, there was no question that the U.S. would be compelled to act militarily. Colin Powell, chairman of the Joint Chiefs of Staff—and the most reluctant of the president's advisors to resort to force—warned President Bush that it would take several months before enough American troops could be airlifted to Saudi Arabia to defend against a massive Iraqi attack.[22] But the biggest problem was getting permission from the Saudis to deploy those troops. The fundamentalist rulers of Saudi Arabia would be very reluctant to invite into their country thousands of foreign soldiers—men and women— with their loose morals, blatant sexuality, and drugs.

When President Bush telephoned Saudi King Fahd on August 3 to warn him of a possible Iraqi attack, the monarch replied that he still had hopes for a negotiated settlement with Saddam. The president persisted, "But if things got worse, your Majesty, would you accept American military aid?"

"If things got worse," the king answered in a resigned tone, "Yes, we'll accept."[23]

At that point, President Bush, despite his previous assurances to King Hussein that he would avoid provoking Saddam and give the Arabs a chance to settle things themselves, entered the fray. He announced he was dispatching American warships to the Gulf and freezing all Kuwaiti assets. Early on August 3—the day after making his commitment to King Hussein—the president also instructed Brent Scowcroft, his national security advisor, to pressure Arab countries to condemn Saddam's invasion.[24] Assistant Secretary of State John Kelly dispatched a tough message to the Egyptian Foreign Ministry in Cairo demanding that Egypt and the other Arab states take a firm stand on the Kuwait affair. According to one source, the message was brutal: "The West has done its duty, but the Arab nations are doing nothing. The United States has sold a lot of arms to Arab countries, especially Egypt. If they do not act, if they do not take a firm stand on the Kuwait affair, they can be sure that in the future they will no longer be able to count on America."[25] The Egyptian Foreign Ministry complied immediately, issuing a communiqué condemning Iraq's invasion of Kuwait. The Arab League, over King Hussein's objections, also passed a resolution condemning Iraq and calling for Saddam Hussein to withdraw his troops unconditionally from Kuwait.[26] Saddam reacted as promised: he announced he would no longer attend the planned mini-summit. The result, he said, was predetermined. The meeting was canceled.

On Saturday, August 4, President Bush met with the Emir of Kuwait, who had fled his country just ahead of the Iraqi troops. The Kuwaitis had once been Bush's benefactors.[27] Thirty years earlier, when he was head of Zapata Off-Shore Petroleum, Bush had drilled the first oil wells off the coast of Kuwait, with the approval of the ruling Al-Sabah family. Now, in August 1990, the president promised not only to drive Saddam out of Kuwait but to restore the emir to his throne.[28]

The Road to War

On Sunday, August 5, 1990, President Bush denounced the Iraqis as "international outlaws and renegades." Having delivered a mortal blow to the Arab solution proposed by King Hussein, he declared that it "obviously has failed." In fact, as many observers close to the events, such as King Hussein, saw it, President Bush never gave the Arab solution a chance to succeed or fail, so eager was he to publicly condemn Saddam Hussein.[29] Moreover, by his vituperative attacks on Hussein, which would escalate over the coming weeks, President Bush provoked the worst of Saddam Hussein's street-fighter character. The day after the invasion, according to the *Washington Post*, Bush had also ordered CIA Director William Webster to undertake covert operations to destabilize the Iraqi regime and overthrow the government of Saddam Hussein.[30]

When asked by reporters on August 5 if he planned to move militarily against Saddam, the president declared, "I will not discuss with you what my options are or might be, but they're wide open, I can assure you of that." Then, with mounting anger, he waved his finger and said, "I view very seriously our determination to reverse this aggression. This will not stand. This will not stand, this aggression against Kuwait."[31]

Colin Powell heard the president's statement on television. He realized that Bush had just set a new goal beyond defending Saudi Arabia; the president now was committing himself to war, if necessary, to drive Saddam from Kuwait. Like Saddam Hussein, Bush was improvising policy as he went. The immediate problem was to convince the Saudis to accept the deployment of hundreds of thousands of American and other foreign troops. To do that, the Bush administration had to persuade King Fahd that there really was a threat. The Saudi king was skeptical. Saudi patrols sent into Kuwait had reported there was "no trace of Iraqi troops heading toward the kingdom."[32]

The task of convincing King Fahd was given to a top-level U.S. delegation, headed by Secretary of Defense Dick Cheney. The delegation flew to Riyadh with the latest satellite photos purporting to show the Iraqi buildup. Though other members of his royal family strongly disagreed with the decision, the Saudi king finally agreed to accept more than 150,000 American soldiers.

The issue of whether or not Saddam was really menacing Saudi Arabia was key to the tragedy that was to unfold. Without that threat, President Bush would not only have been unable to deploy troops in the region, he also would never have been able to put together a coalition to defeat Saddam. That issue, however, has still not been settled. Even Dick Cheney realized that Saddam's intentions were far from clear. As he cautioned his colleagues en route to Riyadh, "We have to be careful. We don't know Saddam is going to invade Saudi Arabia. So let's not go in there and suggest it is inevitable or that we have inside knowledge."[33]

Saddam Hussein and Tariq Aziz were also offering assurances to anyone who would listen that Iraq had no plans to invade Saudi Arabia. Though the Jordanian king was convinced that Saddam was telling the truth,[34] the Iraqi statements were ignored by U.S. officials and almost all the American media. Regular news bulletins instead featured alarming reports of the escalating number of Iraqi troops in "offensive posture."[35]

On August 6, Saddam, wearing his Baath party uniform and a pistol on his hip, met with Joseph Wilson, the U.S. *charge d'affaires* in Baghdad, who was filling in for the vacationing April Glaspie. For an hour Iraqi television cameras recorded the largely one-sided conversation, as Saddam attempted to justify the invasion and fulminated against the Kuwaiti royal family for its attempt to throttle Iraq's economy. But it was clear that Saddam's main purpose was to reassure the Americans that he would guarantee an uninterrupted supply of reasonably priced petroleum and would be pleased to assume responsibility for policing the Gulf. He insisted he was not contemplating any attack against the Saudis. "If you are really worried about Saudi Arabia, your worries are unfounded," the Iraqi dictator said. "But if you are showing that worry in order to worry Saudi Arabia, that is something else. . . . You can offer that assurance to the Saudis and to the world. We will not attack those who do not attack us."[36]

Saddam scoffed that the U.S. did not have the tenacity and will that it would take to drive Iraq from Kuwait—"spilling the blood of ten thousands of [American] soldiers in the Arabian desert." But it was clear to Joseph Wilson that, behind all the bluster, the Iraqi dictator was still attempting to feel out the Americans—still "fishing for clues," as the American diplomat put it, trying to understand what Bush's response would be. Or, as Saddam had asked him, "Do you know something that I don't know about a potential American response?"

Saddam may have still felt, Wilson later wrote, "that the confusing statements coming from different parts of the U.S. government meant there would be no consensus to respond militarily to his invasion of Kuwait."[37]

The White House never responded to Saddam's proposals. Instead, they leaked the confidential message to the U.S. president to the *New York Times*, while Bush claimed he had never received any offer. Saddam only fully comprehended Bush's decision to react militarily when he saw U.S. C-5A military transports bound for Saudi Arabia on CNN.[38]

Meanwhile, on August 6 in New York, the United Nations Security Council voted to impose trade sanctions on Iraq, to be lifted only when Saddam pulled out of Kuwait.

On August 9, 1990, Defense Department spokesman Pete Williams admitted that the Iraqi forces in Kuwait "seem to be in a defensive posture." Indeed, at the end of the first week after the invasion, U.S. military analysts were surprised to see that Saddam Hussein had already begun moving his elite Republican Guard units north, back to Iraq. "They were headed out of Kuwait," one American expert said.[39]

Over the following weeks, a number of news organizations in the U.S. and other countries obtained commercial satellite photographs of the Gulf region from the Soviets and had them examined by skilled photo analysts, veterans of the U.S. intelligence community. They found no sign of the supposed massive Iraqi troop build up anywhere near the Saudi border, nor for that matter anywhere in Kuwait. As one of the analysts, Pete Zimmerman, told Jean Heller of the *St. Petersburg Times*, "The Pentagon kept saying the bad guys were there, but we don't see anything to indicate an Iraqi force in Kuwait of even twenty percent the size the administration claimed."[40] As the story began to gain momentum, the Pentagon denied that estimates of Iraqi troops were inflated; at the same time it discouraged other major American media from investigating further.[41]

After the Gulf War, two expert military authors concluded that apart from the case of one defector who claimed to have a sketch of a battle plan, "there is no other evidence that Baghdad ever intended to do anything more than hold what it had already captured."[42] Also, after the fact, some administration officials admitted that neither the CIA nor the Defense Intelligence Agency thought it probable that Iraq would actually invade Saudi Arabia. One top American commander admitted to *Newsday* that the Pentagon had seriously exaggerated the numbers of Iraqi troops: "There was a great disinformation campaign surrounding this war," he admitted.[43] As Colin Powell himself later conceded, if Iraq had wanted to invade Saudi Arabia, it had a long border with that country; there was no need to go through Kuwait. Finally, if Saddam really had wanted to take Saudi Arabia, he could have done it immediately after he took over Kuwait. The small Saudi forces could never have stopped the Iraqis. Indeed, the greatest fear of American commanders at the beginning of the U.S. buildup in the Gulf was that Saddam Hussein would invade and decimate the small American advanced force.

Whether or not Saddam really coveted Saudi Arabia, nothing would stop the huge deployment of U.S. troops to the Gulf. On August 7, President Bush went on television to address America. "There comes a time in the life of a nation where we are called to find out who we are and what we believe in," he declared. The American troop movements were purely defensive, he said. There were four objectives: Iraq's immediate and unconditional withdrawal from Kuwait; the restoration of the legitimate government of the Emirate; the security of the Gulf region, especially its oil reserves; and the protection of American lives.[44] Immediately after Bush's announcement that troops were being dispatched to the Gulf, Baghdad declared that Iraq had annexed Kuwait to form a new "permanent union."

President Bush also referred to the embargo being imposed on Iraq. But what he did not explain was the role of U.S. troops if the embargo did not convince Saddam to withdraw from Kuwait. His declaration that the deployment in the Gulf would be purely defensive was misleading. From the start, Bush had little faith in the embargo and was determined to go to war once he had enough troops in the region. That, in fact, is what he told French Minister of Defense Jean Pierre Chevenement on August 7, 1990.[45]

According to a later investigation by the U.S. Congress, however, a diplomatic solution satisfactory to the interests of the United States may well have been possible in the period following the invasion, had the White House been interested in diplomacy. For instance, on August 7 Saddam sent a proposal to George Bush via an intermediary, who delivered it to White House Chief of Staff John Sununu. Saddam confirmed that he would withdraw once he had settled his financial dispute with Kuwait's rulers. The Bush White House never replied to the proposal. They were uninterested in any negotiations that would appear to reward the invasion.[46]

President Bush instead ratcheted up the tension. Appeasement doesn't work, he declared, drawing on World War II analogies.[47] It wasn't a tawdry question of oil but of principle: U.N. resolutions had to be scrupulously respected. Aggression would not be tolerated or rewarded. This rhetoric was deployed at a time when U.S. ally Israel had regularly been defying U.N. resolutions by continuing to occupy the West Bank and Golan Heights; Arab leaders were quick to point out what they labeled as hypocrisy.[48]

What drove Bush's refusal to negotiate was not vague principles of international conduct, but the determination to use the invasion of Kuwait as an excuse to destroy Saddam Hussein. As the White House now saw it, the attempt to domesticate Saddam by offering trade and credits had been a disaster. He had played the U.S. for a fool. Worse, he had lied when he assured President Mubarak he had no intentions to invade Kuwait. In fact, it is doubtful that Saddam ever made such a flat-out promise, but Bush believed that he did—and seemed to regard that action almost as a personal slap in the face.[49] Saddam was obviously untrustworthy; for the sake of stability in the Gulf and the security of Israel, he and his military forces had to be destroyed.

It was important to the U.S. and the Saudis—still wary of Saddam's intentions toward their own country—that the force being deployed in the Gulf not appear to be overwhelmingly American. To that end, President Bush and Secretary of State Baker worked day and night, cajoling, arm-twisting, and threatening in order to assemble a broad coalition including other Arab countries. They also needed tough resolutions from the U.N. and the Arab League condemning Saddam. In many cases, their success was due to tens of billions of dollars doled out in aid, loans, and assorted other favors that had nothing to do with idealistic values and everything to do with narrowly focused national self-interest.

Egypt's President Mubarak was the first Arab leader to publicly criticize Saddam Hussein, after receiving a blunt American threat that the annual $2 billion in U.S. aid would terminate if Egypt didn't condemn the Iraqi dictator. Mubarak also agreed to push for tough measures against Saddam at a new Arab summit scheduled for August 10 and to dispatch Egyptian troops to Saudi Arabia as part of a parallel all-Arab force. In return, a grateful U.S. wrote off Egypt's military debts to the tune of $6.75 billion.[50] Another $7 billion of Egyptian debts were forgiven by the Gulf States.[51] The Egyptians also demanded—and received—$200,000 for each military transport ship that passed through the Suez Canal, a sum well above the average fee.[52]

The U.S. was particularly eager to enlist Syria's support—though that country had recently been condemned by the U.S. as a terrorist state. In exchange, the Americans and their allies, intent on rolling back Saddam's occupation of Kuwait, gave Syria a free hand to take control of most of Lebanon.[53] The Syrians also received pledges totaling $5 billion, mainly from other Arab states but including $200 million from the European Community and a loan from Japan of $500 million. The European Community lifted economic sanctions it had imposed against Syria, while Great Britain restored diplomatic relations. In the end it was all symbolic: none of the 18,000 Syrian troops who joined the coalition forces in Saudi Arabia ever fought.[54]

Meanwhile, the United States was also putting together a huge war chest to help pay the costs of the massive military buildup in the Gulf. From one point of view, the nations providing troops in the name of great abiding principles and global security were in effect mercenaries, their services purchased by the fabulously wealthy states of the Gulf, deeply concerned about their own security. The sum collected over the following months came to more than $25 billion. One of the principal donors, Saudi Arabia, paid $4 billion down and another $500 million a month to cover the transportation costs and expenses for the thousands of foreign troops encamped on its soil. The ruling family of Kuwait came up with $5 billion. Japan and West Germany—both heavily dependent on oil from the Gulf—each offered $1.3 billion. Those sums were easily obtained from the oil-producing states. Because of the crisis, the price of petroleum had doubled and OPEC decided to free its members from production quotas.[55]

A more astute leader than Saddam Hussein might have thwarted George Bush's attempts to build and maintain a coalition of such disparate nations. But by his willful arrogance and folly, Saddam played into U.S. hands. On August 9, Iraq announced it was closing its borders and would hold all foreigners in its territory "for security reasons." Saddam had decided to use the eight thousand Western and Japanese nationals who were stuck in Kuwait after the invasion, plus 3,400 more in Iraq, as human shields against the possibility of American air or rocket attacks. To Saddam, an isolated tyrant, surrounded by sycophants, his decision "to play host to the citizens of these aggressive nations" seemed a reasonable move—to ensure peace, as he put it. He was surprised by the wave of international outrage that followed. British Foreign Secretary Douglas Hurd branded the move an example of "the tactics of the outlaw down the ages."[56]

On August 10, at the Arab League meeting in Cairo, Egypt's President Mubarak, predictably, turned down Saddam's appeal for an Arab solution. In reaction, Saddam accused Mubarak of taking orders from foreigners. He had a point: the resolution that approved deploying foreign troops in Arab territories had originally been drafted in English.[57]

Meanwhile the Bush administration continued to reject all Saddam's attempts to negotiate a face-saving withdrawal.[58] Instead, in a speech at the Pentagon on August 15, the president cranked up the rhetoric. Although Bush had vigorously shielded Saddam from sanctions for having used chemical weapons against the Kurds prior to the invasion, he now denounced him as a mass murderer "who has used poison gas against the men, women and children of his own country." The world had long ago learned the dangers of appeasing such tyrants, said Bush.

The president's inflammatory rhetoric alarmed many in the White House. Dick Cheney was concerned that by so viciously attacking Saddam, Bush might actually provoke an Iraqi attack. Colin Powell, on the other hand, was concerned about sending tens of thousands of American troops to Saudi Arabia without any idea of where the situation was heading. He described it as rolling down a highway without knowing which off-ramp to take.[59]

Politically, the crisis could not have come at a better time for Bush. Faced with a mounting budget deficit, the president had been obliged to break his "no new taxes" election vow. Democrats were also having a field day with the spreading savings and loan scandals, which involved the president's son Neil. Bush's poll ratings had been dropping; he was viewed increasingly as somewhat lily-livered, even effete. Here was an opportunity to play macho leader of the world.[60]

President Bush's problem now was to convince Americans that the same Iraqi tyrant whom he had been so assiduously courting for trade and investment until just a couple of weeks earlier had suddenly been transformed into a diabolical enemy worth sending hundreds of thousands Americans halfway around the world to do battle with. The president had to portray the conflict as struggle between absolute good and evil incarnate. American lives and funds were not going to be sacrificed for distant oil fields or to return a corrupt, immensely rich, and autocratic family to its throne.[61]

It boiled down to a major P.R problem. To handle it, the Kuwaiti ruling family financed a mammoth campaign to shape American opinion and get a skeptical U.S. Congress on board. Directing the effort was the world's largest P.R. organization, Hill and Knolton, which was also the most politically wired firm in Washington, DC.[62] Out of nowhere appeared a vocal, well-financed lobbying organization, Citizens for a Free Kuwait. Supposedly independent, it was almost totally backed by Kuwaiti government money. The ensuing propaganda blitz covered universities, churches, and public spaces across the country—everything from bumper stickers, T-shirts, and free clips for the evening news, to the nationwide celebration of Free Kuwait Day. Overnight the American media was awash with lurid tales of Saddam's atrocities, the same tales that the Bush and Reagan administrations had studiously ignored over the past eight years.[63]

Also pushing for decisive military action behind the scenes was the powerful pro-Israel lobby. Reflecting the views of the Israeli government, the lobby advocated immediate, massive American air strikes against Iraqi targets. Right-wing columnist Patrick Buchanan wrote, "There are only two groups that are beating the drums of war in the Middle East: the Israeli defense ministry and its amen corner in the U.S."[64]

The Israelis feared that the fragile alliance being formed against Saddam might fall apart. Indeed, in an attempt to undermine the coalition, Saddam continued to present various proposals for negotiation, but the U.S still demanded a complete and unconditional withdrawal, shutting down the possibility of a face-saving way out.[65]

On the other hand, the thuggish Iraqi dictator continued playing into Bush's hands on the P.R. front. On August 23, 1990, Saddam visited a group of fifteen British hostage families with a television team in tow and amiably explained to the terrified people that their presence was necessary to protect Iraq against military strikes by the United States. As if he were a caring father, Saddam ran his fingers through the hair of one young blond boy. He wanted to make sure, he said, that they were getting enough milk and playing soccer with the Iraqis. Saddam called them "heroes of peace" because they were preventing war. Predictably, the Western world was repelled by the scene.[66]

On August 25, the U.S. obtained Soviet support for a Security Council resolution authorizing the use of force if necessary to implement the previously declared embargo. With the Cold War now over, Saddam Hussein could no longer count on the support of his onetime Soviet allies. The once mighty USSR, in fact, would receive a billion dollars from the Saudis in return for joining the coalition. Saddam Hussein was virtually alone. The U.N. embargo was already throttling

Iraq's economy. Inflation was rising; bread, sugar, tea, and cooking oil were rationed. The country's oil wells were producing at only 20 percent of capacity.[67] Margaret Thatcher announced that the dictator would be charged with crimes against humanity.[68] Saddam, however, continued to hope that the international coalition would unravel in the face of mounting pressure from the Arab street. He was attempting to portray himself as the new Nasser, the new champion of the Arab people against the West and Israel.[69]

Indeed, the coalition's commitment to war was still in question—as was America's. Many key congressmen were not at all convinced that evicting Saddam from Kuwait was worth going to war, and President Bush had already been forced to admit that Saudi Arabia was not imminently threatened. When a group of American senators arrived in Saudi Arabia to talk with regional leaders, the Emir of Kuwait declined to see them. Later, when the autocratic ruler of the United Arab Emirates launched into an endless discourse about the courage of the Kuwaitis, Senator Daniel Patrick Moynihan of New York interrupted, "Your Grace, the Kuwaitis left their wives. They left their servants. They took their money and stuffed it in Swiss bank accounts. That is not my definition of courage."[70] Back in Washington, Senator William Cohen of Maine urged President Bush against sending young Americans to die for the Kuwaitis. "We visited the Kuwaitis," he said, "and we realized that Kuwaitis are willing to fight—until every U.S. soldier has dropped."[71]

On September 17, Iraq came up with another offer to negotiate. Saddam's first deputy prime minister said that Iraq would withdraw from Kuwait if this led to an international conference to solve the Palestinian problem. At the same time, Saddam told another Arab diplomat that he would consider pulling out if he could show some tangible gain for Arabs, such as American endorsement of an international peace conference on the Israel-Palestinian issue.[72] On September 21, after another peace proposal was rejected by the U.S., Saddam Hussein declared, "There is not a single chance for any retreat. Let everybody understand that this battle is going to become the mother of all battles."[73]

The administration's firm line was bolstered on October 1 when Amnesty International issued a shocking report on conditions in Kuwait, based on interviews with scores of people who had recently fled the country. "Their testimony builds up a horrifying picture of widespread arrests, torture under interrogation, summary executions, and mass extra judicial killings," the report concluded. President Bush later said he had read and reread the report, appalled by its revelations. "This is Hitler revisited," said the President.[74] Saddam's atrocities became regular fare in Bush's speeches.

What was happening, as Colin Powell saw it, was that the president—and thus the U.S.—was being painted into a corner by the president's increasingly vituperative portrayal of Saddam Hussein. After one such attack on Saddam, in which the president compared Saddam's taking of hostages to the Holocaust, one of Bush's aides commented, "Got to get his rhetoric under control."[75] The president now wanted the liberation of Kuwait and the destruction of Saddam at almost any cost.[76] It was *mano a mano*, a personal battle between George H. W. Bush and the Iraqi tyrant.

The push for war continued on all fronts. A special hearing was called by the Congressional Human Rights caucus to listen to testimony about Saddam's barbaric nature. The star of the show was a fifteen-year-old Kuwaiti girl, introduced by only her first name, Nayirah, in order, the audience was told, to protect the safety of her family. The young girl recounted how Iraqi soldiers had stormed into the al-Addam hospital in Kuwait City where, she said, she had been working as a volunteer. Tearfully, she described how rampaging soldiers with guns had gone "into rooms where fifteen babies were in incubators. They tore the babies out of the incubators, took the incubators, and left the babies on the floor to die."[77]

That story, which was picked up immediately by the media worldwide, had tremendous impact, not least on wavering members of the U.S. Congress. President Bush was to repeat the horrifying tale at least five times. "I don't believe that Adolf Hitler ever participated in anything of that nature," said Bush. If anything could justify going to war against Saddam, this was it.

The problem was that the story was not true. Kuwaiti medical authorities denied that the incubator incident had ever occurred. It was only after the end of the Gulf War, however, that the deception was finally revealed. It was a total fabrication, right out of the fertile, high-priced imagination of Hill and Knolton, the Kuwaiti ruling family's Washington P.R. firm. Nayirah, the tearful fifteen-year-old girl who had so convincingly recounted the atrocity, turned out to be the daughter of the Kuwaiti ambassador to the United States; she had never been in Kuwait after the invasion. By the time that was discovered, however, the Kuwaiti royal family was securely back on the throne and the folks at Hill and Knolton had earned their pay.

President Bush, meanwhile, continued the media offensive. On October 11, 1990, he made the first of several fateful calls for a popular revolt in Iraq. "We all want Saddam out," he said. "I hope the people of Iraq do something about that."[78] Saddam, however, was continuing to soften his position. He was releasing some of the hostages and no longer defending the takeover of Kuwait. But he still needed a face-saving concession in return for total withdrawal, some kind of agreement, he suggested, for a conference to discuss the Israel-Palestinian problem. He was concerned about a coup or assassination attempt if he pulled out of Kuwait with nothing to show for all the hardships his people had endured because of the embargo. In any case, he told Soviet official Yevgeny Primakov, he worried that certain Western powers were out to destroy him no matter what he did in Kuwait.[79]

The Soviets were only one of several governments around the world still attempting to negotiate some kind of settlement—much to the dismay of the U.S. On October 21, for instance, the defense minister of Saudi Arabia, Prince Sultan bin Abdul Aziz, suggested that it would be a brotherly act for Kuwait to cede or lease the tiny, unpopulated islands of Warba and Bubiyan to the Iraqis, because it would give them a secure outlet to the Gulf. At the time, James Aikens was U.S. ambassador to Saudi Arabia. "I thought it was a brilliant suggestion," he later said.

> The islands themselves were totally worthless and it would give Saddam a face-saving way out. If the U.S. would accept the deal, the crisis would be over. But it didn't work out that way. The U.S. government panicked. Cheney was sent out to rectify the situation. He talked with King Fahd and said 'we have to go for war with Iraq.' So

Prince Sultan was told to shut up. The Saudis disassociated themselves from the proposal. It was taken off the table. Obviously, we
were preparing for the war and any solution would deprive us of a
glorious victory to push Saddam out and punish Saddam. The war
could have been avoided. This would get Saddam off the hook. But
people had decided by then that Saddam must go.[80]

Once again, the decisions were being made by President Bush
and just a few trusted advisors. Even Colin Powell was taken aback
on October 25 when, on a short trip overseas, he heard Secretary of
Defense Cheney declare on television that it might indeed be necessary to dispatch a hundred thousand more American troops to the
Gulf. Powell was shocked. "What is going on?" he asked an aide.
"Goddammit, I'll never travel again. I haven't seen the president on
this." General Schwarzkopf was also surprised. In a recent interview
in Saudi Arabia, he had declared that the sanctions were working, that
they should be given a chance. "Now we're starting to see evidence
that the sanctions are pinching," Schwarzkopf said to a newspaper
reporter. "So why should we say, 'Okay, gave 'em two months, didn't
work. Let's get on with it and kill a whole bunch of people'? That's
crazy. That's crazy. . . . War is a profanity because, let's face it, you've
got two opposing sides trying to settle their differences by killing as
many of each other as they can." On the other hand, Schwarzkopf
had privately said that a prolonged stalemate would be a victory for
Saddam.[81]

On October 31, President Bush would give the go-ahead for the
huge increase in U.S. troops in the Gulf Cheney had predicted. Ultimately, the force would be far greater than the troops the allies assembled for D-Day. But opinion polls showed that Americans were
concerned about the president's handling of the Gulf crisis. The White
House decided to ratchet up the rhetoric again in response. On October 23, Bush declared, "We are dealing with Hitler revisited, a totali-
tarianism and brutality that is naked and unprecedented in modern
times. And it must not stand."[82] Critics immediately asked why, if
Saddam was that despicable, had the Reagan and Bush administrations
backed him for so long?

As late as August 1, 1990, the Bush White House had defended Saddam as "a moderate" and "a pillar of stability" in the Gulf. Now, just three months later, trying to drum up support to destroy the Iraqi dictator, presidential speechwriters cast about for an argument that would hit home: Saddam had to be defeated to defend American jobs, to safeguard global oil supplies, to uphold international law, to defeat aggression. Critics persisted, however, asking why American lives should be sacrificed to safeguard the oil supplies of Germany and Japan, who were providing money to the coalition forces but refusing to send their own troops.[83]

President Bush cited the threat of Saddam's biological and chemical weapons and possible nuclear arms. Yet most experts—and certainly the ones Bush had heeded before the invasion of Kuwait—thought the Iraqi dictator was still many years away from having nuclear weapons.[84] Others, like political analyst Theodore Draper, charged that President Bush's outrage about Saddam's takeover of Kuwait was pure hypocrisy. Wrote Draper, "As to Iraq's naked aggression—a remark requiring selective-memory skills of a high order coming from a government that held all modern records for international aggression, naked or otherwise, and from a man who, less than a year before, had nakedly invaded Panama—both Syria and Israel had invaded Lebanon and still occupied large portions of that country, Israel bombarding Beirut mercilessly in the process, without a threat of war emanating from Washington."[85]

But in a reverse of what would happen in 2003, the White House was having better luck lining up U.N. support for a military attack against Saddam than it was in convincing the public. On November 29, 1990, the U.N. Security Council passed U.N. Resolution 278 authorizing the coalition to drive out Iraqi troops "by all necessary means." The deadline for Saddam to clear out of Kuwait was January 15, 1991, a date chosen to give the coalition forces time to do the job before the Islamic holiday of Ramadan.[86]

The resolution was not passed by the force of Bush's arguments to Security Council members, but by further bribes and arm twisting. Colombia's vote, for instance, was obtained by Washington's promise to end U.S. import restrictions on imported cut flowers.

Chinese support came in exchange for America's taking the heat off Beijing for its atrocious human rights record. As for the Soviets, the U.S. agreed to aid Moscow by helping to prevent the fractious Baltic states from attending a future international conference; the Saudis also came through with a $4 billion loan for the Soviets. The Yemeni delegate was applauded by other Third World nations for voting against the resolution, but a grim-faced James Baker, who had earlier threatened to cancel $70 million in aid to Yemen, declared, "I hope he enjoyed that applause, because this will turn out to be the most expensive vote he ever cast." Within days, the tiny Middle East nation suffered a sharp reduction in U.S. aid.[87] James Baker even conducted talks with the Cuban foreign minister, the first such contact in thirty years. Baker reportedly offered to remove Cuba from the list of terrorist states, which would make the Communist country eligible for U.S. humanitarian aid; the Cubans turned him down.[88]

To mollify those who charged he was hell-bent on war, President Bush suggested a meeting between Secretary of State Baker and Tariq Aziz. But, as if to ensure that his offer was not accepted by the Iraqi dictator, Bush made it clear that any such meeting "would not be sessions to find common ground, to let Saddam save face. He doesn't deserve it." The president said he hoped Saddam got the message that the purpose was not to find a compromise. A compromise would sink the coalition.[89] Over the following weeks, the two sides were never able to find suitable dates. Continued attempts of others to mediate were also coolly received by Washington. Indeed, *Fortune* magazine praised the administration's inflexible strategy: "The President and his men worked overtime to quash freelance peacemakers in the Arab world, France, and the Soviet Union, who threatened to give Saddam a face-saving way out of the box Bush was building."[90]

In the first week in December 1990, in another gesture of compromise, Saddam agreed to release the rest of the hostages. They would be home by Christmas. The only difference that made to Bush was that U.S. military planners no longer had to be concerned about the possibility of killing Americans or other Westerners in their planned raids on Iraq. Saddam was only slowly beginning to understand that his hopes of fracturing the U.S.-led coalition were in vain. When a visiting PLO official showed the Iraqi dictator cover stories in both *Time* and *Newsweek* vividly describing the upcoming battles, Saddam asked his aides why no one had ever shown those stories to him.[91] A devastating attack was really in the offing.

On January 2, 1991, Saddam Hussein modified his negotiating position even further. All he asked now in return for withdrawing from Kuwait was a guarantee that his troops would not be fired on as they retreated. As for the Palestinian question, he simply asked for agreement that the issue would be dealt with in the not-too-distant future. That request was also rejected by the U.S.[92] The president and his military advisers had already chosen the precise time that the air war would be launched against Iraq—January 17, 1991, at 3 in the morning.[93]

By mid-January, as the U.N. deadline loomed, the U.S. had about 100,000 more troops in the Gulf than it had in Europe at any time during the Cold War. The various branches of the military, eager to justify their budgets in the face of cutbacks, all wanted a piece of the coming Gulf action.[94]

As a final gesture to peace, George Bush agreed to send James Baker to meet with Tariq Aziz in Geneva on January 9. Though the meeting lasted several hours, it was a total failure. Baker continued to demand an unconditional withdrawal, a proposal he knew Aziz could never agree to. After glancing at the harshly worded letter from President Bush to Saddam that Baker handed him, Tariq Aziz declared it was so insulting to his president that he would not even accept it.[95] A visit by U.N. Secretary General Javier Perez de Cuellar on January 11 would also prove totally futile.

On January 10, Saddam Hussein heard that the U.S. Congress had voted to give war powers to the president. Why didn't Saddam pull out and save his forces to fight another day? As Saddam told a senior Algerian official, "I have two options: to be killed by U.S. bombs or by Iraqi officers. In the first case I shall be a martyr, in the second a traitor. If I withdraw unconditionally from Kuwait, I shall certainly have to face the second scenario." He had also come to believe that no matter what he did, the Americans—and, as he saw it, the Israelis—were determined to destroy him.[96]

The Storm Breaks

Finally, at almost 3 A.M. Baghdad time on January 17, 1991, just as planned months earlier, Operation Desert Storm was launched. Ironically, the American-led coalition was taking on an enemy force that its own policies, intelligence agencies, arms merchants, and military establishment had done much to create. For instance, some of Saddam's elite forces had been brought to the U.S. in the 1980s for specialized training by the vaunted Green Berets.[97] The Iraqi pilots the coalition faced had been trained in the Soviet Union, Britain, the U.S., and France. Indeed, red-faced French officials later reported that, even after the war began, there were still Iraqi pilots studying in France. Even more embarrassing for the French, their crack French fighter pilots were unable to show off their sophisticated Mirages in the fight against Saddam—because they were almost exactly the same planes they had sold to the Iraqis, and the U.S.-led coalition was concerned that its pilots would be unable to distinguish a French-operated Mirage from an Iraqi one.[98]

An even bigger quandary for the U.S. and its allies was the extremely effective defense radar system that the French firm, Thompson, had sold to Saddam for hundreds of millions of dollars. It incorporated the newest technologies, was linked by buried optical cables, and was extremely resistant to attack. Many of its operators had also been trained by the French. However, since the French were part of the coalition, they provided the military planners with critical information to destroy the radar shield they had built. In the end, they took down their own system. That also crippled the effectiveness of the Roland antiaircraft missiles that the French had sold to Saddam.[99]

Of course, the chemical and biological weapons that the coalition was so concerned about had also been furnished to the Iraqi dictator mainly by European companies and engineers, while the nuclear potential that so worried George Bush was also a product of Western and Eastern aid.

The sustained air attack that opened Operation Desert Storm was the most devastating in history. U.S. military planners originally thought it would achieve its goals in only a few days; instead, the bombardment continued for six horrific weeks. Iraq and its troops in Kuwait were hit with just about every aerial weapon in the Western arsenal—from Vietnam vintage B-52 bombers flying all the way from the United States to the latest Stealth bombers, undetectable by enemy radar and equipped with night-bombing systems. There were RAF Tornadoes carrying cluster bombs to destroy Iraqi runways and Tomahawk sea-launched cruise missiles targeting Iraqi missile sites, communication hubs, command posts, airports, and oil refineries. The coalition would also use cluster bombs, napalm, and fuel air explosives in increasingly lethal raids against Iraqi troops in Kuwait.

U.S. officials claimed that the air war was directed "solely at Iraq's armed force and their lines of supply and command." In fact, the devastation was much more widespread. The goal declared by General Schwarzkopf was not just to drive Saddam from Kuwait but—more important—to annihilate his war-making potential, particularly his elite Republican Guard.[100] The U.S. also aimed to depose Saddam Hussein by provoking a military coup. Many of the bombing targets were specifically selected to inflict maximum damage on Iraq's economy and infrastructure. Iraq's electrical grid was destroyed, which in turn knocked out the country's water purification and irrigation systems. Bridges and industrial plants were demolished.

Antiwar protesters, who had taken to the streets through much of the West, charged that these attacks had nothing to do with military targets and everything to do with destroying Iraq. Iran, with whom Saddam had made peace to protect his flank, protested to the U.N., claiming that the coalition attacks went far beyond the U.N. mandate. "Under no conditions can operations for the liberation of Kuwait justify killing innocent people and destroying economic resources," declared Iran's foreign minister. "Iraq is being savagely attacked."[101] Saddam's air force was no match for the coalition onslaught. Indeed, he soon dispatched most of his surviving fighter planes to Iran, where they remained for the duration of the war.

On January 17, Saddam carried out an earlier threat to hit Israel with his long-range modified scud missiles if he was attacked. His strategy was to provoke the Zionist state into joining the U.S.-led assault. If that happened, he calculated, the Arab members of the coalition would cease their support for the war; the alliance would disintegrate.

The U.S., however, convinced the Israelis to stay out of the conflict, even though the Patriot missiles they supplied to defend the Israelis against Iraqi scuds proved of little worth. Saddam lost his gamble.

The Pentagon was determined to keep tight control of the media. Reporters were restricted to official pools. Military escorts had to be present at all interviews, frequently interrupting when they objected to what was being said. Some reporters had their access to troops cut off after they quoted comments critical of President Bush and the war effort. Most of the media succumbed to the new regulations with remarkably little protest.[102]

The Soviets and a few others continued attempts at mediation, but both Saddam and the U.S. held firm. Despite the punishment his country—one nation against twenty-eight—was taking, the Iraqi dictator clung to the hope that the coalition would ultimately disintegrate. Meanwhile, the massive air raids continued. Over five weeks, coalition planes, primarily American and British, flew a staggering 86,000 sorties against Iraqi targets. Reporters were told by U.S. and British pilots that they were literally running out of important targets. Neither side released casualty figures, but, at the end of the bombing campaign, it was estimated that 29,000 Iraqi civilians and military personnel had been killed, with another 88,000 injured. The Iraqis later claimed that about 13,000 civilians died in the bombings; the U.S. estimated about 9,000.[103] The U.S. didn't dwell on these figures: "That's not really a number I'm terribly interested in," said Colin Powell when asked for a total, in April 1991.

After January 25 Saddam Hussein let in the Western media. His officials gave the reporters tours of the bombed-out areas. The result was a flood of articles graphically describing the damage to military and civilian targets. Though U.S. military briefers had awed the media with videos of "smart" bombs and missiles flying through windows or whizzing down chimneys to hit their target with incredible precision, it turned out that the great majority of bombs and missiles were not so smart at all. Reporters found a tremendous number of destroyed homes, hospitals, and mosques far from any military targets.

Though they were not supposed to be attempting to assassinate Saddam Hussein—to target the Iraqi leader was theoretically in violation of the Geneva Conventions of 1977—the U.S. Air Force made several attempts to hit shelters where he was thought to be with deep penetration bombs. One such attack destroyed an underground bunker; 314 people are believed to have died, 130 of them children. Allied forces were unaware that hundreds of women and children had been routinely using the shelter since the start of Desert Storm.[104]

On February 18, Soviet leader Mikhail Gorbachev, after consulting with the Iraqis, forwarded a peace proposal to President Bush, saying, "It is important to avoid the tragedy of destroying Iraq as a state, of dismembering its territory, to say nothing of human deaths." Saddam Hussein would now agree to withdraw from Kuwait with no preconditions at all. He was, in fact, accepting the original U.N. resolution. But the proposal was immediately rejected by President Bush, who now imposed a new set of Draconian conditions. The Iraqi forces, he stated, would have to pull out of Kuwait *before* a cease-fire was called, and they would have to withdraw completely within four days—which meant they would have to abandon all their tanks and heavy military equipment. They would also have to pay reparations to Kuwait, and the U.N. embargo would still continue, supposedly until all Saddam's WMD were destroyed.[105]

A series of frantic Soviet negotiations with Tariq Aziz narrowed the gap between the new American demands and the Iraqi position. It came down to a few issues that could have been easily resolved through negotiations with a bit more time.[106] But the last thing President Bush and his aides wanted at that moment was a cease-fire and an Iraqi withdrawal. It would leave Saddam Hussein and his military machine battered but unbowed. The Iraqi leader, who had stood up to the might of the Western world, would emerge as triumphant hero of the Arab street.

Refusing the cease-fire left the coalition on the threshold of a great victory. Intelligence reports showed that the Iraqi armed forces had been badly bloodied and were in total disarray. Saddam had set fire to the Kuwaiti oil fields. The U.S.-led coalition had already deployed troops into Kuwait to prepare the ground offensive. This was no time to stop. The goal still had to be the destruction of Saddam and his warmaking ability.

The ground offensive led by the United States was called Operation Desert Sabre. It began on February 24 and was an awesome demonstration of Western military might, meticulously planned for months. The object was to destroy the Iraqi army. Hit from the south and driven out of Kuwait City, Saddam's forces would be obliged to retreat north toward Iraq. At that point, a coalition force storming in from the west would cut off the roads along the Tigris and Euphrates and pulverize Saddam's military machine.

The plan failed. Saddam had already ordered his best units out of Iraq. The remaining forces turned out to be far fewer than the U.S. had originally estimated. Already reeling from the relentless air attack, the army was disintegrating: huge numbers of soldiers had already deserted; tens of thousands more became willing prisoners of the coalition. The Iraqi forces were pushed out of Kuwait City and sent scurrying back to Iraq much more quickly than planned.

Large numbers of fleeing soldiers, driving any conveyance they could get their hands on, from stolen cars to pickup trucks and buses, fled up the main road back to Basra and Iraq. As they neared the Mitla ridge, the head and tail of the column were hit by U.S. ground attack fighters. They were trapped. Though General Schwarzkopf had earlier declared that he would not attack a retreating army, what followed was a bloody slaughter.[107] Scores of U.S. and British planes swooped in to bomb and strafe the blocked vehicles, imprisoned bumper to bumper for more than two miles. They were hit with fuel air explosives and napalm and cluster bombs that could shred anything in the area of a football field. Some terrified Iraqi soldiers managed to scramble away into the desert. Thousands more were killed in their vehicles, many burned to cinders.

The slaughter continued for forty hours. It was, in the words of Colin Smith of *The Observer*, "one of the most terrible harassments of a retreating army from the air in the history of warfare." Tony Clifton of *Newsweek* wrote,

> The group of vehicles we hit included petrol tankers and tanks, so the tanks exploded in these great foundations of white flame from the ammunition. . . . You could see the little figures of soldiers coming out with their hands up. It really looked like a medieval hell—the hell

you see in Bosch, because of the great red flames, and then these weird little contorted figures. . . . Next morning we went up to see what we'd done. There were bodies all over the place. And I remember at one point looking down at the car track and I was up to my ankles in blood. The tracks had filled with blood, and there were very white-faced men going round saying, 'Jesus. Did we really do this?'[108]

There were other similar slaughters as well, but it was Mitla Ridge that received the attention. Viewing the first awesome television images of the carnage, Bush and his advisors, always leery of shifting public opinion, began to push for an end to the hostilities. As the president put it, "We need to have an end. People want that. They are going to want to know we won and the kids can come home. We do not want to screw this up with a sloppy, muddled ending."[109]

In any case, the latest word from General Schwarzkopf was that the great bulk of Saddam's troops had been destroyed. Members of the coalition had agreed to drive the Iraqis from Kuwait, not to carry the conflict to Iraq itself. The mission was accomplished. They agreed to end hostilities after one hundred hours of fighting.

It was a nice round number.

On March 3, 1991, in a tent at the Iraqi desert village of Safwan, General Schwarzkopf and Saudi General Khalid Bin Sultan accepted the surrender of the Iraqi forces from two Iraqi commanders. Saddam Hussein had not been obliged to attend.

In briefing American commanders the previous October, General Schwarzkopf had been explicit about their mission. Saddam's elite Republican Guard was not to be defeated or routed, they were to be destroyed. But despite a half year of planning and the enormous resources and manpower invested by the American-led coalition, they missed their goal. Surveillance photos showed that more than half the Republican Guards' forces, along with their tanks and armor, had slipped through the noose and escaped back to Iraq. And Saddam Hussein was still in power.

On March 1, before those intelligence reports had reached the White House, a reporter asked President Bush, "I'm struck by how somber you feel. And I was wondering, aren't these great days?"

"You know," the president replied, "to be very honest with you, I haven't yet felt this wonderfully euphoric feeling that many of the American people feel. And I'm beginning to. I feel much better about it today than I did yesterday. But I think it's that I want to see an end. You mentioned World War II—there was a definitive end to that conflict. And now we have Saddam Hussein still there—the man that wreaked this havoc upon his neighbors."[110]

And Saddam would still be there for twelve more years. Meanwhile, the groundwork was being laid for an even more bloody tragedy.

CHAPTER SEVEN

Betrayal: The Shiite and Kurd Uprisings February 1991–April 1991

There's another way for the bloodshed to stop, and that is for the Iraqi military and the Iraqi people to take matters into their own hands and to force Saddam Hussein to step aside.

—President George H. W. Bush, February 15, 1991

Do I think that the United States should bear guilt because of suggesting that the Iraqi people take matters into their own hands, with the implication being given by some that the United States would be there to support them militarily? That was not true. We never implied that.

—President George H. W. Bush, April 16, 1991[1]

The most horrendous crime attributed to Saddam is the slaughter of possibly hundreds of thousands of Iraqis—mainly Shiites, but also Kurds—who rose up in rebellion following Saddam's disastrous defeat in Kuwait in February 1991. For twelve years the account of the bloody repression that followed the uprising was veiled in fear. The families of those who had "disappeared" were too terrified to search for their relatives. Appeals to local authorities for information were brutally rebuffed. Those who had witnessed the killings were too frightened to talk. Human rights organizations were barred from Iraq.

It was only after the disintegration of Saddam's regime in April 2003 that the full horror was slowly unearthed. Throughout the country, Iraqis began to excavate the mass graves. Some were relatively small, containing the tattered remains of a few score bodies. Other sites were huge. One revealed the remnants of at least two thousand people. There were still vestiges of the cords that had bound their hands and the blindfolds that had covered their eyes.

The newly uncovered sites were soon thronged by Iraqis picking through the grisly rubble, looking for anything—a skull with a lock of hair, the decaying fragments of a billfold or shirt or shoe—anything that might explain the fate of a missing father or brother or son or daughter. Visiting American civilian and military officials stopped by to express their outrage. Here was graphic evidence of the Hitler-like brutality of Saddam Hussein. Who could doubt that the U.S.-led invasion of 2003 had been necessary?

Forensic experts for the special Iraqi tribunal meticulously examined the sites. Everyone supposed that the major charge to be brought against Saddam Hussein and his lieutenants would be perpetrating this appalling slaughter.

There was another component to the case, however, that the special Iraqi tribunal would never fully explore: how the U.S. government and its allies, by their actions and inaction, were complicit in these massacres. The question is fundamental not just for apportioning responsibility for the terrible aftermath of the uprising itself, but because repressing that uprising prevented the overthrow of Saddam Hussein and set the stage for the tragic present in Iraq. As it turns out, the U.S. not only incited and then abandoned the rebellion; it actually enabled the brutal repression.

The Explosion

The uprising was an explosion of Shiite fury pent up over decades of repressive Sunni rule. Shiites were disproportionately represented in the lower ranks of the army and suffered appalling losses in the war against Iran and the economic privations that followed. On the heels of that came Saddam's disastrous invasion of Kuwait, the U.N. embargo on all trade with Iraq, and then the devastating air raids of the American-led coalition, which destroyed Iraq's infrastructure and reduced the once thriving oil-rich country to Third-World status.

The uprising—or intifada, as it came to be called—began on February 27, 1991. It was sparked by demoralized, shell-shocked Iraqi soldiers fleeing Kuwait, the majority of them Shiites, furious at the suffering and sacrifices they had been forced to endure because of yet another foolhardy foreign adventure by Saddam Hussein. Many saw their plight as the newest sinister plot by Saddam to destroy the Shiites. The Iraqi dictator had already ordered his predominately Sunni Republican Guard out of Kuwait; now he was content to let the coalition forces annihilate the regular army. They had never been much more than cannon fodder.

As one Shiite officer later recalled, "We had to desert our tanks and vehicles to avoid aerial attacks. We walked a hundred kilometers toward the Iraqi territories, hungry, thirsty, and exhausted." The first town they reached inside Iraq was Zuhair. "In Zuhair we decided to put an end to Saddam and his regime. We shot at his posters. Hundreds of retreating soldiers came to the city and joined the revolt; by the afternoon, there were thousands of us."[2] Backed up by civilian mobs, they stormed the headquarters of the Baath party and the security services. Thus was launched the Shiite intifada—the uprising that Saddam Hussein had feared for so many years.[3]

By 5 A.M. on March 1, the intifada had spread to the sprawling southern city of Basra near the mouth of the Tigris and Euphrates. At the entrance to the city was a huge poster of Saddam gazing benignly over his people. Enraged, an Iraqi tank commander trained his gun turret on the Iraqi tyrant and pulverized the image, to the acclaim of the other retreating soldiers.[4] Then, again, supported by throngs of euphoric civilians, they rampaged through the city, attacking Baath Party offices and freeing hundreds of political prisoners from a secret underground complex. Some prisoners had been held in barbaric conditions for more than a decade. Baath party officials and security officers fled for their lives. Many never escaped the mob's fury; some were literally torn to bits.

Over the next few days the revolt spread through the Shiite heartland of southern Iraq. One after another, the holy cities of Najaf,

Karbala, and Kufa fell to the rebels. Some local army garrisons simply dissolved as officers and soldiers deserted to the rebels. One of the thousands of civilians who joined the intifada was Zainab al-Suwaij, the granddaughter of a venerated Shiite Ayatollah. She lived in Karbala, and had just completed high school, but in Saddam's Iraq, she later said, there was no hope for her or her friends. When the first rebels appeared in Karbala the beginning of April she dashed into the street to join them. The gunfire went on for less than an hour; most of the loyalist soldiers fled for their lives. "They were knocking on doors, asking people to give them civilian clothes, because they were afraid of being killed. Most of those who remained in the city were killed. The feeling of the people was just wonderful. There was a hope they would get rid of Saddam and it would be over and we would build a new Iraq."

Within a few hours they had taken the city, but they had no idea what to do next. "We were not organized, we didn't have any leadership," said Zainab. "We didn't have enough weapons or anything like that."[5]

But they also never thought they would be taking on Saddam Hussein and his massive apparatus of repression on their own. For several weeks they had heard the president of the United States calling on the people of Iraq to rise up. On February 15, 1991, in a speech at the Raytheon Missile Plant in Massachusetts, while the war was still going on, President Bush declared: "There's another way for the bloodshed to stop, and that is for the Iraqi military and the Iraqi people to take matters into their own hands and to force Saddam Hussein to step aside."[6]

The president's call to the Iraqi people was not a careless rhetorical flourish. The Bush White House had been hoping that the devastating aerial bombardment of Iraq's infrastructure and the U.N. embargo would finally provoke the country's military leaders to rid themselves of Saddam Hussein. To encourage the process, President Bush had also ordered the CIA to fund Iraqi opposition groups. Now, in a very calculated address, the president was calling on "the people of Iraq" themselves to revolt. Those additional words had been penciled into the speech before it was delivered.[7] To make doubly sure the message got through, the president repeated the same appeal later that day. It wasn't the first time President Bush had made such a call. On October 11, 1990, he had declared, "We all want Saddam removed. I hope the Iraqi people do something towards that."[8]

Over the following weeks, the president's February 15 speech was broadcast and rebroadcast across Iraq. It was delivered via the Voice of America, Radio Monte Carlo, the BBC, and two clandestine CIA-backed radio stations, the Voice of Free Iraq and Radio Free Iraq.[9] The CIA-backed stations continued broadcasting similar calls to arms until at least March 3, when the truce agreement was signed with Iraq. Another was printed on the backs of replicas of Iraqi twenty-five-dinar notes that were dropped by U.S. aircraft flying out of Turkey.[10]

On February 24, 1991, after the coalition ground offensive was launched, the Voice of Free Iraq, which now claimed—almost certainly falsely—to be broadcasting from Baghdad, intensified its calls for an uprising. It announced that Saddam Hussein had already smuggled his family and wealth out of Iraq and was now preparing to flee the country himself. It was time to act, the broadcast urgently declared: "Honorable sons of Iraq . . . Stage a revolution now before it's too late. . . . Hit the headquarters of the tyrant and save the homeland from destruction."[11]

Thus in the first few days of March 1991, President Bush's call to revolt continued to reverberate as the intifada spread across southern Iraq. Implicit in that call, the rebels believed, was a U.S. intention to aid a popular uprising. As a Shiite leader, Sayid Majid al-Khoie, said later, "The biggest reason for the intifada was that they [the rebels] thought that the Americans would support them. They knew that they couldn't beat Saddam on their own. They thought that they could get control of the cities and that the Americans would stop the army from intervening."[12]

Meanwhile, as the Shiite revolt spread through the south, the Kurds in northern Iraq also erupted. They had been preparing an uprising for several weeks, but their plans were overtaken by events. The revolt began March 5 in the Kurdish mountain town of Rania. Several young Kurds had returned home after deserting the retreating army in Kuwait.[13] When Iraqi police tried to arrest them, the local militia rose up. In a few hours they had control of the town. Also fired by Bush's call for an uprising, the Kurdish revolt spread rapidly to the provincial capital of Sulaimaniya.[14]

In Sulaimaniya the people broke into the dreaded stone citadel of the Central Security Headquarters. They were outraged by what they found in its dank underground warren of prison cells: "Dried blood, metal supports, meat hooks, piano wire, and other torture paraphernalia, and a special building where Kurdish girls were said to have been raped. Trapdoors led to underground cells where the prison's liberators found recently strangled naked women and children and barely conscious prisoners, some of whom had been detained for more than a decade."[15]

The Kurdish *pesh merga*, who had lost three thousand of their men fighting to take Sulaimaniya, reacted by killing at least four hundred government loyalists sheltering in the fortress. According to one account, "Those who had survived the fighting were tried and executed on the spot by the people using iron saws and knives even as they screamed and sobbed." Similar bloodcurdling displays of popular vengeance took place in two other Kurdish centers that fell to the uprising.[16]

The Kurdish leaders were ecstatic in victory. "One second of this day is worth all the wealth in the world," exclaimed Massoud Barzani.[17] Shortly afterward, U.S. Senate staff member Peter Galbraith arrived in newly liberated Kurdistan with a small group of foreign journalists. "There was this enormous sense of euphoria," he said later. "For the first time, the Kurds were controlling their own destiny."[18] The Kurds saluted the American president, who, they said, had inspired their victory, with the honorific title "Haji": "Haji Bush," they shouted to the U.S. journalists.[19]

The fate of Iraq teetered in the balance by mid-March, a few days after Saddam's surrender to the U.S-led coalition. The rebels in the north and south held fourteen of Iraq's eighteen provinces. Baghdad was still quiet, but there were rumors that Saddam really was preparing to flee. Advance units of the American-led coalition were still deployed deep into southern Iraq, just south of Najaf and Karbala. The intifada seemed on the verge of triumph. But it was not to be.

The Bush administration had failed to achieve the goals it set for itself when it decided to go to war in the Gulf. True, Saddam's forces were expelled from Kuwait. But the real objective was to destroy the Iraqi dictator and demolish his military potential. At the close of hostilities on February 27, in a televised briefing, General Norman Schwarzkopf claimed triumph for the American-led coalition. Those enemy forces not already annihilated were hopelessly trapped. "The gates are closed," he claimed, "on their military machine." In fact, the gates had never been fully closed. On March 1, after the cease-fire, American intelligence analysts concluded that more than half of Saddam's elite Republican Guard had escaped back to Iraq along with much of their armor and artillery. Some of Saddam's troops were even permitted to return and pick up their weapons after the cease-fire.[20] More important, most of Saddam's senior officers also slipped through the coalition dragnet. As for Saddam Hussein himself, he was still alive and well and defiant in Baghdad.

In his briefing, Schwarzkopf also announced that coalition forces would not be going to Baghdad. In Washington, Assistant Defense Secretary Paul Wolfowitz was furious at the general's admission. It was true there were no plans to take the Iraqi capital, but, by gratuitously making that information public, Schwarzkopf managed to both reassure the Iraqi dictator and undermine those still hoping for a military coup.[21]

Indeed, after the disastrous rout of his forces in Kuwait, Saddam Hussein fully expected that the coalition would advance to Baghdad to finish the job. As Saddam's intelligence chief, General Wafiq al-Samarrai, later said, "Before the cease-fire, he [Saddam] felt that his doom was very close by. He sat before me and he was almost in tears, not crying, but almost in tears." The dictator's despair, however, was swept away on February 28, when President Bush, announcing the cease-fire, also declared a halt to the advance of the coalition. As Saddam now saw it, by simply surviving he had defeated the enemy. "He was feeling himself as a great, great hero," said General Samarrai. "He started to go like 'We won, we won!' He was laughing and kidding and joking and talking about Bush."[22]

It became obvious that, though the U.S. had meticulously planned the military campaign against Saddam Hussein, the Bush administration had no plans for the aftermath. Thomas Pickering, who was then U.S. ambassador to the United Nations, revealed later, "We had wonderfully prepared combat activities, and we had absolutely no idea what to do in the post combat phase. There was no policy, no examination of what we should do; no examination of how we should deal with the future, except that we didn't want to go to Baghdad."[23]

One reason for the lack of planning, according to Chas Freeman, the U.S. ambassador to Saudi Arabia at the time, was that "the White House was terrified that any leaks about any U.S. plans might unhinge the huge and unwieldy coalition that George Bush had put together to support the war. So officials were discouraged from writing, talking, or even thinking about what to do next."[24]

Indeed, on March 3, when General Schwarzkopf met his defeated Iraqi counterparts in the Iraqi desert town of Safwan to sign a truce agreement, he had no directives from Washington on how to proceed. "He should have had instructions," said a Bush administration official, "but everything was moving so fast the process broke down. The generals made an effort not to be guided. It was treated as something that was basically a military decision, not one to be micromanaged."[25] The U.S. also didn't insist that Saddam Hussein attend the Safwan meeting and accept personal humiliation for the defeat. American officials didn't know what they would do if Saddam refused.

The priority for Schwarzkopf at Safwan was not to shape the political future of Iraq. His goal was the immediate return of all prisoners of war held by the Iraqis and the withdrawal of coalition forces from the area as soon as possible. The Iraqis were also told that no military aircraft flights would be allowed. After dealing with those matters, Schwarzkopf asked if there were any other items the Iraqis wished to raise. Lt. General Sultan Hashim Ahmad, the chief of staff of the Ministry of Defense, pointed out that many Iraqi roads and bridges had been damaged in the conflict; therefore, the Iraqis would like permission to use their helicopters to transport government and military officials. Magnanimously, Schwarzkopf gave his okay. The Iraqi general appeared taken aback by the American's ready assent. "So you mean even the helicopters that are armed in the Iraqi skies can fly, but not the fighters?" he asked, not quite believing what the American commander had so quickly conceded.

"Yeah," Schwarzkopf replied. "I will instruct our Air Force not to shoot at any helicopters that are flying over the territory of Iraq where we are not located." It was a fateful decision. Though Schwarzkopf saw no threat to coalition forces, those helicopters would prove devastating against the intifada. There is no way that the General's command could not have known of the Shiite revolt, which had broken out three days earlier and was already sweeping through southern Iraq, just a few kilometers away from front-line American units. It was obvious, however, that Schwarzkopf had little interest in the matter. He wanted out just as quickly as he could redeploy his troops.[26]

When the Iraqis complained that coalition forces had moved further into Iraq since the cease-fire was declared, General Schwarzkopf promised, "There will not be one single coalition force member in the recognized borders of Iraq, as soon as, as rapidly as we can get them out."[27]

"It was an extraordinary assurance," two American military experts later concluded. "The United States might have used its occupation of southern Iraq to press for further demands. It might have insisted that the Iraqis reach a new political accommodation with the Shiites and Kurds, or at least not attack them. It might even have pressed for the removal of the Saddam Hussein regime. But it did none of this."[28] There were two American Army corps deep into southern Iraq, the U.S. controlled the skies, Saddam's forces were demoralized and in disarray, and revolt was beginning to sweep the country, yet Schwarzkopf and the Bush administration let the opportunity slip through their fingers.

Assured by the Americans themselves that they would be withdrawing as soon as possible, Saddam and his generals set out to rally their forces and quash the uprising. They were abetted by the chaotic state of the intifada. The rebels were totally disorganized, lacking leadership, arms, and communication equipment. No group really knew what the others were up to. In addition, the horrific tales of vengeance wreaked by Shiites and Kurdish mobs against Sunnis from the Baath Party, the intelligence apparatus, and the military were enough to convince many wavering government officials that this was no time to turn against Saddam.

There were also disturbing signs that Iran might be attempting to gain control of the southern rebellion. Some Shiites who had been exiled in Iran were returning to join the intifada under the leadership of Mohammed Baqir al-Hakim, descendent of a prominent Iraqi religious family. In Iraqi towns on the Iranian border, posters of al-Hakim were plastered on the walls alongside images of the Ayatollah Khomeini. Proclamations purporting to speak for al-Hakim claimed control of the uprising. There were rumors that the Badr Brigade, a pro-Iranian military group of Iraqi Shiites, was also joining the intifada.[29] The specter of an Iranian-dominated fundamentalist regime taking over in Iraq terrified Iraqi Sunnis, as well as many Shiites. Saddam played on those fears by claiming that the uprising was, in fact, being run from outside Iraq.

By March 9, 1991, Saddam's forces were ready to move against the uprising. They would go after the south first, the holy city of Karbala, where young Zainab al-Suwaij had taken part in the revolt. As Zainab and her friends saw it, the revolt seemed to have stalled. Their euphoria had waned. The American troops camped nearby had made no move to aid them. Meanwhile the Baghdad government was broadcasting threatening proclamations from Saddam Hussein.

"We rose up," Zainab recalled years later. "It was a great victory. We felt so great! And then, we were waiting for help—the help that America promised to give to Iraqis."

When I pointed out that President Bush had never specifically said that America would help the uprising, Zainab replied, "Well, that's what was understood among the people. And we needed help."[30] Though short of weapons, food, and medicines, the rebels still clung to the hope that threats of a counterattack by Saddam were just propaganda. On March 9, however, Saddam's forces hit Karbala with a massive attack. The rebels were hopelessly outgunned, their light weapons no match for Saddam's helicopter gunships, tanks, and artillery.[31] "We couldn't figure out why, if the war had ended and Saddam is not allowed to fly his planes, why are the helicopters flying?" said Zainab. "Why are the Americans and the coalition army, why are they letting them fly?" The

American troops, she said, were just twenty minutes away from Karbala, "but help never came and people started being killed. We had the feeling of being betrayed."

As Saddam's forces tightened their grip on Karbala, they ordered the people to leave the shelter of the city. Then they used helicopters to attack the fleeing civilians, in some instances pouring kerosene over them and setting it aflame with tracer bullets, as American observation planes circled overhead.[32]

Why didn't the U.S. intervene? Because the last thing General Schwarzkopf, Colin Powell, and the majority of their civilian masters in Washington wanted was for American troops to become sucked into internal Iraqi conflicts. The Americans felt they had completed—if imperfectly—their task of expelling Saddam Hussein from Kuwait. Granted, the Iraqi dictator was still in power with half his elite Republican Guard still intact, but becoming embroiled in the uprising, the Americans believed, was a recipe for disaster. They had managed to hold the shaky international coalition together long enough to expel Saddam. Their principal Arab allies, the Saudis and Egyptians, would never support what would be, in effect, an American invasion of Iraq, and U.S. congressional leaders had been doubtful about the enterprise from the beginning.

There was also the fear that, if victorious, the uprising would lead to Iraq splintering into its ethnic components: a Shiite state allied with Iran in the south and an independent Kurdish state in the north, which would mean endless turmoil for the Turks, who had their own restive Kurdish population to deal with. There were those reports that Iranian-backed Shiites had already infiltrated the uprising; if it turned out that by aiding the intifada the Bush administration was actually paving the way for fire-breathing Islamists allied with Iran to take over Iraq, the domestic political fallout would be devastating.

Such nightmarish scenarios were the backdrop to the White House debate over how to deal with the uprisings. The president's call for the Iraq people to rise up had been a tactical move to weaken Saddam. The White House never expected they would actually attempt to seize power. The U.S. wanted the downfall of the Iraqi tyrant, but they wanted him replaced not by a seething civilian cauldron they could not control but by another strong military figure who could hold his fractious country together, a leader who—above all—would be more sympathetic to American interests.[33]

Earlier, at the end of February 1991, when Peter Galbraith attempted to arrange for Kurdish leaders to discuss their plans for an uprising with a top administration official, he was rebuked by a deputy. Said Galbraith, "She was furious with me. 'You are interfering in administration policy and that is unacceptable,' she said. And I said, 'Surely we want to get rid of this regime,' and she said, 'No, our policy is to get rid of Saddam Hussein, not the regime.' Well, these were nuances that may have made sense to her and perhaps to the first President Bush, but they were not nuances that made any sense to either Kurds or Shiites."

Thus, the uprising that Bush had called for a few weeks earlier was now viewed as a threat to the U.S. and its allies in the region. As Secretary of State James Baker declared, "We are not in the process now of assisting or giving arms to these groups that are in uprising against the current government. We don't want to see a power vacuum develop in Iraq. We want to see the territorial integrity of Iraq preserved. So do all the other coalition partners."[34]

There were some in the Bush administration, like Paul Wolfowitz, who also argued that the United States should support the rebellion. He was not talking about sending American troops to Baghdad but funneling arms to the rebels and modifying the ceasefire agreement to ban the Iraqi military from flying their helicopters. The Shiites of Iraq, he insisted, were different from those of Iran. Aiding them would not mean expanding the radical Islam of Khomeini.

The White House position, however, was based not on hard intelligence or facts, but rumor, fear, and a caricatured view of Iraq and the region. The men around President Bush knew little about the country they had spent billions of dollars to defeat, as would be the case in 2003. The word "Shiite" was a bogeyman, conjuring images of the American embassy hostages in Iran and the 1983 suicide bombing of the marine barracks in Lebanon. There was little room or patience for the idea that the Shiites of southern Iraq were an independent people in their own right, that they had recently fought for eight years against their coreligionists in Iran. Many Shiite religious leaders of Iraq had also long disagreed with Khomeini's concept of a theocratic state ruled over by Shiite clerics.

American policy makers knew little of Iraq's opposition groups, because for years there had been a ban on U.S. officials meeting with Iraqi dissidents. One reason had been the fear of annoying America's then-ally, Saddam Hussein, while the ban on State Department contacts with Iraqi Kurdish dissidents was out of deference to Turkish President Ozal. The upshot was that in 1991, top American officials were ignorant of the personalities and movements behind the uprising. All considerations paled beside the threat, real or imagined, of a radical Shiite takeover or the creation of an independent Kurdish state.[35] The powerful pro-Israel lobby also weighed into the deliberations in Washington. One official in Jerusalem noted, "We don't want a Shiite-based regime in Iraq, which would be even more militant than Saddam against Israel."[36]

In fact, there was little likelihood of Iran hijacking and radicalizing the revolt. Though some Iraqi Shiites who had been exiled in Iran came back to join the uprising, their numbers were limited. Nor is there any convincing evidence that Iran was sending substantial arms or men to aid the Shiites in the south. Indeed, there were Iraqi opposition leaders who later claimed that that evidence of Iranian influence in the uprising had been planted by Saddam's secret police, the Mukhabarat. "He sent his own Mukhabarat to the south with pictures of Khomeini," said one secular opposition leader. "The Badr Brigade never came. We talked to the Iranians. They swear by the Koran that they didn't send the pictures." An Iranian Islamic exile supported that view. The Iranians, he said, "encouraged the uprising and then betrayed it. They only let a few people cross the border to help, and they would not let them bring arms. They certainly did not put up posters—they were terrified of an American reaction."[37]

Later, in justifying their abandonment of the rebellion, the White House would claim they had been obliged by their allies to reject the uprising. "It was never our goal to break up Iraq," President Bush explained. "Indeed, we did not want that to happen, and most of our coalition partners (especially the Arabs) felt even stronger on the issue."[38] In fact, on March 5, 1991, the Saudis told Secretary of State

Baker, who had flown to Riyadh, that they were not at all happy that the war was ending with Saddam Hussein still in power. They suggested secretly arming the Shiites and Kurds to keep the rebellion going and keep pressure on the Iraqi dictator.[39] This advice was ignored—the White House had made up its mind.

The Uprising Smashed

When Saddam's brutal counterattack against the rebellions began, the order was given to American troops already deep inside Iraq and armed to the teeth not to assist the rebellion in any way—though everyone knew that they were condemning the intifada to an awful defeat. Thanks to their high-flying reconnaissance planes, U.S. commanders would observe the brutal process as it occurred.

At the time, Rocky Gonzalez was a Special Forces warrant officer serving with U.S. troops in southern Iraq. Because he spoke Arabic, he was detached to serve with the Third Brigade of the 101st Infantry when the ground war began. There were about 140 men in his unit, which was stationed at Al Khadir on the Euphrates, just a few kilometers from Karbala and Najaf.

Rocky was one of the few Americans who could actually communicate with the Iraqis. When the intifada erupted, the Americans prompted the rebels to raid the local prison in Karbala and free the Kuwaitis who were being held there. "We didn't think there was going to be a lot of bloodshed," said Gonzalez, "but they executed the guards in the prison." Prior to the uprising, the rebels had also been feeding intelligence to the Americans on what Saddam's local supporters were up to.

From their base, Rocky and his units watched as Saddam's forces launched their counterattack against the rebel-held city. Thousands of people fled toward the American lines, said Gonzalez.

> All of a sudden, as far as the eye could see on Highway Five, there was just a long line of vehicles, dump trucks, tractors—any vehicle they could get—coming to us in streams.
>
> The rebels wanted aid, they wanted medical treatment, and some of the individuals wanted us to give them weapons and ammunition so they could go and fight. One of the refugees was wav-

ing a leaflet that had been dropped by U.S. planes over Iraq. Those leaflets told them to rise up against the regime and free themselves. They weren't asking us to fight. They felt they could do that themselves. Basically they were just saying, 'We rose up like you asked us, now give us some weapons and arms to fight.'[40]

The American forces had huge stocks of weapons they had captured from the Iraqis. But they were ordered to blow them up rather than turn them over to the rebels. "It was gut-wrenching to me," said Gonzalez. "Here we were sitting on the Euphrates River and we were ordered to stop. As a human being, I wanted to help, but as a solider I had my orders."

Ironically, according to a former U.S. diplomat, some of the arms that were not destroyed by American forces were collected by the CIA and shipped to anti-Soviet rebels in Afghanistan, who at the time were being clandestinely backed by the U.S.[41]

A Shiite survivor of the uprising later said he had seen other American forces at the river town of Nassiriya destroy a huge cache of weapons that the rebels desperately needed. "They blew up an enormous stock of arms," he said. "If we had been able to get hold of them, the course of history would have been changed in favor of the uprising, because Saddam had nothing left at that moment."[42]

Indeed, Saddam's former intelligence chief, General Wafiq al-Samarrai, later recounted that the government forces had almost no ammunition left when they finally squelched the revolt. "By the last week of the intifada," he said, "the army was down to two hundred and seventy thousand Kalashnikov bullets." That would have lasted for just two more days of fighting.[43]

In his autobiography, General Schwarzkopf, without giving details, alludes to the fact that the American-led coalition aided Saddam to crush the uprising. According to his curious reasoning, expressed in another interview, the Iraqi people were not innocent in the whole affair because "they supported the invasion of Kuwait and accepted Saddam Hussein."[44]

Iraqi survivors of the intifada also claimed that U.S. forces actually prevented them from marching on Baghdad. "American helicopters landed on the road to block our way and stopped us from continuing," they said. "One of the American soldiers threatened to kill us if we didn't turn back." Another Shiite leader, Dr. Hamid al-Bayatti, claimed that the U.S. even provided Saddam's Republican Guard with fuel. The Americans, he charged, disarmed some resistance units and allowed Republican Guard tanks to go through their checkpoints to crush the uprising.[45] "We let one Iraqi division go through our lines to get to Basra because the United States did not want the regime to collapse," said Middle East expert William Quandt.[46]

The U.S. officials declined even to meet with the Shiites to hear their case. As Peter Galbraith said, "These were desperate people, desperate for U.S. help. But the U.S. refused to talk to any of the Shiite leaders: the U.S. embassy, Schwarzkopf, nobody would see them, nor even give them an explanation."[47]

The stonewalling continued even when evidence that Saddam was using chemical weapons against the rebels emerged. "You could see there were helicopters crisscrossing the skies, going back and forth," Rocky Gonzalez said. "Within a few hours people started showing up at our perimeter with chemical burns. They were saying, 'We are fighting the Iraqi military and the Baath Party and they sprayed us with chemicals.' We were guessing mustard gas. They had blisters and burns on their face and on their hands, on places where the skin was exposed," he said. "As the hours passed, more and more people were coming. And I asked them, 'Why don't you go to the hospital in Karbala,' and the response was that all the doctors and nurses had been executed by the Iraqi soldiers, 'so we come to you for aid.'"

One of the greatest concerns of coalition forces during Desert Storm had been that Saddam would unleash his WMD. U.S. officials repeatedly warned Iraq that America's response would be immediate and devastating. Facing such threats, Saddam kept his weapons holstered—or so the Bush administration led the world to believe.

Rocky's suspicion that Saddam did resort to them in 1991 was later confirmed by the report of the U.S. government's Iraq Survey Group (ISG),[48] which investigated Saddam's WMD after the U.S.-led invasion in 2003 and concluded that Saddam no longer had any WMD. Almost universally ignored by the media, however, was the finding that Saddam *had* resorted to his WMD during the 1991 uprising.[49] The "regime was shaking and wanted something 'very quick and effective' to put down the revolt." They considered then rejected using mustard gas, as it would be too perceptible with U.S. troops close by. Instead, on March 7, 1991, the Iraqi military filled R-400 aerial bombs with sarin, a binary nerve agent. "Dozens of sorties were flown against Shiite rebels in Karbala and the surrounding areas," the ISG report said. But apparently the R-400 bombs were not very effective, having been designed for high-speed delivery from planes, not slow-moving helicopters. So the Iraqi military switched to dropping CS, a very potent tear gas, in large aerial bombs.

Because of previous U.S. warnings against resorting to chemical weapons, Saddam and his generals knew they were taking a serious risk, but the coalition never reacted. The lingering question is why. It's impossible to believe they didn't know about it at the time. There were repeated charges from Shiite survivors that the Iraqi dictator had used chemical weapons. Rocky Gonzalez said he heard from refugees that nerve gas was being used. He had also observed French-made Iraqi helicopters—one of which was outfitted as a crop sprayer—making repeated bomb runs over Najaf.[50] Gonzalez maintained that, contrary to what the ISG report said, many of the refugees who fled to U.S. lines were indeed victims of mustard gas. "Their tongues were swollen," he said, "and they had severe burns on the mucous tissue on the inside of their mouths and nasal passages. Our chemical officer also said it looked like mustard gas." Gonzalez suggested that local Iraqi officials, desperate to put down the uprising, may have used mustard gas without permission from on high. "A lot of that was kept quiet," he said, "because we didn't want to panic the troops. We stepped up our training with gas masks, because we were naturally concerned."

Gonzalez's unit also passed their information on to their superiors. "There was no way that officers higher didn't know what was happening," Gonzalez said. "Whether those reports went above our division, I have no idea." Gonzalez's former commander turned down my request for an interview. At the time, few subjects were more sensitive than Saddam's potential use of WMD. It's difficult to believe that reports from Gonzalez's unit weren't flashed immediately up the chain of command in the Gulf and Washington.

There were other American witnesses to what happened. U.S. helicopters and planes flew overhead, patrolling as Saddam's helicopters decimated the rebels. Some of those aircraft provided real-time video of the occurrences below. A reliable U.S. intelligence source confirmed that such evidence does indeed exist.[51]

On March 7, Secretary of State Baker warned Saddam not to resort to chemical weapons to repress the uprising. But why, when the U.S. was notified that the Iraqi dictator actually *had* resorted to chemical weapons, was there no forceful reaction from the Bush administration? One plausible explanation is that denouncing Saddam's use of chemical weapons would have greatly increased pressure on the U.S. president to come to the aid of the Shiites.

Instead, the American decision to turn its back on the intifada gave a green light to Saddam Hussein's ruthless counterattack. General Wafiq al-Samarrai learned of the decision after Iraqi units intercepted frantic conversations between two Islamic rebels near Nassariya. One told the other that he had gone to the Americans to ask for support, and twice was rebuffed. "They say, 'We are not going to support you because you are Shiites and are collaborating with Iran.'" After hearing that message, al-Samarrai recalled, "The position of the regime immediately became more confident. Now [Saddam] began to attack the intifada."[52]

The repression when it came was as horrendous as everyone knew it would be. "Women were being raped. People were being shot in the streets and just left to rot there," Zainab al-Suwaij recounted. "The citizens were forbidden to bury the bodies. Many of them were eaten by the dogs. The government ordered people out of Karbala to take the road to Najaf. They were slaughtered and executed along the roadway. Many of those killed were teenagers."

As an object lesson to his people, Saddam Hussein himself ordered Iraqi television to record and broadcast scenes of the repression: appalling scenes of captured Shiites, some with ropes around their necks, being kicked and beaten and insulted, threatened with pistols and machine guns, a few pleading for mercy. Most of them, eyes downcast, are eventually dragged away to execution.

The Bush administration attempted to disengage itself from any responsibility. They were helped by the fact that there were no graphic news reports in the West of the slaughter that was taking place. U.S. intelligence agencies had their own accounts and explicit images, but they weren't sharing them with the press or the public. Anonymous government figures, wise in the ways of *realpolitik*, were making statements such as, "It is far easier to deal with a tame Saddam Hussein than with an unknown quantity."[53]

On March 13, 1991, when asked by the press about Iraq's using helicopters to smash the revolt, President Bush declared, "These helicopters should not be used for combat inside Iraq." The attacks had to stop, he warned, before there could be any "permanence to the cease-fire." But immediately after that declaration, two top White House aides took Bush aside to explain that the cease-fire agreement did not ban Iraqi helicopter flights after all. The president issued no further warnings.

On March 17, General Robert Johnston, Schwarzkopf's deputy, reiterating the ban announced at the cease-fire, again advised the Iraqi generals that they were not allowed to fly their fixed wing aircraft— even if it was just to move them back to their main bases. "You fly, you die," the Iraqis had been warned. However, with regard to the helicopters being deployed against the insurgency, General Johnston merely told the Iraqis that the U.S. "was not pleased."[54] Saddam continued to use the helicopter gunships, without any further reaction from Washington. Though the U.S.-led coalition shot down two Iraqi jets to enforce the ban on fixed-wing aircraft, they never destroyed a single Iraqi helicopter.[55] A few administration officials, such as Paul Wolfowitz, continued to push for a total ban on all aircraft until he received an irate phone call from Colin Powell telling him to stop implying to the press that the question of forbidding Iraqi helicopter flights was still being discussed.[56] To close the issue, it was made clear that the U.S. had modified its policy on Iraqi helicopters: they could be shot down, but "only if they posed a threat to coalition forces." What the gunships did to the Iraqis was now irrelevant.

The final decision to walk away from the Shiite uprising was made on March 26, when President Bush met with seven senior advisors.

Domestically, the judgment seemed to make eminent sense. The U.S.-led coalition appeared to have won an impressive victory. Saddam's naked aggression had been defeated, with very few coalition casualties.[57] True, the Shiites were being brutally hammered in the South, but few Americans had any sympathy for the Shiites—nor any knowledge of the slaughter going on.

As for the Kurdish rebellion, that seemed to be dangerously out of hand. On March 20, the *pesh merga* had seized the petroleum rich region of Kirkuk. That infuriated the Sunnis and heightened concerns about the ultimate stability of Iraq. At the time, however, Kurdish leaders were telling anyone who would listen that they had no intention of setting up an independent Kurdistan. They realized it wouldn't be feasible. The problem was that the Bush administration never heard such assurances; for years, as we've seen, the State Department had a ban on meetings with Kurdish leaders for fear of offending the government of Turkey. But now, while Washington was still refusing to meet with any of the Kurdish leaders, Turkish President Ozal was attempting to contact the Iraqi Kurds himself to negotiate future relations.[58]

As far as the Kurds went, the Bush administration was flying blind. "We didn't know diddly," one State Department official later admitted. "No one had the foggiest idea of whom to talk to, and no one even knew who the Kurds were."[59] The White House knew only that they were a menace.

The March 26 meeting in the White House came to the conclusion that it was time to put the genii back in the bottle and walk away from both the Shiites and the Kurds.[60] Following the meeting, a Bush spokesman announced, "We don't intend to involve ourselves in the internal conflict in Iraq."[61] The unanswered question remained: If Saddam really was worse than Hitler, as the president had repeatedly claimed, how could Bush now justify leaving him in power?

Veiling the administration's cynicism behind the always-ready cloak of anonymity, one unidentified American official admitted that Washington decision makers "don't approve of what Saddam Hussein is doing, but they are not unhappy to see him have to do the dirty work."[62] Another "senior official" elaborated to reporters that Bush believed that "Saddam will crush the rebellions and, after the dust settles, the Baath military establishment and other elites will blame [Saddam] not only for the death and destruction from the war, but the death and destruction from putting down the rebellion. They will emerge then and install a new leadership."[63] "We never made any promises to these people," another official blandly declared. "There is no interest in the coalition in further military operations."[64]

President Bush himself was asked if any rebel groups had requested help from the United States. "Not that I know of," said the president. "No, I don't believe that they have. If they have, it hasn't come to me."

In fact, after the White House meeting, two of the president's top officials, Brent Scowcroft and Richard Haas, were dispatched to Riyadh to tell the Saudis that there would be no clandestine aid to the uprisings. Three days after the Americans arrived, that message was passed on to one of the leaders of the Shiite rebellion, Sayid Majid al-Khoie.[65] The same message was also transmitted to Hoshyar Zibari, a top aide to Kurdish leader Mustafa Barzani, who had earlier been brought by the Saudis to Riyadh to discuss full-blown cooperation with the uprising. After the Americans departed, the Saudis handed Zibari an airline ticket back to London. Any hope of collaboration for the Kurds had ended.[66]

On March 29, having disposed of the Shiites, and confident in the knowledge that the U.S. would not back the Kurds, Saddam Hussein ordered his forces north. Remembering past chemical attacks, the Kurds were terrified of the new offensive. "Tens of thousands of people suddenly were moving out of their homes," said Peter Galbraith, who was there at the time.

> The streets and the roads out of the Iraqi towns were scenes that must have been reminiscent of refugees leaving Paris in June 1940. There were cars packed with people and furniture all heading for the mountains and a sense of disbelief and betrayal about the first President Bush. I couldn't believe it. I was also incredibly angry. Here was a sea of humanity, two million people moving to the mountains. Thousands ended up dying, and this is something where my country

was completely responsible. We had called for this uprising, we had made it possible. And then for geostrategic reasons that had no connection with human life we had allowed Saddam to destroy the uprising.[67]

Air Force Monthly afterward described the experiences of two American F-15 pilots obliged to watch as Iraqi helicopters attacked a terrified column of Kurdish refugees. "As the gunships worked over the column with bombs and machine guns, the pilots repeatedly radioed the U.S. command post in Saudi Arabia, asking permission to take out the Iraqi machine. When the reply came back from their controller in the negative, the pilots had to back off and allow Saddam Hussein's henchmen to do their worst."[68]

Kurdish leaders dispatched a message to President Bush: "You personally asked the Iraqi people to rise up against Saddam Hussein's brutal dictatorship," then abandoned them to "the night of Saddam Hussein's tyranny."[69] For its part, the Bush administration issued a stream of anonymous justifications for refusing to help. "It probably sounds callous, but we did the best thing not to get near the Kurdish revolt," said one U.S. official. "They're nice people, and they're cute, but they're really just bandits. They're losers."[70] The Americans were not the only members of the coalition turning their back on the uprising. British Prime Minister John Major primly declared, "I don't recall asking the Kurds to mount this particular insurrection."[71]

Escaping from Kurdistan into Turkey on April 1, 1991, Peter Galbraith immediately gave videos he had shot of the dramatic Kurdish exodus to television reporters. He was himself repeatedly interviewed, and called for America to help: "Basically I delivered the message that this uprising was called for by the U.S. president. Bush had compared Saddam Hussein to Adolf Hitler, and here we had a new Holocaust taking place in Iraq, and we were doing nothing to stop it."[72]

In the age of instant television, it was a public relations disaster for the White House. The president was on a golfing vacation, where he piously declared, "I do not want to push American forces beyond our mandate. Of course, I feel a frustration and a sense of grief for the innocents that are being killed brutally, but we are not there to intervene." Juxtaposed to that declaration on the TV screen were the piti-ful images of thousands of Kurdish men, women, and children huddled on the frozen mountainsides of eastern Turkey. Outraged American columnists decried America's betrayal of the Kurds. There was also growing pressure from Turkey itself. The last thing the Turks wanted was more troublesome Kurds on their territory.

Finally, Secretary of State Baker was dispatched to assess the situation. It took just a few minutes on the ground, surrounded by a sea of desperate refugees and a gaggle of aggressive reporters, for Baker to realize that Bush had no choice. After first dispatching shipments of medicine and food, on April 16, the American president ordered U.S. troops into northern Iraq to establish a protected enclave for the Kurds and warned Saddam to stay clear. He also declared a no-fly zone forbidden to all Iraqi planes—and helicopters. Saddam Hussein immediately complied.

Though finally obliged to intervene in the north, President Bush was still attempting to rewrite history. "Do I think that the United States should bear guilt because of suggesting that the Iraqi people take matters into their own hands, with the implication being given by some that the United States would be there to support them militarily?" he asked. "That was not true. We never implied that."[73]

The haven created in the north quickly expanded, under U.S. protection. Ironically, the very thing that President Bush had sought to avoid by not supporting the uprising—that is, an autonomous Kurdistan—he ultimately created precisely by not supporting the uprising.

In the south, however, where there was no television coverage, the slaughter of the Shiites continued. It is estimated that at least 100,000 were killed—men, women, and children—between March 1991 and September 1991. They were placed in ranks and shot at close range, or summarily executed during house-to-house searches. According to Amnesty International, "Suspected rebels in Najaf were lined up, blindfolded with their hands bound, and shot in front of their families. Other detainees were doused with petrol and set alight, while a further large number were detained in a local hotel which was subsequently destroyed by heavy artillery." Other refugees told of Iraqi soldiers "throwing patients and others out of hospital windows," while doctors and medical staff were shot for having given medical assistance to wounded rebels. In other places prisoners were thrown into the river with their hands tied together and a weight around their legs. Others were reportedly blindfolded with their hands tied, then buried alive in a public garden.[74]

A few months earlier, when his goal was to inflame American public opinion against Saddam, George Bush had made frequent references to earlier Amnesty reports describing the savagery of the Iraqi regime. But when Amnesty attempted to call the world's attention to the dreadful repression of the Shiites following the 1991 uprisings—even as that slaughter was still going on—there was a deafening silence from the White House. It was now an internal Iraqi affair.[75]

As White House spokesman Marlin Fitzwater said in late March 1991, "I think it's safe to assume that in the kind of warfare being conducted by the rebel forces and the Kurds, as well as by the government of Iraq, as well as by other groups, that there are all sorts of atrocities and war repercussions taking place—yes. But it is our belief that the best policy is not to involve ourselves in those internal conflicts."[76]

"All of the efforts to debilitate Saddam and to create problems for him in order to remove him from Kuwait were justified," Thomas Pickering later told me, defending President Bush's calls for an uprising—even though the U.S. couldn't follow up afterward to help the people who rose up. "In war and love, all's fair," Pickering said wryly.[77]

In July 1991, Amnesty International warned of the plight of tens of thousands of Shiites who had sought refuge in the marshes of the Euphrates Valley in southern Iraq.[78] It took more than a year, however, for President Bush to declare a no-fly zone to protect those Shiites from air attack, and when he finally did, Saddam's military got around the flight ban by draining the swamps where the Shiites had taken shelter and then decimating them with ground troops.

Many Shiites came to believe that this vast carnage must have been the result of a diabolical plot between Saddam Hussein and the Americans to destroy the Shiites. "When that kind of catastrophe befalls a people," said Peter Galbraith, "they can't say that it was just a screw up by the American president. There has to be a greater meaning. So they assumed it was intentional, and twelve years later the second President Bush reaped the whirlwind in the south of Iraq. The second Bush administration, having no comprehension of this history, assumed that American forces would be seen as liberators. The reason that didn't happen is that twelve years later the Shiites still didn't trust the United States. George [W.] Bush is still paying the price for the incredibly casual and callous decision of his father."[79]

In explaining why he had refused to back the uprising, George H. W. Bush would later say, "We were concerned that the uprisings would sidetrack the overthrow of Saddam, by causing the Iraqi military to rally around him to prevent the breakup of the country."[80] In other words, the White House was afraid that the high-level military coup they hoped would lead to stable regime change would be stymied by a popular uprising.

But this face-saving analysis is not only counterintuitive; several former officials think it was dead wrong. According to Peter Galbraith, at the very moment when the Iraqi military were waiting to see which way the U.S. was going to go, the U.S. sent the wrong signal. At the height of the uprising, a group of Iraqi army officials approached a dissident group of Iraqi exiles with an offer of cooperation. All the would-be defectors were looking for was "a sign that the sponsors of the rebellion had the support of the U.S."[81]

The State Department, however, refused to meet any groups of the opposition, and this public snub was read as a clear indication that the U.S. did not want the popular rebellion to succeed. Said Galbraith, "The military waited to see what was the attitude of the U.S. and what they saw was that the U.S. was allowing helicopters to fly. They saw that the U.S. was allowing Iraqi tank units to move south to crush the uprising. So they understood that the U.S. wanted the uprising to fail, and no one was going to put his life on the line for a failed uprising. But had the Bush administration adopted a different position, had it simply shot down the helicopters, the uprising would have succeeded."[82]

Rocky Gonzalez, who spoke extensively with defeated Iraqi troops, also felt that they would have gone over to the rebels if the U.S. had given some sign of support to the uprising. "The Iraqi military saw our destructive capability," said Gonzalez. "They saw they were beaten as a military force. A lot of them would have gone over immediately to the anti-Baath groups and joined their ranks if they had seen a green light, in my opinion. And perhaps—who knows—we wouldn't have gone in a second time."

"In other words," as Peter Galbraith put it, "it was not the rebellions that destroyed the possibility of a coup. Abandoning the rebellions made it almost inevitable that there would not be a coup acceptable to Washington."[83]

Such speculation, however, was soon put aside. Operation Desert Storm was heralded as an extraordinary victory. Despite the predictions of thousands of casualties, only 146 American soldiers had been killed in action, thirty-five of them by friendly fire.[84] General Schwarzkopf returned a conquering hero to an ecstatic ticker-tape parade up lower Broadway in Manhattan. President Bush's ratings in the polls soared.

But Saddam Hussein could no longer count on the West for financial and military assistance. In fact, he had been transformed from a useful U.S. pawn in the game of Middle East politics to an enemy of the free world. The draconian embargo that had been imposed by the United Nations Security Council after Saddam invaded Kuwait would continue. From the beginning, the U.S. let it be known that the embargo, supposedly designed to force Saddam to open his country to U.N. weapons inspectors, would never be lifted as long as Saddam Hussein remained in power.

For Iraq and its people, things would only get worse.

CHAPTER EIGHT

Embargo : The U.N. Sanctions
August 6, 1990–May 22, 2003

The most lethal weapons of mass destruction to hit the people of Iraq were the sanctions imposed by the U.N. Security Council in August 6, 1990. They cut off all exports and imports between Iraq and the rest of the world; that meant everything—from food and electric generators to vaccines, hospital equipment, and even medical journals. Since Iraq imported 70 percent of its food, and its principal revenues were derived from the export of petroleum, the sanctions had an immediate and catastrophic impact on the country.

Maintained primarily by the United States and Great Britain, they would remain in place for almost thirteen years and were responsible for the deaths of from 500,000 to one million Iraqis, a huge proportion of them children. Two U.N. administrators who oversaw humanitarian relief in Iraq during that period consider the sanctions to have been a crime against humanity, as massive as any of the crimes committed by Saddam Hussein.

Punish the People

At first, the declared purpose of the sanctions was to oblige Saddam to withdraw from Kuwait. In that they failed. But on April 3, 1991, after the U.S.-led coalition had driven out the invading forces, the Security Council voted to keep sanctions in place. The new declared goal was to force Saddam Hussein to permit United Nations weapons inspectors to search for and destroy Iraq's vaunted weapons of mass destruction.

From the beginning, it was evident that, for the United States and England, the underlying objective of the sanctions was not the elimination of Saddam's weapons of mass destruction but of Saddam Hussein himself, though that goal went far beyond anything authorized by the Security Council. As President George H. W. Bush announced at a White House press briefing on April 16, "Do I think the answer is now for Saddam Hussein to be kicked out? Absolutely, because there will not be—may I finish, please?—there will not be normalized relations with the United States, and I think this is true for most coalition partners, until Saddam Hussein is out of there. And we will continue the economic sanctions."[1] The president and his successors, as well as Britain's prime ministers, would repeat that mantra over the following years.[2]

At first both Saddam and his enemies thought the sanctions would be temporary. By January 1991, before the outbreak of the Gulf War, the people of Iraq, particularly the poor and the young, were already devastated by the cuts. When the Gulf War ended, the CIA estimated the dictator would be toppled within six months.[3] They calculated that the sanctions, added to Saddam's devastating defeat, would finally provoke the military coup for which they'd long been hoping.

The effect of the sanctions was magnified by the massive destruction wrought by the war. Secretary of State James Baker had warned Iraqi Foreign Minister Tariq Aziz on January 9 that if Saddam did not immediately withdraw from Kuwait, "We will return you to the pre-industrial age." Between January 16 and February 27, the American-led coalition hit Iraq with 88,000 tons of bombs, an explosive tonnage equivalent to seven Hiroshima-sized atomic bombs. It was an intensity of attack that had no parallels in the history of warfare.[4]

At the time, U.S. spokesmen claimed they were confining their raids to military targets. The destruction of many civilian sites, they said, was regrettable but unavoidable "collateral damage." At a breakfast meeting with reporters long after the war, then Defense Secretary Richard B. Cheney maintained that every Iraqi target was "perfectly legitimate" and added, "If I had to do it over again, I would do exactly the same thing."[5]

In fact, according to several American officers responsible for the air war, the bombing campaign deliberately set out to destroy Iraq's vital civilian infrastructure.[6] As one reporter wrote, "The worst civilian suffering, senior officers say, has resulted not from bombs that went astray, but from precision-guided weapons that hit exactly where they were aimed—at electrical plants, oil refineries, and transportation networks."[7]

Punishing Iraqi civilians was justified by the claim that they shared responsibility for Saddam's invasion of Kuwait. "The definition of innocents gets to be a little bit unclear," said a senior Air Force officer. "They do live there, and ultimately the people have some control over what goes on in their country."[8] Such casuistry may have assuaged the conscience of those responsible for the destruction, but it had nothing to do with reality: Saddam ruled by terror and assassination, not by consulting the views of his people.

The idea, as we have seen, was to create such devastation and pain that the Iraqi military would overthrow the Iraqi dictator. To that end, the bombing campaign also ravaged Iraq's radio and television stations, telephone exchanges, water-treatment facilities, irrigation networks, and factories. One estimate of the replacement value of Iraqi assets destroyed in the war was at least $200 billion.[9] Two weeks into the air campaign, General Schwarzkopf declared, "We never had any intention of destroying 100 percent of all the Iraqi electrical power," because such a course would cause civilians to "suffer unduly." The campaign might never quite have achieved 100 percent, but of twenty electrical generating plants, seventeen were seriously hit; eleven of those were totally destroyed. The Al Hartha power plant south of Basra, for instance, was demolished beyond repair early on. Despite that fact, U.S. bombers returned to hit the plant twelve more times.[10]

It was estimated that it would take five years for those power centers to be rebuilt, and that considerable foreign aid would be necessary—which was an additional goal of the bombing campaign. As a top Air Force planner said, "Big picture, we wanted to let people know, 'Get rid of this guy and we'll be more than happy to assist in rebuilding. We're not going to tolerate Saddam Hussein or his regime. Fix that, and we'll fix your electricity.'"[11]

Glib expressions such as "fix your electricity" purposely ignored the awful impact of the destruction. It wasn't just a question of inconvenience, of lights out at night or refrigerators not working. The cascading effect of the ruined electrical grid would prove far more lethal than all the bullets and smart bombs of the Gulf War. The cataclysm of the war, added to the eight months of sanctions that had already been in force, meant that the people of Iraq faced a survival crisis that Martti Ahtisaari, the U.N. undersecretary general, described as "of apocalyptic proportions." It was impossible, he said in March 1991, "for the Iraqi authorities even to measure the dimensions of the calamity, much less to respond to its consequences."[12]

The situation would not have been as grave if Iraq had still been a Third-World country, a peasant society. But thanks to the petroleum boom, the country had become a highly urbanized, industrializing nation. Its people for the first time had access to potable water and one of the best hospital and medical systems in the Middle East. Three quarters of Iraq's population lived in the cities; they were dependent on electricity not only to power their factories and homes but for their water treatment plants, sewage treatment facilities, and irrigation systems.

In short, the bombing campaign and the sanctions were part of the same strategy. "People say, 'You didn't recognize that it was going to have an effect on water or sewage?'" said a U.S. Air Force planning officer. "Well, what were we trying to do with sanctions—help out the Iraqi people? No. What we were doing with the attacks on infrastructure was to accelerate the effect of the sanctions."[13]

The CIA had calculated that, amidst all this destruction, Saddam would remain in power for a matter of months at most after the war. They were wrong. His dictatorship proved far too ruthless and durable. But the sanctions remained, crippling Iraq even further. For the next twelve years, they blocked the imports of vital spare parts needed to restore the country's shattered infrastructure and the education and medical care systems.[14]

Since it is a war crime under the Geneva Conventions to starve a civilian population or block its access to medicine, the sanctions made an exception for "supplies intended strictly for medical purposes, and, in humanitarian circumstances, foodstuffs." The U.S. and Britain would point to that exception as evidence that sanctions were a civilized way of putting pressure on Saddam, while sparing his people, but that was more official deceit. In order to import food and medicines, Iraq had to have the money to pay for them. But, immediately after the invasion of Kuwait, the U.S. and other Western countries froze all Iraq's overseas assets and prohibited Iraq from exporting petroleum. Iraq was able to "smuggle" some relatively small amounts of petroleum to its neighbors, but there was no way the country could generate the huge amounts needed for food and other vital imports.

Further, the sanctions were controlled by a Security Council committee made up of the five permanent and ten rotating members of the council. Every item to be exported from or imported into Iraq had to be okayed by all fifteen members, which meant that any one member intent on throttling Iraq could object to any article, either blocking it entirely or raising enough questions to delay its shipments for months on end, with virtually the same effect. This is precisely the policy followed by the United States and Great Britain, who came to dominate the committee. To relieve committee members of the need to defend their actions publicly, deliberations were kept secret.[15]

An American professor of philosophy, Joy Gordon, later spent three years studying the sanctions program and managed to obtain access to the confidential internal documents. "What they show," she wrote in her 2002 report, "is that the United States has fought aggressively throughout the last decade to purposefully minimize the humanitarian goods that enter the country. Invoking security concerns—including those not corroborated by U.N. weapons inspectors—U.S. policymakers have effectively turned a program of international governance into a legitimized act of mass slaughter."[16]

The United States prevented Iraq from obtaining crucial materials to restore its civilian infrastructure, often simply by prohibiting the import of one key part. For example, Iraq was permitted to import a sewage-treatment plant, but denied permission to bring in a generator to power it. Because Iraq's water treatment plants had been ravaged by bombing, the people were forced to return to the rivers for drinking water, as they had for thousands of years past. Meanwhile, 300,000 tons of raw sewage were spewing daily into its rivers with—as the U.S. well knew—disastrous impact on the nation's health.[17] A study for Harvard University in September 1991 found that more than half the people tested were exposed to dangerous fecal contamination in their drinking water.[18]

Those contaminated waters became in their own way a weapon of mass destruction, a biological killer as lethal as anything Saddam had attempted to produce. Shortly after the end of the Gulf War, there were widespread outbreaks of severe child and infant dysentery. Typhoid and cholera, which had been virtually eradicated in Iraqis, were also filling the hospital wards. Child mortality rates were soaring. Iraq would soon have the worst child mortality rate of all 188 countries measured by UNICEF.

In October 1991, an English journalist accused the Americans and British of waging their own form of biological warfare. "We know about cholera but we destroy power plants and electricity supply, we deny by embargo the means for immediate repair. That is different from deliberately seeding and spreading the cholera virus only in the most etiolated fashion. It is different in the way that manslaughter is different to murder. . . . In this most lackadaisical and morally laidback way, we are killing people."[19]

The list of items blocked because they could conceivably be used to fabricate weapons of mass destruction or for other ulterior motives was as long as it was often absurd. A request to ship baby food to Iraq was blocked by the United States because that food could also be consumed by adults. Heart attack pills were vetoed because they contained a milligram of cyanide which—given tens of thousands of pills—could presumably add up to a lethal weapon; chlorine vital for treating the country's water supply was blocked for years because it could also be used for chemical weapons. Also declared verboten: spare parts for incubators, hospital air conditioning units, filters for water treatment plants, vaccines, children's clothes, cotton swabs and gauze for medical use, Ping Pong balls from Vietnam, and funeral shrouds. As President George H. W. Bush had promised when he was asked by reporters in August 1990 if the sanctions would cover food and other essentials: "Just watch: everything, everything."[20] The U.S. and Britain even blocked attempts to define what "humanitarian need" really meant.[21]

The sanctions bureaucracy itself was enough to discourage the most determined of traders. From the first request by an exporter to sell something to Iraq to the moment the item actually arrived in Baghdad or Basra, two years often dragged by. If in the interval a change of model or price intervened, it was necessary to start the whole process over again. This gauntlet was not the fault of a punctilious U.N. bureaucracy but simply another measure employed by the U.S. and Britain to throttle Iraq.[22] Iraqi engineers cannibalized ruined power plants and sewage treatment facilities to keep others going, but it was a losing game. Their makeshift repairs broke down; there were soon no more parts to cannibalize.[23]

There is no question that U.S. planners knew what the awful impact of the sanctions on top of the wholesale destruction of civilian infrastructure would be. The health calamity had first been predicted and was then carefully followed by the Pentagon. In January 22, 1991, after six months of sanctions and as the bombing campaign was about to get underway, the Pentagon's Defense Intelligence Agency produced a detailed nine-page study chillingly entitled "Iraq Water Treatment Vulnerabilities as of 18 January."[24]

According to the report, Iraq's rivers "contain biological materials, pollutants, and are laden with bacteria." Chemicals for water treatment, the DIA study noted, "are depleted or nearing depletion." Because of the sanctions, chlorine supplies were "critically low." Unless the water is purified with chlorine, "epidemics of such diseases as cholera, hepatitis, and typhoid could occur."

The sanctions thus posed a deadly challenge to Iraq:

> With no domestic sources of both water treatment replacement parts and some essential chemicals, Iraq will continue attempts to circumvent United Nations sanctions to import these vital commodities. Failing to secure supplies will result in a shortage of pure drinking water for much of the population. This could lead to increased incidences, if not epidemics, of disease.
>
> Unless water treatment supplies are exempted from the U.N. sanctions for humanitarian reasons, no adequate solution exists for Iraq's water purification dilemma.

Because pharmaceutical manufacturers and food processing facilities require very pure water, those industries were also threatened.

This was only one of several DIA studies made over the following months chronicling the lethal impact of the bombing and sanctions on the population of Iraq. Another report dated January 22 looked at "Effects of Bombing on Disease Occurrence in Baghdad." Concluding the obvious, it predicted there would be an upsurge in diseases throughout Iraq. The impact would affect "particularly children."[25] The DIA cautioned there was a P.R. downside: the Iraqi government may "blame the United States for public health problems created by the military conflict."[26]

Another DIA report, from February 21, 1991,[27] confirms that "conditions are favorable for communicable disease outbreaks, particularly in major urban areas affected by coalition bombing. . . . Most likely diseases during next sixty–ninety days (descending order): diarrheal diseases (particularly children); acute respiratory illnesses (colds and influenza); typhoid; hepatitis A (particularly children); measles, diphtheria, and pertussis (particularly children); meningitis, including meningococcal (particularly children); cholera (possible, but less likely)." The author of the report cautions once again that the Iraqi government might "propagandize increases of endemic diseases."

Similar DIA documents were prepared in March and May.[28] By June 1991, the reports were cataloging rather than predicting epidemics:

> Source observed that Iraqi medical system was in considerable disarray, medical facilities had been extensively looted, and almost all medicines were in critically short supply. . . . In one refugee camp at least 80 percent of the population has diarrhea. . . . Cholera, hepatitis type B, and measles have broken out. . . . In the south, 80 percent of the deaths were children (with the exception of Al Amarah, where 60 percent of deaths were children).[29]

Contaminated water was the major killer of young Iraqis. Added to that was a disastrous shortage of food, which meant malnutrition for some, starvation and death for others. Without the money to import food, Iraq only averted total chaos with the rationing system imposed by the government in September 1990. A World Health Organization (WHO)/Food and Agriculture Organization study in February 1991, before the Gulf War was over, estimated that the daily per-capita calorie intake had fallen from the pre-sanction levels of 3,340 calories per person to less than 1,000 calories—one third of the WHO recommended levels.[30] The U.N. undersecretary general reported in March 1991 that "widespread starvation was a real possibility.[31]

There was a third component to the killing machine created by the war and the sanctions. Just as the health of Iraqis was being assaulted by severe food shortages and contaminated drinking water, the medical system, once the country's pride, was careening toward total collapse.

Already by March 1991, hospitals suffered major shortages of everything from electricity to run their air conditioners to incubators, surgical devices, syringes, intravenous fluids, ambulances, and the most basic drugs. Before sanctions, Iraq had imported 80 percent of its medicines. Afterward, drug imports slowed to a trickle. Pharmacies were massively depleted.[32] Medical supplies like spare parts for X-ray machines and incubators were either vetoed outright by members of the Sanctions Committee—mainly the U.S. and Britain—or subject to lengthy and deliberate bureaucratic delays.

In one outrageous example, more than fifty separate consignments of medicines and thousands of tons of infant formula and milk powder that had been purchased by the Iraqi government *before* the sanctions were instituted were held up by governments that refused to authorize shipment. As early as February 7, 1991, the Red Crescent Society of Iraq estimated that the medical and food shortages caused by the blockade in addition to the bombing, which had destroyed the only plant for making infant formula in the country, had already resulted in 3,000 infant deaths.[33] One American health professional said that many hospitals had been reduced to "mere reservoirs of infection."[34]

Because of malnutrition and the lack of medical facilities, what used to be minor medical problems became virtual death sentences. Babies were dying in incubators after power failures; other infants would grow up crippled with cerebral palsy because of insufficient oxygen supplies.

Lacking medicines, some pharmacies were obliged to refuse service to 90 percent of the people seeking treatment.[35]

From April 28 to May 6, a Harvard medical team visited Iraq and concluded the country was experiencing "an emergency public health catastrophe."[36] One doctor told the team, "We have lost patients because we don't have any instruments. We can't monitor cardiac patients because the monitors don't work. We have radiological equipment but no x-ray paper." The resident pediatrician at Basra General Hospital reported that over a third of Iraqi children between the ages of one and two were now malnourished. Outpatient visitors were coming to the hospital just to get formula, but the hospital didn't even have enough for its own patients.[37]

On September 23, 1991, President Bush would declare, "Our argument has never been with the people of Iraq. It was and is with a brutal dictator whose arrogance dishonors the Iraqi people. We must keep the United Nations sanctions in place as long as he remains in power. This is not to say that we should punish the Iraqi people."[38]

Yet, as American officials well knew, that is exactly what U.S. policy was doing. Denis Halliday, the former U.N. humanitarian coordinator for Iraq who ultimately resigned in protest of the sanctions, declared that "the U.S. theory behind the sanctions was that if you hurt the people of Iraq and kill the children particularly, they'll rise up with anger and overthrow Saddam."[39]

A country that had managed to achieve European levels of growth in the 1980s was being rammed back to sub-Saharan status. The once thriving middle class—which would have been the focal point of opposition to Saddam Hussein—was being annihilated.[40] Street corners teemed with people selling jewelry, carpets, rare books, TVs, clothing—anything to be able to buy food and medicines. Without access to hard currency, no one could travel. Most communication with the outside world was cut off.[41] A mass exodus of foreign contractors, engineers, nurses, and doctors added to the collapse. There was an explosion of crime and prostitution. Smuggling and kickbacks caused by the sanctions were creating a new flamboyant class of the wealthy. Corruption flourished in all ranks of what had formerly been a government known for its relative honesty. It was a question of survival.

bomb. Administration "hard-liners," the report added, worried that "the first sign of a 'smoking gun' . . . may be a mushroom cloud."[33]

The next day, the Sunday morning talk shows were blanketed with top administration officials primed to talk about the previously classified information. Condoleezza Rice allowed that "there will always be some uncertainty about how quickly he [Saddam] can acquire nuclear weapons." But, she said, using the marketing slogan the administration had settled upon, "we don't want the smoking gun to be a mushroom cloud."[34]

"Imagine," said Donald Rumsfeld, "a September Eleventh with weapons of mass destruction. It's not three thousand—it's tens of thousands of innocent men, women, and children."[35]

The aluminum tubes would become the key to the administration's case for war.[36] The public, however, had no way of knowing that the tubes had been the subject of heated debate within the intelligence community, with strong dissents from experts from the State Department and the Department of Energy, who had the most direct experience in the field. Contrary to analysts in the CIA and DIA, they maintained that the tubes were not at all suitable for enriching uranium. More likely, they were destined for use as conventional battlefield rockets—which later turned out to be the case.[37] However, it was the CIA's view that prevailed; dissenting scientists were expected to remain silent.[38]

The downplaying and suppression of information that might undermine the push for war became standard practice. Regardless of the uncertainty around the exact status of Saddam's weapons of mass destruction program, it was clear that the greatest threats of terrorism and WMD came from other nations. However, even as the administration trumpeted the supposedly imminent nuclear threat from Saddam, they buried the fact that U.S. intelligence agencies had uncovered a much graver threat from North Korea and Pakistan. In June 2002, the CIA had revealed to President Bush and his key advisors that, since 1997, Pakistan had been "sharing sophisticated technology, warhead design information, and weapons-testing data with North Korea, including how to conceal their nuclear research from the U.S. and South Korea."[39] The Bush administration sat on the CIA report; the White

By the summer of 1991, the United Nations was in the absurd position of attempting to raise funds to stave off the humanitarian crisis in Iraq, even as that crisis was being caused by the U.N. Security Council's own sanctions. As one U.N. worker put it, "We first break their legs; then we offer them a crutch."[42]

In the face of mounting domestic and foreign criticism, Washington introduced a new Security Council resolution in August 1991. It would allow Iraq to sell $1.6 billion of oil to purchase vital humanitarian supplies. In fact, that resolution was a public relations ploy. As an official in the Bush administration admitted to the *New York Times*, the resolution "was a good way to maintain the bulk of sanctions and not be on the wrong side of a potentially emotional issue."[43] The $1.6 billion represented less than a quarter of the $6.8 billion that the U.N.'s own investigative commission reported was urgently needed by the country. In addition, a third of the money generated by the petroleum sales would not go to relieve the humanitarian crisis, but to petroleum-rich Kuwait as reparations for Iraq's invasion as well as to the United Nations itself to pay the expenses of the U.N. weapons inspectors in Iraq. Finally, the entire scheme would be administered by the Sanctions Committee and the U.N., which meant there was no guarantee the funds would be disbursed according to Iraq's real needs. This was, after all, the same committee that had blocked the import of disinfectants, sanitary towels, and syringes.

Iraq rejected the proposal, saying it was inadequate and an attack on its national sovereignty; Iraq would become nothing more than a "U.N. trusteeship." In fact, Saddam hoped to negotiate a deal with the Security Council that would give him more power; he was using his own people as pawns. The U.S. was playing the same game and refused any serious changes. The standard reply of U.S. officials to anyone asking about the damage being caused by the sanctions was that a band of international do-gooders, leftist journalists, and anti-Americans was swallowing the lies of Saddam's propagandists and wildly exaggerating the plight of the people of Iraq.

Certainly Saddam was hoping to create such overwhelming revulsion for the sanctions abroad that the United States and Britain would finally be forced to back down. The United States, however, was also still using the horrors of the sanctions to provoke the Iraqis to overthrow Saddam. Indeed, the horrors were considerable. In October 1991, a report by a Harvard team of lawyers and international public health specialists estimated that deaths among children under 5 had nearly quintupled since the Gulf War; almost one million children were malnourished and as many as 100,000 were currently starving to death.[44] Yet by the fall of 1991, many American officials already realized they were backing a failed policy. As a senior U.S. official privately admitted to a reporter, a popular uprising against Saddam "is the least likely alternative."[45]

The Sanctions under Clinton

Though the official reason for maintaining the sanctions was to oblige Saddam to give up his WMD, the Americans were not overly concerned about the problem. They felt they had already destroyed Iraq's major weapons facilities. In fact, their bombs and rockets had missed many key installations, which their intelligence agencies didn't even know existed. They had no knowledge, for instance, that Saddam's scientists had made great progress in enriching uranium and had developed sophisticated binary chemicals, biological weapons, and a missile with a range in excess of 1200 miles.[46]

Saddam realized his enemies ignored much of what his scientists had accomplished, and he was eager to rebuild his WMD program. He initially assumed the sanctions would be short lived; in the meantime, he counted on corrupting the weapons inspectors from the newly formed United Nations Special Commission (Unscom) and infiltrating the organization with his spies. As he told his intelligence chief General Wafiq al-Samarrai, "The Special Commission is a temporary measure. We will fool them and we will bribe them and the matter will be over in a few months."[47] He also figured that, though the U.S. and Britain might be intent on maintaining the sanctions, the other great powers, eager to do business with Iraq, would soon lose patience.

Saddam's strategy was to give up his standard chemical weapons, since their existence was already well known, but to conceal his advances in other areas. However, in June 1991, armed with information from a defector, the Unscom inspectors discovered several "calutrons," centrifuges to enrich uranium, that Saddam's engineers had clandestinely developed.[48] At that point the Iraqis decided to secretly destroy the remainder of their forbidden weapons in their entirety in order to keep the extent of their capabilities hidden. That way, they calculated, they could at least preserve the technical knowledge their scientists had amassed for use in the future, once Unscom had left the country.[49] Saddam was also concerned that if he admitted he had destroyed all his WMD, his enemies—especially Iran—might be emboldened to attack; his putative arsenal of WMD, as he saw it, was also useful in keeping the ever restless Shiites in line.

Over the following years, uncovering what Iraq's WMD programs had been up to became a game of cat and mouse: Unscom would accumulate new leads; the Iraqis would issue blanket denials and attempt to stymie inspections, then reluctantly give way under Unscom persistence and American threats of military action. The Iraqis would issue a revised "complete" list of what their WMD program had once entailed, swear that was it—and then the process would start all over again.

Those tactics provided the U.S. and Britain with all the ammunition they needed to maintain the sanctions. On the other hand, those two powers gave the Iraqi dictator little incentive to cooperate with Unscom. The U.S. and Britain continued to make it clear that only his departure would bring the end of sanctions. That stand was certainly far beyond the authorized goals of the U.N. Security Council resolution 687, which declared that once Iraq had complied with the demands of the Unscom inspectors, the sanctions "shall have no further force or effect."[50] But the judgment of whether or not Iraq complied would not be based on any objective standards but on the views of the members of the Security Council itself—and not necessarily the views of the majority. A vote to end the sanctions could be vetoed by any permanent council member acting on its own criteria, no matter what the degree of Iraq's cooperation. This meant that, in theory at least, the U.S. could maintain sanctions on Iraq forever. The only reason for Saddam to cooperate with the inspectors was to build up enough sympathy with the world community to oblige the U.S. and Britain to back off.

The people of Iraq were hostage to that standoff. They hoped that when Bill Clinton became president on January 20, 1993, U.S. policy might change, but by March 1993, it was clear those hopes were illusory. White House press secretary Dee Dee Myers announced, "It is inconceivable that Saddam Hussein could remain in power if he complied with all the U.N. sanctions." Whatever compliance there had been was simply a cynical ploy by Saddam. The dictator could never be trusted.[51]

President Clinton was intent on proving that he, too, could be tough with Saddam. On June 27, he authorized a barrage of twenty-three tomahawk missiles against Baghdad. The attack was belated retaliation for an alleged attempt by Saddam to assassinate former president George Bush during a celebratory visit to Kuwait in April 1993. Though the million dollar missiles targeted the headquarters of the Iraqi intelligence service, a couple went off track: eight civilians were killed, including Iraq's most gifted artist. It later turned out that the evidence for the supposed bomb plot—which had been supplied to the FBI by the Kuwaitis—was tenuous at best.[52] But few Americans paid attention to such fine points. The day after the attack, Clinton's approval rating jumped 11 percent.[53]

Meanwhile the U.S. and Britain continued moving the goal posts, changing the definition of what would constitute compliance with the U.N. resolution in order for Iraq to have sanctions removed. In July 1993, the U.S. ambassador to the U.N., Madeleine Albright, declared Saddam would first have to abandon his WMD research and that Rolf Ekeus, the head of Unscom, would have to monitor Iraq for another six to twelve months to verify the abandonment of those programs. That was just the first step. The second was that Baghdad would have to prove its "readiness to rejoin society." Such determinations as the U.S. put forward were deliberately vague; nothing would remove the sanctions but the fall of Saddam.

In 1993, an employee of the U.S. Census Bureau almost lost her job when she attempted to publicize the deadly effects of the sanctions. Beth Osborne Daponte estimated that Iraqi life expectancy at birth had dropped from sixty-eight years in prewar Iraq to forty-seven years by 1992. Sixty thousand of those excess deaths, she said, were children under five. When the Census Bureau refused to issue Daponte's report, she objected; except for the intervention of the American Civil Liberties Union, she would have been fired.[54]

One of the NGOs attempting to bring medical supplies to Iraq was the British charity Medical Aid for Iraq (MAI). In early 1993, it noted that hospitals now lacked even the most basic supplies; one doctor described Iraq as "a concentration camp with a population of 18 million, one third of which are children—of whom at least a hundred thousand are already dead, not from war but from hunger."[55]

On May 31, 1994, *The Times* of London published the anguished letter of a British physician, Dr. Harvey Marcovitch, who had been working in Iraq. It was entitled "Saddam's Atrocity—Or Ours?" He described the desperation of families attempting to buy medicines for their children: "Parents sell their belonging and even their homes, and even after bringing in the drugs the children are dying from uncontrolled infection."[56]

In December 1994, another MAI team reported that "the government's food rations, which were already inadequate, were cut again by a third. The wards were filled with sick and dying children for whom the hospitals could do virtually nothing. There was a reduced need for insulin: so many diabetic children have died. With no treatment available, many children were now being kept to die at home.[57]

Those reports were no more alarming than the situation described by the *New York Times* on October 25, 1994:

Children lie on filthy hospital beds, murmuring in pain as they die of diarrhea and pneumonia. Some of the Arab world's finest artists peddle their work for as little as $12 a painting. A 50-year-old retired policeman, victim of a stroke a year ago, limps from merchant to merchant in a food market looking for what he can afford on a pension driven down by inflation to the equivalent of $2 a month, barely enough to buy one chicken. . . . Unable to sell its oil and buy food, medicine and spare parts except under United Nations conditions that it refuses to accept, Iraq faces famine and economic collapse.[58]

Saddam and His WMD

Rather than weakening Saddam, the sanctions seemed to consolidate his hold on power. The rationing system set up by the government became vital to the survival of the Iraqi people, even though it provided less than a third of a person's nutritional requirements. Iraqis were so obsessed with simply keeping their families alive that there was little interest or energy to plot the overthrow of one of the most ruthless dictatorships on the planet.[59] "The people didn't hold Saddam responsible for their plight," Denis Halliday said. "They blamed the US and the UN for these sanctions and the pain and anger that these sanctions brought to their lives."[60]

Meanwhile, the sanctions had little impact on Saddam and his extended family. Wrote the *New York Times*, "Mr. Hussein, his two sons and potential political heirs, Uday and Qusay, and his Tikriti family clan continue to rule Iraq virtually as royalty. Behind the walls of sumptuous palaces and cordons of security men, Mr. Hussein remains invulnerable to public dissent, protected by an intelligence and security apparatus directed by Qusay and a handful of first cousins and other relatives."[61]

Saddam, however, was not invulnerable to high-level defections. In early 1995 his chief of military intelligence fled and, debriefed by Unscom inspectors, revealed the full extent of the dictator's discontinued biological weapons program—a program Saddam had denied ever having. On August 7, 1995, another, final blow to Saddam's WMD ambitions was delivered by his son-in-law, General Hussein Kamel, who had been in charge of Iraq's WMD programs. He suddenly showed up in Jordan along with his brother and Saddam's two daughters and asked for asylum. It was a stunning humiliation for Saddam and an unbelievable breakthrough for Unscom. As soon as they discovered his defection, the Iraqis attempt to preempt his expected revelations by turning over a huge trove of records detailing Iraq's WMD programs that they had concealed for years. It was Hussein Kamel, they claimed, who had been hiding them.[62]

The new information revealed Iraq's impressive progress with biological and binary chemical weapons, but it didn't lead to the actual recovery of any WMD. On the contrary, Hussein Kamel informed the startled inspectors that Iraq had secretly destroyed its prohibited weapons four years earlier.[63] That revelation brought a major shift in what was demanded of Iraq. Unscom insisted it was now up to Iraq to document the demise of every last Scud missile and vial of anthrax. Since the destruction had been carried out secretly and in no organized fashion by a small group of Saddam's most trusted forces, there was little documentation. How to prove a negative?

The problem was compounded by the fact that the U.S. now seemed unwilling to believe anything the Iraqis said, but were quick to credit any rumor of nonconventional weapons. Scott Ritter, a Marine Corps intelligence officer who worked with Unscom from September 1991 until 1998, reported that CIA officials regularly brought forward new claims of hidden WMD conveyed to them by exile groups. When Unscom inspectors reported back that the stories didn't check out, Washington refused to listen. Said Ritter, "The US intelligence community, when it came to Iraq, seemed interested only in maintaining the perception that the Iraqis were not telling the truth, regardless of what the facts showed."[64]

As the U.S. saw it, there was no way Saddam Hussein could ever be trusted. Even if many or all of his WMD had been destroyed, the scientists and engineers who had created those weapons were still in Iraq. As soon as the Unscom inspectors left, Saddam could be counted on to resume his diabolical quest. No one was safe as long as the Iraqi dictator remained in power.

By now it was clear that sanctions and the terrible sacrifices they were exacting from the people of Iraq would not rid the world of Saddam Hussein. But rather than ending the sanctions or simply modifying them to target those items truly crucial to building WMD, the Clinton administration continued its futile policy: decimating an entire nation in order to destroy one leader.

President Clinton had inherited the secret "lethal finding" signed by George H. W. Bush in October 1991, which authorized the CIA to work with Iraqi opposition groups to overthrow Saddam. The policy was known as "containment plus." At the beginning of the Clinton administration, the CIA had been relatively inactive in Iraq; now it was ordered into the fray. The result was a series of abject failures. After a disastrous attempt to work with the Kurds in northern Iraq in the spring of 1995, the CIA decided it would focus on orchestrating a coup in Baghdad. That scheme, controlled out of

Amman, Jordan, involved a network of military and government officials close to the Iraqi dictator.[65]

It also involved several Unscom inspectors, whom the CIA used as cover. Saddam Hussein had always charged that Unscom was a nest of spies, though most in the West wrote those accusations off as propaganda. But according to Scott Ritter, beginning in the summer of 1991, CIA agents pretending to be experts from the U.S. Department of State were planted with Unscom. Their true identity was unknown to most Unscom personnel. Over the following years, while supposedly aiding Unscom, the CIA operatives collected intelligence that went far beyond the scope of weapons inspection. Said Ritter, "Despite the assurances given by the U.S. government that the inspectors provided would do only the bidding of Unscom as set forth by the chief inspector, the reality was quite different. Each inspector worked for his or her own office back in Washington."[66]

Under Bill Clinton, U.S. policy makers continued to manipulate Unscom and its inspections for their own purposes. They were less interested in revealing Saddam's WMD program than in discrediting—and in the end destroying—Unscom to attain their own tactical ends. Thus, in 1996, CIA agents used their Unscom cover to intercept the communications of Saddam and his personal security forces so they could target their precise location for the coup they were organizing against Saddam from Amman.[67] Thanks to their Unscom role, the coup plotters were also able to communicate secretly with covert allies in Saddam's special presidential guard.[68]

But the CIA's plans to use Unscom in this coup went much further. The attack would be launched under cover of an American missile strike against the commanders of Saddam's personal security forces. The pretext for that strike would be a confrontation between Iraqi authorities and Unscom inspectors, a confrontation deliberately provoked by Unscom. Saddam's security units would be decapitated; the road would be open for the CIA-backed plotters in Iraq to take action.

The CIA plan began like clockwork: an Unscom team demanded access to facilities of Saddam's special Republican Guard. The Iraqis refused. On June 12, 1996, the Security Council deplored the refusal. Tension built. U.S. planes and missile ships were in position; everyone was primed. Then things fell apart. Saddam's own agents had infiltrated the plotters. At the key moment, they moved in, rounding up eight hundred people in all, including members of the tyrant's domestic staff: his cook, for instance, who was supposed to poison the Iraqi dictator. Reportedly, Iraqi intelligence agents couldn't resist one last radio transmission to the CIA controllers in Amman: "We have arrested all of your people," they crowed. "You might as well pack up and go home."[69] Indeed, the U.S. and British agents who had worked undercover on the Unscom team were recalled by their respective governments.

Saddam's spies had uncovered Unscom's role in the affair.[70] They understood, however, that most of the people running Unscom had no idea they were being used. Since the Iraqis still hoped for a favorable report from the inspectors, they decided to allow Unscom to continue its work.[71]

The CIA engaged in another disastrous operation that same year in northern Iraq. Though the U.S. had refused to back the Kurdish uprising in 1991, in 1996 a team of American agents was dispatched to Kurdistan to coordinate the efforts of Kurdish tribes and the Iraqi National Congress (INC), an exile organization headed by Ahmad Chalabi and financed from the outset by the CIA. Unfortunately, the two principal Kurdish tribes went to war against each other, which provoked one of the tribal leaders to call upon Saddam to intervene in the struggle. The sad tale ended with the U.S. refusing to honor the pledge made by George H. W. Bush in 1991 to protect the Kurdish enclave. Saddam moved his troops northward long enough to slaughter about two hundred hapless members of the INC, who had counted on U.S. protection.

After such a debacle, with U.S. presidential elections just a few weeks away, it was necessary for Bill Clinton to be seen doing something. On September 2 and 3, 1996, he sent forty-four cruise missiles from U.S. warships in the Persian Gulf to destroy Iraqi military targets. The Kurds might have questioned the symbolism of this "retaliation" against Saddam, as the targets were in southern Iraq, four hundred miles away from Kurdistan, but those were the sites—radar and missile installations—that the U.S. military had been itching to take out. The U.S. also extended the unilaterally declared no-fly zone in the south seventy-five miles further north. "We have choked Saddam in the south," U.N. Ambassador Madeleine Albright trumpeted unconvincingly. "We really whacked him."[72]

On September 19, CIA Director John Deutsch gave a more sober view of the recent U.S. failures. "Saddam," he admitted to the Senate Intelligence Committee, "is politically stronger now in the Middle East than he was before sending his troops into northern Iraq in recent weeks." Deutsch also confirmed that there was little possibility of Saddam being overthrown in the near future.[73]

In short, after spending several years and a hundred million dollars, the CIA and its exile allies had failed miserably in their attempts to overthrow Saddam. Despite that, the U.S. continued to maintain the lethal sanctions on the people of Iraq as if they could somehow achieve what the professionals had so ignominiously botched. As former U.S. ambassador to the U.N. Thomas Pickering admitted to me, the U.S. simply had no other policy.[74]

The Road to Nowhere

By March 1996, according to the WHO, child mortality had increased 600 percent since sanctions were imposed.[75] The regional manager of the World Food Program, Mona Hamman, declared that "70% of the population has little or no access to food. . . . Nearly everyone seems to be emaciated. . . . We are at the point of no return. The social fabric of the nations is disintegrating. People have exhausted their ability to cope."[76]

In 1996, a *60 Minutes* correspondent asked Madeleine Albright whether the value of the sanctions justified the deaths of half a million children in Iraq, "more children than died in Hiroshima." Was that price worth it?, the correspondent asked. "I think that is a very hard choice," Albright replied, "but the price, we think, the price is worth it."[77]

President Clinton himself reiterated in November 1997, "We are not interested in seeking a relaxation of sanctions as long as Saddam Hussein is in power. Sanctions will be there until the end of time, or as long as he [Saddam Hussein] lasts."

Many of the Unscom inspectors, however, were increasingly convinced they had uncovered the full extent of Saddam's WMD program.

In addition, there was mounting domestic and international pressure to do away with sanctions altogether. The coalition put together by George H. W. Bush, focused solely on driving Saddam from Kuwait, was no more. The Clinton administration was obliged to come up with a compromise that would allow the U.S. to keep a stranglehold on Iraq. It was embodied in Security Council Resolution 986 which, after considerable haggling, was finally accepted by Iraq on May 1996. Under its provisions, Iraq would be permitted to sell $1 billion worth of petroleum every ninety days.

It was billed as a major humanitarian measure: Oil for Food. In fact there was much less to the program than was claimed by its Western sponsors. According to the resolution, at least 30 percent of the funds generated by oil sales would, as with the last such program, go to Kuwait and the U.N. Many of those payments to Kuwait in fact went to American contractors doing business with that country.[78] That left $2.8 billion a year remaining to pay for 20 million Iraqis, which comes to $2 per Iraqi per week, less than thirty cents a day.

Further, the program was soon expanded to cover not just food, but all "humanitarian products." This meant that those thirty cents a day had to pay for everything from imported wheat and rice to vital spare parts for water-treatment plants and electric generators.[79] Compared to the needs of the shattered country, the new funds were a pitiful drop in the bucket. Denis Halliday, an Irish Quaker who oversaw disbursement for the U.N. of supplies purchased by the petroleum money, calculated that it would take ten to twenty years to rebuild Iraq's ravaged infrastructure. The electrical power system alone would require $10 billion.[80]

From the beginning the program was snarled in the tangle of new regulations imposed by Britain and the United States;[81] everything the country imported with those new revenues still had to run the Kafkaesque gauntlet of the Sanctions Committee. It took ten months before the first food supplies purchased by the program arrived in Iraq—at a time when children were dying at the rate of 4,500 per month.[82]

Meanwhile, U.S. conservatives, aligned with Iraqi exile leader Ahmad Chalabi, continued to push the Clinton administration for more aggressive action against Saddam. In February 1998, forty prominent Americans, including three former secretaries of defense, signed an open letter to Clinton warning that Saddam and his WMD still posed an imminent threat. As the pressure mounted from the Republican-dominated Congress, Clinton finally signed the Iraq Liberation Act, allocating $97 million for training and equipping the Iraqi opposition.[83]

That political pressure also drove the White House to continue manipulating Unscom's inspections as a means of destroying Saddam. In March 1998, American officials secretly arranged for Unscom's compliant new head, Australian Richard Butler, to provoke another confrontation with Iraq. It would give President Clinton a pretext to demonstrate he was still standing up to Saddam. The target of the next Unscom inspection would be Iraq's Ministry of Defense, a site so sensitive that the White House was certain the Iraqis would never allow the inspectors access. Butler briefed Scott Ritter, who would be leading the inspection. "We have to have a crisis with Iraq by this date," he said, according to Ritter. "I have been told that the U.S. has a bombing campaign prepared which needs to be completed in time for the Muslim religious holiday that begins on March 11."[84]

"I sat there stunned," Ritter wrote. "What I was observing was nothing less than total collusion between a United Nations official, Richard Butler, and the USA over military action that had not been sanctioned by the Security Council."[85] American officials were attempting to provoke an incident that would enable the United States government to declare that Unscom inspections were dead.

On March 8, as instructed, Ritter brought his team to the Ministry of Defense and demanded entry. Meanwhile, a British communication expert with Unscom fed the waiting CIA team the coordinates of the location of top Iraqi officials, including those closest to Saddam. Those coordinates were entered into the guidance system of cruise missiles being prepared for launch. But just as the U.S. was ready to let fly, the Iraqis, who by now grasped what was happening, announced that the Unscom inspectors could enter the Defense Ministry. Another chance to take out Saddam bit the dust.

The next Unscom team included structural engineers whose secret mission was to examine the potential vulnerability of Saddam's places to air attack. Unscom, said Ritter, had become "little more than an espionage tool to be used by the CIA to spy on Saddam Hussein."[86]

By October 1998, however, there was the feeling in Unscom that the inspections were finally nearing an end; there was nothing more to find. France, Russia, China, and U.N. Secretary General Kofi Annan were pushing for one final review to wind up the inspection process. Their idea was that instead of demanding that Iraq account for every last weapon it claimed to have destroyed, the U.N. would shift the burden of proof. Now it would be up to the accusers—the U.S. and England—to present convincing evidence that Iraq was still cheating. That effort was blocked by the British ambassador to the United Nations, Sarah Graham-Brown. As president of the Security Council, she dispatched a toughly worded letter to Baghdad demanding that Saddam let Unscom inspectors go anywhere and enter any facility they wanted, no matter how sensitive.[87] But at the same time, American and British leaders again publicly declared that, contrary to the original U.N. sanctions resolution, whether Saddam cooperated or not made no difference—the sanctions would be maintained as long as he was in power.[88]

The Iraqi dictator reacted angrily to Graham-Brown's letter, declaring that he would no longer cooperate with Unscom. The U.S. would later use that statement as proof that Iraq was to blame for ending inspections. In fact, Saddam sent a counterproposal, declaring Iraq was ready to continue cooperating—but pushed for a clear guarantee that, in return for Iraq's compliance, sanctions would end.

The U.S., however, planning another attack on Saddam, reacted to this unwanted diplomatic breakthrough by distorting the Iraqi response. Saddam, they claimed, was still thumbing his nose at the U.N. On November 11, after being warned by the acting U.S. ambassador to the U.N. that he would be wise to clear his people out of harm's way, Richard Butler directed Unscom inspectors to leave Baghdad. U.S. officials would later claim that Saddam ordered them out; in fact, they left to avoid the threatened American attack.

Once again, however, the U.S. was forced to abort its plans. On November 14, American B-52 bombers had already taken off from Louisiana bound for Baghdad when Tariq Aziz announced Iraq's agreement to renew the Unscom inspections.[89] On November 18, Unscom inspectors were back in Iraq.

In the end, the U.S. achieved its long-desired confrontation when twelve Unscom inspectors attempted to search a Baath Party regional headquarters in Baghdad on a trumped-up lead.[90] After objecting, the Iraqis finally agreed to admit the Unscom team, but stipulated that it be limited to four inspectors. The U.S. demanded that twelve more inspectors be admitted. "This time it worked," said Ritter. "The demand was denied."

Citing Iraq's intransigence, on December 14, 1998, Richard Butler—consulting with Clinton's national security advisor, Sandy Berger—wrote a starkly pessimistic report to the Security Council claiming that no progress had been made in the past few weeks.[91] U.N. Secretary General Kofi Annan tried to temper Butler's extreme views with a cover letter saying that the situation presented "a mixed picture." When the U.S. delegation to the U.N. received its copy of Annan's letter, a senior delegate later told reporters, "We tore it up."[92]

On December 15, the acting ambassador to the U.N., Peter Burleigh, again cautioned Richard Butler to be "prudent" with the safety and security of Unscom staff. Once again, the Unscom inspectors left on American advice—they were not thrown out by Saddam Hussein.[93]

On December 16, President Clinton unleashed Operation Desert Fox: four days of intensive American bombing and missile strikes. American officials said the strikes were in reprisal for Saddam's rejection of the inspection process—a breakdown that the U.S. had done so much to engineer. In what many took as more than coincidence, the strikes began on the same day the U.S. House of Representatives was to begin debate on the president's impeachment for the Monica Lewinsky affair.

William Arkin, a U.S. military analyst who studied the Desert Fox strikes, concluded their primary aim had nothing to do with suspected WMD sites, but instead with targeting Saddam Hussein's security apparatus—thanks in part, as the Pentagon later admitted, to intelligence supplied by Unscom.[94] Lasting only four days, Desert Fox did nothing to destabilize Saddam or make an effective show of U.S. strength; all it did was destroy Unscom. As Richard Butler himself wrote, it was "hard not to see Desert Fox as a failure, particularly because of its brevity. If one uses the test of looking rationally at outcomes, without ascribing motives, it could be argued that the death of Unscom also became U.S. policy, because that is what has happened."[95]

In December 1999, after months of wrangling, a new U.N. resolution created a new inspection force, Unmovic. Though the U.S. continued to claim it had information that Saddam's WMD program was still alive and well and menacing, it didn't seem particularly eager to get Unmovic inspectors back to Baghdad. Clinton was leaving office, and a well-functioning U.N. inspection program would only undermine the still-unannounced resolve of the George W. Bush administration to invade Iraq.

Meanwhile, the people of Iraq would continue to pay the price for Saddam's having endured. In September 1988, Denis Halliday quit as United Nations humanitarian coordinator in Iraq, after holding the job for one year. He refused, he later told me, to administer a program that was responsible for the deaths of anywhere between 500,000 to one million Iraqis, mostly children, but also adults—a program he referred to as "genocide."[96]

In 1999, responding to growing international and domestic pressure, the U.S. and Britain agreed to remove the limits on Iraq's oil sales under the sanctions. There would be more food available, but the sanctions still wreaked terrible hardships. The simple fact is that Iraq didn't have much petroleum to sell. The country's ability to pump oil had been crippled by the bombings and sanctions. Of the $64 billion earned during the period of the Oil for Food program, because of contracts blocked by the Sanctions Committee and payments that were obliged to go to Kuwait and the U.N., only $28 billion actually arrived in Iraq. That amounted to $170 per person per year, which, as one analyst pointed out, is less than one half the annual per capita income of Haiti, the most destitute nation of the Western Hemisphere. Iraqi diplomats pointed out that the sum was also far less than what the U.N. budgets for dogs used in Iraqi de-mining operations (about $400 per dog per year on imported food).[97]

A few years later, in an Orwellian slight of hand, British and American leaders would attempt to blame those appalling conditions on Saddam

Hussein, rather than the sanctions. In fact, on March 27, 2003, British Prime Minister Tony Blair actually cited the dramatic increase in infant mortality to *justify* the invasion. As if the sanctions didn't exist, he declared that 400,000 Iraqi children had "died because of the nature of the regime under which they are living. Now, that is why we're acting."[98]

On March 25, 2003, Andrew Natsios, the administrator for the U.S. Agency for International Development, declared, "Water and sanitation are the principal reasons children have died at higher rates than they should have for a middle-income country. It is a function of a deliberate decision by the regime not to repair the water system or replace old equipment with new equipment, so in many cases people are basically drinking untreated sewer water in their homes and have been for some years."[99]

On October 7, 2002, President Bush blamed the woes of the Iraqi people on Saddam's unquenchable desire for weapons. "The world has also tried economic sanctions," Bush declared, "and watched Iraq use billions of dollars in illegal oil revenues to fund more weapons purchases, rather than providing for the needs of the Iraqi people."[100]

There is no question that Saddam ripped off money during the sanctions regime to attempt to rebuild his military machine and support his lavish lifestyle and that of his sons, but that point obscures the basic issue: Iraq's needs were enormous. Its economic output had plunged from $60 billion a year to $13 billion. Even if Saddam had invested everything he skimmed from the sanctions into rebuilding his country and feeding his people, those sums would have never prevented the colossal devastation that sanctions brought about. It should also be noted that, although Saddam took in about $10 billion by smuggling petroleum to neighboring countries, the Volcker Commission set up to investigate charges of corruption under the sanctions regime found that the great bulk of those illicit activities were known—and accepted—by the U.S.-dominated Sanctions Committee. Because the other countries involved in the smuggling—Turkey, Jordan, and Syria—had powerful allies on the Security Council, the delegates closed their eyes to what was going on.[101]

The same was true of the estimated $1.8 billion that Saddam raked off from the Oil for Food program. It came from the power he had been granted by the Security Council to decide who could buy Iraq's petroleum, and who would get contracts for relief aid. Everyone knew the system was an invitation for Saddam to demand a commission from each deal; it was a bribe of sorts to get Saddam's consent to a more humane program that would temper the mounting criticism worldwide of the sanctions regime. Rights to purchase Iraqi petroleum were also used as payoffs to Iraq's allies around the world.[102]

On the other hand, when U.S. officials claimed Saddam was ripping off humanitarian shipments, the U.N. responded with figures that demonstrated that, to the contrary, the distribution system was working extremely well. The Americans, however, were not interested in such facts. "They ignored the studies," said Hans Von Sponeck, who had replaced Denis Halliday as head of U.N. humanitarian operations in Iraq. "The Americans continued to argue that food never reached the people, that the medicines were never put on the market. They ridiculed the Unicef mortality figures, they considered it Iraqi propaganda."

In 2000, Von Sponeck also quit his post. "My conscience said that I can not be associated with such a program," he declared. German born, with a fine sense of moral outrage, Von Sponeck had thought that by bringing the awful reality of the sanctions to the attention of Security Council members, he could convince them to moderate their policies. But the powers who controlled the Security Council were not interested in being told how woefully inadequate the program was, said Von Sponeck, "because that would have added tremendous moral pressure on the Council to do something about it."[103] Nor were most American officials interested in the problem. When Von Sponeck briefed State Department officials and described the desperate plight of the Children's Hospital in Baghdad, they replied, "Oh, you went to the propaganda hospital."

"No one listened," said Von Sponeck, "because the Oil for Food program was not meant to run well. It was made to be a daily reminder of a punishment. The Oil for Food program was a fig leaf of the international conscience."

The situation was exacerbated by the continued determination of the U.S. and Britain to block "dual-use" items critical to Iraq's health system and rebuilding its infrastructure. As of July 2001 more than $5 billion worth of such goods were on hold.[104] Even as U.N. inspectors determined that Saddam's WMD programs were history, the U.S. increasingly blocked humanitarian supplies. For every contract directed at rehabilitating the water system that was unblocked in August 2001, three new contracts were put on hold. Between the spring of 2000 and the spring of 2002, holds on humanitarian goods tripled.[105]

Confronted by growing outrage over the sanctions at home and abroad, the administration of George W. Bush proposed a switch to "smart sanctions" that would supposedly target Saddam and his family rather than the people of Iraq.

Conceivably, a program of "smart sanctions," whose goal really was to block imports of key components for WMD programs—particularly the development of nuclear weapons—might have been effective in conjunction with continued U.N. inspections. But that is not what the U.S. and Britain had in mind. Instead, they continued their futile attempts to use the sanctions as a way of provoking the overthrow of Saddam Hussein himself. Ironically, the suffering that policy continued to cause the people of Iraq was one of the main factors leading to undermining the sanctions—the rest of the world was no longer willing to go along with such ruthless measures.

Indeed, the program of "smart sanctions" that was finally set up by the U.N. in May 2002 was still rigged to give the U.S. and Britain the power to veto imports into Iraq that they considered potentially dangerous. For instance, they continued blocking the import of vaccines desperately needed to combat the diseases killing thousands of children a month. The vaccines, according to U.S. officials, had dangerous dual-use potential—until the *Washington Post* and Reuters revealed the scandal and the U.S. abruptly announced it could lift the ban.

In May 2002, Unmovic inspectors reviewed the holds that had been placed on $5 billion worth of goods and found that very few of them were truly security concerns. As a result, hundreds of such purposeless holds were finally lifted. That should have had an immediate and beneficial impact on Iraq. It didn't. To the end, the U.S. and Britain continued to come up with new machinations to block Iraq's sales of petroleum as well as the import of humanitarian supplies.[106]

By the time the sanctions were finally removed on May 22, 2003, after the U.S.-led invasion, an entire generation of Iraqis had been decimated by the failed policy. A Unicef study in 1999 concluded that half a million Iraqi children perished in the previous eight years because of the sanctions—and that was four years before they ended. Another American expert on sanctions in 2003 estimated that the sanctions had killed between 343,900 to 529,000 young children and infants.[107] The exact number will never be known. It was, however, certainly more young people than were ever killed by Saddam Hussein.

A few individuals who have studied the matter, including former U.S. attorney general Ramsey Clark, and two officials who administered the U.N.'s humanitarian relief program in Iraq, Hans Von Sponeck and Denis Halliday, argue that the sanctions constituted a crime of war against the people of Iraq, and that the U.S. and Great Britain should be charged.

According to the articles of the Geneva Convention:

1. Starvation of civilians as a method of warfare is prohibited.
2. It is prohibited to attack, destroy, remove or render useless objects indispensable to the civilian population . . . foodstuffs, crops, livestock, drinking water installations, and supplies and irrigation works, for the specific purpose of denying them for their sustenance value to the civilian population.[108]

The studies by the Pentagon's Defense Intelligence Agency of the devastating impact of the bombings and sanctions on the health of millions of Iraqis cited earlier in this chapter indicate that American planners knew well what they were doing. This prickly issue has received virtually no attention from the American media. It will certainly not be dealt with at the trial of Saddam Hussein.

Beyond the massive deaths and destruction of infrastructure, the sanctions had another, equally devastating, but less visible impact. Drawing on comparisons with other devastated countries such as Uganda, Sudan, and Mozambique, a group of Harvard medical researchers found that the children of Iraq were "the most traumatized children of war ever described." Four out of five children interviewed were fearful of losing their families; two thirds doubted whether they themselves would survive to adulthood. The experts concluded that a majority of Iraq's children would suffer from severe psychological problems throughout their lives. "The trauma, the loss, the grief, the lack of prospects, the feeling of threat here and now, that it will all start again, the impact of the sanctions, make us ask if these children are not the most suffering child population on earth."[109]

It is that generation of children, it should not be forgotten, that is coming to power in Iraq today.

CHAPTER NINE

The Noble Lie : The Invasion of Iraq
January 2000–March 19, 2003

On March 17, 2003, President George W. Bush, in a television address to the nation, declared that he had ordered military action against Iraq. Rather than implement a more targeted form of sanctions to keep Saddam disarmed, Bush would engage in what he solemnly called a preemptive action to defend the American people from the Iraq-Al-Qaeda nexus. There was "no doubt that the Iraq regime continues to possess and conceal some of the most lethal weapons ever devised."[1] The U.S. was not going to sit back and wait for Iraq to turn it over to its terrorist allies. Yet the charges the president used to justify the invasion had already been strongly challenged or contradicted by America's own intelligence agencies, which had failed to find any connection with Al-Qaeda or 9/11 and had serious doubts about the threat of Saddam's weapons of mass destruction program.

In fact, it was not these particular security concerns but ideology coupled with an almost primal desire to demonstrate American power in the aftermath of 9/11 that finally led to Saddam's ouster. A small group of ideologues in the executive branch—the neoconservatives—had succeeded in creating an imaginary threat that allowed them to hijack the foreign policy of the most powerful nation on the globe and take it in an alarming new direction. They believed that, in the wake of the Cold War, America must use its unequaled power to reshape the world. In pursuit of that goal, they would play on the fears of the American people, the cowardice of its elected representatives, the timidity of the media, and the messianic instincts of an American president with a profound belief that his foreign policy was an expression of God's will. They would target Saddam, not because he was the most imminent threat to America's security, but because he wasn't.

Backdrop to War

The neoconservatives, some of whom had been radical leftists in the 1960s and 1970s, regarded themselves as a revolutionary vanguard. They were unabashed advocates of in-your-face American power, global dominance, and "benevolent hegemony." With the end of the Cold War, neoconservatives believed, multilateral organizations like the United Nations could no longer be counted on to preserve world peace and stability; the role fell instead to the globe's only surviving superpower.[2] The U.S. was obliged to use its status and, if necessary, its military power to stop the spread of nuclear arms and thwart the emergence of any potential rival—if need be, by preemptive action. The world had become too dangerous a place to wait for foes to attack: with its overwhelming military superiority, America now had the ability to take out potential enemies before they could even launch an assault. To advance these ideas, the neocons formed a think tank, the Project for the New American Century (PNAC). Among the signers of their mission statement in 2000 were Donald Rumsfeld, George W. Bush's brother Jeb Bush, Paul Wolfowitz, and Dick Cheney.

These men were crucial in determining the makeup of the George W. Bush administration. Cheney, who would become the most influential vice president in modern American history, oversaw staffing for the administration and filled key posts with neoconservative ideologues. Their influence was particularly pervasive at the Pentagon under Secretary of Defense Donald Rumsfeld. Paul Wolfowitz was made deputy secretary of defense, the second most powerful post in the Pentagon; Douglas Feith, a fervid neoconservative supporter of Israel's hard-line Likud Party, became the influential undersecretary for policy. They were joined in the administration by other backers of Israel's radical right, Richard Perle and David Wurmser.

In 2000, as self-appointed private counselors to Israeli Prime Minister Benjamin Netanyahu, they had written a study, "A Clean Break: A New Strategy for Securing the Realm," advocating that Israel abandon the "land for peace" negotiating policy as bankrupt.[3] Israel should instead impose terms on the Palestinians through military force.

The neocons were similarly determined to use their new power in Washington for a wide range of goals, from ensuring the security of Israel and American control over the oil of the Gulf to preventing nuclear proliferation, replacing tyranny with democracy, and ensuring a stable peace.[4] They were also determined to topple Saddam Hussein. "Whoever inherits Iraq," they wrote, "dominates the entire Levant strategically."[5] In September 2000, in fact, the PNAC issued a new declaration in which the authors made it clear that overthrowing Saddam was just a means to a strategic end: "While the unresolved conflict with Iraq provides the immediate justification," they bluntly stated, "the need for substantial American force presence in the Gulf transcends the issue of the regime of Saddam Hussein."[6] The roots of this policy are deep. Wolfowitz had Saddam in his sights as early as 1991, when he had argued that the U.S., rather than abandoning the Shiite and Kurd rebels, should have helped them remove Saddam. Since then, Saddam had continued to tyrannize his people and flout U.N. inspectors while protecting his WMD. Once the sanctions collapsed, Saddam would reemerge as a major threat to Israel and the rest of the region. He had to be destroyed.[7] Working together with other similarly minded officials strategically placed throughout the Bush administration, Wolfowitz and the other neocons would lead the country inexorably toward that goal.

They had a willing audience in George W. Bush. Even before he was elected, Bush was talking privately in 1999 about the political benefits of attacking Iraq.[8] He would destroy Saddam Hussein, as his father never could. There was also an element of revenge: he believed the charge that the Iraqi tyrant had attempted to assassinate George H. W. Bush when the former president visited Kuwait after the first Gulf War. "He tried to kill my dad," the younger Bush frequently said.[9]

When George W. Bush took office in January 2001, the view of some of his advisors, such as Secretary of State Colin Powell, was that

Saddam Hussein had been so weakened by sanctions that he did not represent a serious menace to anyone. He no longer possessed any significant weapons of mass destruction, and whatever future ambitions he had could be contained with a more focused program of "smart" sanctions.[10] The U.S. needed to get on with more vital global issues. In his first briefings to the president, CIA director George Tenet barely mentioned Iraq.[11]

But long before 9/11, from the first high-level National Security Council meeting on January 20, 2001, Bush made it clear his chief concerns were not terrorism, China, Russia, or the threat of nuclear proliferation from North Korea and Iran. He had three prime objectives: getting rid of Saddam Hussein, tilting to Israel's Ariel Sharon, and reinforcing the strength of the United States in the Middle East. "From the very first instance, it was about Iraq," said Bush's treasury secretary, Paul O'Neill. "It was all about finding a way to do it. That was the tone of it. The president saying: 'Go find me a way to do this.'"[12]

A way presented itself in the aftermath of the 9/11 attacks on New York and Washington. Wolfowitz and Rumsfeld immediately suggested that Al-Qaeda couldn't be acting on its own; Saddam must be involved.[13] On the evening of September 12, 2001, President Bush told a small group of advisors at the White House, "I know you have a lot to do and all . . . but I want you, as soon as you can, to go back over everything, everything, see if Saddam did this. See if he's linked in any way. . . . I want to know any shred."[14]

What was driving Bush and Rumsfeld and the neocons as much as any desire to finally destroy Saddam Hussein was a much broader determination to hit back, to demonstrate to the world that, despite 9/11, the United States was still the preeminent power on the globe to be reckoned with—and to be feared. Going after the Taliban and Bin Laden in Afghanistan was just the prelude. The administration wanted a bigger, more impressive target. Saddam was ideal, even if he did not represent the greatest threat to global security at that moment. Indeed, North Korea and Iran, with their ongoing nuclear weapons programs, were a much more ominous threat than Saddam Hussein, who had no active WMD program at all. But North Korea and Iran would also be much more daunting military opponents; Saddam's forces, on the other hand, had been crippled by the first Gulf War and the decade of sanctions. Invading Iraq was doable—which is why it was done.[15]

President Bush's antiterrorism chief, Richard Clarke, who vainly argued against targeting Saddam at that time, later wrote, "I doubt that anyone ever had the chance to make the case to him [Bush] that attacking Iraq would actually make America less secure and strengthen the broader radical Islamic terrorism movement. Certainly he did not hear that from the small circle of advisors who alone are the people whose views he respects and trusts."[16]

On November 21, 2001, based on the president's orders, Donald Rumsfeld instructed General Tommy Franks, who was already overseeing military operations in Afghanistan and the hunt for Bin Laden, to begin secretly drawing up a plan for attacking Iraq.[17] By December 1991, unnamed senior American diplomats in the Middle East were already announcing that military action against Saddam was just a matter of time.[18]

A month later, in his State of the Union address, the president branded Iraq part of an "Axis of Evil." "The United States of America," he warned "will not permit the world's most dangerous regimes to threaten us with the world's most destructive weapons."[19] At West Point on June 1, 2002, the president publicly proclaimed his sweeping new policy of preemption. The U.S. had the unilateral right, Bush declared, to overthrow any government in the world it judged a threat to American security. The menaces of terrorism and weapons of mass destruction had become so horrific that the United States could no longer sit and wait for the threat to become immediate. "If we wait for threats to fully materialize, we will have waited too long," Bush declared.[20] Ideally, the U.S. would carry out this policy within the framework of the United Nations; if not, it would act with ad hoc "coalitions of the willing"; if necessary, it would go it alone. Officials quickly dubbed this the "Bush Doctrine." The subtext was America would do whatever it thought was right for the benefit of its people and the world at large.

The president still publicly maintained he had made no decision about invading Iraq, but by August 2002, General Franks had spent close to $700 million quietly preparing the military groundwork in the Gulf. The CIA had spent $189 million for the same effort.[21] That same month, the first phase of the war was initiated under the guise of protecting the no-fly zones of southern Iraq. British and American planes launched an intensive bombing campaign targeting Iraq's sophisticated air defense capabilities, without the authorization of the U.N. Security Council. Tony Blair had already promised the president he would back a move against Saddam.

President Bush, however, had no congressional green light for the military action he had planned. Indeed, the Americans and British were still attempting to cobble together a convincing case as to why the military buildup in the Gulf, which had already taken on a momentum of its own, was really necessary. The neocons in the administration realized that their overarching goal of establishing a U.S. presence in the Middle East and making the region safer for Israel was not something that the American people would be willing to go to war to achieve. Many neocons were followers of philosopher Leo Strauss, a refugee from Nazi Germany. One of the major themes of his work was the vulnerability of liberal democracies in an increasingly hostile world.[22] Strauss maintained that statesmen must depend on the counsel of wise advisors. He also espoused the Platonic idea of "the noble lie," according to which enlightened philosophers may have to create useful myths to propagate their policies, because the man in the street—and even many leaders—might not be wise enough to act correctly on the basis of the truth alone. The threat of Saddam's WMD and his supposed links to Al-Qaeda became that noble lie.

As Paul Wolfowitz admitted many months after the U.S. invaded Iraq, "The truth is that, for reasons that have a lot to do with the U.S. government bureaucracy, we settled on the one issue that everyone could agree on, which was weapons of mass destruction."[23] That issue, however, would not be enough. A preemptive strike against Iraq could only be justified within the context of the president's war on terrorism. Saddam had to be linked to 9/11, Al-Qaeda, and the fearful image of wild-eyed suicide bombers ready to turn Saddam's WMD against the West.

It was a great marketing concept, but there was no solid intelligence to back it up. On July 23, 2002, after lengthy conferences in Washington with U.S. officials, Tony Blair's intelligence chief, Richard Dearlove, reported that "Bush wanted to remove Saddam through military action, justified by the conjunction of terrorism and WMD. But the intelligence and facts were being fixed around the policy." According to the memo, "It seemed clear that Bush had made up his mind to take military action, even if the timing was not yet decided. But the case was thin. Saddam was not threatening his neighbors, and his WMD capability was less than that of Libya, North Korea, or Iran."[24]

Cheney, Rumsfeld, and the neoconservatives, however, were convinced that the evidence against Saddam was there. It was the intelligence organizations, with no agents of their own in Baghdad, who in their slipshod, irresolute fashion were unable to find it. Convinced they could do a better job, the neocons set up their own secret intelligence bureau in the Pentagon, which became known as the Office of Special Plans. Its staffers would bypass the professional analysts to assess the raw intelligence data themselves and pass on what they considered relevant to the decision makers on high.

To head up the office, they chose hard-line ideologues already committed to overthrowing Saddam and bolstering the State of Israel. Abram Shulsky, a former aid to Richard Perle, was appointed to direct the office, reporting directly to Douglas Feith and his assistant William Luti. The staff soon mushroomed to 110 people. They had close ties with intelligence units from Israeli Prime Minister Ariel Sharon's office and were also a conduit for raw intelligence from defectors and exile groups, such as Ahmad Chalabi's highly political Iraq National Congress. CIA analysts had found much of this information questionable or false, but it was funneled directly to the White House anyway. One former Pentagon official described the process as "propaganda, not information."[25]

The Battle for Congress

This cherry-picked, unverified information would be used to bulldoze Congress into authorizing the use of military force to get rid of Saddam.[26] Another special office, the White House Iraq Group, was set up in September 2002 to coordinate the campaign. In Nashville, Tennessee, on August 26, Vice President Cheney had already kicked off the drive for war. He warned darkly of a Saddam "armed with an arsenal of these weapons of terror," who could "directly threaten America's friends throughout the region and subject the United States or any other nation to nuclear blackmail." Cheney warned, "The risks of inaction are greater than the risk of action."[27] Colin Powell was surprised by the vice president's vehemence; Cheney seemed to him single-mindedly dedicated to action against Saddam.[28]

Because the pro-Israel lobby was one of the most powerful pressure groups in Washington, the purported threat that Saddam represented to the Zionist state became part of the administration's sales pitch. On September 19, President Bush told eleven House members that, regarding the war on terror, the biggest threat "is Saddam Hussein and his weapons of mass destruction. He can blow up Israel, and that would trigger an international conflict."[29] On September 26, the president warned another group of congressmen that "Saddam Hussein is a terrible guy who's teaming up with Al-Qaeda. He tortures his own people and hates Israel."[30]

Many leading congressmen at first resisted the drive to invade Iraq, but they quickly yielded to the no-holds-barred campaign launched by the administration. Democratic politicians were increasingly reluctant to challenge the president,[31] who characterized any dissent based on factual intelligence into a lack of patriotism. The Democrat-controlled Senate, he charged, "is not interested in the security of the American people."[32]

The 9/11 anniversary was exploited to the hilt for the administration's saber-rattling campaign. The White House leaked a story based on classified documents to the *New York Times*, which produced the desired front-page headline on September 8: "U.S. Says Hussein Intensifies Quest for A-Bomb Parts." The language was stark and menacing: "Mr. Hussein's dogged insistence on pursuing his nuclear ambitions, along with what defectors described in interviews as Iraq's push to improve and expand Baghdad's chemical and biological arsenals, have brought Iraq and the United States to the brink of war." The most damning evidence, according to the report, was that Iraq had attempted to obtain thousands of high-strength aluminum tubes that could be used in centrifuges to enrich uranium for a nuclear

House didn't want to divert the focus from Saddam Hussein, and Pakistan had become a vital ally in President Bush's war on terrorism.

For the same reason, the Bush White House downplayed news of a disastrous meeting between U.S. and North Korean officials in October 2002, when the North Koreans insisted on their right to develop nuclear weapons. The White House acknowledged the crisis only after it had won congressional backing for an attack on Saddam Hussein—and only after it learned that word had already been leaked to the press. Bush officials also denied there was any serious concern about Iran's nuclear program, though they knew it was far more menacing than anything Saddam might have in the works.

CIA officials also suppressed important information on the status of Saddam's weapons of mass destruction that had been obtained by a daring secret operation devised by CIA veteran Charles Allen. He convinced family members of Iraqi weapons scientists who were living abroad to return to Iraq and secretly question their scientist relatives about Saddam's WMD programs. The roughly thirty Iraqi weapons scientists who were thus debriefed stated unanimously that Saddam no longer had any WMD, nor the means to make them. Those reports, however, were squelched by the CIA and never transmitted to the State Department, Pentagon, or White House.[40]

In fact, before the administration's public relations offensive began, U.S. intelligence agencies had held a fairly mild view of Saddam's capabilities. In his January 2002 review of global weapons-technology proliferation, CIA Director George Tenet warned of growing menace from North Korea and Iran, but didn't even mention Iraq. A month later, the *New York Times* reported that the CIA had found "no evidence that Iraq has engaged in terrorist operations against the United States in nearly a decade, and the Agency is also convinced that President Saddam Hussein has not provided chemical or biological weapons to Al-Qaeda or related terrorist groups."[41] The International Atomic Energy Agency (IAEA) had also concluded that, though they still had doubts about whether or not Iraq had destroyed all its previous stocks of WMD, its present nuclear capabilities were virtually nil. The IAEA had no convincing evidence that Iraq was reconstituting its nuclear program—nor did U.S. intelligence agencies.[42]

Similarly, the CIA and other intelligence agencies believed Iraq still possessed considerable amounts of biological and chemical weapons, but they had no idea how much or what condition they were in, since they also reported that substantial stocks of WMD had been destroyed by U.N. weapons inspectors in the 1990s. There was no consensus about whether Iraq was rebuilding its facilities and producing new weapons. The CIA had never declared unequivocally that Saddam possessed weapons of mass destruction,[43] but all of these questions and dissents were silenced when the administration began the hard sell.

The Bush administration also distorted intelligence to establish a link between Saddam Hussein and Al-Qaeda. On September 25, 2002, for instance, President Bush gave a speech conflating the two. "You can't distinguish between Al-Qaeda and Saddam," the president declared. "The danger is, is that they work in concert. The danger is that Al-Qaeda becomes an extension of Saddam's madness and his hatred and his capacity to extend weapons of mass destruction around the world."[44] Donald Rumsfeld claimed "bulletproof" evidence of a connection and insisted his charges were "accurate and not debatable." When queried further, the defense secretary replied dismissively, "That happens to be a piece of intelligence that either we don't have or we don't want to talk about."[45]

Much of the "bulletproof" evidence was based on a solitary Czech informant who claimed he saw 9/11 hijacker Mohammed Atta meet with a top Iraqi intelligence official in Prague on April 2001. The White House pounced on the unconfirmed report and leaked it to friends in the media. On December 9, 2001, Dick Cheney declared that the Atta meeting was "pretty well confirmed."[46] Over the following weeks and months, U.S., Czech, and other foreign intelligence experts disputed the so-called Prague connection. Top CIA and FBI officials reported that "there was no evidence Atta left or returned to the United States at the time he was supposed to be in Prague." Even FBI Director Robert S. Mueller III, a Bush political appointee, admitted in April 2002 that the agency had found nothing to back up the claim after an exhaustive search.[47] Nevertheless, administration hawks continued to voice the discredited charges with the fervor of the faithful.[48]

As part of the growing congressional debate, the Senate Intelligence Committee asked the CIA for an updated National Intelligence Estimate (NIE) on Iraq, reflecting the views of all major U.S. intelligence agencies. The CIA and its director, George Tenet, already on the defensive after 9/11, had long been the focus of intense administration pressure. They were repeatedly ridiculed for their inability to find proof of Saddam's deadly potential. Cheney and his deputy, Lewis "Scooter" Libby, made repeated trips to the Agency, badgering Tenet and his analysts to reexamine their intelligence for the evidence they were certain was there.[49] There were increasing complaints from unnamed agents to the media that George Tenet was failing to shield his analysts from the political heat.[50]

A classified version of the new NIE was released to the Senate Intelligence Committee on October 2, 2002. Its opening paragraphs, stating that "Baghdad has chemical and biological weapons," seemed to substantiate the administration's case. But deeper in, the report was honeycombed with dissents and qualifiers. The stark conclusions, it turned out, were actually very ambiguous, based not on believable first-person sources but vague suppositions.

Evidence that Saddam Hussein might offer his WMD to terrorists for attacks on the U.S. or its allies—the administration's main justification for a preemptive strike—was undercut with a host of "ifs," "mights," and "woulds": "Saddam, if sufficiently desperate, might decide that only an organization such as Al-Qaeda—with worldwide reach and extensive terrorist infrastructure, and already engaged in a life-or-death struggle against the United States—would perpetrate the type of terrorist attack that he would hope to conduct. In such circumstances, he might decide that the extreme step of assisting the Islamist terrorists in conducting a CBW [chemical or biological weapons] attack against the United States would be his last chance to exact vengeance by taking a large number of victims with him."[51] Just in case it was still not clear how inferential the conclusion was, the report added the additional qualifier that there was "low confidence" in such speculation. The State Department's intelligence bureau filed its own eleven-page addition—more like a rebuttal—to the NIE's views on Saddam's nuclear threat. The available evidence, it declared, did not add up to "a compelling case" that Iraq has "an integrated and comprehensive approach to acquire nuclear weapons."

On October 4, however, CIA Director Tenet released to the whole Congress a declassified version of the NIE report, a White Paper that played up the administration's argument and left out or consigned to footnotes most of the qualifications and dissenting views that undermined the case. For instance, it referred once again to the aluminium tubes as evidence that Saddam "remains intent on acquiring" nuclear weapons. And it stated—incorrectly—that "all intelligence experts agree that Iraq is seeking nuclear weapons and that these tubes could be used in a centrifuge enrichment program." The NIE also stated flat out that Saddam had "begun renewed production of chemical warfare agents." Yet the Pentagon's own Defense Intelligence Agency (DIA) had specifically cast doubt on that claim.

Democratic Senator Bob Graham of the Senate Intelligence Committee, who had seen the original NIE report with all its qualifications and reservations as well as earlier skeptical reports from other intelligence agencies, was furious with the sanitized version that Tenet had publicly released. He demanded that the CIA declassify dissenting portions. The White House refused to okay most of the request.

Instead, the White House increased the drumbeat of disinformation. On October 7, 2002, in a major address in Cincinnati, President Bush warned again of the aluminum tubes as proof of Saddam's nuclear program and talked chillingly of another supposed weapon: unmanned aerial vehicles that could be used by Saddam to spread WMD across the United States. Saddam's "alliance with terrorists could allow the Iraqi regime to attack America without leaving any fingerprints." The president also divulged that "Iraq has trained Al-Qaeda members in bomb making and poisons and gases. The danger is already significant, and it only grows worse with time."[52]

Yet a year earlier, the administration's top military experts told the White House that they "sharply disputed the notion that Iraq's unmanned aerial vehicles were being designed as attack weapons."[53] Similarly, the president's claim that Iraq had trained Al-Qaeda terrorists was based on the interrogation of one high-ranking member of Al-Qaeda whom the DIA had identified as a probable fabricator months before the president's Cincinnati speech. In February 2002, the DIA had concluded that the man "was intentionally misleading the debriefers."[54]

Nevertheless, the president's alarming charges, which he claimed reflected the consensus of his advisors and the intelligence community, hit home. Most of the media ignored the doubts expressed publicly by a handful of former government analysts and investigative reporters. The vote in Congress was a Kafkaesque farce. Five of the nine Democrats on the Senate Intelligence Committee, who had seen the original National Intelligence Estimate, voted against the resolution. But because the administration refused to declassify the report, the dissenting Democrats were not allowed to divulge what they knew to their colleagues on Capitol Hill.[55] On October 10, 2002, by a vote of 296 to 133, the House passed a resolution empowering the president to use the U.S. armed forces in Iraq "as he deems to be necessary and appropriate." In the Senate, Edward Kennedy was one of the lone voices of dissent. The administration, he declared, had neither proven its case against Iraq, nor given any indication of what the cost to the U.S. would be. Bush's new doctrine of preemptive war, he said, was "a call for 21st century American imperialism that no other nation can or should accept." On October 11, however, by a vote of 77 to 23, the Senate also authorized the president to use the military as "necessary-and-appropriate" to defend against "the continuing threat posed by Iraq." The White House had its victory.[56]

Much later, in July 2004, with the U.S. hopelessly mired in Iraq, the Senate Select Committee on Intelligence condemned the White Paper that the CIA had released in October 2002.[57] The committee concluded that "the 28-page public document turned estimates into facts, left out or watered down the dissent within the government about key weapons programs, and exaggerated Iraq's ability to strike the United States." The committee also accused the CIA of selectively declassifying material that would support the administration's case while withholding information that would have weakened it. In doing so, the White Paper "misrepresented [the intelligence community's] judgments to the public," the Senate panel concluded. The Senate committee's chairman, Republican Pat Roberts, declared that had

Congress known before the vote to go to war what his committee had since discovered about the intelligence on Iraq, "I doubt if the votes would have been there."[58]

Convincing the U.N.

The next step for the Bush and Blair administrations was to get a forceful U.N. resolution condemning Iraq if it didn't agree to new weapons inspections.[59] According to the confidential Downing Street memo of discussions among Tony Blair and his top advisors the previous July, Blair was concerned about finding a convincing pretext for resorting to war. The tactic finally agreed upon was simple. "We should work up a plan for an ultimatum to Saddam to allow back in the U.N. weapons inspectors. This would also help with the legal justification for the use of force. The prime minister said that it would make a big difference politically and legally if Saddam refused to allow in the U.N. inspectors."[60]

In other words, they would demand that Saddam readmit weapons inspectors, not from a sincere desire to resolve the problem of his supposed WMD, but to provide the U.S. and Britain with the excuse they needed to go to war. In November 2002, however, Saddam foiled those tactics by agreeing to accept Unmovic inspectors back in Iraq.

The U.S. and Britain remained convinced they would have their casus belli: the inspectors would ultimately fail to account for Saddam's WMD. On November 15, they persuaded the Security Council to vote for a resolution declaring that if Saddam continued to violate his obligations to get rid of his WMD, he would face "serious consequences"—a threat that fell short of the tougher wording the U.S. had wanted; on the other hand, the resolution passed unanimously. The meaning of "serious consequences" was left ambiguous. Most members of the Security Council, including the British, assumed that there would have to be a second resolution to authorize any invasion of Iraq.[61] As the U.S. saw it, however, it now had all the authorization it needed. Dick Cheney and the neocons in the Bush administration viewed the entire U.N. process with contempt; there was nothing the Unmovic inspectors could find that would convince them that Saddam should be left in power.

A few in the administration realized that there was one niggling problem. The U.S. still lacked solid evidence of the imminent threat supposedly posed by Saddam. On December 19, 2002, after General Franks updated President Bush and his advisors on the latest war preparations, Condoleezza Rice asked CIA Director Tenet how strong the agency's case for Saddam's WMD was and what could be said publicly.[62] Coming so late in the game, it was an astounding question: Rice, the president's national security advisor, whose scaremongering talk of "mushroom clouds" had been so much a part of the drumbeat for war, was only now verifying the strength of the intelligence justifying the huge military invasion that by this time was all but unstoppable. As Rice saw it, "something was missing."[63]

It was still missing on December 21, when CIA Deputy Director John McLaughlin briefed the president and his top advisors on the threat represented by Saddam. The presentation was intended to summarize an airtight case, but even his willing audience was unconvinced. As Andrew Card saw it, "the presentation was a flop." As a former advertising executive, Card was particularly concerned about problems "of marketing. The examples didn't work, the charts didn't work, the photos were not gripping, the intercepts were less than compelling."

"Nice try," said the president. "I don't think this is quite—it's not something that Joe Public would understand or would gain a lot of confidence from." It was at this crucial moment that Bush turned to Tenet for reassurance and was told by the head of the CIA, "Don't worry. It's a slam dunk!" The president instructed his aides to put together a compelling dossier he could present to the public to justify the coming invasion. According to Bob Woodward's fly-on-the-wall account, Bush repeatedly admonished Tenet, "Make sure no one stretches to make our case."[64]

But Bush's nine-word admonition to Tenet could not possibly have terminated the process of distortion and lies that had been going on for months. Administration officials had not only been stretching to make their case, they'd been pressuring the intelligence community itself to distort information.[65] In fact, the entire exchange between Bush and Tenet rings false: Bush's supposed warning not to distort intelligence sounds like a Mafia Don talking theatrically loud to a confederate after discovering that the Feds are secretly recording the meeting. Indeed, Tenet and the U.S. intelligence agencies would ultimately be made the scapegoats for the disastrous decision to invade Iraq.

Bush may indeed have been oblivious to much of the debate within the intelligence community, a captive of his Oval Office cocoon and lack of curiosity. His former treasury secretary, Paul O'Neill, described the president as disengaged from the issues and apparently uninterested in dialogue with advisors.[66] The agenda on Iraq was essentially set by Dick Cheney and Donald Rumsfeld.

Bush's former counterterrorism chief, Richard Clarke, later wrote,

> It was clear that the critiques of him as a dumb, lazy rich kid were somewhere off the mark. When he focused, he asked the kind of questions that revealed a results-oriented mind, but he looked for the simple solution, the bumper sticker description of the problem. Once he had that, he could put energy behind a drive to achieve his goal. The problem was that many of the important issues, like terrorism, like Iraq, were laced with important subtlety and nuance. These issues needed analysis, and Bush and his inner circle had no real interest in complicated analyses; on the issues that they cared about, they already knew the answers; it was received wisdom.[67]

Ridding the world of Saddam, in fact, seemed to have become a mission the president had been entrusted by God. "Going into this period," Bush later recalled, "I was praying for strength to do the Lord's will. . . . I'm surely not going to justify war based upon God. Understand that. Nevertheless, in my case I pray that I be as good a messenger of His will as possible."[68] As he told PLO leader Mahmoud Abbas on June 4, 2003, "God told me to strike at Al-Qaeda and I struck them, and then he instructed me to strike at Saddam, which I did, and now I am determined to solve the problem in the Middle East. If you help me I will act, and if not, the elections will come and I will have to focus on them."[69]

Even if President Bush had no idea what was going on, certainly his top aides did: several of them were part of the problem. Other advisors who might have objected to the lying and manipulation of facts, such as Colin Powell and Condoleezza Rice, chose to follow wherever the president led. In any case, the president really no longer had the option to back out. The massive U.S. military buildup in the Gulf had achieved a momentum of its own—the same fateful dynamic that helped impel his father, George H. W. Bush, to war in the Gulf in 1991.

With no real resistance from CIA leadership, the process of massaging intelligence continued. In January 2003, according to an analyst in the CIA's Counter-Proliferation Division, their unit chief gave marching orders to his staff. "He said, 'You know what—if Bush wants to go to war, it's your job to give him a reason to do so.'"[70]

Meanwhile, the special bipartisan 9/11 Committee of the U.S. Congress had concluded by the end of 2002 that there were no links between Saddam Hussein and 9/11 or between Saddam and Al-Qaeda. Each piece of evidence the administration had cited to substantiate its case had been demolished by the Senate investigators. But the committee was not allowed to make its findings public.[71] Disputes between the committee and the Bush administration over which parts of the study could be declassified ensured that the report was not publicized until well after the invasion of Iraq was terminated.

"The reason this report was delayed for so long—deliberately opposed at first, then slow-walked after it was created—is that the administration wanted to get the war in Iraq in and over . . . before [it] came out," said Democratic Senator Max Cleland, a member of the committee. "Had this report come out in January like it should have done, we would have known these things before the war in Iraq, which would not have suited the administration."[72]

On January 25, Cheney's assistant Scooter Libby gave a lengthy presentation of George Tenet's "slam dunk" case to Rice, Wolfowitz, Colin Powell's deputy, Richard Armitage, and other top administration aides. Armitage was "appalled at what he considered overreaching and hyperbole. Libby was drawing only the worst conclusions from fragments and silky threads." Wolfowitz, on the other hand, who had never doubted the links between Saddam and Al-Qaeda, thought the presentation first rate. "He subscribed to Rumsfeld's notion that lack of evidence did not mean something did not exist."[73]

The U.N. weapons inspectors had a different take on the question. On January 27, Hans Blix, the chief inspector, gave an interim report to the Security Council. Though Iraq had not "come to a genuine acceptance" of the disarmament expected of it, said Blix, overall the cooperation was good and the inspectors had uncovered no new WMD or production sites. The problem was Iraq was still tasked with proving itself innocent, obliged to account for all the WMD it claimed to have destroyed in the early 1990s. No one was being asked to prove those arms still existed.

As for the search for nuclear weapons, the director general of the International Atomic Energy Agency, Mohammed El Baradei, reported, "We have to date found no evidence that Iraq has revived its nuclear weapons program." Though his work was still not completed, he was optimistic, he said. "We should be able within the next few months to provide credible assurance that Iraq has no nuclear program."

Such rosy assurances infuriated the White House. Cheney and the president were convinced that inspections were a farce, the inspectors dupes of Saddam Hussein. Rather than being cautioned by such positive findings, Bush was ever more determined to go to war.[74] None of his top advisors suggested putting on the brakes.

On January 28, 2003, in his State of the Union address, the president launched a bitter attack against Saddam Hussein, substituting fear for facts. The biological weapons that Saddam had been unable to account for, Bush declared, were "enough to subject millions of people to death by respiratory failure."[75] The president then ominously revealed, "The British government has learned that Saddam Hussein recently sought significant quantities of uranium from Africa."[76]

In fact, just a few months earlier, on the insistence of CIA Director Tenet, the White House had deleted that same claim from the speech that Bush gave in Cincinnati because the accusation was totally unsubstantiated and appeared to be probably untrue. The CIA had even dispatched former U.S. Ambassador Joseph Wilson to Niger to investigate. He returned to report that the allegation didn't hold water. Though the claim was finally excised from the speech Bush gave in October, over the following months administration officials from Condoleezza Rice to Colin Powell to Donald Rumsfeld continued to cite the story as if it were fact,[77] and there it was again in the president's State of the Union address. Condoleezza Rice would later explain that it had been an unfortunate but trivial slip—"only sixteen words." But the lawyerly way in which the charge was phrased and carefully attributed to British rather than American intelligence belies the claim that it was an innocent mistake.

With the date they had already set for the invasion fast approaching, the administration searched for a great communicator to present the case to the world. The choice was Colin Powell; the forum, the U.N. Security Council. Powell was ideal for the mission. He was known as a reluctant warrior, leery of attacking Iraq, intelligent, personable, and trustworthy; a man who could as easily have been a Democrat as a Republican. Flattered when the president asked him to take on the task, Powell agreed, like the dutiful soldier he had always thought himself to be.

He would be fronting for a policy he didn't believe in, crafted by government officials, several of whom he came close to despising. Cheney, he told Bob Woodward, "took intelligence and converted uncertainty and ambiguity into fact."[78] It was Cheney and Rumsfeld, however, who were calling the shots in the administration. President Bush never even asked Powell—the former chairman of the Joint Chiefs of Staff—point blank whether or not the U.S. should invade Iraq. On the other hand, though Powell cautioned the president what the consequences of overthrowing Saddam would be—"You know that you're going to be owning this place?"—Powell never took it upon himself to advise Bush that he was making a grievous error.[79]

What Powell didn't know was that on the night before his speech to the U.N., a top CIA official attempted unsuccessfully to alert him to further flaws in the intelligence. Tyler Drumheller, who headed the CIA's spy activities in Europe, had learned from German intelligence that a key CIA source for claims about Iraq's WMD, known by his code name of "Curveball," had been judged mentally unstable, unreliable, and not to be trusted. As late as the night before Powell's presentation, Tyler spoke to Tenet by phone and alerted him to the problem. But Tenet ignored the warnings; the false claims remained.[80]

In fact, George Tenet sat squarely behind Powell on February 5, when the secretary of state delivered his seventy-minute speech to the Security Council. There was no indication from the authoritative delivery that followed that Powell himself had doubts about the intelligence he was relaying. Indeed, in some cases, when he played the tape of intercepted conversations between two Iraqi military officials that might have related to hiding evidence of "forbidden ammo," Powell added his own unsubstantiated interpretations to the much more ambiguous conversations he was presenting.

Although he had earlier refused to include several White House claims in his address, like the supposed "Prague connection"—which he referred to privately as "garbage"—Powell assured the Security Council that there was a "sinister nexus between Iraq and the Al-Qaeda terrorist network."[81] He also repeated the threadbare allegation—disputed by his own State Department intelligence experts—that Saddam's attempts to obtain aluminum tubes were conclusive proof of his drive for nuclear weapons.

Almost every claim made by Powell later turned out to be false. Indeed, at the time Powell gave his speech, U.S. intelligence agencies knew that many of his charges were flimsy at best. So did Powell. Prior to his U.N. presentation, Powell admitted to British Foreign Secretary Jack Straw that he was "apprehensive" about the "at best circumstantial evidence" he was to present. Said Powell, "I hope the facts, when they come out, will not explode in our faces."[82]

There was no such concern in the White House. Powell's performance was judged a marketing triumph, demolishing whatever obstacles still remained to the rush to war. Though a few reporters and intelligence specialists immediately pounced on the errors and inaccuracies in his claims, their views went unheeded by the general public. Almost universally, columnists and editorialists reacted to Powell's theatrics with euphoric reviews. The *New York Times* hailed Powell's "powerful" and "sober, factual case." Under the title "Irrefutable," the *Washington Post* editorialized that "it is hard to imagine how anyone could doubt that Iraq possesses weapons of mass destruction." On CNN, General Amer al-Saadi, Saddam Hussein's scientific advisor, was permitted to deliver a rebuttal of Powell's case. But, as if to apologize for having granted airtime to the Iraqi, the CNN anchor, Paula Zahn then introduced James Rubin, a former State Department spokesman, with the words, "You've got to understand that most Americans watching this were either probably laughing out loud or got sick to their stomach. Which was it for you?"

"Well, really, both," Rubin replied."[83]

All along most of the mainstream press and television had been either enthusiastic cheerleaders for the government's misinformation campaign or fearful of raising the serious questions that were out there. "There was an attitude among editors: Look, we're going to war, why do we even worry about all the contrary stuff?" said the *Washington Post*'s Pentagon correspondent Thomas Ricks.[84]

Yet there were knowledgeable insiders around who were very willing to talk to reporters. Some in the media, like Knight Ridder's Washington bureau, ran stories based on their charges.[85] *Newsweek* seriously questioned several of Colin Powell's claims to the U.N. But such reports were relatively rare and usually buried or given short shrift. These critical reports were swept away by what *Newsweek* correspondent Chris Dickey describes as "a tsunami of news" created by the explosion of new cable channels, Internet sites, niche magazines, blogs, talk shows, and all-news radio and TV.[86]

Stories pushing administration claims, however, were front-page material. Most investigative reporters were more intent on uncovering evidence that supported rather than debunked the administration's case. The White House kept them occupied with a steady stream of classified intelligence documents and contacts with defectors whose credentials turned out to be paper thin.[87] In addition, sympathetic reporters were rewarded with timely leaks, unusual access, background interviews, and seats on official flights, while those thought to be hostile to the administration were frozen out from the access on which they depended for their stories. And in Congress, the lack of significant or prominent Democrat opposition to the march to war meant there were no investigators on the Hill ready to talk, no dramatic hearings reporters could cover.[88]

If a major issue was going to be generated, the media would have had to create it on their own, and in the face of vicious attacks on their patriotism from the likes of Fox News, Rush Limbaugh, and the *Weekly Standard*. Gradually most journalists chose to muzzle themselves. The closer the invasion became, the more reluctant editors were to ask tough questions. Few editors wanted to take responsibility for challenging the national security alarms raised by a popular administration.

Powell's speech was intended to wring a new resolution from the Security Council that would cut short the inspection process and explicitly authorize military action against Iraq. U.S. diplomacy was being driven by an invasion timetable that had been drawn up months ago by U.S. military planners. The window for military action was now. Temperatures would soon be soaring in the Gulf. Quick U.N. backing would enable the U.S. to assemble a coalition of countries to take part in the invasion, as George W. Bush's father had done in 1991.

This time, however, the White House had a much tougher sell. Encouraged by optimistic reports from the U.N. inspectors, several key countries—among them France, Germany, and Russia—argued that Unmovic should be given time to complete its work. "If Iraq were to cooperate even more fully," said Hans Blix on February 14, after another upbeat report, "the period of disarmament through inspection could still be short."[89]

The White House continued to ridicule the inspections as farce; the moment for such games was over. Those arguing for more time were derided as naive at best, treacherous at worst. France, Germany, and Russia were attacked on the talk shows as the "axis of weasels."

The inspectors' greatest obstacle, Hans Blix later revealed, was no longer Saddam Hussein but George Bush's obsession with overthrowing the Iraqi dictator no matter what the inspectors found. As Blix wrote, "Although the inspection organization was now operating at full strength, and Iraq seemed determined to give it prompt access everywhere, the United States appeared as determined to replace our inspection force with an invasion army."[90]

Little known at the time was the fact that, behind the scenes, Canada was attempting to hammer out a compromise.[91] From frequent conversations with the U.N. inspectors, the Canadians knew that they were increasingly skeptical that Saddam had any important stocks of WMD. The demand for a few more weeks to finish the task made eminent sense. The Canadians came up with a compromise deadline of forty-five days for the inspectors to report that either they were convinced that something was being hidden or that Saddam was no threat. "The Americans and British thought even forty-five days was too much," a Canadian close to the negotiations told me. "I think they would have disagreed with any number. They were looking at the weather. Our forty-five days didn't work with that."[92]

Unable to get a second Security Council resolution justifying immediate action against Iraq, the Bush administration abruptly declared it did not need any new authorization from the U.N. since, it claimed, previous resolutions already gave the U.S. all the legal grounds it needed to invade Iraq. On March 19, 2003, with support from Congress and American public opinion won through a relentless campaign of distorted information, the huge U.S.-led attack was launched. After three weeks of fighting, the Coalition of the Willing toppled the government of Saddam Hussein. As Colin Powell had earlier warned the president, the U.S. now "owned the place."

CHAPTER TEN

Full Circle : The Occupation
April 2003–August 2006

From the beginning, the modern nation of Iraq was a volatile jumble of peoples and tribes cobbled together by its British occupiers for their own purposes, and for the following eighty years foreign powers continued to intervene. They promoted coups, exploited resources, financed revolts, sold billions of dollars of arms to Iraq and its enemies, and throttled the country with economic sanctions. Finally, in April 2003, occupying troops returned to Baghdad. This time, they vowed they would remain just long enough to clean up the mess left by Saddam Hussein's twenty-four years of tyranny and turn the country over to honest, democratically minded leaders. A new era was dawning for Iraq. It was not, unfortunately, to be the rosy era of national healing that President Bush and his ally Tony Blair had promised. By August 2006 it appeared to be an unmitigated disaster for all concerned.

Costs and Consequences

What would be the cost of Bush and Blair's massive armed venture? Almost three and a half years after the invasion, there were only tentative answers. First, the price in human lives: 15,000 to 30,000 Iraqi soldiers were estimated to have died in the fighting, though the U.S. claimed it had no exact figures. "We don't do body counts," said American General Tommy Franks.[1] The Pentagon also claimed to have no running count of civilian casualties, certainly a much greater number. Various groups attempting to keep track determined that by August 2006 anywhere from 38,000 to more than 100,000 civilians had died during the invasion and the years of occupation.[2] Indeed, according to the United Nations, Iraqis were being murdered as a result of religious and sectarian violence at the rate of 100 a day.[3] The proportionate number in the United States would be 33,000 Americans stabbed, shot, garroted, beheaded, and blown up every month.

Those appalling figures, the result of a war ostensibly waged to protect the world from terrorism, are probably greater than the sum of all the people ever killed by terrorist attacks. The amount of property damage during the fighting and in the looting and destruction that followed was in the tens of billions of dollars.

The casualty figures for the United States were considerably lower. As of the end of August 2006, some 2,620 American soldiers had been killed and more than 19,300 wounded, many of them crippled for life. The British lost 115 military personnel in the same period, as did all the other members of the coalition combined.[4]

To get an idea of the ongoing financial cost to the United States, one could consult an Internet site, Costofwar.com, which featured a whirring count of the money spent each second by the U.S. in Iraq. The hundreds of dollars flash by too rapidly to follow; the thousands change about once a second. At noon on August 26, the amount had reached $309,847,570. The National Priorities Project, which hosts the counter, also allows the viewer to instantly calculate what that money could have provided if, instead of being spent in Iraq, it was dedicated to other causes: $309 billion, for instance, could fund all world hunger efforts for the next thirteen years; all basic immunization programs around the globe for the next one hundred and three years; or—if spent in the U.S. alone—the salaries of an additional 5.4 million public school teachers for one year or health insurance for more than 185 million American children.

The ultimate cost of the war would be much higher. According to a report coauthored by a Nobel Prize-winning economist, it could range from $1 trillion to $2.6 trillion.[5] Much of that money wouldn't be used to rebuild Iraq. Hundreds of millions, for instance, would go to lifetime disability payments for injured American soldiers; another portion would pay for higher petroleum prices due to the war.[6]

On the other hand, for several mammoth American corporations, there was a bright side. One third of $1 billion dollars a week that the U.S. was spending in Iraq went to U.S. companies like Halliburton, Bechtel, and DynCorp, which were awarded multibillion-dollar contracts. The deals covered more than just reconstruction: the Pentagon began outsourcing a wide range of tasks that had once been performed by the military itself, including managing military bases, training the Iraqi police, delivering the mail, and cooking and serving millions of hot meals for U.S. troops. These contract employees, often sporting army fatigues with civilian patches on their shoulders, became part and parcel of army life in Iraq.[7]

With as much as 20 percent of the money in Iraq being spent on security, that business also experienced a windfall. More than 25,000 private armed security guards worked in the country in June 2006. Many of them were former American and British soldiers eager to return to Iraq at five or six times the salaries they made in the army, sometimes paid to protect U.S. officials. Many were pocketing as much as $1,000 a day. More than 340 of them had also been killed by the summer of 2006.[8]

Were the invasion and occupation worth the huge costs in treasure and lives? We first have to consider what they accomplished. The proposition that Saddam and his WMD represented an incalculable menace to the West, and that therefore anything spent to destroy the menace was justified, no longer holds up—it is now clear that Saddam posed no such threat. The excuse that it was all the result of an honest mistake or faulty intelligence, an error that any well-meaning government might have made, also doesn't bear scrutiny in light of the campaign of lies and distortions that the White House used to justify overthrowing Saddam.

The argument that Saddam Hussein was linked to the threat of international terrorism proved to be similarly hollow. Indeed, the invasion and occupation of Iraq turned out to be a propaganda gift to Al-Qaeda and other radical Islamist groups, which spun the intervention to stimulate hatred of the United States throughout the Arab world and used the insurgency in Iraq as a training camp for thousands of potential jihadis.

The fallback argument of the Bush administration hinged on the inherent value of overthrowing a ruthless tyrant. Not only did this free the people of Iraq from one of the world's most oppressive regimes but, the White House claimed, it would also engender a new spirit of democracy across the region. The jury is still out on that proposition, but by mid-2006 the outlook was not very promising. As a terrified university professor in Basra told a reporter in June 2006, "I cannot talk with you. I haven't joined a party and no militia is protecting me."[9]

More than three years after George Bush declared mission accomplished for the "Coalition of the Willing," though Saddam Hussein was on trial in Baghdad, human rights abuses were even more horrific than they had been when the despot held power.[10] Nearly every morning mangled bodies surfaced in Sunni and Shiite neighborhoods around Baghdad and Basra, their killers unknown, though many were suspected to be linked to the Ministry of the Interior. Many bodies bore marks of torture—badly beaten faces, gagged mouths, and rope burns around the neck.

"Under Saddam, if you agreed to forgo your basic right to freedom of expression and thought, you were physically more or less OK," said John Pace, the former director of the human rights office for the U.N. Assistance Mission to Iraq. "But now, no. Here, you have a primitive, chaotic situation where anybody can do anything they want to anyone." Now, he said, no one was safe from abuse. "It extends over a much wider section of the population than it did under Saddam."[11]

At the beginning of June 2006, Iraq's Ministry of Health confirmed that 6,002 bodies, most of them victims of violence, had been delivered to Baghdad's main morgue in the first five months of the year. The great majority of them had been summarily executed, garroted, or shot, many with their hands tied behind their back. Some showed evidence of torture, with arm and leg joints broken and skulls pierced by electric drills. Morgue authorities in turn were being threatened by both government-backed militias and insurgents not to investigate the deaths. The former Baghdad morgue director charged that most of the killings were carried out by Shiite militias linked to the Ministry of the Interior, which runs the country's police force. Many of the ministry's forces were trained and financed by the United States.

As if to confirm the director's allegations, on June 5, 2006, police officers delivered nine severed heads to the morgue in the provincial capital of Baquba in the same fruit boxes in which they had been found in the village of Hadid. Notes found with the bodies explained that the dead were Sunnis murdered in retaliation for the earlier killings of five Shiites, four of them doctors. The American ambassador himself, Dr. Zalmay Khalilzad, conceded in June that security in Baghdad was getting worse, not better.

The U.S. itself was also directly accused of human rights violations. Earlier in the year, Amnesty International issued a scathing report, charging that thousands of detainees were being held by the U.S.-led Multinational Force (MNF)—some for more than two years without charges. The MNF detainees, said Amnesty, were "trapped in a system of arbitrary detention that denies them their basic rights."[12] Such charges were just for starters. Ever since the invasion, American forces had been charged with using excessive, indiscriminate firepower against civilians, killing hundreds, possibly thousands of innocent people.

As for promises that the invasion would open the way for the restoration of Iraq's shattered economy, by the summer of 2006 only a fraction of the $30 billion committed by the U.S. to rebuild the country had been put to work. This was due as much to the total lack of security as to the incompetence of the occupiers and the new Iraqi authorities. The country still lacked reliable electricity, water, and other services.[13] In many areas, unemployment rates exceeded 50 percent. Inflation was skyrocketing. Oil production had slumped to 2.2 million barrels a day, compared to 2.5 million barrels a day before 2003. And Iraqis had to queue for hours—sometimes days—to fuel their cars, while huge amounts of oil were being smuggled out of the country. Hundreds of thousands of middle-class professionals had fled the country, including 12,000 of Iraq's 34,000 doctors; 2,000 other doctors had been murdered.[14]

Those Iraqis who remained lived in a constant state of apprehension, hostage to the rampant violence and killings. Kidnapping had become a major economic activity, with children often the target. One banker who didn't flee was kidnapped after his seven bodyguards were killed.[15] In March 2006, the Ministry of Education cautioned children not to accept candy from strangers because it "might contain explosives." The warning was provoked when several people were killed after a box of sweets blew up in a Baghdad tea shop.[16]

U.S. investigators—once outraged about the monies that Saddam Hussein skimmed from the Oil for Food program in the 1990s—were now searching for more than $9 billion of the money earmarked for rebuilding Iraq in the first year of the occupation. It had somehow vanished into thin air.

Meanwhile, the country's new government and its American occupiers were isolated from the rest of the nation, holed up behind the thick concrete blast walls, barbed wired, and checkpoints of Baghdad's Green Zone. Iraq's newly elected leaders, obsessed by narrow sectarian tribal and religious issues, fear of the future, and the desire for revenge, continued their frenetic maneuvering for power as the country teetered on the edge of civil war.

How It Happened

The war was over within three weeks. It was soon clear that President Bush's arguments for invading Iraq—Saddam's WMD and links with Al-Qaeda—were bogus, as many had maintained before the invasion. But the same doctrinaire arrogance that had led the country to war continued to shape the disastrous U.S. occupation that followed.[17]

Long before the invasion, experts had warned of the grave problems to be encountered. In October 2001, expecting it would be tasked with overseeing the occupation, Colin Powell's State Department launched a wide-ranging effort called the Future of Iraq project, enlisting dozens of international experts and Iraqi exiles. They spent $5 million to examine the problems likely to be confronted in post-Saddam Iraq. The result of the conferences, study groups, and seminars filled several thousands of pages—some of it of little immediate use, but some very incisive, predicting the likelihood of an insurgency, the total breakdown of law and order, and the danger that, if security were not reestablished, the entire enterprise could fail.[18]

The project and its recommendations were almost totally ignored by the Bush administration in its prewar planning, as were the recommendations of experienced think tanks and NGO's. The White House had decided that Donald Rumsfeld's Pentagon would run postwar Iraq. The studies and predictions of the State Department and many others offering counsel were brushed aside, as was the advice of top Pentagon generals that, to ensure success, the U.S. would have to commit 350,000 to 500,000 troops.[19] They were not needed so much for the actual attack as for the postwar occupation. It would be vital, the generals argued, to establish order, put down any unrest and looting, and let Iraqis know there was someone reliable in charge as quickly as possible. Impatient with such concerns, Rumsfeld and his deputy Paul Wolfowitz insisted that 150,000 troops would be more than enough. After all, this was a new age of modern, highly mobile warfare, streamlined, quick, and efficient.[20]

As Rumsfeld and Wolfowitz saw it, there would be no need of long-term planning, nor for the military to worry about such issues as policing and security. There would be no need, in fact, for any large numbers of U.S. troops to hang around after the invasion. There was no way the U.S. would become enmeshed in the kind of expensive "nation building" that the Republicans had derided the Clinton administration for undertaking in Kosovo and Bosnia. As soon as possible, the task of governing Iraq would be handed over to Iraqis themselves. The Iraqis that Wolfowitz and Douglas Feith had particularly in mind were the exiles of Ahmad Chalabi's Iraqi National Council, who had assured the administration that the invasion would be a cakewalk. One important matter was taken care of before the first shot was fired: Dick Cheney's former employer, Halliburton, was awarded a $7 billion, no-bid contract to rebuild Iraq's oil industry.[21]

The man who was first selected by the Pentagon to oversee the interim American administration was Jake Garner, a retired lieutenant general chosen largely because of the impressive job he had done in providing disaster relief to the Kurds in northern Iraq in 1991. In April 2003, he was dispatched to Iraq with a similar mission in mind: providing short-term emergency support for refugees and extinguishing fires in the oil fields, while essentially relying on Iraqi institutions to bounce back into action quickly. Such details as postinvasion security and humanitarian assistance would be left to the Iraqis themselves, with the assistance of the U.N., NGOs, and other nations, which would naturally pitch in to help out. As Larry Di Rita, Donald Rumsfeld's representative on Garner's team, declared, "We're giving them their freedom. That's enough. We don't owe the people of Iraq anything. We're going to set up an interim government, hand over power to them, and get out in 3 to 4 months. All but 25,000 soldiers will be out by the beginning of September 2003."[22]

When Garner's team arrived in Baghdad on April 18, however, it found that the government it had hoped to help back to its feet had simply disintegrated, as had the military and police. The entire infrastructure was in shambles. They were confronting a California-sized nation in ruins, with an insurgency already threatening to spread. To deal with it, Garner had a staff of about three hundred people and very little money. They had arrived with no serious plans, not even a decent organizational chart of the Iraq government ministries. As for the U.S. military, now that it had achieved its breathtakingly quick victory over Saddam, it was already anxious to withdraw.

John Sawers, Tony Blair's envoy to Baghdad, was outraged. In a confidential memo to Downing Street in May he labeled the U.S. operation "an unbelievable mess." He said that "Garner and his top team of 60-year-old retired generals" were "well meaning but out of their depth." They possessed "no leadership, no strategy, no coordination, no structure, and [were] inaccessible to ordinary Iraqis."[23]

As the State Department study had predicted, looting broke out as soon as Baghdad fell. The U.S. military, with no orders to maintain security or protect property other than the Petroleum Ministry, simply stood by. "Stuff happens," commented Donald Rumsfeld in the Pentagon. He dismissed the mounting chaos as the natural response of Iraqis suddenly gaining their freedom.[24] He was already refusing to send additional American troops to help handle the situation. The result was an escalating rampage of theft and destruction that inflicted billions of dollars worth of damage to buildings and property across the country—more even than the devastation caused by the war itself. Unchecked, the growing anarchy established a sense of insecurity and fear that came to pervade much of the country and undermined all attempts to rebuild Iraq and install a representative government.

By May 12, 2003, within three weeks of his arriving in Baghdad, Jake Garner was replaced by L. Paul Bremer, a retired diplomat with considerable experience in government but little in the Middle East. He had been abruptly summoned to become Iraq's chief civilian administrator at the head of the Coalition Provisional Authority (CPA). When he arrived in Baghdad, American troops were still standing by as looting continued.[25]

From the start the CPA was desperately short of experienced staff, interpreters, transportation, communications facilities, and ideas. Several months after Bremer arrived, the CPA was still only 50 percent staffed; it never reached 70 percent. There was no institutional memory—most of the personnel stayed for only a few months before they rotated back to the States. Few had any knowledge of Arabic or Iraq or the specialized skills needed for the jobs they filled. Most of the foreign governments that the Bush administration assumed would join in to help after the invasion didn't; the few that did soon fled as the security situation worsened. Meanwhile, garbage littered the streets, potable water was a luxury, and regular blackouts reminded Iraqis that electrical output was still below prewar levels.[26]

Before the war, experts who warned that the cost of the occupation and of rebuilding Iraq could run into the hundreds of billions of dollars were either silenced by the Bush administration or dismissed from their posts. Now, pushed by Bremer, who realized there was no way out, the president was obliged to ask Congress for an emergency appropriation. But by August 24, 2004, ten months after the money had been appropriated, only $400 million of the $18.4 billion had been spent. Despite the desperate need, the appropriations had been hobbled by Washington bureaucracy. When money did get through, it was often distributed with few controls or records.[27] Emergency funds were being doled out to Iraqis by American officials in stacks of hundred-dollar bills. Engineers trained in removing mines were now attempting to fix water filtration plants and sewer systems. Rocketing security costs were soon consuming as much as a fifth of the budget of many projects.

One example of American reconstruction that disappeared into waste and incompetence was a $75.7 million project called the Fatah pipeline crossing. Its goal was to restore a vital set of large oil pipelines crossing the Tigris River north of Baghdad that had been destroyed by bombs during the invasion. It was a key component of a $2.4 billion, no-bid reconstruction project that a subsidiary of Halliburton, Kellogg Brown, and Root (KBR) had been awarded by the army in 2003. Restoring the pipeline complex at Fatah would enable Iraq to increase petroleum exports, and thus help pay for its own reconstruction, as well as provide gas and heating oil to Iraqis. The idea was to re-lay the pipeline in a tunnel under the river.

From the outset, however, experts had warned that the tunneling project could never succeed because the underground terrain was situated on a fault line. Suggestions for other solutions were ignored. When the ground did indeed prove unstable, the Fatah project still went ahead, despite the huge costs and a contract that enabled idle crews to bill up to $100,000 per day for waiting on standby. According to U.S. officials, KBR attempted to keep the U.S. government ignorant of the growing debacle until the entire budget had been spent. Meanwhile, the U.S. Army Corps of Engineers, which was supposedly administering the project, permitted the disaster to continue for months, notwithstanding warnings from individual Corps officers. The failed project cost Iraq about $5 million a day in potential fuel exports. Despite a scathing report by U.S. government inspectors, Halliburton received little more than a slap on the wrist. That was not unusual. In February 2006, the Army Corps of Engineers also agreed to pay Halliburton most of its fees on a large fuel supply contract in Iraq, even though Pentagon auditors had found that more than $200 million of the charges were questionable.[28]

The Iraqi people had expected the great American superpower, after sweeping Saddam from office, to get the country up and running again. Instead, Iraq sank even further into chaos. Security became more of a luxury than air conditioning. The goodwill with which most Iraqis had originally greeted the coalition quickly dissipated, and things only got worse.

The Insurgency

From the outset the Bush administration misread the threat of the insurgency. It was not, as many later claimed, planned ahead of time by Saddam Hussein. Saddam never thought that the U.S. would actually dare to invade the capital. Ultimately, he reasoned, the coalition would leave him in power just as they had in 1991. Nor did the Iraqi tyrant attempt to prepare any last-ditch guerrilla effort when he finally understood he was wrong.[29] Certainly, foreigners linked with Al-Qaeda, the other enemy in the region identified by the White House, became active in the insurgency—the Jordanian Abu Musab al-Zarqawi chief among them. But there were many insurgent groups, and the reason for their growing success was often the actions of the U.S. itself.

As the invasion threatened, Saddam dispatched thousands of paramilitary fighters, Fedayeen, to the south. They were Baath party members much more fiercely loyal to Saddam than was his regular army. American front-line commander William Wallace, impressed by the Fedayeen's unexpectedly tough resistance and suicide attacks in Najaf and Nasiriya, wanted to pause and wipe them out before proceeding to Baghdad. Various American pundits also warned that the chief threat would not be Saddam's Republican Guard, but a long guerrilla war against the occupation. But General Tommy Franks, driven by Rumsfeld's obsession with a quick, dramatic victory, came close to firing General Wallace for suggesting that he slow the pace. Instead, Franks ordered U.S. forces to bypass the resistance—a bump in the road—and race on to the capital.[30] Rumsfeld also continued to resist calls for an immediate increase in troops for Iraq. The assumption was that once Saddam had fallen, resistance would collapse.

Another preinvasion assumption of the Pentagon was that the U.S. occupiers would be able to turn to Iraqis themselves—the military, police, and civilian bureaucracy—to play the major role in restoring the country after the hard-line Baathists had been purged from their ranks. Once in Baghdad, however, Paul Bremer instituted a series of draconian measures that ignored those plans and instead drove thousands more Sunnis to the insurgents' camp. One of Bremer's first acts—on May 23—was to disband the Iraqi army, dismissing hundreds of thousands of soldiers and officers without pay. He would argue that the army had already ceased to exist; it had simply dissolved in the face of the coalition attack. But preinvasion studies by the State Department and Pentagon had warned against just such measures. Bremer's edict had been okayed by Rumsfeld, but caught other key members of the administration, like Colin Powell and Condoleezza Rice, completely by surprise.[31] There should have been an attempt, critics argued, to recall the officers and reform the ranks after purging the true Saddam loyalists. Although Bremer later agreed to pay the former soldiers, the dismissed officers and men had been transformed virtually overnight from a force that might have played a key role in restoring security into a disgruntled mass of thousands of trained, armed men ready to support, if not actually join, a growing Sunni insurgency.[32]

With a similar decree, Ambassador Bremer decimated the Iraqi civilian administration. Everyone who had been in the top four levels of the Baath Party was dismissed. That meant that about 35,000 of the most experienced civil servants, engineers, teachers, university professors, and hospital administrators were told not to bother showing up for work. The measure had been pushed by Shiite exile leader Ahmad Chalabi, who was intent on wiping out all traces of the Baath Party. The fact that Iraqis had been obliged to join the party simply to advance in Saddam's Iraq made no difference. Their careers destroyed, cut out of power, they, too, became sympathetic to the insurgency.[33]

The insurgents were also aided in their recruiting by the often brutal tactics of U.S. soldiers, who were mostly untrained in urban warfare; largely ignorant of the country and its religion and language; frequently without interpreters or any method of communicating with the people other than raised voices, gestures, and force. They had been told that, once Baghdad had fallen, they would soon be heading home. Now, in the furnace of an Iraqi summer, they were the targets of an unseen enemy, confronting the increasingly hostile population they had supposedly come to liberate. Despite repeated pleas from their commanders, American forces were not furnished with enough armored vehicles and vests to confront the mounting threat. In the heart of Baghdad or other cities, they were tempted to respond to occasional rifle shots with devastating fire from mortar, artillery, and tanks. Lacking firm intelligence, they would sweep up thousands of young Iraqis and hold them without charges. CNN captured one furious young G.I. screaming at a group of Iraqis, "We're here for your fucking freedom. Now back up."[34] Woefully undermanned, American forces were like firemen racing from one blaze to the next.[35]

Paul Bremer's repeated pleas to Rumsfeld and Bush for more American troops were ignored; at times, Rumsfeld didn't even answer the requests.[36] Determined to start rotating U.S. troops out of Iraq, the military launched a crash program to train new Iraqi police and military in record time.

Before the invasion, the U.S. Justice Department supported a plan to deploy thousands of American civilian trainers to rebuild the police force.[37] The Bush administration, however, rejected the idea, arguing it would create an overwhelming American presence in Iraq; they would rely instead on the existing police force to enforce the law. As it turned out, the police force disintegrated as U.S. and coalition troops advanced through the country. Eighty percent of the Iraqi police abandoned their posts, leaving the field open to looting, crime, and the fledgling insurgency. By the time General Garner and other American officials arrived in Baghdad, sixteen of twenty-three major government ministries had already been stripped bare.

With chaos mounting, the Justice Department recommended sending 6,600 police trainers. That number was slashed to 1,500 by Washington, and then the program was never enacted. Though the plans were ready, U.S. officials in Baghdad told reporters they had never received the funding. The White House's hope that other countries would step in to train the police proved chimerical. Those other countries—many of them miffed by the Bush administration's unilateral decision to invade Iraq in the first place—were not ready to send their own trainers into harm's way. Thus, in the turbulent first eight months of the occupation—the crucial period for establishing a sense of law and order—the United States deployed a total of 50 police trainers in the entire country.

From the beginning, those few American instructors—themselves requiring military protection—were overwhelmed by the task. One man, for instance, was dispatched to train a unit with 4,000 officers to guard power plants and other utilities. Another was charged with setting up a border patrol for the entire country. New recruits received about four weeks of training; nearly half that time was spent waiting for instructions to be translated.

The administration paid no attention to repeated warnings by Paul Bremer that the quality of police training was poor; they were intent on increasing the number of trainees regardless of their qualifications. "They were just pulling kids off the streets and handing them badges and AK-47's," Bremer later said.[38]

The new force was also wracked by corruption and infiltrated by various tribal and sectarian gangs who hoped to hijack the police force for their own ends. Thousands of trainees themselves had criminal records, but the Americans lacked the staff to do anything about it. In many areas, equipment was also a problem. "They had rusted Kalashnikovs, which they cleaned with gasoline," said one American advisor. "Most of their weapons did not work. And they got paid very little. They'd sell their bullets to feed their families."

Despite Bremer's warnings, the Bush administration continued to push the myth that the newly trained Iraqi police and military would shortly be taking the place of American forces. Disregarding their own intelligence reports, American leaders publicly downplayed the menace of the growing insurgency. "The dead-enders are still with us," Rumsfeld declared on August 25, 2003, "those remnants of the defeated regimes who'll go on fighting long after their cause is lost."[39]

In October 2003, a major National Intelligence Estimate warned that the insurgency that Rumsfeld had written off in fact had deep roots, was likely to get worse, and could result in civil war.[40] It was fueled by local conditions, said the report, and drew its strength from profound grievances, including the presence of U.S. troops. The rebels were largely disaffected Sunnis upset at being locked out of government posts and denied a role in determining the country's future.

The insurgency got everyone's attention in April 2004, when four American security guards working for a private security company in

Fallujah, in the Sunni Triangle west of Baghdad, were torn apart by an enraged crowd and publicly hung by a bridge over the Euphrates. Outraged at the appalling TV images, President Bush ordered a reluctant U.S. Marine commander stationed outside Fallujah to reoccupy the city and hunt down and arrest the killers.[41] The resulting scenes of American troops smashing their way back into the city further inflamed Iraqis and brought threats from Iraq's U.S.-appointed interim leaders that they would quit the council if the U.S. didn't pull back. Iraqi security forces sent to the scene had shown themselves, in Paul Bremer's words, "to be ineffective or worse."[42]

In short, the first year of the occupation was a disaster, strengthening the insurgency and confirming the views of Iraqis that the coalition was unable to provide them the security they desperately wanted. As sentiments against the Americans mounted, large numbers of Sunnis and Shiites who had considered themselves secular turned to their Muslim beliefs as a new symbol of resistance; the mosques gained in strength as the credibility of the CPA collapsed. The American forces were no longer liberators; they were occupiers.

Lacking troops on the ground to deal with the spreading problem, the U.S. turned increasingly to the Air Force to pulverize suspected insurgent targets with rockets and bombs. Enormous collateral damage, civilian deaths, and mounting bitterness among Iraqis were inevitable.[43]

Iraqis were further outraged in April 28, 2004, when pictures of the mistreatment and torture of prisoners by American troops at the Abu Ghraib prison were broadcast around the world. American authorities had long known of serious problems in the U.S.-run prison system.[44] Paul Bremer had voiced his concerns to U.S. Army Commander Ricardo Sanchez; he never heard back. The problem was complex: American troops lacked the personnel and training to deal with the thousands of Iraqi prisoners they had indiscriminately rounded up; at the same time, statements and doctrine handed down from top Pentagon officials actually encouraged the offenses.[45]

Evidence of torture and brutality continued to surface. In the eyes of many Iraqis, not only was the great American superpower unable to restore the electricity and sewage systems or impose a modicum of law and security, it was now itself guilty of some of the same brutal tactics as Saddam Hussein. As Bremer told Condoleezza Rice, "The message to most Iraqis is that the Coalition can't provide them the most basic government service: security. We've become the worst of all things—an ineffective occupier."[46]

On June 28, 2004, the situation still deteriorating, the CPA handed over formal sovereignty to the interim government of Ayad Allawi. The U.S. would continue to rule behind the scenes, but with steadily diminishing authority. In a very fundamental way, Iraq was coming apart. The sentiment of nationhood that all Iraqi leaders—including Saddam Hussein—had attempted to inculcate over the past eighty years was being ripped asunder. It was being destroyed by the random killings, death squads, bombings, and all-pervasive fear. Iraq's Shiites, Kurds, and Sunnis, who had increasingly commingled in marriage, schools, offices, and the marketplace, were reconsidering who they really were. Terrified of outsiders, unable to count on national police or the military, and certainly not on the occupation troops, they were obliged to provide for their protection by turning back to their tribes, religions, or ethnic groups—or to their own militias. By 2004 there were already nine major militias operating in Iraq, with tens of thousands of members. These were grassroots forces, without uniforms, bases, or any serious training. They set up makeshift checkpoints throughout the country, guarded hospitals, mosques, and airports, and—just as often—persecuted their rivals under the guise of "neighborhood watches."[47]

By mid-2006 they posed a double threat to the future of Iraq. First, they were often brutal, bullying gangs themselves, disturbing order, sowing insecurity, and torturing their enemies. At the same time, these members of the Iraqi army and police who cruised around in official cars and carried government-issued weapons were, by their sectarian revenge killings, destroying the very national institutions whose uniforms they were wearing.[48] A 2006 internal police survey conducted northeast of Baghdad found that 75 percent of Iraqis did not trust the police enough to tip them off to insurgent activity.[49]

Some of the militias had existed well before the fall of Saddam. In the north, the Kurdish *pesh merga* had long led the fight for autonomy and resistance to Baghdad. Many enlisted in the ranks of the new Iraqi army after Saddam's fall. It was a way for them to ensure their influence over a key institution and make certain it would never again be turned against them. In Kirkuk in the north, Kurds began attacking the Arab population so they could claim that city and its surrounding oil wealth as part of their domain.[50]

In the Shiite south, with the collapse of the national government, local militias also took over the policing of their communities. One of the largest groups, the Badr organization, was led by Abdul Aziz al-Hakim, who had originally fought Saddam Hussein from exile in Iran. When the Shiites won control of the Iraqi government in the spring of 2005, they took over the Ministry of Interior, purged its top Sunni officials, and filled the ranks of the country's police with thousands of young Badr militants.

From one point of view, their putting on an Iraqi uniform was an encouraging sign of national unity. In practice, however, the Shiites were intent on turning the Ministry of the Interior into their own sectarian force.[51] Shiite militias were soon discovered running death squads and torture chambers in Ministry buildings. Families of Sunnis who had disappeared or been murdered charged that their relatives had been picked up by men wearing police uniforms and driven away in official vehicles, never to be seen alive again. The most notorious units were the police paramilitary forces, which numbered more than 17,000 men.

Another Shiite militia group, the Mahdi Army, filled one of the main units of the police's public order brigades. They were also accused by many Iraqis, especially Sunni Arabs, of torture and extrajudicial killings. Most were recruited from poorer Shiite areas of Baghdad.

The leader of the Mahdi Army was Moktada al-Sadr, the fiery descendant of a prominent Shiite clerical family. When Saddam fell in the summer of 2003, the young cleric's radical mix of religion, nationalism, and anti-Americanism was an instant success among the aimless, unemployed Shiite youth. As the American occupiers and establishment Shiites looked on, reluctant to challenge the young demagogue, he created within a few months a force of several thousand young men. By the time U.S. troops finally moved against him in the spring of 2004, it was too late. His militiamen fought the Americans to near standstill; overnight he gained a reputation as a fearless, outspoken nationalist.

Though they privately despised him, Iraqi political leaders now courted his support. In the parliamentary elections in 2005, he won more seats in the 275-person legislature than any other political leader. He also gained power over key posts in the south of the country, as well as the ministries of transportation and health, giving him control of tens of thousands of government jobs.

By the spring of 2006, the Mahdi Army controlled the Shiite section of eastern Baghdad known as Sadr City and the southern city of Basra. Government forces had vanished. Thousands of Sadr's aggressive young followers, many of them teenagers in shiny soccer jerseys, volunteered for street cleanup operations and donated blood after Friday prayers. They also wore flak jackets and packed grenade launchers and AK-47s as they patrolled the neighborhood; they enforced random roadblocks, detaining whomever they wanted. Mosques blared warnings on loudspeakers for American troops to stay out of the area. Increasingly, the Americans were doing just that.[52]

Sadr's Mahdi followers also enforced a fairly harsh Islamic fundamentalism everywhere from university campuses to liquor stores. But even Iraqis who detested his fervid religious views and were suspicious of his ties with the political and religious leadership in Iran appreciated the Mahdi Army's attempts to act as a force of order—if not law.[53]

His, however, was only one of the Shiite and criminal groups battling for control of cities like Basra. By June 2006, corruption there had become so pervasive that the 135-member internal affairs unit established to police the police was itself operating as a ring of extortionists, kidnappers, and killers. The police chief in Basra complained publicly that he could not trust most of his men and that corruption was rampant, but he was powerless to fire—never mind prosecute—even the most outrageous offenders. Murders in Basra were being committed almost hourly.

As the Shiite militias grew in strength, Shiite communities increasingly became the targets of the more radical groups of the Sunni insurgency, who were intent on provoking a civil war.[54] Such was the announced goal of Abu Musab al-Zarqawi, who decried Shiites as apostates and called for their annihilation by the same ferocious means—beheadings, mass executions, and suicide car bombings—that his followers used against the occupying "Crusader" forces. There were increasingly bloody attacks against Shiite leaders, mosques, and even funeral processions. On February 22, 2006, an enormous explosion destroyed the golden dome of the Askariya Shrine in Samarra. Enraged, Shiite militias reacted just as the radical insurgents had hoped: storming out of their own communities to launch a wave of bloody attacks against Sunni mosques, religious leaders, and, often, any hapless individual who crossed their path. More than a thousand people were killed, many for no other reason than that they were Sunni.

The Iraqi police, under the control of the Shiite minister of the interior, stood by as the mayhem spread. The American army, supposedly in Iraq to maintain peace and security, was ordered to remain in their quarters as retributive violence flared across the country.[55]

The Sunnis, who had no militias, felt more vulnerable than ever. They would push to form their own local defense forces. As one senior Sunni political leader said, "The Kurds have their militia, and they're part of the army. The Shiites run the government. We've been left alone with our mosques in the field."[56]

As many saw it, more than three years after the invasion, civil war had already broken out. Instead of entering an era of peace and democracy, as President Bush and Prime Minister Blair had promised, Baghdad seemed to be turning into a new Beirut. With foreign reporters usually too terrified to venture out on their own, the outside world was increasingly dependent for information on Iraqi bloggers, like the Mesopotamian who described the savagery of his own Baghdad neighborhood:

> The confusion and conflict between the Americans, the army, and the Ministry of Interior is producing a situation where the citizens don't know anymore whether the security personnel in the street are friends, enemies, terrorists, or simply criminals and thieves. Everybody is wearing the same uniforms. Whole sections of the city have virtually fallen to gangs and terrorists, and this is especially true for the Sunni-dominated neighborhoods. People and businesses are being robbed and employees kidnapped en masse in broad daylight and with complete ease as though security forces are nonexistent,

although we see them everywhere. I don't know anymore what can be done to rescue the situation.[57]

Ironically, many of the 120,000-member police and commando force of the Ministry of the Interior had been trained by American military advisors and financed by the United States. The idea was that the new Iraqi security force would take the place of U.S. forces eager to pull out. Instead, the U.S. had created something of a Frankenstein's monster, arming and training one side, the Shiites, in an impending civil war.

Alarmed by the situation, the same American ambassador who had been pressing for the private militias to be dissolved and disarmed, Zalmay Khalilzad, threatened to end U.S. payments for the government units. He demanded that the ministry weed out officers and soldiers whose primary allegiance was to a sect rather than the state and that the ministry itself be freed from control by radical Shiites. Shiite leaders retorted there was no way they would give up their hold over the ministry that Saddam had used so ruthlessly against their people.

"Anybody who has a militia now has power," said Adnan Pachachi, a former foreign minister and member of the newly elected Iraqi Parliament. "The Mahdi Army, Badr, the insurgents—these are the ones who wield power. They have weapons, they can move around, and they are determined. It's not a question of political personalities, but of arms and weapons."[58]

Meanwhile, having dismissed the Sunni-led army after the fall of Saddam, American forces were now doing their utmost to attract Sunnis back to the ranks of the police and military. It was only in the spring of 2006, three years after the invasion, that Bush administration officials finally began putting the necessary resources into training the Iraqi police, dispatching 3,000 American soldiers plus private DynCorp contractors. The effort, however, may have come too late to halt the spiral of violence, which had taken on a momentum of its own. The same may be true for a belated effort to train and equip the new Iraqi army.

Full Circle

There are those for whom the invasion of Iraq was definitely worthwhile. One of the Bush administration's major concerns was to transform Iraq from a centrally planned to a market economy. During his reign in Baghdad, Paul Bremer accomplished that task by fiat virtually overnight. The new guidelines he imposed were incorporated firmly into Iraq's interim constitution, and the economic restructuring they mandate is well under way. Legislation governing everything from banking and investment to copyrights, business ownership, and trade was all similarly modified according to U.S. objectives, with very little say from the Iraqi people.[59] One of the main measures was to privatize all of Iraq's 192 state-owned industries (with the exception of oil extraction) and open the country to foreign investment.

Contracts for the reconstruction of Iraq were carefully directed to American corporations. With the Iraqi government denied the right to give preference to Iraqis, some 150 U.S. companies won contracts totaling more than $50 billion. Halliburton had the largest, worth more than $11 billion, while 13 other U.S. companies were earning more than $1.5 billion each. Those contractors answered to the U.S. government rather than the Iraqi people, many of whom were upset about their failure to provide water, sanitation, and electricity at prewar levels.[60]

In 1921, when Winston Churchill and his group of experts met in the Semiramis Hotel in Cairo to establish the artificial state of Iraq and decide who they would put in charge of their creation, they had a couple of key concerns in mind. They needed military bases, not just to dominate Iraq but to maintain their sway over the entire strategically vital region. They were also determined to control Iraq's potentially vast petroleum resources.

Eighty-five years later, in 2006, Iraqis could be forgiven if they thought their country had come full circle. American strategists had been concerned about U.S. dependence on Saudi Arabia for bases in the region; Iraq could resolve that problem—just as it had for the British. Even as the American occupiers continued to issue vague denials of any interest in establishing permanent military facilities in Iraq, the Pentagon was spending hundreds of millions of dollars building new bases that appeared to be anything but temporary.[61] The largest was the sprawling air base and logistics center at Balad, north of Baghdad. By mid-2006, the U.S. had poured close to a quarter of a billion dollars into the facility and was planning tens of millions of dollars more, including a major road system and a 13-foot-high security fence that would stretch for 12.4 miles. The base was billed as the Americans' strategic air center for the entire region.

Indeed, Balad was only one of several sophisticated complexes being developed by the Pentagon across the country. Another $110 million was earmarked for the Tallil airbase near the southeastern city of Nasiriya, including a new dining hall for six thousand troops. The huge sums involved finally prompted some congressmen to suspect that the money the Pentagon had been requesting for supposedly short-term, emergency needs in Iraq was actually destined for much more permanent ends.

"The Iraqis believe we came for their oil, and we're going to put bases on top of their oil," said Democratic Representative Tom Allen, a critic of the administration's approach. "As long as the vast majority of Iraqis believe we want to be there indefinitely, those who are opposed to us are going to fight harder, and those who are with us are going to be less enthusiastic."

The Bush administration refused to define its long-term plans. In June 2006, however, Republicans in Congress killed a provision in a war-funding bill that would have put the United States on record as *against* establishing permanent U.S. bases in Iraq.

The question of oil, of course, had been paramount from the beginning. Long before the invasion, American oil companies understood that toppling Saddam could be a business bonanza, allowing them to supplant countries like France and Russia, which had been granted lucrative oil deals under Saddam.[62] The potential was enormous: not only would Iraq's existing wells require complete revamping, but the country also boasted huge deposits in the south that had yet to be developed. The American companies would have the inside track—providing the country held together.

In March 2006, President Bush vowed that by the end of the year, U.S. troops would begin pulling out of Iraq. By then, he assured the American people, the security of most of the country would be taken over by Iraqi forces—the army and the police trained by the United States. Just a few months earlier, however, according to the U.S. government's own estimate, not a single unit of the Iraqi army was capable of operating on its own without U.S. support. A few days later, the American president conceded what experts had long been saying— that U.S. troops would still be in Iraq in 2009, when a new American president took office.[63]

Meanwhile, the U.S. was building the largest embassy in the world on the banks of the Tigris. Referred to, ironically, as George W.'s palace, its twenty-one buildings would cover an area larger than Vatican City. Though Iraqis had to tolerate frequent cuts in electricity, outrageous delays to be connected to the water system, and interminable lines to fuel their cars, the new U.S. embassy, which was due to open June 2007, boasted its own power and water plants to supply a population that would be the size of a small town. Details of the complex were veiled in tight security, but reports were that behind the ten-foot-thick perimeter walls, diplomats and staff would enjoy spacious apartments, the largest swimming pool in Iraq, a gymnasium, tennis courts, a cinema, restaurants run by major U.S. food chains, a beauty salon, and a recreation hall to rival anything in the U.S. According to a State Department spokesman, the size reflected the "massive amount of work still facing the U.S. and our commitment to see it through."[64]

In June 2006, the Americans claimed to have demonstrated that commitment when they finally tracked down and killed Abu Musab al-Zarqawi, the most infamous of the insurgent leaders. His disappearance, however, did little to calm the situation. Indeed, his notoriety may have been due as much to the $25 million price tag put on his head by the United States as to his vicious tactics. He was only one of many Sunni insurgent leaders, several of whom were said to have been dismayed by the violent attacks he engineered against Shiite civilians. They viewed themselves as Arab nationalists fighting to end the U.S.-led occupation. At the same time, they feared for their future under a Shiite-dominated government—although the most radical Shiite militias were also increasingly determined to drive out the occupiers. They seemed to have broad support: according to a poll taken in January 2006, 88 percent of Sunnis and 41 percent of Shiites in Iraq supported attacks against the American-led coalition.[65]

As many had foreseen, the occupation itself was now part of the problem, fueling the insurgency and failing to deliver on promises of security and peace. With frightened young American troops finding themselves patrolling the cities and villages of a hostile civilian population, the situation was similar in some ways to Vietnam sixty years before. Unsurprisingly, similar calamaties occurred.

One such tragedy happened in the Sunni village of Haditha in November 2005, when a roadside bomb killed a young marine lance corporal. The brief report released to the press at the time claimed that twenty-three Iraqis—eight insurgents and fifteen civilians—were killed by the blast and the firefight that followed. A few months later, *Time* magazine, furnished with pictures of the casualties, questioned the official account, and subsequent investigations pieced together a very different story. Following the bomb attack, there was no battle with insurgents. Instead, according to Iraqi witnesses, the U.S. marines moved into the village to exact revenge, methodically executing twenty-four civilians—men, women, and children—with shots to the head and chest at point blank range even as they pled for mercy, the mothers trying to shield their children. The girls killed inside one family's house were ages 14, 10, 5, 3, and 1, according to death certificates.[66] It appeared that reports on the crime were first falsified, then ignored or squelched up the chain of military command.

Haditha may have been just the tip of the iceberg. Even as that story was breaking, American troops near the troubled city of Samarra shot and killed two Iraqi women, including one who might have been pregnant and on her way to a hospital, after their car disobeyed what the American military command said were repeated warnings to stop. Meanwhile, the U.S. was investigating charges that seven marines dragged a man from his home west of Baghdad, shot him, and then planted a rifle and a shovel near the body to make it appear as if he were burying a bomb.[67] Relatives claimed he had refused earlier American requests to provide information about insurgent attacks.

Provoked by Haditha, Iraq's new prime minister Nuri Kamal al-Maliki, a Shiite, gained political points by denouncing what he characterized as habitual attacks by troops against Iraqi civilians. Such violence, he declared, had become a "regular phenomenon" by many troops in the American-led coalition who "do not respect the Iraqi people." "They crush them with their vehicles and kill them just on suspicion," he declared. Attacks on civilians, he said, would play a role in future decisions on how long to ask American forces to remain in Iraq.[68]

Other Iraqi leaders called on the U.S. to turn over evidence of the Haditha killings so that Iraqis themselves could investigate the case. They were ignoring the fact that—unlike Saddam Hussein and his henchmen—U.S. troops in Iraq were not subject to the jurisdiction of Iraqi courts.

Yet even as the new prime minister may have bolstered his political standing by condemning the American occupation, he—and most of the elite—realized, as the Iraqi elite had realized during the British occupation eighty-five years earlier, that the only thing keeping them in power and holding their country together were roughly 150,000 foreign troops.

More than three years after the invasion, the newly elected representatives to the country's parliament were still bitterly feuding. The Kurdish nationalists demanded assurances of autonomy; the Sunnis a share of the power; many of the Shiite fundamentalists, who held the majority of the seats, an Islamic state. And all were at loggerheads over who would control the country's vast petroleum wealth.[69] They were all also battling for influence and privilege within their own ranks.

It was considered something of a triumph that in June 2006, five months after the Iraqis elected a new government, Shiite Prime Minister Nuri Kamal al-Maliki finally managed to appoint ministers of the Interior and Defense. Whether the government—itself beholden to major Shiite sectarian groups—would actually have the will to cleanse the security forces of the militias and criminal gangs that had taken control of them was another question.

By mid-2006, like an unstable chemical compound, Iraq's fractious peoples seemed on the verge of detonating, with shock waves that would reverberate throughout the entire region. Even if the country held together, the possibility of a radical Shiite government with the sort of fundamentalist overtones and links to Iran that the U.S. had feared in 1991 now seemed very real. The dream of establishing any kind of democratic regime seemed evermore illusory.

Some of the more thoughtful neoconservatives in the United States who had earlier cheered on Bush's invasion of Iraq were having serious second thoughts. Francis Fukuyama, author of *The End of History* and one of the early, celebrated proponents of neoconservatism, announced in the spring of 2006 that the philosophy had "evolved into something I can no longer support." The war in Iraq was unwarranted and poorly conceived. Its failure, he said, demonstrated "the danger of good intentions carried to extremes." Democracy cannot be imposed from without. He concluded, "It seems very unlikely that history will judge either the intervention [in Iraq] itself or the ideas animating it kindly."[70]

Publicly, at least, George W. Bush and his top officials revealed no such misgivings. On June 13, 2006, encouraged by the killing of Zarqawi and Prime Minister Maliki's apparent resolve, President Bush flew into Baghdad. He wanted to look Maliki "in the eye," he said, and show America's support for the new government.

The president's six-hour visit demonstrated the daunting extent of the task Bush was attempting to bequeath to Iraq. More than three years after the invasion, with 135,000 American troops on the ground, the president's trip was arranged with all the stealth of a trip to a deadly war zone—which Iraq still was. Even Maliki wasn't informed of the plan until just before Air Force One landed at the Baghdad airport. From there the president was flown directly by armored Nighthawk helicopter to the heavily fortified Green Zone, as a force of 85,000 Iraqi and American troops fanned out across Baghdad in yet another attempt to quell the mounting anarchy and bloodshed.

Before dark the president—again under tightest security—was hustled back to the Baghdad airport. The next day, back in the White House Rose Garden, Bush, without defining what success in Iraq would mean, declared that it "depends upon the Iraqis." The U.S. would continue to offer help, but it would no longer shoulder the burden of running the country. "If the Iraqis don't have the will to succeed, they're not going to succeed. We can have all the will we want, I can have all the confidence in the ability for us to bring people to justice, but if they choose not to take the—make the hard decisions and to implement a plan, they're not going to make it."[71]

There was something more than vaguely disingenuous about all this. From the establishment of the modern nation of Iraq, foreign powers had prevented Iraqis from making just this sort of hard decision. George W. Bush was just the latest in a long line of outsiders complicit in the country's bloody history stretching back to the British, who first stitched the makeshift country together in order to control its strategic location and the vast oil wealth that was to prove a curse rather than a bounty to Iraq's peoples. It was an edifice almost doomed to autodestruct. Indeed, what followed was an appalling series of failed rebellions, ruthless reprisals, cynical manipulations, and great power betrayals. There was the longest war of the twentieth century; the hypocrisy of Halabja; the abandonment of hundreds of thousands of Shiites and Kurds in 1991; the years of murderous U.N. sanctions; and finally the trumped-up, illegal invasion of 2003 and the disastrous occupation that followed.

The U.S.-led coalition had a chance in the first months after the 2003 invasion to restore a sense of order and reassure Iraq's fractious peoples. Instead, because of a combination of ignorance and arrogance at the highest levels of the Bush administration, they failed to seize the opportunity, opening the way to spiraling mayhem that drove Iraqis back to their tribal and religious loyalties. Instead of calming their centripetal passions and fears, the U.S. played into the hands of the insurgents and radical militia leaders, spinning the anarchy to an even higher pitch.

And, now, driven by domestic political pressure, George Bush had the gall to announce that it would be up to Iraqis to resolve the mess left by nearly a century of foreign abuse. Or, as Donald Rumsfeld, the official who had ensured that the U.S. never had enough troops on the ground to secure Iraq, noted when asked who would have to deal with the problem if civil war broke out, replied, the plan was to "have the Iraqi security forces deal with it, to the extent that they are able to."[72]

But, after the enormous sacrifice in treasure and human lives, politically there was now no way that the Bush administration could pack up and leave. President Bush made that clear at a press conference on August 21st, 2006. It was one day after Sunni Arab gunmen killed 20 religious pilgrims and wounded 300 others who had gathered in Baghdad for a Shiite holiday.

The President's rambling, disjointed remarks not only underscored the bankruptcy of his administration's handling of Iraq, but the never-neverland that the president of the United States seemed to inhabit:

Reporter: But are you frustrated, sir?

The President: Frustrated? Sometimes I'm frustrated. Rarely surprised. Sometimes I'm happy. This is—but war is not a time of joy. These aren't joyous times. These are challenging times, and they're difficult times, and they're straining the psyche of our country.[73]

Failure to remain, Bush said, would throw open the door to the terrorists, yet that terrorist threat—the thousands of insurgents and suicide bombers and bloody religious and sectarian chaos—were a product of the Bush administration's own calamitous policies. When one of the journalists pointed that out, the President—as if emerging from three years in a time capsule—first repeated the now shopworn and discredited claim that Saddam had represented a deadly threat because he had the capacity to produce WMD and had links with terrorist leader Abu Musab al-Zarkawi. Then the president pressed on.

You know, I've heard this theory about everything was just fine until we arrived, and kind of 'we're going to stir up the hornet's nest' theory. It just doesn't hold water, as far as I'm concerned. The terrorists attacked us and killed 3,000 of our citizens before we started the freedom agenda in the Middle East.

Asked what Iraq had to do with the attack on the World Trade Center, Mr. Bush responded testily, "Nothing," adding—as if his words could somehow erase his government's past lies and distortions—that "nobody has ever suggested in this administration that Saddam Hussein ordered the attacks."

The president also repeatedly cited the threat to freedom in Iraq if the U.S. withdrew. But that lofty cause was nothing but political window dressing. Indeed, allowing the people of Iraq a real choice in their future had always been a *threat* to the U.S. and other great powers, not a goal. What counted was which local leaders would gain control of the region and its resources and how amenable they would be to great power interests. Not if they were freely elected.

The past eighty years of history certainly proved the point.

END NOTES

Introduction : The Trial of Saddam

1. Robert Parry, *Trick or Treason: The October Surprise Mystery* (New York: Sheridan Square Press, 1993), 167.

2. The preliminary charges brought against Saddam on July 1, 2004 were:

1. The executions of 148 men and boys at Dujail following the assassination attempt against Saddam in 1982.
2. The slaughter of Shiites and Kurds following their uprising in March 1991.
3. The Anfal Campaign waged against the Kurds in 1998.
4. The gassing of 5,000 Kurds at Halabja in 1998.
5. The massacre of some 8,000 members of the Kurdish Barzani tribe in 1983.
6. The invasion of Kuwait in August 1990.
7. Killing thousands of political activists over thirty years.

These seven were preliminary charges to be further investigated and refined by teams of lawyers and researchers. In a procedure roughly similar to the way indictments are handed down in the U.S., evidence then has to be presented to a judge to decide whether a trial is justified. (At the beginning of April 2006, while the Dujail trial was still going on, Saddam was formally charged with the death and deportation of thousands of Kurds during the Anfal Campaign of the 1980s.) In theory, the former dictator and his lieutenants could face trial for at least each of these seven accusations, but because of the chaotic nature of the Dujail trial, it seems highly unlikely that the Iraqi government would be interested in six more similar events. BBC News, "Charges Facing Saddam Hussein, July 1, 2004," via http://news.bbc.co.uk/2/hi/middle_east/3320293.stm.

3. *Washington Post*, May 28, 1998, B4.

4. In the fall of 2004, the documentary was broadcast in several countries, though not the United States.

Chapter 1 : Beginnings

1. William R. Polk, *Understanding Iraq* (New York: Harper Collins, 2005), 77.

2. Many insights throughout this chapter thanks to Peter Sluglett; Said K. Aburish, *Saddam Hussein* (London: Bloomsbury, 2000), 2.

3. Judith S. Yaphe, *The View from Basra*, in Simon, Reva and Eleanor Tejirian, *The Creation of Iraq* (New York: Columbia University Press, 2003), 19.

4. George G. Gruen, *The Oil Resources of Iraq*, in Simon Tejirian, ibid., 114.

5. Ibid., 115.

6. Ibid.

7. Ibid.

8. Polk, 73–74.

9. Yaphe, 27.

10. Polk, 74.

11. John Bulloch and Harvey Morris, *Saddam's War* (London: Faber & Faber, 1991), 58.

12. Their dispute began on the prophet Muhammad's death in 630, over the question of who would succeed him. Those who much later become known as Sunnis—who now account for about 85 percent of all Muslims—chose to follow one of Muhammad's closest confidants, his father-in-law Abu Bakr, naming him their leader, or caliph. Those who later became the Shiites believed that the rightful successor was the prophet's cousin and son-in-law Ali, who became caliph between 656 and 661. Bitterness grew between the two rival branches. First Ali was murdered; then his son, Hussein, along with his family and a small group of followers, was slaughtered. Hussein's head was cut off and delivered to the Sunni caliph in Damascus. Memories of that massacre, which are commemorated annually in what are known as passion plays, are still vivid for millions of Shiites. In time, many Sunnis came to despise the Shiites as traitorous apostates, although the sectarianism currently afflicting Iraq is a phenomenon largely created by Saddam Hussein in the 1980s. Peter Sluglett.

13. Polk, 77.

14. Sir Martin Gilbert (ed.), *Winston S. Churchill*, vol. IV (London: Heinemann, 1975), 504–505, in Christopher Catherwood, *Winston's Folly* (London: Constable, 2004), 92.

15. Churchill to Trenchard, August 29, 1920, from the Chartwell Papers at the Churchill Archive Centre, Churchill College, Cambridge. Quoted in Catherwood, 85.

16. Geoff Simons, *Iraq: From Sumer to Saddam* (London: St. Martins Press, 1994), 179–181.

17. Churchill to Lloyd George (not sent), August 31, 1920 (Chartwell, ibid.), quoted in Catherwood, 88.

18. Catherwood, 128.

19. Churchill to Shuckburgh, July 9, 1921, quoted by Catherwood, 128.

20. Catherwood, 163–164.

21. Sandra Mackey, *The Reckoning* (New York: W. W. Norton, 2002), 113.

22. Catherwood, 193.

23. George Packer, *The Assassins' Gate* (New York: Farrar, Straus and Giroux, 2005), 334.

24. Catherwood, 186.

25. Ibid.

26. Ibid., 205.

27. Packer, 333.

28. Quoted in Omissi, *Air Power*, 154. The draft of the Air Staff's "Notes on the Method of Employment of the Air Arm in Iraq," presented to Parliament in August 1924, carried this sentence almost verbatim. Later drafts omitted it and stressed air control's humaneness, Lawrence to Liddell Hart, June 1930, quoted in Mack, *A Prince of Our Disorder*, 385. See also Omissi, *Air Power*, 164–165. Cited in "The Defense of Inhumanity: Air Control and the British Idea of Arabia," Priya Satia, *The American Historical Review*, vol III, no. 1, February 2006.

29. Wilson to the chief of the general staff, Mesopotamia, March 4, 1920, in Air Staff, "Memo on effects likely to be produced by intensive aerial bombing of semicivilised people," n.d., 58212, CO 730/18, PRO; Trenchard, maiden speech to the House of Lords, 1930, quoted in Townshend, "Civilization and 'Frightfulness,'" cited in Priya Satia, "The Defense of Inhumanity." Ibid.

30. For an excellent discussion of this period, see Peter Sluglett, *Britain in Iraq 1914–1932* (London: Ithaca Press, 1976), 20–40.

31. CP 235 (25), May 11, 1925: CO 730/82/22162, cited in Sluglett. Ibid., 89.

32. F. H. Humphreys to Sir John Simon, December 15, 1932, AIR 8/94, PRO; emphasis added. *See also* Air Ministry to CID, November 26, 1921, FO 730/18, PRO. Cited in "The Defense of Inhumanity." Ibid.

33. Mackey, 119.

34. Ibid., 136.

35. Aburish, 27.

36. Mackey, 137.

37. Aburish, 29. That claim, according to Peter Sluglett, is specious. Kuwait had never been part of Iraq, had never paid taxes to Istanbul, and had never had an Ottoman administrator. See Peter Sluglett, "The Resilience of a Frontier: Ottoman and Iraqi Claims to Kuwait, 1871 to 1990," *International History Review*, 24, 2002, 783–816.

38. Ibid., 30.

39. Ibid., 39.

40. Ibid., 41.

41. On July 19, 1958, still discussing the possibility of intervention, U.K. Foreign Secretary Selwyn Lloyd sent a secret telegram (number 1979, dated July 19, 1958) to Prime Minister Harold Macmillan, declaring, "The advantage of [immediate British occupation] would be that we could get our hands firmly on Kuwait oil [however] the effect upon international opinion and the rest of the Arab world would not be good." Instead he suggests it would be better to set up "a kind of Kuwaiti Switzerland where the British do not exercise physical control" but must be prepared to "take firm action to maintain our position in Kuwait" as well as the other Gulf states (Saudi Arabia, Bahrain, Qatar) and that the U.S. agrees with the U.K. "that at all costs these oil fields must be kept in Western hands." Telegram no. 1979, July 19, 1958, to prime minister from secretary of state, from Washington; File FO 371/132 779. "Future Policy in the Persian Gulf," January 15, 1958, FO 371/132 778, cited in Noam Chomsky, *Deterring Democracy* (Boston: South End Press, 1992), ch. 6.

42. William Quandt, "Lebanon, 1958, and Jordan, 1970," in Barry Blechman and Stephen Kaplan, eds., *Force Without War* (Brookings Institution, 1978), 238 and 247.

Chapter 2 : A Presentable Young Man

1. UPI, "Saddam Key in Early CIA Plot," April 10, 2003, by Richard Sale; also Richard Sale, UPI intelligence reporter, interview by author, Connecticut, April 2004. Sale has written extensively on the U.S. intelligence community. His information comes from background interviews over the years with American intelligence officials.

2. *Foreign Relations of the United States* (Washington: Government Printing Office, 1945), vol. 8, 45.

3. Said K. Aburish, *Saddam Hussein* (London: Bloomsbury, 2000), 54.

Palestinian journalist Aburish's biography of Saddam is one of the most informed on the early life of the Iraqi leader.

4. Sale article and interview; see also Aburish, 54.

5. UPI, Sale. According to Sale, "Adel Darwish, Middle East expert and author of 'Unholy Babylon,' said the move was done 'with full knowledge of the CIA,' and that Saddam's CIA handler was an Iraqi dentist working for CIA165–167 and Egyptian intelligence. U.S. officials separately confirmed Darwish's account. Darwish said that Saddam's paymaster was Capt. Abdel Maquid Farid, assistant military attaché at the Egyptian Embassy who paid for the apartment from his own personal account. Three former senior U.S. officials have confirmed that this is accurate."

6. Ibid., and Aburish, 46–48.

7. Richard Sale, interview with author. Several top U.S. intelligence officials confirmed Saddam's training to him on background.

8. Mackey, 27; and Charles Tripp, *A History of Iraq* (Cambridge: Cambridge University Press, 2000), 165–167.

9. Roger Morris, "A Tyrant 40 Years in the Making," *New York Times*, Op-Ed, March 14, 2003.

10. *Le Monde*, February 5, 1963, 5.

11. Mackey, 191.

12. Batatu quotes King Hussein as confirming that "what happened in Iraq on February 8 had the support of American intelligence." H. Batatu, *The Old Social Classes and the Revolutionary Movements of Iraq* (Princeton, 1978), 985–986, cited in Marion Farouk-Sluglett and Peter Sluglett, *Iraq Since 1958* (London: Tauris, 2001), 297; also Aburish, 60.

13. Andrew and Patrick Cockburn, *Out of the Ashes* (New York: Harper Collins, 1999), 74. The declassified papers of the British Cabinet of 1963 also disclose that the coup was backed by the CIA and the British. *The Guardian*, London, January 1, 1994, 5.

14. Michel Despratx, interview by author, Paris, May 20, 2004. For a TV documentary co-reported with the author, Despratx interviewed several former Iraqis who were active in the Baath Party around the time of the 1963 coup. Despratx supplied tapes and transcripts of those interviews.

15. UPI Sale and inteview; also Morris, *New York Times*. Aburish, 58.

16. Aburish, 58.

17. Ibid., 61.

18. Hatef Abdallah interview with Michel Despratx; transcript provided to author. Abdallah is now the headmaster of a primary school in Baghdad.

19. UPI, Sales.

20. "Transcript: U.S. OK'd 'Dirty War,'" *Miami Herald*, December 4, 2003. See also National Security Archives Web site: http://www.gwu.edu/~nsarchiv/NSAEBB/NSAEBB104/index.htm.

21. Abdallah interview with Michel Despratx.

22. Aburish, 59.

23. Ibid., 62.

24. Sluglett, 100; Aburish, 71.

25. Sluglett, 100–101.

26. According to Aburish, the negotiator for the U.S. was Robert Anderson, the former secretary of treasury under Eisenhower. Ibid., 74.

27. Ibid., 75; Sluglett, 113.

28. Aburish, 73.

29. Morris, *New York Times*.

30. Aburish, 74.

31. Methods of torture seemed limited only by human imagination—cigarettes were snuffed out in eyeballs, machines were employed to chop off human limbs, and victims were hung from meat hooks while torturers flayed or burned the skin off their backs. Despratx interviews; Mackey, 210–211; see also Kanan Makiya, *Republic of Fear* (Berkeley: University of California Press, 1998).

32. Biographic sketch of Saddam Hussein by British embassy, Baghdad, November 15, 1969; Public Record Office, London, FCO 17/871 via http://www.gwu.edu/~nsarchiv/NSAEBB/NSAEBB107/index.htm.

33. Telegram from British embassy, Baghdad, to Foreign and Commonwealth Office, "Saddam Hussein," December 20, 1969. Source: Public Record Office, London, FCO 17/871. via http://www.gwu.edu/~nsarchiv/NSAEBB/NSAEBB107/iraq02.pdf.

34. Sluglett, 145–148.

35. Aburish, 101. Concerned about maintaining the country's oil production level, Saddam excluded the Basra oil company, which was the sister company of the IPC.

36. Ibid., 106. Also Mackey, 229.

37. Christine Moss Helms, quoted in Mackey, 229.

38. Mackey, 229.

39. Jonathan Randal, *After Such Knowledge, What Forgiveness* (New York: Farrar, Straus and Giroux, 1997), 145.

40. Mackey, 225.

41. Transcript, "Secretary's Principals and Regionals Staff Meeting,"

April 28, 1975 (excerpt). Source: National Archives, RG 59, Department of State Records, Transcripts of Secretary of State Henry A. Kissinger Staff Meetings, 1973–1977, via http://www.gwu.edu/~nsarchiv/NSAEBB/NSAEBB107/index. htm.

42. Memorandum of conversation, Henry Kissinger et al. with Iraqi Minister of Foreign Affairs Sa'dun Hammadi, December 17, 1975. Source: National Archives, RG 59, Department of State Records, Records of Henry Kissinger, 1973–1977, Box 13, December 1975 NODIS Memcons via http://www.gwu .edu/~nsarchiv/NSAEBB/NSAEBB107/index.htm.

43. Aburish, 147.

44. Kenneth Timmerman, *The Death Lobby* (New York: Bantam Books, 1992), 20. This is probably the best work on the arming of Saddam.

45. Ibid., 60.

46. Ibid., 76.

47. Aburish, 146.

48. Ibid.

49. Timmerman, 72.

50. Ibid., 86.

51. Aburish, 137.

52. Ibid., 139.

53. For extensive coverage of German-Iraq relations, see Hans Leyendecker and Richard Rickelmann, *Marchands de Mort* (Paris: Olivier Orban, 1991).

54. Timmerman, 81; Aburish, 139; also Iraq Supplier Database, Iraq Watch, via http://www.iraqwatch.org/search/search_db.asp?sc=supplier&qu= chemical+weapons&sm=exact.

55. Iraq Suppliers Database; also DIA "Chemical Weapons in Iraq" 1991, via http://www.gulflink.osd.mil/declassdocs/dia/19950825/950825_53270053_ 91r.html.

56. Khidhir Hamza, "Inside Saddam's Secret Nuclear Program," September (vol. 54, no. 5), *Bulletin of the Atomic Scientists*, October 1998, 26–33.

57. Timmerman, 58.

58. Ibid., 61.

59. Dan Ravi and Yossi Melman, *Every Spy a Prince* (Boston: Houghton Mifflin, 1990), 250; and John Cooley, *An Alliance Against Babylon* (London: Pluto Press, 2005), 160.

60. Hamza, 26–33.

61. David Albright, Corey Gay, and Khidhir Hamza, "Development of the Al-Tuwaitha Site," Institute for Science and International Security, April 26,

1999, via http://www.isis-online.org/publications/iraq/tuwaitha.html; and Iraq Watch, Suppliers Index.

62. Accounts of the July 1979 purge of the Baath are drawn from Coughlin, 155–159; Sluglett, 206–207; and Aburish, 172.

63. Coughlin, 154.

64. Aburish, 168.

Chapter 3 : The Tilting Game

1. Mohammed Heikal, "Illusion of Triumph," 81, cited in Aburish, 252.

2. Tripp, 220–222.

3. Aburish, 187.

4. Jimmy Carter, State of the Union Address, 1980, via www.jimmycarter library.org. Jimmy Carter had already dispatched an envoy to Baghdad in 1977 with an offer of conciliation as part of an overall plan to "aggressively challenge" the Soviets for influence in radical states.

5. Barry Rubin, "The United States and Iraq," in *Iraq's Road to War*, ed. Amatzia Baram and Barry Rubin (New York: St. Martin's Press, 1993), 256.

6. Ibid., 256.

7. Aburish, 189.

8. Robert Perry, telephone interview with author, April 19, 2004. Haig's memo can be found on Perry's Web site, www.consortiumnews.com/archive/ xfile5.html.

9. James Aikens, interview with author, Bowie, Maryland, May 13, 2004.

10. Richard Sale, interview with author.

11. Ibid.

12. In July 1980, the *New York Times* reported there was a meeting in Amman between Zbigniew Brzezinski and Saddam. Brzezinski later flatly denied any such meeting took place. Aburish, 187. See also Timmerman, 112.

13. According to Bani Sadr, the plan of attack was drawn up by American, Israeli, and Iraqi officials meeting in the Hotel Raphael in Paris's Sixth Arrondisement. His intelligence agencies, he said, had managed to buy a copy of the plan prior to the invasion, and the Soviets provided the same plan a few days later to Iraq's ambassador in Moscow. See also Dilip Hiro, *The Longest War* (New York: Routledge, 1991), 71.

14. R. P. H. King, "The United Nations and the Iran-Iraq War, 1980–1986," in *The United Nations and the Iran-Iraq War*, ed. Brian Urquhart and Gary Sick (New York: Ford Foundation, August 1987).

15. Aburish, 195.

16. John Kifner, "Iraqis Stalled by a Tenacious Enemy," *New York Times*, February 28, 1986.

17. Andrew and Leslie Cockburn, *Dangerous Liaison* (New York: HarperCollins, 1991), 318–323. Also, Hiro, *The Longest War*, 71–72.

18. Mohammed Heikal, *Illusions of Triumph*, 81, cited in Aburish, 252.

19. William Staudenmaier, "Military Policy and Strategy in the Gulf War," Parameters, *Journal of the U.S. Army War College*, vol. 12, no. 2, 28, quoted in Samir al-Kihalil, *Republic of Fear* (London: Hutchinson Radius, 1989).

20. "Iraq Court Hears Testimony of Witness A," *International Herald Tribune*, December 6, 2005.

21. Firas Mahmood Ya'koob, quoted in Baghdad blog, http://www .casi.org.uk/analysis/2004/msg00576.html; also "Prosecutors in Hussein Case tie him to order to kill 148." *New York Times*, March 1, 2006.

22. Aburish, 207.

23. Cockburn, 322–323.

24. Cooley, 157.

25. Seymour M. Hersh, "The Iran Pipeline: A Hidden Chapter; U.S. Said to Have Allowed Israel to Sell Arms to Iran," *New York Times*, December 8, 1991, 1.

26. Ibid.

27. Ibid; also Murray Waas and Craig Unger, "Annals of Government— How the U.S. Armed Iraq," *The New Yorker*, November 2, 1992. This article provides an excellent review of the entire period.

28. Cockburn, 319.

29. In 1982, George P. Shultz would replace Haig as secretary of state and become a key member of the pro-Iraq faction. Waas and Unger.

30. Ibid.

31. Cooley, 156.

32. Baram and Rubin, 256.

33. Ibid.

34. Friedman, 5.

35. Ibid., 8.

36. "How U.S. Arms and Technology were transferred to Iraq," ABC News *Nightline*, Show No. 2690, September 13, 1991.

37. Aburish, 204.

38. Friedman, 7.

39. Timmerman, 19–20, 47–48, 58–60.

40. SIPRI Report, Stockholm, 1987. These countries were Austria,

Belgium, Brazil, Britain, Bulgaria, Chile, China, Czechoslovakia, East Germany, France, Greece, Hungary, Italy, the Netherlands, North Korea, Pakistan, Poland, Portugal, South Africa, the Soviet Union, Spain, Sweden, Switzerland, the U.S., West Germany, and Yugoslavia.

41. Timmerman, 257; and Bruce Jentleson, *With Friends Like These* (New York: Norton, 1994), 33. Saddam's involvement with terrorists was limited to extremist Palestinian groups—he never had any ties with Al-Qaeda, as the U.S. would finally admit in 2004.

42. Aburish, 287.

43. Friedman, 24–25.

44. Howard Teicher, Affadavit to U.S. District Court, Southern District of Florida, January 31, 1995, via Georgetown National Security Archives (NSA): http://www.gwu.edu/~nsarchiv/NSAEBB/NSAEBB82/ and http://www.gwu.edu/~nsarchiv/NSAEBB/NSAEBB82/iraq61.pdf.

45. Friedman, 27.

46. Ibid., 28.

47. Timmerman, 187.

48. Teicher Affidavit, 12–13.

49. Timmerman, 262.

50. From Teicher via NSA, http://www.gwu.edu/~nsarchiv/NSAEBB/NSAEBB82/

51. Friedman, 48–55.

52. The Chilean's business deals were wide-ranging. In 1983, for instance, Cardoen was arrested during a sting operation in Florida by U.S. agents intent on breaking up a ring smuggling night-vision goggles to Cuba and Libya. Fearful that the arrest might interfere with Cardoen's ability to continue supplying cluster bombs to Saddam, the CIA intervened to halt the prosecution. CIA director William Casey directed the secretaries of state and commerce to make sure that the vital export licenses required by Cardoen were not denied. From Teicher affidavit.

53. ABC *Nightline* broadcast, 1991.

54. Ibid.

55. Cooley, 178.

56. Ibid., 171. Citing Loretta Napoleoni; Friedman, 37.

57. Ibid., 104.

58. Friedman, 116.

59. Ibid., 104.

60. Ibid., 33.

61. State Department memo from Johnathan Howe to Shultz, November 18, 1983, via http://www.gwu.edu/~nsarchiv/NSAEBB/NSAEBB82/iraq24.pdf.

62. National Security Directive 114, via http://www.gwu.edu/~nsarchiv/NSAEBB/NSAEBB82/iraq24.pdf.

63. Description of Rumsfeld meeting with Tariq Aziz in memo in NSA collection, "Shaking Hands with Saddam Hussein: The U.S. Tilts toward Iraq, 1980–1984," NSA Electronic Briefing Book No. 82, edited by Joyce Battle, February 25, 2003, via http://www.gwu.edu/~nsarchiv/NSAEBB/NSAEBB82/iraq26.pdf; and Friedman, 28.

64. Declassified State Department document, http://www.gwu.edu/~nsarchiv/NSAEBB/NSAEBB82/iraq32.pdf.

65. Rumsfeld meeting with Saddam Hussein, State Department notes, via http://www.gwu.edu/~nsarchiv/NSAEBB/NSAEBB82/iraq31.pdf.

66. No corporation had closer ties to the Reagan administration. Caspar Weinberger, Reagan's secretary of defense, had worked there; so had George Shultz, who went directly from Bechtel to become secretary of state.

67. State Department memo from Baghdad to Rumseld, January 10, 1984. Memo in NSA collection, "Shaking Hands with Saddam Hussein: The U.S. Tilts toward Iraq, 1980–1984," via http://www.gwu.edu/~nsarchiv/NSAEBB/NSAEBB82/iraq37.pdf.

68. Samir al Khalil, *Republic of Fear* (Berkeley: University of California Press, 1989), 284. Wrote one reporter, "The Iraqi guns kept up a heavy fire which cut down the Iranians like swathes of corn under a sickle. . . . 'We crushed the Iranians like insects,' said an Iraqi soldier, jubilation showing through the exhaustion on his face. He squatted in a frontline trench he was sharing with three dusty Iranian corpses, which, after two days, remained unburied. In the hot sun, the Iraqis' own dead still lay in the open where they had fallen, their limbs convulsed in death agonies."

69. Joseph Trento, interview by author, Washington, DC, May 12, 2004.

70. William Eagleton, interview by author, Paris, January 9, 2006.

71. Peter Galbraith, interview by author, Washington, DC, May 16, 2004.

72. Briefing Notes for Rumsfeld visit to Baghdad, March 1984. Memo in NSA collection, "Shaking Hands with Saddam Hussein: The U.S. Tilts toward Iraq, 1980–1984," via http://www.gwu.edu/~nsarchiv/NSAEBB/NSAEBB82/iraq48.pdf.

73. Teicher affidavit.

74. Department of State press briefing, March 19, 1984, via http://www.gwu.edu/~nsarchiv/NSAEBB/NSAEBB82/iraq47.pdf.

75. Patrick E. Tyler, "Officers Say U.S. Aided Iraq in War Despite Use of Gas," *New York Times*, August 18, 2002.

76. Bob Woodward, "CIA aiding Iraqi in Gulf War," *Washington Post*, December 15, 1986, A1.

77. *Sunday Times*, February 26, 1984, cited in *Republic of Fear*, 284.

78. Jon Swain, *Sunday Times*, March 4, 1984, cited in *Republic of Fear*, 284.

79. Timmerman, 277.

80. Ibid., 278–279.

81. *Time*, July 25, 1983, cited in Hiro, *The Longest War*, 121.

82. Timmerman, 276–277.

83. *New York Times*, April 3, 1984, quoted in *Republic of Fear*, 63.

84. Amnesty International, op. cit.

85. Timmerman, 287.

86. Waas and Unger.

87. Ibid.

88. Ibid.

89. Bob Woodward, *Veil* (New York: Simon & Schuster, 1987), 408–409.

90. The Iranians were upset over U.S. insistence that all the hostages be liberated before any more arms were delivered and at what they considered to be inflated prices for the weapons. (In fact, the second part of the White House's convoluted operation had already swung into action: money obtained from the illegal weapons sales to Iran was being diverted by the White House to fund another clandestine—and illegal—operation, the support of the Contras in Nicaragua.)

91. Quoted in Waas and Unger.

92. Waas and Unger. According to Howard Teicher, similar strategic advice from the Americans was transmitted to Saddam via other European and Middle Eastern heads of states.

93. Ibid.

94. Stephen Pelletiere, *Iraq and the International Oil System* (Washington, DC: Maisonneuve Press, 2004), 195–196.

95. "Keeping Either Side from Winning," *New York Times*, January 12, 1987, and Woodward, *Veil*, 444.

96. Timmerman, 344.

97. Friedman, 38.

98. Timmerman, 362–364; Friedman 273–278.

99. Phil Hearse, who writes for the British socialist journals *Militant* and *Socialism Today*.

100. Cited by Pilger, 93, and Timmerman, 105.

101. Friedman, 87.

102. In fact, most major transactions were monitored by the CIA, the British Ministry of Defense, and other Western intelligence agencies. See Waas and Unger; also Friedman, 5, 86, 132–133.

103. Sale interview.

104. Rocky Gonzalez, interview by author, Sierra Vista, Arizona, May 10, 2004.

105. "Public War/Secret War," ABC News *Nightline*, July 1, 1992, via http://homepage.ntlworld.com/jksonc/docs/ir655–nightline-19920701.html.

106. Reagan White House officials were doing the same thing in Central America in Honduras, Nicaragua, and El Salvador. Much of this information was developed by John Barry, an investigative reporter for *Newsweek*, in 1992. John Barry and R. Charles, "Sea of Lies," *Newsweek*, July 13, 1992.

107. Friedman, 40.

108. Bob Woodward, "CIA Aiding Iraqi in Gulf War," *Washington Post*, December 15, 1986. Also, Friedman, 40.

109. Rick Francona, former Defense Intellegence Agency (DIA) officer stationed in Baghdad, interview with author, Newark, New Jersey, April 17, 2004.

110. "Public War/Secret War."

111. Friedman, 40.

112. "Public War/Secret War."

Chapter 4 : Halabja

1. Randal, 213.

2. President Bush, weekly radio address, March 17, 2003, 1:15 P.M., via http://www.scoop.co.nz/stories/WO0303/S00226.htm.

3. Michael Despratx, interview with former Baathist General Hatef Abdallah, Baghdad, May 2004; notes provided to author. Also, UPI, Sales.

4. Randal, 148.

5. Ibid., 160.

6. Ibid., 166.

7. The Pike Report, reprinted as "The Select Committee's Investigative Record," *The Village Voice*, February 16, 1976, 85.

8. Randal, 4–5, 56.

9. Ibid., 229, quoting from secret Iraqi government documents seized by the Kurds in their abortive uprising of 1991.

10. Randal, 232.

11. Ibid., 17.

12. Christopher Drew and Treasha Mabile, "Desert Graves in Northern Iraq Yield Evidence to Try Hussein," *New York Times*, June 7, 2005. By annihilating Kurdish villages, al-Majid's vicious campaign was also devastating Iraq's wheat production; luckily for Saddam, the U.S. was ready and eager to meet any shortfalls with huge shipments of subsidized American grain via agricultural credits courtesy of the Reagan and Bush administrations. By this point, Iraq had become America's powerful wheat industry's most valuable export market.

13. Randal, 213.

14. Bob Woodward, "CIA Aiding Iraq in Gulf War," *Washington Post*, December 15, 1986, 1.

15. Samantha Power, *A Problem from Hell* (New York: Harper Perennial, 2003), 188.

16. David Hirt, *The Guardian*, March 23, 1988.

17. Patrick E. Tyler, "Poison Gas Attack Kills Hundreds," *Washington Post*, March 24, 1988, A1; also "Poison Gas in Iraq," *Los Angeles Times*, March 24, 1988.

18. Andrew Gowers and Richard Johns, *Financial Times*, March 23, 1988.

19. Iraq at first tried to blame the attacks on Iran, as did a study issued by the DIA. But the explanation was by no means credible, even to the Iraqis themselves—a captured Iraqi intelligence memo dated April 11, 1988, refers to a videocassette on sale in Sulaimniyah showing "the Iraqi chemical attack on Halabja."

20. "The Gulf: The Battle, the War," *Washington Post*, April 20, 1988, A20. (I do not know author.)

21. Power, 186.

22. Quoted in Power, 186.

23. Document 0423 in National Security Archive, Iraqgate Collection, and 00453 cable of August 1987, quoted in Power, 351.

24. Rick Francona, interview with author, Secaucus, New Jersey, May 17, 2004.

25. Ibid.

26. Power, 200.

27. John Pilger, *The New Rulers of the World* (London: Verso, 2003), 67. Iraq soon became Britain's third largest market for machine tools, with which the Iraqis turned out a wide range of weapons.

28. Power, 209.

29. Morton Abramowitz, "Swan Song for Iraq's Kurds?," top secret cable from Assistant Secretary of State for Intelligence and Research Morton

Abramowitz to Secretary of State George Shultz, September 2, 1988, as document 00626 in National Security Archive (NSA) Collection, Iraqgate.

30. Power, 209.

31. Ibid.

32. For instance, in September 1988, when *Washington Post* correspondent Jon Randal managed to get a rare graphic photograph of a badly scarred survivor of Saddam's chemical attack, the reply from his foreign desk was a yawn. "Much to my stunned disappointment," Randal wrote later, "my foreign editor refused the $200 asking price for it." The *New York Times* buried its story on page 15.

33. Randal, 214.

34. Power, 198.

35. Author's interview with Peter Galbraith.

36. Power, 199.

37. William Safire, "Stop the Iraqi Murder of the Kurds," *New York Times*, September 5, 1988, A21.

38. "Murder Within Sovereign Borders" (editorial), *New York Times*, September 5, 1988, A20.

39. David Ottaway, "U.S. Concern is Expressed to Baghdad," *Washington Post*, September 7, 1988, A24.

40. Galbraith interview with author.

41. State Department Briefing, Federal News Service, September 8, 1988.

42. Power, 211.

43. Galbraith interview.

44. According to State Department officials interviewed by Human Rights Watch reported in Human Rights Watch Annual Report for 1988, available at hrw.org.

45. Power, 221.

46. Ibid.

47. Cable from U.S. embassy, Baghdad, to State Department, "Minister of Industry Blasts Senate Action," September 13, 1988, from NSA collection, "Saddam Hussein—More Secret History," via http://www.gwu.edu/~nsarchiv/ NSAEBB/NSAEBB107/.

48. Power, 220.

49. There were others who called for a special session of the U.N. Security Council to condemn Iraq. The U.S. neatly sidestepped the issue by joining nine other nations in demanding instead a "fact-finding mission"—though by this time the U.S. knew all the facts. Missions in 1986, 1987, and 1988 had concluded that Iraq had used illegal chemical weapons against Iranian troops. Despite those findings, the Security Council had taken no action.

50. Brian Cloughley, "Colin Powell's Shame," Counterpunch 9/20/2003 via http://counterpunch.org/cloughley09202003.html; see also Secretary Colin L. Powell, Halabja, Iraq, September 15, 2003, Press Release, U.S. Department of State at www.state.gov.

51. Human Rights Watch Report on Iraq for 1988.

52. Power, 234.

Chapter 5 : Signals

1. Milton Viorst, "A Reporter At Large: After the Liberation," *The New Yorker*, September 30, 1991, 66; also Viorst, *Sandcastles*, 280.

2. Salinger, 69.

3. BBC News, "Charges Facing Saddam Hussein," July 1, 2004, via http://news.bbc.co.uk/2/hi/middle_east/3320293.stm.

4. Baram, 6.

5. Mackey, 278.

6. For the postwar situation see Aburish, 258–279; Baram, 8.

7. Kenneth Pollack, *The Threatening Storm* (New York: Random House, 2002), 27; Aburish, 261.

8. Pollack, 27; Aburish, 279.

9. Pierre Salinger and Eric Laurent, *Secret Dossier* (New York: Penguin, 1991), 1–2; also see Henry Schuler, "Congress Must Take a Hard Look at Iraq's Charges Against Kuwait," *Los Angeles Times*, December 2, 1990, Op-Ed.

10. Aburish, 270.

11. Michael Gordon and Bernard Trainor, *The Generals' War* (New York: Little, Brown, 1994), 10.

12. Waas and Unger.

13. Timmerman, 399.

14. Its members at this time ranged from petroleum giants Mobil, Exxon, Texaco, and Occidental to defense contractors such as Lockheed, Bell Helicopter-Textron, and United Technologies, and included other assorted members of the Fortune 500—AT&T, General Motors, Bechtel, and Caterpillar.

15. Friedman, 133.

16. Ibid., 134.

17. Power, 233.

18. "Guidelines for U.S.-Iraq Policy," 6, secret State Department internal paper, January 20, 1989, reproduced as 00761 in National Security Archives, ed. Iraqgate.

19. Human Rights Watch, 1989 report. Some excerpts: "For years execution has been an established Iraqi method for dealing with perceived po-

litical military opponents of the government. . . . In some case, a family only learns that one of its members has been executed when the security services return the body and require the family to pay a fine. . . . Thousands of political prisoners continued to be arbitrarily arrested and detained. . . . Relations, including children of suspects, are said to be held as hostages to compel confessions."

20. Ibid.

21. Power, 234.

22. This tale is very well told in Alan Friedman, *Spider's Web* (London: Faber & Faber, 1993), 153–154; see also Bruce W. Jentleson, *With Friends Like These* (New York: Norton, 1994), 107–109.

23. Friedman, 155.

24. Timmerman, 441: Encouraged by the Department of Commerce, on June 4, 1989, Marshall Wiley, head of the U.S.-Iraq Forum, arrived in Baghdad with a delegation of twenty-three of America's major corporations. It was an invitation-only affair, limited to senior executives from Fortune 500 companies with annual sales of at least half a billion dollars. They talked trade and business opportunities during a two-hour meeting with Saddam Hussein himself.

25. Waas and Unger.

26. Michael Gordon and Bernard Trainor, *The Generals' War* (Boston: Back Bay Books, 1995), 10.

27. Timmerman, 420.

28. Ibid., 401.

29. Ibid., 418.

30. Russ W. Baker, "Iraqgate," *Columbia Journalism Review*, March/April 1993.

31. Friedman, 86, 132–133.

32. Russ Baker.

33. Ibid.

34. Martin Tolchin, "U.S. is Criticized on Iraq Loan Case," *New York Times*, October 6, 1992.

35. Neil A., Lewis, "Judge Scoffs at Defense of Bush on Iraq," *New York Times*, August 24, 1993.

36. Judge Shoob had repeatedly demanded that the government name a special prosecutor to look into the whole affair. But when one of the government prosecutors pointed to an investigation that had been earlier carried out by a former Federal judge, Frederick B. Lacey, who had concluded that there was no necessity for a special prosecutor, Judge Shoob was incensed.

"If Judge Lacey had investigated the Teapot Dome scandal," he said, referring to the 1922 scandal that almost toppled President Warren G. Harding, "he would have given out a medal instead of a jail sentence." Ibid.

37. Friedman, 283.

38. Waas and Unger.

39. Ibid.

40. Gordon and Trainor, 11

41. Friedman, 136.

42. Notes of Baker-Aziz meeting, ibid., 136–139.

43. Pollack, 21; Salinger, 38.

44. Power, 234.

45. Friedman, 153.

46. Though Congress had tried to block the measure because of the violations, President Bush signed a waiver determining that the prohibition "was not in the national interest of the United States." Ibid., 157.

47. Jentleson, 100–119; Aburish, 269.

48. Friedman, 134.

49. Salinger, 2; Aburish, 271.

50. John Bulloch and Harvey Morris, *Saddam's War* (London: Faber & Faber, 1991), 9.

51. Jentleson, 143.

52. *Washington Post*, August 19, 1990; G. Henry Schuler, "Congress Must Take a Hard Look at Iraq's Charges Against Kuwait," *Los Angeles Times*, December 2, 1990.

53. "Kuwaiti Intelligence Memorandum, Labeled Top Secret," *Los Angeles Times*, November 1, 1990, 14.

See also George Lardner, Jr., "Iraqi Charges Alleged Kuwaiti Memo Proves a CIA Plot Against Baghdad," *Washington Post*, November 1, 1990, A30; according to the *Washington Post*, the Kuwaiti minister of foreign affairs fainted when confronted with the document by his Iraqi counterpart at an Arab summit meeting in mid-August.

54. Viorst, 251.

55. Aburish, 272.

56. Timmerman, 471.

57. Aburish, 272.

58. Avner Yariv, "Israel Faces Iraq," in Baram and Rubin, 245–246.

59. U.S. News, *Triumph Without Victory* (New York Random House, 1992), 17.

60. Aburish, 273.

61. Salinger, 7.

62. Ibid., 11.

63. Gordon Thomas, *Gideon's Spies* (New York: Thomas Dunne, 1999), 174; Aburish, 275.

64. Baram, 11.

65. Aburish, 274–275; Friedman, 158.

66. Friedman, 159; Baram, 11.

67. Bob Woodward, *The Commanders* (New York: Simon & Schuster, 1991), 202–204.

68. Ibid.

69. Salinger, 21.

70. Ibid.

71. Salinger, 23.

72. Randal, 82–83.

73. Ibid., 82.

74. Salinger, 22.

75. Douglas Waller, "Glass House," *The New Republic*, November 5, 1990, cited in Power, 558.

76. U.S. News, *Triumph Without Victory*, 11.

77. Power, 235.

78. Aburish, 276. Information based on Aburish's conversations with an unidentified Iraqi intelligence officer.

79. Saddam was not the only one to see Kuwait's actions in such terms. The director of the Center for Strategic and International Studies, G. Henry Schuler, described these policies as "economic warfare" against Iraq. G. Henry Schuler, "Congress Must Take a Hard Look at Iraq's Charges against Kuwait," *Los Angeles Times*, December 2, 1990.

80. Baram, 16.

81. Salinger, 32; Aburish, 278. Salinger's source was a PLO delegate at the meeting.

82. Joseph Wilson, *The Politics of Truth* (New York, Carroll & Graf, 2004), 122. This incident was relayed to Ambassador Wilson by Nizar Hamdun, who later became a close friend of the ambassador.

83. Aburish, 282.

84. Ibid.

85. Viorst, 279.

86. Ibid., 278.

87. Ibid. Nathaniel Howell, phone interview with author, January 16, 2006.

88. Viorst, 284.

89. Ibid., 280.

90. Aburish, 279; also Dilip Hiro, *Desert Shield to Desert Storm* (New York: Authors Choice, 2003), 429.

91. Gordon, 14.

92. Ibid.,18.

93. U.S. News, *Triumph Without Victory*, 30.

94. High-level Egyptian officials told Milton Viorst that Mubarak had indeed been mistaken, even though after the invasion Mubarak accused Saddam of lying about his intentions. Viorst, 342.

95. Friedman, 134. As Representative Henry Gonzalez concluded in July 1992 after a congressional investigation, "The Bush administration deliberately, not inadvertently, helped to arm Iraq by allowing U.S. technology to be shipped to Iraqi military and to Iraqi defense factories. . . . Throughout the course of the Bush administration, U.S. and foreign firms were granted export licenses to ship U.S. technology directly to Iraqi weapons facilities despite ample evidence showing that these factories were producing weapons." Representative Henry Gonzalez of Texas, testimony before the House, Congressional Record, July 27, 1992. Representative Henry B. Gonzalez cited in John King, *Arming Iraq: A Chronology of U.S. Involvement*, March 2003, Iran Chamber Society, via http://www.iranchamber.com/history/articles/arming_iraq.php.

96. Gordon and Trainor, 4.

97. *Washington Post*, October 21, 1992, cited in Baram, 19.

98. Baram, in Baram and Rubin, 19; Gordon and Trainor, 18.

99. Gordon and Trainor, 23.

100. Baram, in Baram and Rubin, 21. As Baram, a specialist on Iraq and Saddam, put it, "Due to Saddam's personal cordiality and because he intentionally blurred his threat somewhat, Glaspie completely misread the situation." Baram, 20.

101. Nathaniel Howell, phone interview with author.

102. Baram, in Baram and Rubin, 24.

103. Later April Glaspie disputed its accuracy, claiming to have given Saddam more warnings than indicated on the transcript, but her own cables to Washington gave no such indication. Gordon and Trainor, 21.

104. Murray Waas, "Who Lost Kuwait? How the Bush Administration Bungled Its Way to War in the Gulf," *The Village Voice*, January 22, 1991, 35; Elaine Sciolino with Michael Gordon, "Confrontation in the Gulf," *New York Times*, September 23, 1990, A1.

105. William Safire, *New York Times*, September 17, 1990, 23.

106. Pollack, 35.

107. Wilson, 100–102.

108. Elaine Sciolino with Michael Gordon, "Confrontation in the Gulf," *New York Times*, September 23, 1990, A1.

109. Salinger, 65.

110. Ibid., 67.

111. Ibid.

112. Bob Woodward, *The Commanders* (New York: Simon & Schuster, 2002), 217.

113. Aburish, 282; Baram, 23.

114. Salinger, 69.

115. Years later, I asked Congressman Lee Hamilton what his impression of U.S. policy would have been if *he* had been Saddam Hussein listening to Kelly's testimony. "Saddam Hussein looked on Kuwait as if it were a province of Iraq," said Hamilton. "He was looking for an excuse to go in, and I think he did not understand clearly, unambiguously that the United States would oppose any effort by Iraq to move into Kuwait. We did not draw a firm line in the sand. It's not difficult. What is clear to me is at the highest levels of the U.S. government we did not convey strongly and clearly to Saddam Hussein that we would react militarily if he went across that border." Hamilton interview with author, Washington, DC, May 13, 2004.

116. Wilson, 104.

117. Quoted in Barry Lando & Michael Despratx, "Iraq's Crimes and Collusions," *Le Monde Diplomatique*, November 2004.

118. As Colin Powell, then chairman of the Joint Chiefs of Staff, later explained, "There are lots of things going on in Washington in any day and that particular day we had foreign visitors in town. Part of my day was spent with the president of Togo, and it just did not gel early enough for us to deal with as a single problem that required immediate effort on our part to send a deterrent message to Saddam Hussein. And it was only late afternoon, early evening when all of the pieces came together, and it was clear that some kind of message had to go back to Saddam Hussein immediately. But by then it was too late." There is even some reason to believe that Saddam's final decision to invade may have been made impulsively, based on a miscalculation of U.S. reaction, even as the United States had miscalculated his action. One military account of the war says that Iraqi units were surprised by the order to invade Kuwait, which they received less than half a day before the attack. The Americans could take some comfort from the fact that the British were no smarter. British ministers

received an assessment from the Cabinet Office the day before the invasion to the effect that Iraq would not invade. Theodore Draper, "The True History of the Gulf War," *New York Review of Books*, January 30, 1992.

119. Woodward, 223.

120. Gordon, 29.

Chapter 6 : No Exit

1. Pollack, 27.

2. Viorst, *Sandcastles*, 344; Gordon and Trainor, 29–32.

3. Baram, in Baram and Rubin, 22.

4. Viorst, 344–345; see also Dilip Hiro, *Desert Shield to Desert Storm* (London: Authors Choice Press, 2003), for an excellent detailed account of this period.

5. Salinger, 91.

6. Kenneth Pollack, *The Threatening Storm* (New York: Random House, 2002), 36–38.

7. Woodward, *The Commanders*, 213.

8. Salinger, 99.

9. Woodward, *The Commanders*, 225.

10. Salinger, 91.

11. Woodward, *The Commanders*, 225.

12. Ibid., 226. Bush expressed no concerns about the vast resources of the Saudis, who were staunch U.S. allies.

13. Salinger, 106.

14. Gordon and Trainor, 37.

15. Woodward, *The Commanders*, 231.

16. Michael Emery, "How Mr. Bush Got His War," in Greg Ruggiero and Stuart Sahulka, eds., *Open Fire* (New York: New Press, 1993), 39, 40, 52, based on Emery's interview of King Hussein, February 19, 1991, in Jordan. (Revised version of article in *The Village Voice*, March 5, 1991.)

17. Viorst, 309.

18. Salinger, 97; also Michael Emery, *The Village Voice*, 1991.

19. Salinger, 102; Viorst, 309.

20. Salinger, 109.

21. Ibid.

22. Woodward, *The Commanders*, 254; Salinger, 101. Ironically, throughout the crisis, Colin Powell, though a four-star general, would repeatedly urge military restraint. He argued that the immediate task should be limited to defending Saudi Arabia from a possible Iraqi attack.

23. Salinger, 111.

24. Hiro, *Desert Shield to Desert Storm*, 106; Judith Miller, "Mideast Tensions: King Hussein on Dashed Hopes," *New York Times*, October 16, 1990, A1.

25. The State Department later denied any such message was sent to Cairo that day, but according to Pierre Salinger, "a highly placed and eminently trustworthy Egyptian source is adamant that he himself saw the message." Salinger, 112.

26. Salinger, 117.

27. Craig Unger, *House of Bush, House of Saud* (New York: Scribner, 2004), 33.

28. Woodward, *The Commanders*, 255.

29. Viorst, 310; Hiro, *Desert Shield to Desert Storm*, 114–115.

30. Hiro, *Desert Shield to Desert Storm*, 113.

31. Woodward, *The Commanders*, 260.

32. Emery.

33. Woodward, *The Commanders*, 266.

34. Viorst, 309.

35. Hiro, *Desert Shield to Desert Storm*, 131.

36. Wilson, 121–125; Salinger, 139, 142. Wilson does not directly quote Saddam regarding the Saudis. Salinger, however, does.

37. Wilson, 123.

38. Ibid., 125.

39. Unger, 140.

40. Jean Heller, "Photos Don't Show Buildup," *St. Petersburg Times*, January 6, 1991, A1. Unger, 140. Also, author's interview with photoanalyst Peter Zimmerman and Jean Heller, by phone April 12, 2004. As Zimmerman told me, "I was not able to see anything there that indicated armored forces on the border or near the border with Saudi Arabia." Nor, he said, were there any traces of such forces having been there in the past few weeks.

41. Unger, 140.

42. Gordon and Trainor, 65.

43. Unger, 140.

44. Salinger, 156.

45. Aburish, 296. Also author's interview with Jean Pierre Chevenement, Paris, April 17, 2004.

46. Robert Parry, "The Peace Feeler That Was," *The Nation*, April 15, 1991, 480–482.

47. Woodward, *The Commanders*, 275.

48. As Jordan's King Hussein said, "How can you expect us to be enthusiastic about Security Council Resolution 660, which requires Iraq to quit Kuwait immediately, when Security Council Resolution 242 requiring Israel to evacuate the occupied territories has been on the books, unenforced, for twenty-three years?" Emery.

49. Woodward, *The Commanders*, 240.

50. Hiro, *Desert Shield to Desert Storm*, 119.

51. Theodore H. Draper, "The True History of the Gulf War," *New York Review of Books*, January 30, 1992, 38–45; and Emery.

52. Gordon and Trainor, 59.

53. Aburish, 289.

54. Daniel Pipes in *Foreign Affairs* (Fall 1991), 41. Martin Yant, *The True Story of the Gulf War* (New York: Prometheus Books, 1991), 215.

55. Hiro, *Desert Shield to Desert Storm*, 169–170.

56. Hiro, 145.

57. Aburish, 290; Salinger, 165; and according to several of the delegates at the meeting.

58. On August 12, 1980, Saddam again announced his willingness to withdraw in accord with U.N. resolutions, saying he would do so in return for Israel accepting to obey similar U.N. resolutions demanding Israel's withdrawal from the occupied territories. Saddam's attempt at linkage was rejected by all, even the other Arab countries, but it played well on the Arab street. Over the following days Saddam made repeated offers to withdraw under varying conditions. They were all refused outright by the Bush administration. There could be no preconditions. Salinger, 174; and Emery.

59. Gordon and Trainor, 281.

60. Hiro, *Desert Shield to Desert Storm*, 143.

61. As a Jordanian official told Milton Viorst, "Americans talk of democracy but in Saudi Arabia and Kuwait, America is tying itself to the ugliest image of nondemocracy in the world. You are not protecting a society; you are protecting a class, or maybe a family business." Viorst, 247.

62. Craig Fuller, the head of its Washington office, had also headed Bush's staff when Bush was vice president. Hill and Knolton assigned a small army of their executives, 119 in all, across the United States. Unger, 136.

63. Unger, 136.

64. *Sunday Times*, September 23, 1990, cited in Hiro, *Desert Shield to Desert Storm*, 156.

65. August 22, 1980, *New York Times*; Aburish, 293. One proposal was sent to Brent Scowcroft. In exchange for Iraq withdrawing from Kuwait and allowing

the foreigners to leave, Iraq would receive the lifting of the economic sanctions that the U.N. had imposed; a "guaranteed access" to the tiny but key islands of Bubiyan and Warba; and full control of the Rumaila oil field, which extended slightly into Kuwaiti territory. In addition, Iraq's proposal included an oil agreement advantageous to both the U.S. and Iraq and a joint plan to "alleviate Iraq's economic and financial problems" and "jointly work on the stability of the gulf." The White House rejected the bid, saying there "was nothing in this particular proposal which merited their pursuit." Hiro, 147.

66. Hiro, *Desert Shield to Desert Storm*, 154.

67. Ibid., 173.

68. Aburish, 292.

69. Ibid., 292–293. Indeed, from day to day, American officials sent out conflicting signals. On August 31, 1990, at a news conference in Saudi Arabia, for instance, General Schwarzkopf assured reporters, "There is not going to be any war unless the Iraqis attack." As Schwarzkopf knew, however, his superiors were very much considering taking the offensive once they had enough troops on the ground.

70. Gordon and Trainor, 288.

71. Woodward, *The Commanders*, 289.

72. Hiro, *Desert Shield to Desert Storm*, 193.

73. Woodward, *The Commanders*, 297; Hiro, *Desert Shield to Desert Storm*, 193.

74. Hiro, *Desert Shield to Desert Storm*, 216.

75. *Los Angeles Times*, November 6, 1990, 4.

76. Woodward, *The Commanders*, 302.

77. John MacArthur, "Remember Nayirah, Witness for Kuwait?" *Seattle Post Intelligencer*, January 12, 1992, D1; also Unger, 136–140.

78. Gordon and Trainor, 130.

79. Hiro, *Desert Shield to Desert Storm*, 244.

80. James Aikens, interview with the author, Bowie, Maryland, May 15, 2004.

81. Woodward, *The Commanders*, 313.

82. Hiro, *Desert Shield to Desert Storm*, 245.

83. Ibid., 267.

84. Ibid., 252.

85. Draper.

86. Gordon and Trainor, 156.

87. *Washington Post*, November 25, 1990, C4.

88. Hiro, *Desert Shield to Desert Storm*, 257–258.

89. Woodward, *The Commanders*, 338.

90. *Fortune* magazine (New York), February 11, 1991, cited in "Killing Hope: U.S. Military and CIA interventions since World War," William Blum, at Third World Traveler via http//www.thirdworldtraveler.com/Blum/Iraq_KH.html.

91. Aburish, 299.

92. Ibid., 300.

93. Woodward, *The Commanders*, 353.

94. According to former assistant secretary of defense Lawrence Korb, the army would have twice as many divisions on the ground as it did in Europe; two thirds of the entire combat power of the Marines would be there. Lawrence Korb, Op-Ed, *Washington Post*, November 25, 1990, C4.

95. Salinger, 208–209.

96. Ibid., 211.

97. Joe Trento, interview by author, Washington, May 12, 2004, and with Rocky Gonzalez, former special forces warrant officer, Sierra Vista, Arizona, May 10, 2004. Among the instructions they received was counterinsurgency training. There was concern at the time that if Saddam's army was overwhelmed by the Iranians, Iraqi units might have to go underground to wage a guerrilla operation against the Iranians. It is unclear to what extent those Iraqi soldiers later used that training against American troops—not just in 1991, but in the current occupation, as well.

98. Rick Francona, interview with author.

99. Ibid., also Gordon and Trainor, *The Generals' War*, 108–110.

100. Gordon and Trainor, ibid., 289–290.

101. *International Herald Tribune*, January 22, 1991, cited in Hiro, *Desert Shield to Desert Storm*, 331.

102. Hiro, *Desert Shield to Desert Storm*, 330.

103. Patricia Axelrod, "Clean Lies, Dirty Wars," *Reno News and Review*, October 10, 2002; Hiro, *Desert Shield to Desert Storm*, 371. See also Gordon and Trainor, 308–331.

104. "Flashback: Desert Storm," BBC, January 15, 2001.

105. Hiro, *Desert Shield to Desert Storm*, 368.

106. *International Herald Tribune*, February 20, 1991, 1; *Independent*, February 21 and 22, 1991, 1.; Hiro, 268–369. Saddam fully accepted the terms of the original Security Council resolution passed after his invasion. Other issues now were question of timing of the withdrawal and the amount of military hardware that would be left behind.

107. After-the-fact report by Michael Evans, *The Times*, March 23, 1991, cited in Aburish, 305.

108. Hiro, *Desert Shield to Desert Storm*, 388.

109. Gordon and Trainor, 416.

110. Presidential press conference on the Persian Gulf War, White House, March 1, 1993, cited in Gordon and Trainor, 433.

Chapter 7 : Betrayal

1. Andrew Cockburn and Patrick Cockburn, *Out of the Ashes*, op. cit., p. 42.

2. Ibid., 15.

3. For a very good study of the uprising, see "Endless Torment, the 1991 Uprising in Iraq and Its Aftermath," Human Rights Watch Report, 1992 via http://www.hrw.org/reports/1992/Iraq926.htm; and Faleh Abd al-Jabba, "Why the Uprisings," *Middle East Report*, May–June 1992.

4. Mackey, 287.

5. Zainab al-Suwaij, interview with author, Boston, May 5, 2004.

6. CNN's Special Report, "The Unfinished War: A Decade Since Desert Storm," hosted by Brent Sadler, January 16, 2001, on CNN and CNN International.

7. Andrew and Patrick Cockburn, *Out of the Ashes*, 13.

8. Aburish, 307.

9. Gordon and Trainor, 435; Andrew and Patrick Cockburn, *Out of the Ashes*, 13. General Schwarzkopf made a similar call for the Iraqi people "to rise up in revolt."

10. Aburish, 307, citing Pilger, 51; Richard Denis Johnson, *Propaganda Materials of the Persian Gulf War*, Salt Lake City, Utah: 1995, leaflets E10 and E11.

11. Quoted in Philip Taylor, 239. See also the study "Operations Against Enemy Leaders," by the Rand Corporation, California, 66–71.

12. Andrew and Patrick Cockburn, *Out of the Ashes*, 23.

13. Ibid., 19; Randal, 39.

14. Randal, 39.

15. As journalist Jon Randal described the scene; Randal, 41. Randal also quotes "a letter from a purported eyewitness in Sulaimaniya who recounted how on March 8, 1991, the population 'tore their victim's bodies to shreds to avenge what was done in Halabja and other places. The cries of the cowards penetrated to the skies, but there was no mercy shown to these despicable and deviant men.'

... Seven hundred security and party men died in the assault on the Central Security Headquarters building."

16. Randal, 41.

17. Ibid., 41.

18. Peter Galbraith, interview with author.

19. Randal, 45.

20. Gordon and Trainor, 435.

21. Ibid., 418.

22. Interviewed by PBS for *Frontline*.

23. Thomas Pickering interview with author, Roslyn, Virginia, May 12, 2004. Somewhat incredulously, I asked the former ambassador, "Deploying hundreds of thousands of troops without any idea of what you're going to do?" "Yep, fairly convincingly so." "How could that have happened?" "Well, it happened thirteen years later, in 2003. Why ask the question about 1991?"

24. Andrew and Patrick Cockburn, *Out of the Ashes*, 33.

25. Gordon and Trainor, 444.

26. Ibid., 446–447.

27. Ibid.

28. Ibid.

29. Andrew and Patrick Cockburn, *Out of the Ashes*, 22–23.

30. Author's interview with Zainab al-Suwaij.

31. Gordon and Trainor, 448.

32. Andrew and Patrick Cockburn, *Out of the Ashes*, 23.

33. Gordon and Trainor, 449–459; Said Aburish, 307–311; Andrew and Patrick Cockburn, 35–41; as well as author's interviews with Peter Galbraith and former State Department official David Mack, interviewed by phone, May 12, 2005.

34. Michel Despratx and Barry Lando, "Iraq: Crimes and Collusions," *Le Monde Diplomatique*, November 2004.

35. Galbraith interview.

36. *Newsweek*, April 15, 1991.

37. Andrew and Patrick Cockburn, *Out of the Ashes*, 22.

38. Gordon and Trainor, 456.

39. Randal, 98. Said Chas Freeman, the U.S. ambassador to Saudi Arabia at the time, "The behavior of the Iraqi Shiites in the Iran-Iraq war convinced the Saudis that the Shiites were not Iranian surrogates. Washington was obsessed by that idea, and attributed it to the Saudis." Andrew and Patrick Cockburn, 40.

40. Rocky Gonzalez, interview with author, Sierra Vista, Arizona, May 10, 2004.

41. Andrew and Patrick Cockburn, *Out of the Ashes*, 39.

42. Interviews with Michel Despratx, Baghdad, May 2004.

43. Andrew and Patrick Cockburn, *Out of the Ashes*, 29.

44. Hussein Al Shami, *The Iraqi Crisis: The View from Within*, 98, cited in Aburish, 308.

45. Interviews with survivors of the uprising by Michel Despratx, Baghdad, May 2004.

46. Mackey, 352–353.

47. Peter Galbraith interview. Galbraith added, "I taught later at the National War College and we would discuss this with officers who had served in Iraq and this was a searing experience for them, to have come into Kuwait and Iraq as liberators and then see they couldn't do anything to help those who were being massacred before their eyes."

48. Iraq's Chemical and Biological Warfare Programme, Vol. 3. Comprehensive Report of the Special Advisor to the DCI on Iraq's WMD, September 30, 2004, via http://www.cia.gov/cia/reports/iraq_wmd_2004/chap5.html.

49. A notable exception is Juan Cole in his October 7, 2004, "WMD Myth Meant to Deter Iran" on his blog, "Informed Comment," via http://www.juancole.com/.

50. What were they spraying? Rocky said he thought it might have also have been sulfuric acid. A truck driver came in to their aid station one day with a broken arm. "He said he was driving a chemical tanker with sulfuric acid coming from Syria going to Baghdad. He told me the sulfuric acid was to be used on the people there. I asked, 'Why sulfuric acid?' He said they didn't have any other chemicals. The sulfuric acid was given to them by the Syrians." The burns on the refugees fleeing to American lines, he said, could have been sulfuric acid burns.

51. Author's interview by phone, September 20, 2004.

52. Andrew and Patrick Cockburn, *Out of the Ashes*, 20.

53. Randal, 100.

54. Rick Francona, interview with author. Francona had attended the meeting between General Johnston and the Iraqi generals.

55. Randal, 100.

56. Gordon and Trainor, 456; Brent Scowcroft had discussed with Secretary of Defense Dick Cheney grounding Saddam's helicopters, but they decided not to because it would appear to be undercutting Schwarzkopf. Later, however, in their jointly authored book, George Bush and Scowcroft wrote, "In retrospect, since the helicopters were being used offensively, not for communications, Schwarzkopf would not have been undercut and, psychologically, it might have been salutary to have rapped the Iraqis on the knuckles at their first transgression."

57. *Washington Post*, March 27, 1991, cited in Andrew and Patrick Cockburn, *Out of the Ashes*, 40.

58. Randal, 93–95.

59. Randal, 98.

60. Former French ambassador Eric Rouleau wryly observed, "The Americans indeed wanted Saddam Hussein to be replaced, but by them, in order to control the country. What good is it to have made a war if you leave the power with people that you don't know?" Rouleau interview with author, Paris, April 20, 2004.

61. Andrew and Patrick Cockburn, *Out of the Ashes*, 40–41.

62. Joseph Fitchett, *International Herald Tribune*, March 17, 1991, cited in Randal, 101.

63. *Washington Post*, March 29, 1991, cited in Andrew and Patrick Cockburn, *Out of the Ashes*, 41.

64. Devroy and Moore, *International Herald Tribune*, April 15, 1991, cited in Randal, 99.

65. When the Shiite rebel leaders were told that they would not be supported, one asked the Saudi prince who had informed him, "Why are you so worried about the Shiites?" "We can't do anything to help you," replied the Prince. "The Americans don't want to remove Saddam. They say 'Saddam is under control. This is better than somebody we don't know about. We are worried about Iran.'" Quoted in Andrew and Patrick Cockburn, *Out of the Ashes*, 41.

66. Randal, 99.

67. Galbraith interview with author.

68. "Saddam Next?" *Air Forces Monthly*, May 2002, 20, cited in Milan Rai, *War Plan Iraq* (London: Verso, 2002), 79.

69. Andrew and Patrick Cockburn, *Out of the Ashes*, 41.

70. *Newsweek*, April 15, 1991, cited in Mackey, 350.

71. Independent Television News, April 4, 1991, cited in John Pilger, *The New Rulers of the World* (London: Verso, 2003), 80.

72. Galbraith interview.

73. Andrew and Patrick Cockburn, *Out of the Ashes*, 42.

74. Amnesty International, "Iraq: Human Rights Violations Since the Uprising. July 1991." AI Index MDE, May 14, 1991.

75. Jon Randal compares the calls for uprising and subsequent abandonment to the same tactics used by the Radio Free Europe—also financed by the CIA—in 1956 toward the Hungarians, whom they urged to rise up against their

Soviet-backed regime, then stood by as the revolt was brutally crushed by So-viet tanks. Randal, 33.

76. Milan Rai, *War Plan Iraq* (London:Verso, 2002), 81.

77. Thomas Pickering interview with author, Roslyn, Virginia, May 2004.

78. Amnesty International, "Iraq: Human Rights Violations Since the Uprising. July 1991."

79. Galbraith interview. There were many in the administration who felt that Bush Senior had betrayed the Iraqis, like James Aikens, who had served in Iraq and as the U.S. ambassador to Saudi Arabia. Once the U.S. decided to move, Aikens said, they should have aided the uprising. When I pointed out that President George H. W. Bush had claimed there was no U.N. mandate for going any further, Aikens replied, "The fact that there was not a U.N. mandate doesn't bother us usually. But we still could have gone into Basra under the existing mandate, but none of these things did we do. We betrayed the Iraqis and the Iraqis remembered that. They have no reason to trust us. They may still detest Saddam, but they are not going to look at the United States as their savior. The U.S. president today has the same name as the American president who betrayed them in their eyes. Bush is not a welcome name throughout all of southern Iraq." James Aikens interview with author.

80. Gordon and Trainor, 456.

81. Quoted by Associated Press, May 2, 1991; also Galbraith interview with author.

82. Galbraith interview with author.

83. AP report, May 2, 1991.

84. Gordon and Trainor, 457.

Chapter 8 : Embargo

1. President George H. W. Bush, April 16, 1991, White House Briefing, via http://www.presidency.ucsb.edu/ws/index.php?pid=19479.

2. In May 1991, White House spokesman Marlin Fitzwater also declared that "all possible sanctions will be maintained until he [Saddam Hussein] is gone." Prime Minister John Major sent the same message. Britain, he said, would veto any U.N. attempt to weaken sanctions against Iraq "for so long as Saddam Hussein remains in power." As the *Independent* wrote, "The Prime Minister's remarks caused little surprise at the U.N., where it has long been felt that the coalition allies were moving the goalposts to drive President Saddam from power. It has become clear that the sanctions put in place to force Iraq out of Kuwait are now being used to overthrow President Saddam. Mr. Major's

statement comes at a time of growing unease at the U.N. that the allies' hard line against the Iraqi leader is beginning to take a toll of hunger and disease among Iraq's civilian population."

3. Andrew and Patrick Cockburn, 95.

4. Geoff Simons, *The Scourging of Iraq* (London: Palgrave, 1998), 5.

5. Barton Gelman, "Allied Air War Struck Broadly in Iraq," *Washington Post*, June 23, 1991, A1.

6. Simons, 11.

7. Gelman, "Allied Air War," *Washington Post*.

8. Ibid.

9. Amy Kasslow, "Shifting Fortunes in the Arab World," *Christian Science Monitor*, June 26, 1991, 7, cited in Simons, 12.

10. "The War We Left Behind," WGBH *Frontline*, October 29, 1991.

11. Gelman, "Allied Air War," *Washington Post*.

12. Report from Martti Ahtisaari, U.N. undersecretary general for administration and management, to the U.N. secretary general, March 1991, quoted in Simons, 29.

13. Gelman, "Allied Air War," *Washington Post*.

14. Simons, 110.

15. Simons, 113–114.

16. Joy Gordon, "Cool War," *Harper's Magazine*, November 2002.

17. Ibid.

18. Ross B. Mirkarimi, "The Environmental and Human Health Impacts of the Gulf Region with Special Reference to Iraq," The Arms Control Research Center, San Francisco, now Arc Ecology, May 1992.

19. Simons, 172. The team from Harvard that had put out an alarming report in 1991 returned in 1996. The water purification plants, it warned, "are now operating at extremely limited capacity. . . . The sewage system has virtually ceased to function." It was estimated that one quarter of the children were suffering from malnutrition. It took an average two weeks' salary to buy a single chicken.

20. Colin Hughes, "U.S. Insists Iraq Cordon Is Not an Act of War," *The Independent*, London, August 14, 1990.

21. Simons, 115.

22. Ibid., 113–122.

23. By the summer of 1991, for instance, the Rustamiya sewage treatment plant just outside Baghdad, which served three million people, had been down for eight months. The plant was sending raw sewage—about fifteen million gallons per hour—directly into the Tigris. Meanwhile, in Baghdad's Amara

hospital, typhoid and infectious hepatitis were reaching epidemic proportions. The children's wards were overflowing.

24. "Iraq Water Treatment Vulnerabilities," via www.gulflink.osd.mil/ declassdocs/dia/19950901/950901_511rept_91.html+&hl=en. The Dia Document, one of several pertaining to the health situation in Iraq, was discovered by Thomas Nagy (see note 26) on a site maintained by the Pentagon for Gulf War veterans.

25. The DIA documents were circulated to the headquarters of American and British forces responsible for what would be forty days of devastating bombing and missiles attacks just getting underway.

26. Thomas Nagy, "The Secret Behind the Sanctions," *Progressive*, September 2001. http://www.progressive.org/0801issue/nagy0901.html.

27. It is actually dated February 21, 1990, but the year is a typographical error and should be 1991.

28. "Medical Problems in Iraq," dated March 15, 1991; "Status of Disease at Refugee Camps," dated May 1991, via www.gulflink.osd.mil/declassdocs/dia.

29. "Health Conditions in Iraq," June 1991, via www.gulflink.osd.mil/ declassdocs/dia.

30. United Nations Children's Fund (UNICEF), "Children and Women in Iraq: A Situation Analysis," March 1993.

31. "The Impact of War on Iraq," report to the secretary-general on humanitarian needs in Iraq in the immediate post-crisis environment by a mission to the area led by Mr. Martti Ahtisaari, undersecretary general for administration and management, United Nations, New York, March 20, 1991, cited in Simons, 30; see also *Frontline*, October 29, 1991.

32. Simons, 18.

33. Eric Hoskins, "The Truth Behind Economic Sanctions: A Report on the Embargo of Food and Medicines to Iraq," in Ramsey Clark et al., *War Crimes: A Report on United States War Crimes Against Iraq* (Washington, DC: Maisonneuve Press, 1992), 165.

34. Simons, 16, 61.

35. Report by Middle East Action Network (MEAN) team, following visits to children's hospitals in Baghdad, April 24, 1991, cited in Simon, 154.

36. Ibid.

37. *Frontline*, October 29, 1991.

38. Ibid.

39. Denis Halliday, interview by author in Brussels, March 17, 2004.

40. Andrew and Patrick Cockburn, *Out of the Ashes*, 115.

41. Ibid., 117.

42. Simons, 99–100.

43. *New York Times*, August 15, 1991; Simons, 100; *Frontline*, October 29, 1991.

44. Simons, 18.

45. Andrew and Patrick Cockburn, *Out of the Ashes*, 44.

46. Ibid., 95.

47. Ibid., 96.

48. *60 Minutes*, CBS, segment produced by the author, November 17, 1991.

49. Andrew and Patrick Cockburn, *Out of the Ashes*, 101.

50. Paragraph 22 of Security Council Resolution 687, April 3, 1991.

51. Simons, 55.

52. *New York Times* editorial, June 28, 1993. When brought to trial in Kuwait, the men accused of the plot recanted their earlier confessions and claimed they'd been tortured by the Kuwaitis. The claim that there were striking similarities between the mechanism of the bomb destined for President Bush and devices used by the Iraqis turned out to be false.

53. Seymour M. Hersh, "A Case Not Closed," *The New Yorker*, November 1, 1993.

54. Simons, 161.

55. Ibid., 111.

56. *London Times*, May 31, 1994.

57. Simons, 170.

58. Youssef M. Ibrahim, *New York Times*, October 25, 1994, A1.

59. *Harvard International Review* analysis, quoted by James Bovard. "Sanctions seem to have bolstered Saddam's domestic popularity. He uses the sanctions to demonize the West and to rally support for his leadership; they have been a convenient scapegoat for internal problems."

60. Denis Halliday interview with author, Brussels, March 17, 2004.

61. Ibrahim, *New York Times*, October 25, 1994, 1.

62. Cockburn, *Out of the Ashes*, 199.

63. In the buildup to the 2003 invasion, President George W. Bush would repeatedly cite Kamel's testimony, omitting the point that the programs he described had been discontinued and their products destroyed.

64. Ritter, 73.

65. Cockburn, 228; Jim Hoagland, "Saddam Prevailed," *Washington Post*, September 29, 1996.

66. Ritter, 54.

67. This was also reported by Barton Gellman in the *Washington Post*. See Gellman interview in "Spying on Saddam," *Frontline*, April 27, 1999.

68. Ritter, 154.

69. In fact, the CIA had been informed the operation was compromised, but decided to forge ahead nevertheless. Cockburn, 229.

70. Ritter, 167. As Iraq had also charged, Unscom was working closely with Israeli intelligence. The top inspectors provided transcripts of intercepts and highly classified U2 photographs gathered for Unscom's purposes, but which included specific details of Saddam Hussein's most sensitive installations and palaces—to be analyzed by Israeli photo interpreters in Tel Aviv. The Israelis in turn provided Unscom with sophisticated intercept equipment and intelligence for Unscom to act upon.

71. Ibid., 169. That wasn't the first time the U.S. administration attempted to manipulate the place and timing of Unscom inspections in order to create a confrontation that could be used as justification for direct military action. In 1992, with George H. W. Bush in power, Ritter was stunned, he said, on the eve of one particularly sensitive inspection to see a *New York Times* report that President Bush and National Security Advisor Brent Scowcroft had "approved a plan calling for demanding [sic] access to Iraq's ministry of military industrialization. . . . If Iraq officials barred access to the building, as they have already threatened to do, unidentified American officials say that American-based aircraft would swiftly bomb the ministry."

72. *International Herald Tribune*, "We had choked Saddam Hussein in the South," September 9, 1996.

73. Cockburn, *Out of the Ashes*, 244; *Washington Post*, September 20, 1996; Deutch's testimony. For all the machinations and at least a hundred million dollars spent by the CIA, the U.S. was unable to hit Saddam or any close family members. Ironically, the only moderately successful attack was brought off by a small clandestine group of dedicated Iraqis with no ties whatsoever to the CIA who managed to ambush Saddam's brutal son Uday in December 1996. Though hit by nine bullets, Uday survived.

74. Thomas Pickering, interview with author.

75. Simons, 217.

76. Ibid., 215. The U.S. government meanwhile seemed intent on making it as onerous as possible for NGOs and charities trying to alleviate the desperate situation. For instance, on January 2, 1996, the U.S. Treasury sent an official letter to the American NGO Voices in the Wilderness. The NGO, one of the most outspoken critics of sanctions, was planning to deliver anticancer

medications to Baghdad's Al Mansour Children's hospital. Treasury warned officers of the NGO that without a special license to export medical supplies and travel to Iraq they might face civil penalties up to $250,000 per violation and added, "Criminal penalties for violating the Regulations range up to 12 years in prison and $1 million in fines."

77. *60 Minutes*, CBS, May 12, 1996.

78. Simons, 233.

79. Hans Von Sponeck, interview with author, Brussels, March 17, 2004.

80. Cockburn, *Out of the Ashes*, 135.

81. Simons, 232. Another reason for the delays was international oil companies' skittishness; they were nervous about the impact that new Iraqi petroleum could have on the international market.

82. Denis Halliday interview; and Hans Von Sponeck interview.

83. Hersh, *Chain of Command*, 166.

84. Ritter, 271. As Ritter later recounted, Butler "made it clear that his instructions came directly from Clinton's national security advisor, Sandy Berger."

85. Ritter, 272.

86. Ibid., 277.

87. Rai, 47.

88. Ibid., 48.

89. Ibid., 49.

90. Richard Butler claimed that the inspectors had solid information that "dismantled missiles were being stored in wooden boxes hidden underground the Baath Party offices." According to Scott Ritter, Butler's claim was just a pretext to provoke another showdown. Ritter, 287.

91. The *Washington Post* reported that U.S. officials played "a direct role in shaping Butler's text during multiple conversations with him at secure facilities at the U.S. Mission to the United Nations." Cited in Rai, 53.

92. Rai, 53.

93. Ibid., 55.

94. William Arkin, *Washington Post*, January 17, 1999, cited in Rai, 55; Rai, 56.

95. Ibid.

96. Halliday, interview with author.

97. Joy Gordon, *Harper's* magazine; in addition, according to Hans Von Sponeck, huge amounts of supplies shipped to Iraq—many from supposedly reputable firms—were of such shoddy quality that they couldn't be used.

98. March 27, 2003, Blair–Bush joint press conference at the White House.

West Wing Connections, via http://merln.ndu.edu/merln/pfiraq/archive/wh/20030327-3.pdf.

99. Andrew S. Natsios, U.S. Agency for International Development administrator, released by the Office of the Spokesman, Washington, DC, March 25, 2003, via http://www.globalsecurity.org/wmd/library/news/iraq/2003/iraq-030325-19051pf.htm.

100. "President Bush Outlines Iraqi Threat, Remarks by the President on Iraq," Cincinnati Museum Center–Cincinnati Union Termina, Cincinnati, Ohio, White House press release, October 7, 2002, via http://www.whitehouse.gov/news/releases/2002/10/20021007-8.html.

101. Joy Gordon, "Iraq: The Real Sanctions Scandal," *Le Monde Diplomatique*, February 2005.

102. Though the Volcker Committee faulted the U.N. for failing to properly audit the Oil for Food program, they also pointed out that the fault lay—once again—with the U.S.-controlled Security Council, which, though warned about the rampant fraud, was never willing to provide the funds necessary for proper oversight. Ibid.

103. Von Sponeck interview. Von Sponeck says he attempted to inform the Security Council on several occasions, not only about the sanctions but also the devastation being caused by U.S. and British bombing raids in the self declared no-fly zones in southern Iraq after Desert Fox.

104. Joy Gordon, "Cool War," *Harper's* magazine.

105. Ibid.

106. Ibid.

107. Columbia University professor Richard Garfield, an epidemiologist and an expert on the effects of sanctions, cited in James Bovard.

108. Geneva Protocols 1, article 54.

109. "Public Health in Iraq After the Gulf War," Harvard study team report, May 1991, quoted in Simons, 18–19. Because of the huge outflow of educated professionals over the past few years—which continues to this day—as of April 2006 there was one child psychiatrist for the entire country.

Chapter 9 : The Noble Lie

1. "President Says Saddam Hussein Must Leave Iraq Within 48 Hours: Remarks by the President in Address to the Nation," White House Press Office Release, March 17, 2003, via http://www.whitehouse.gov/news/releases/2003/03/20030317-7.html.

2. Dilip Hiro, *Secrets and Lies* (London: Politico's, 2004), 6–7.

3. "A Clean Break: A New Strategy for Securing the Realm," via http://www.israeleconomy.org/strat1.htm.

4. Ibid.; also George Packer, *The Assassin's Gate* (New York: Farrar, Straus and Giroux, 2005), 20.

5. "A Clean Break" (see note 3).

6. Project for New American Century. Documents via http://www.newamericancentury.org/AttackIraq-Nov16,98.pdf and http://newamerican-century.org/RebuildingAmericasDefenses.pdf.

7. Packer, 24–27.

8. Russ Baker, "War on My Mind," Guerrilla News Network, October 27, 2004, via http://www.gnn.tv/articles/article.php?id=761.

9. Packer, 45.

10. Colin Powell news conference, February 21, Cairo, Egypt.

11. Bob Woodward, *Plan of Attack* (New York: Simon & Schuster, 2004), 12.

12. Interviewed on *60 Minutes*, CBS News, January 11, 2004.

13. Richard Clarke, *Against All Enemies*, 30–31; Woodward, *Plan of Attack*, 25.

14. Clarke, 32.

15. Michael Gordon and Bernard E. Trainor, *Cobra II* (New York: Pantheon, 2006), 14.

16. Clark, 243–244.

17. Woodward, *Plan of Attack*, 1.

18. As one American diplomat in the Middle East was quoted by *Newsweek*, "The question is not if the United States is going to hit Iraq; the question is when." December 31, 2001, 24.

19. Despite the flurry provoked by that speech, the president continued to deny he was planning to attack Saddam. In February 2002, however, he ordered General Franks to commence a secret but massive military build up in the Gulf. The next month, as Condoleezza Rice was meeting with three senators, President Bush poked his head into her office to interject, "Fuck Saddam. We're taking him out!" In June 2002 Rice advised a State Department official who was cautioning against going to war in Iraq, "Save your breath. The president has already made up his mind." Packard, 45.

20. Woodward, *Plan of Attack*, 132.

21. Ibid., 139.

22. Hersh, 219.

23. Packer, 61.

24. "Secret Downing Street Memo, From: Matthew Rycroft, Date: 23 July 2002," London, *Sunday Times*, May 1, 2005, via http://www.timesonline.co.uk/article/0,,2087-1593607,00.html.

25. Karen Kistiakowski, interview by phone with author, April 12, 2004. Kistiakowski is now a retired Air Force officer who served in the Pentagon's Near East and South Asia (NESA) unit nearby Shulsky's office. She was also shocked by the constant parade of Israeli officials who were given access to what were usually top secret areas of the Pentagon.

26. Woodward, *Plan of Attack*, 168.

27. Ibid., 164.

28. Ibid., 175.

29. Ibid., 186.

30. Ibid., 188. CIA analysts, however, were skeptical of the Israeli reports, knowing they had strong biases about the Arab world. CIA officials discounted or contradicted much of the Israeli information, which infuriated Wolfowitz and other neocons in the administration.

31. Parry, ConsortiumNews.com; and Woodward, 189. One exception was former vice president Al Gore, who delivered a tough-minded broadside against the Bush Doctrine. "I am deeply concerned that the course of action that we are presently embarking upon with respect to Iraq has the potential to seriously damage our ability to win the war against terrorism and to weaken our ability to lead the world in this new century," Gore said on September 23, 2002. *Sunday Times*, January 26, 2003, 1.

32. Woodward, *Plan of Attack*, 189.

33. *New York Times*, September 8, 2002, 1.

34. Fox News, September 8, 2002.

35. Ibid.

36. On September 12, 2002, President Bush himself, in a speech to the U.N. General Assembly, said that "Iraq has made several attempts to buy high-strength aluminum tubes used to enrich uranium for a nuclear weapon"—evidence, he added, of its "continued appetite" for such a weapon. Quoted in Joby Warrick, "U.S. Claim on Iraqi Nuclear Program Is Called Into Question," *Washington Post*, January 24, 2003, A1.

37. *USA Today*, July 31, 2003.

38. John B. Judis and Spencer Ackerman, "The Selling of the Iraq War," *The New Republic*, June 30, 2003.

39. Hersh, 303.

40. James Risen, *State of War* (New York: Free Press, 2006), 89–91. As one

scientist told his sister, "We don't have the resources to make anything anymore. We don't even have enough spare parts for our conventional military. We can't even shoot down an airplane. We don't have anything left. If the sanctions are ever lifted, then Saddam is certain to restart the programs. But there is nothing now."

41. Judis and Ackerman.

42. David Sirota and Christy Harvey, "In These Times," August 3, 2004: In February 2001, the CIA delivered a report to the White House that said: "We do not have any direct evidence that Iraq has used the period since Desert Fox to reconstitute its weapons of mass destruction programs." The report was so definitive that Secretary of State Colin Powell said in a subsequent press conference, Saddam Hussein "has not developed any significant capability with respect to weapons of mass destruction."

43. Woodward, *Plan of Attack*, 194.

44. http://www.whitehouse.gov/news/releases/2002/09/20020925-1.html. On the same day, Condoleezza Rice insisted, "There clearly are contacts between Al-Qaeda and Iraq."

45. Arianna Huffington, "Osama Who?," September 30, 2002, available at http://www.commondreams.org/views02/1001-08.htm.

46. Judis and Ackerman.

47. "We ran down literally hundreds of thousands of leads and checked every record we could get our hands on, from flight reservations to car rentals to bank accounts," but found nothing, said Mueller. In September 2002, the CIA delivered a classified report to Cheney that also cast serious doubt that the Atta meeting ever took place. The intelligence services of American allies in Europe were also very skeptical of the alleged Iraq-Al-Qaeda connection. Ibid.

48. Ibid. The influential neocon chairman of the powerful Defense Policy Board, Richard Perle, declared that "the [Prague] meeting was one of the motives for an American attack on Iraq."

49. According to Judis and Ackerman in the *New Republic*, "Richard Perle and other members of the Defense Policy Board, who acted as quasi-independent surrogates for Wolfowitz, Cheney, and other administration advocates for war in Iraq, harshly criticized the CIA in the press. The CIA's analysis of Iraq, Perle said, 'isn't worth the paper it is written on.'"

50. Ibid.

51. Woodward, *Plan of Attack*, 199.

52. Ibid., 202.

53. Judis and Ackerman, *The New Republic*, wrote, "Specifically, the Air Force's National Air and Space Intelligence Center correctly showed the drones

in question were too heavy to be used to deploy chemical/biological-weapons" spray devices.

54. Risen, *State of War*, 28–29. According to James Risen, the prisoner, Ibn al-Shaykh al-Libi, had been secretly handed over by the Americans to the Egyptians for questioning in January 2002. The tactic, known as rendition, had become standard U.S. policy for prying information out of terrorists by entrusting them to other intelligence agencies less reluctant to use torture. But once back in U.S. custody, Libi claimed that his statements regarding Iraq's links with Al-Qaeda and training terrorists to use explosive and chemical weapons had been fabricated by him to avoid brutal treatment.

55. Judis and Ackerman.

56. Woodward, *Plan of Attack*, 203–204.

57. Dana Priest, "Report Says CIA Distorted Iraq Data," *Washington Post*, July 12, 2004, A1.

58. Priest, *Washington Post*. The public support Bush enjoyed might have disappeared, too, based as it was on the same misinformation. Indeed, according to a Gallup poll in November 2002, 59 percent of Americans favored an invasion; only 35 percent were against. In a December *Los Angeles Times* poll, Americans thought, by a 90 percent to 7 percent margin, that Saddam was "currently developing weapons of mass destruction." And, in an ABC/*Washington Post* poll, 81 percent thought Iraq posed a threat to the United States.

59. Though Vice President Cheney had argued against going to the U.N., Colin Powell convinced Bush that he would be in a much stronger position if he had the Security Council's backing. The British, who were eager to back the U.S., also insisted that they would have a much easier time with their own Parliament if there was also a new U.N. resolution, as did the Canadians.

60. The secret Downing Street memo, *London Sunday Times*.

61. Sir Jeremy Greenstock, the British ambassador to the U.N., put this position bluntly on November 8, the day Resolution 1441 was passed: "There is no 'automaticity' in this resolution. If there is a further Iraqi breach of its disarmament obligations, the matter will return to the Council for discussion as required. . . . We would expect the Security Council then to meet its responsibilities." Quoted in Mark Danner, "The Secret Way to War," *New York Review of Books*, June 9, 2005.

62. Woodward, *Plan of Attack*, 244.

63. Even the dean of hawks, Paul Wolfowitz, was privately admitting that evidence of Saddam's WMD was gossamer. "It's like the judge said about pornography," Wolfowitz told a group of NATO ambassadors, "I can't define it, but I will know it when I see it." Woodward, *Plan of Attack*, 245.

64. Ibid., 250.

65. On October 11, 2002, for instance, one unnamed intelligence official confided to the *Los Angeles Times*, "Analysts feel more politicized and more pushed than many of them can ever remember. . . . The guys at the Pentagon shrieked on issues such as the link between Iraq and Al-Qaeda. There has been a lot of pressure to write on this constantly and not to let it drop." Two days earlier, on October 9, in England, the *Guardian* ran a lengthy article charging that the case presented by President Bush against Saddam Hussein "relied on a slanted and sometimes entirely false reading of the available U.S. intelligence." "Officials in the CIA, FBI and energy department are being put under intense pressure to produce reports which back the administration's line." James Bamford, *A Pretext for War* (New York: Anchor, 2005), 336.

66. Andrew Gumbel, *Independent*, January 12, 2004.

67. Clark, 243–244.

68. Woodward, *Plan of Attack*, 379.

69. Arnow Regular, "Road map is a life saver for U.S., PM Abbas tells Hamas," *Ha'aretz* (Tel Aviv, Israel), June 24, 2003, 1.

70. Bamford, 334–336. Later, testifying before Congress, Vincent Cannistraro, who had headed the CIA's Counterterrorism Unit, stated that Cheney and Libby went to the CIA to push mid-level analysts to find support for the administration claims. They were particularly after proof that Saddam was trying to build a nuclear weapon. "They were looking for those selective pieces of intelligence that would support the policy," Cannistraro said.

71. Shaun Waterman, "9/11 Report: No Iraq Link to Al-Qaida," United Press International, July 23, 2003.

72. UPI, July 25, 2003.

73. Woodward, *Plan of Attack*, 290.

74. Ibid., 294.

75. There was no mention of the fact that—even if Saddam still possessed such weapons, which was extremely doubtful—U.S. intelligence agencies had long ago concluded that it was extremely unlikely the Iraqi dictator would ever use them against the United States.

76. Woodward, *Plan of Attack*, 294.

77. "Speculation, Fact Hard to Separate in Story of Iraq's 'Nuclear' Tubes," Bill Nichols and John Diamond; "Iraq-Niger Uranium Chronology," by Paul Kerr, Arms Control Association, August 11, 2003; "White House 'Lied About Saddam Threat,'" Julian Borger, *Guardian*, July 10, 2003.

78. Woodward, 292. Powell later told Bob Woodward that "it was a sepa-

rate little government that was out there—Wolfowitz, Libby, Feith and Feith's 'Gestapo office,'" as Powell privately called it.

79. Woodward, *Plan of Attack*, 251.

80. Risen, 116–119.

81. U.S. Secretary of State Colin Powell Addresses the U.N. Security Council, February 5, 2003, the White House via http://www.whitehouse.gov/news/releases/2003/02/20030205-1.html. On the same day Powell delivered his U.N. speech, British intelligence leaked a comprehensive report finding no substantial links between Iraq and Al-Qaeda. The BBC reported that British intelligence officials maintained "any fledgling relationship [between Iraq and Al-Qaeda] foundered due to mistrust and incompatible ideologies." Hubert Wetzel, "Doubts Mount on Powell's Evidence to UN," *Financial Times*, July 29, 2003.

82. *Guardian*, May 31, 2003, quoted in Dilip Hiro, *Secrets and Lies*, 135.

83. Quoted in Michael Massing, "Now They Tell Us," *New York Review of Books*, February 26, 2004.

84. Ibid.

85. The Knight Ridder's Washington bureau was one of the few major organizations to assign reporters the time and give them the space to dig into the story. On October 8, 2002, for instance, it published a vivid account of the rising discontent among national security officers. "While President Bush marshals congressional and international support for invading Iraq," the article began, "a growing number of military officers, intelligence professionals, and diplomats in his own government privately have deep misgivings about the administration's double-time march toward war." Michael Massing. CBS's *60 Minutes* also broadcast a report in December 2002 challenging the government's claims about the aluminum tubes.

86. Chris Dickey, interview with author, Paris, January 15, 2006.

87. Indeed, the Post's own ombudsman, Michael Getler, would complain that one prominent story relaying a White House claim that al-Qaeda had gotten hold of a nerve agent from Iraq was so obviously thin that it should never have been allowed on the front page. Michael Massing.

88. The media was particularly weak in covering the U.N. inspectors, who were now back in Iraq and increasingly skeptical of the claims that Saddam still represented a major threat to the world. Michael Massing.

89. Woodward, *Plan of Attack*, 17.

90. Hans Blix, *Disarming Iraq* (London: Bloomsbury, 2004), 228.

91. Author's interview with a top Canadian official who was close to the negotiations.

92. "So we lost any hope of coming up with the right wording," said the Canadian official. "The U.N. inspectors would probably have come in with a report saying the country is clean. By then also Chirac from France was convinced it was useless to try and improve any draft resolution, that the decision had already been made. Instead of trying to play a game with the U.S., he just said no. We found that it was becoming too much of an emotional issue with our neighbors," the Canadian official told me. It's not that the Canadians didn't think Saddam was capable of building a hidden arsenal of WMD, it was that the U.S. and the British had not proven their case.

Chapter 10 : Full Circle

1. John Steele, "Body Counts," *The Guardian*, May 28, 2003.

2. The figures on the Web site Iraq Body Count, http://www.iraqbody count.net, are conservative: their estimate requires at least two sources per casualty. They calculate civilian deaths as of October 1, 2006 to be between 43,000 and 49,000 people. A study published in the *Lancet* arrived at much higher numbers by extrapolating from a few, carefully studied regions; it concluded that more than 100,000 civilians had died by October 2004. See "Study Puts Iraqi Deaths of Civilians at 100,000," *International Herald Tribune*, October 29, 2004.

3. Dexter Filkins, "Chaos Undercuts Tack Pursued by U.S.," *New York Times*, August 6, 2006.

4. Iraqi Coalition Casualty Count, via http://icasualties.org/oif/Stats.aspx.

5. Nobel Prize-winning economist Joseph E. Stiglitz and Harvard lecturer Linda Bilmes, study cited in "Iraq War May Cost U.S. $2.6 Trillion," ABC News online, January 10, 2006.

6. Cited in Stiglitz and Bilmes study, ABC News online.

7. Michael Dobbs, "Halliburton Deals Greater than Thought," *Washington Post*, August 28, 2003.

8. David Barstow, "Security Companies: Shadow Soldiers in Iraq," *New York Times*, April 19, 2004.

9. Sabrina Tavernise and Qais Mizher, "Oil, Politics and Bloodshed Corrupt an Iraqi City," *New York Times*, June 13, 2006, 1.

10. According to John Pace, outgoing director of the human rights office at the U.N. Assistance Mission for Iraq, quoted in "Baghdad Official Who Exposed Executions Flees," *The Guardian*, March 2, 2006.

11. "Iraq Now Less Safe," *Courier News*, March 3, 2006, news.com.au, via http://www.thecouriermail.news.com.au/story/0,20797,18331125–954,00.html.

12. *Beyond Abu Ghraib: Detention and Torture in Iraq*, http://web.amnesty. org/library/index/engmde140012006, March 6, 2006.

13. Patrick Cockburn and Raymond Whitaker, "Iraq: The Reckoning," *The Independent*, March 12, 2006.

14. Iraq Index, Brookings Institute, via http://www.brookings.edu/iraqindex.

15. Cockburn and Whitaker.

16. "Gunmen Kill 8 in Iraqi Raid," *New York Times*, March 29, 2006, 1.

17. For an excellent study of this period see James Fallows, "Blind into Baghdad," *The Atlantic*, January/February 2004; also Gordon and Trainor, *Cobra II*; and Packer.

18. For the final report of several of the study groups see "Reports from the Future of Iraq Project," http://www.thememoryhole.org/state/future_of_iraq/. State Department officials had even foreseen the human rights abuses that would plague the occupation. In a February 7, 2003, memo to Undersecretary of State Paula Dobriansky, three senior department officials noted the U.S. Central Command's (CENTCOM) "focus on its primary military objectives and its reluctance to take on 'policing' roles," but warned that "a failure to address short-term public security and humanitarian assistance concerns could result in serious human rights abuses, which would undermine an otherwise successful military campaign, and our reputation internationally." The memo adds "We have raised these issues with top CENTCOM officials."

19. Fallows, *The Atlantic*; Gordon and Trainor, *Cobra II*, 26, 101–102.

20. Washington, DC, August 17, 2005. Newly declassified State Department documents show that government experts warned CENTCOM in early 2003 about "serious planning gaps for post-conflict public security and humanitarian assistance," well before Operation Iraqi Freedom began.

21. "Beyond the Call of Duty," *Time*, October 24, 2004.

22. Packer, 133.

23. Gordon and Trainor, *Cobra II*, 574–577.

24. Fallows, *The Atlantic*. On April 11, when asked why U.S. soldiers were not stopping the looting, Donald Rumsfeld said, "Freedom's untidy, and free people are free to make mistakes and commit crimes and do bad things. They're also free to live their lives and do wonderful things, and that's what's going to happen here."

25. Paul Bremer, *My Year in Iraq* (New York: Simon & Schuster, 2006), 13.

26. Pauline Jelinek, "Postwar Iraq Chaos Blamed on Poor Planning," Associated Press, February 27, 2006.

27. Packer, 243.

28. James Glanz, "Rebuilding of Iraqi Pipeline as Disaster Waiting to Happen," *New York Times*, April 25, 2006, 1.

29. See Gordon and Trainor, *Cobra II*, 55–74, for discussion of Saddam's views.

30. Ibid., 317–318.

31. Ibid., 483.

32. Ibid., 481–485.

33. Ibid., 479.

34. Packer, 219.

35. In April 2004, during a military briefing on the attempts of U.S. marines to retake Fallujah, the American military spokesman, Brigadier General Mark Kimmitt, said U.S. forces had no estimate of Iraqi casualties, but he described the campaign as "a clean war." When an Iraqi reporter said that Iraqis watching Arab television channels like Al Jazeera had the impression that "what is happening in Falluja is killing children," General Kimmitt replied, "Change the channel to a legitimate, authoritative, honest news station." Cited in "Washington Urges Media Freedom—But Not for Al Jazeera," Inter Press Service, May 26, 2004.

36. Bremer, 10.

37. Michael Moss and David Rohde, "Misjudgments Marred U.S. Plans for Iraqi Police," *New York Times*, May 21, 2006, A1.

38. Ibid.

39. Quoted in "The Real Story of the Insurgency," *The Nation*, March 3, 2005.

40. Warren P. Strobel and Jonathan S. Landay, "Intelligence Agencies Warned About Growing Local Insurgency in Late 2003," Knight Ridder newspapers, February 28, 2006.

41. Packer, 323.

42. Bremer, 354.

43. Tom Lasseter, "U.S. Military Airstrikes Significantly Increased in Iraq," Knight Ridder newspapers, March 14, 2006.

44. Beginning in June 2003, Amnesty International and other human rights organizations had briefed top American officials in Baghdad and Washington, including Condoleezza Rice and Colin Powell, giving them chapter and verse on specific cases of brutal punishments. Author's interview with Amnesty in Washington, May 8, 2004.

45. Seymour Hersh, *Chain of Command* (London: Penguin, 2004), 51. (For full study of this issue, see pages 1–72.)

46. Bremer, 358.

47. Matt Sherman, "Iraq's Little Armies," *New York Times*, March 9, 2006.

48. Edward Wong and Sabrina Tavernise, "Sectarian Bloodshed Reveals Strength of Iraq Militias," *New York Times*, February 24, 2006.

49. Iraq Index, Saban Centre for Middle East Policy, The Brookings Institute, via http://www.brookings.edu/iraqindex.

50. Patrick Cockburn, "Battle for Baghdad 'has already started,'" *The Independent*, March 25, 2006.

51. Wong and Tavernise.

52. Borzou Daraghi, "Radical Iraqi Cleric Expands His Reach," *Los Angeles Times*, March 13, 2006.

53. Ellen Knickmeyer, "Sectarian Violence Changes Face of Conflict for Iraqis," *Washington Post*, March 13, 2006, A1.

54. The Ministry of the Interior was not the only department to have its own security guards and police forces. Another unit, called the Facilities Protection Service, which guards pipelines and other infrastructures in Iraq, ballooned from 4,000 men in 2003 to more than 140,000, its forces—virtually independent gunslingers—spread among more than a dozen ministries.

55. Jeffrey Gettleman, "Shiite Vigilantes in Baghdad Beat and Kill 4 Men Accused of Attacks," *New York Times*, March 13, 2006.

56. Mahmoud al-Mashhadany, a senior official in the main Sunni political bloc, quoted in Wong and Tavernise.

57. Quoted by AndrewSullivan.com.

58. Ibid.

59. These new laws can be changed, but only with a two-thirds majority vote in the National Assembly, and with the approval of the prime minister, the president, and both vice presidents. The constitutional drafting committee has, in turn, left each of these laws in place.

60. Antonia Juhasz, "Bush's Economic Invasion of Iraq," *Los Angeles Times*, August 14, 2005.

61. Peter Spiegel, "Bush's Requests for Iraqi Base Funding Make Some Wary of Extended Stay," *Los Angeles Times*, March 24, 2006.

62. Dan Morgan and David B. Ottaway, "U.S. Drillers Eye Huge Petroleum Pool," *Washington Post*, September 15, 2002, A1.

63. Patrick Cockburn and Raymond Whitaker, "Iraq: The Reckoning," *The Independent*, May 12, 2006.

64. Daniel McGrory, "Baghdad Anger at Bush's Undiplomatic Palace," *The Times* of London, May 4, 2006; Leila Fadel, "Embassy? What Embassy? *Philadelphia Inquirer*, May 21, 2006.

65. Iraq Index, 46.

66. Ellen Knickmeyer, "In Haditha, Memories of a Massacre," *Washington Post*, May 27, 2006, A1.

67. "Investigations of U.S. Troops in Iraq," *International Herald Tribune*, June 2, 2006.

68. Richard A. Opell, Jr., "Iraq Assails U.S. for Strikes on Civilians," *New York Times*, June 2, 2006, A1.

69. Edward Wong, "Iraq Leader Warns U.S. to Stop Interfering," *New York Times*, March 30, 2006, A1.

70. Francis Fukuyama, "Neoconservatism has evolved into something I can no longer support," *The Guardian*, February 22, 2006.

71. Michael A. Fletcher, "Bush Sees Progress in Iraq," *Washington Post*, June 15, 2006, A23.

72. "Rumsfeld: Iraqis to Deal with Civil War," Associated Press, March 8, 2006.

73. White House Press Office, August 21, 1960, via http://www.whitehouse.gov/news/releases/2006/08/20060821.html.

BIBLIOGRAPHY

Books

Aburish, Said. *Saddam Hussein: The Politics of Revenge*. London: Bloomsbury, 2000.

Bamford, James. *A Pretext for War*. New York: Anchor, 2005.

Baram, Amatzia and Barry Rubin. *Iraq's Road to War*. New York: St. Martin's Press, 1993.

Blix, Hans. *Disarming Iraq*. London: Bloomsbury, 2004.

Blum, William. *Rogue State*. Monroe, ME: Common Courage Press, 2000.

Bremer, Paul. *My Year in Iraq*. New York: Simon & Schuster, 2006.

Bulloch, John and Harvey Morris. *Saddam's War*. London: Faber & Faber, 1991.

Catherwood, Christopher. *Winston's Folly: Imperialism and the Creation of Modern Iraq*. London: Constable, 2004.

Chatterjee, Pratap. *Iraq, Inc.: A Profitable Occupation*. New York: Seven Stories Press, 2004.

Chomsky, Noam. *Deterring Democracy*. Boston: South End Press, 1992.

Clark, Ramsey. *War Crimes: A Report on United States War Crimes Against Iraq*. Washington, DC: Maisonneuve Press, 1992.

Clarke, Richard A. *Against All Enemies*. New York: Free Press, 2004.

Cockburn, Andrew and Leslie Cockburn. *Dangerous Liaison: The Inside Story of the US–Israeli Covert Relationship*. New York: HarperCollins, 1991.

Cockburn, Andrew and Patrick Cockburn. *Out of the Ashes*. New York: HarperCollins, 1999.

Cockburn, Andrew and Patrick Cockburn. *Saddam Hussein: An American Obsession*. London: Verso, 2002.

Cohen, Roger and Claudio Gatti. *In the Eye of the Storm*. London: Bloomsbury, 1991.

Cooley, John. *An Alliance Against Babylon*. London: Pluto Press, 2005.

Coughlin, Con. *Saddam: The Secret Life*. London: Macmillan, 2002.

Diamond, Larry. *Squandered Victory*. New York: Times Books, 2005.

Eisendrath, Craig and Melvina Goodman. *Bush League Diplomacy*. New York: Prometheus Books, 2004.

Francona, Rick. *Ally to Adversary*. Annapolis, MD: Naval Institute Press, 1999.

Friedman, Alan. *Spider's Web*. London: Faber & Faber, 1993.

Gordon, Michael and General Bernard Trainor. *The Generals' War*. New York: Little, Brown, 1991.

Gordon, Michael and General Bernard Trainor. *Cobra II*. New York: Pantheon, 2006.

Graubard, Stephen. *Mr. Bush's War*. New York: Hill & Wang, 1992.

Halberstam, David. *War in a Time of Peace*. New York: Touchstone, 2002.

Hersh, Seymour. *The Samson Option*. London: Random House, 1991.

Hersh, Seymour. *Chain of Command*. London: Penguin, 2004.

Hiro, Dilip. *The Longest War: The Iran-Iraq Military Conflict*. New York: Routledge, 1991.

Hiro, Dilip. *Desert Shield to Desert Storm*. New York: Authors Choice Press, 2003.

Hiro, Dilip. *Iraq*. London: Granta Books, 2003.

Hiro, Dilip. *Secrets and Lies*. New York: Politico's, 2004.

Hoffmann, Stanley. *Gulliver Unbound*. Lanham: Rowman and Littlefield, 2004.

Human Rights Watch. *Endless Torment: The 1991 Uprising in Iraq and Its Aftermath*. New York: Human Rights Watch, 1992 via www.hrw.org/reports/1992/Iraq926.htm.

Human Rights Watch. *The Anfal Campaign in Iraqi Kurdistan: The Destruction of Koreme*. New York: Human Rights Watch, 1993.

Jentleson, Bruce W. *With Friends Like These*. New York: W. W. Norton, 1994.

Johnson, Richard Denis. *Propaganda Materials of the Persian Gulf War*. Salt Lake City, UT: Schiffer, 1995.

Kagan, Robert. *Of Paradise and Power*. New York: Knopf, 2003.

Klare, Michael T. *Resources Wars*. New York: Owl, 2001.

Knightley, Philip. *The First Casualty*. London: André Deutsch, 1975.

Laurent, Eric. *Tempête du désert*. Paris: Presse Pocket, 1991.

Leyendecker, Hans and Richard Rickemann. *Marchands de mort*. Paris: Olivier Orban, 2000.

Ludot, Emmanuel. *Saddam Hussein, présumé coupable*. Paris: Carnot, 2004.

MacArthur, John. *Second Front*. New York: Hill & Wang, 1992.

Mackey, Sandra. *The Reckoning: Iraq and the Legacy of Saddam Hussein*. New York: W. W. Norton, 2002.

Makiya, Kanan. *Republic of Fear*. Berkeley: University of California Press, 1989.

Packer, George. *The Assassins' Gate*. New York: Farrar, Straus and Giroux, 2005.

Parry, Robert. *Trick or Treason: The October Surprise Mystery*. New York: Sheridan Square Press, 1993.

Pelletiere, Stephen. *Iraq and the International Oil System*. Washington, DC: Maisonneuve Press, 2004.

Phillips, David. *Losing Iraq*. New York: Westview Press, 2005.

Phillips, Kevin. *American Dynasty*. London: Allen Lane, 2004.

Pilger, John. *The New Rulers of the World*. London: Verso, 2003.

Polk, William R. *Understanding Iraq*. New York: HarperCollins, 2005.

Pollack, Kenneth. *The Threatening Storm*. New York: Random House, 2002.

Power, Samantha. *A Problem from Hell: America and the Age of Genocide*. New York: Harper Perennial, 2003.

Rai, Milan. *War Plan Iraq*. London: Verso, 2002.

Randal, Jonathan. *After Such Knowledge, What Forgiveness*. New York: Farrar, Straus and Giroux, 1997.

Raviv, Dan and Yossi Melman. *Every Spy a Prince*. Boston: Houghton Mifflin, 1990.

Risen, James. *State of War*. New York: Free Press, 2006.

Ritter, Scott. *Guerre à l'Irak*. Paris: Le Serpent à Plumes, 2002.

Ritter, Scott. *Iraq Confidential*. Clevedon, U.K.: Tauris, 2005.

Salinger, Pierre and Eric Laurent. *Guerre du Golfe, le dossier secret*. Paris: Presspocket, 1991.

Salinger, Pierre and Eric Laurent. *Secret Dossier*. New York: Penguin, 1991.

Simon, Reeva Spector and Eleanor H. Tejirian. *The Creation of Iraq: 1914–1921*. New York: Columbia, 2004.

Simons, Geoff. *The Scourging of Iraq*. London: Palgrave, 1998.

Sluglett, Peter. *Britain in Iraq, 1914–1932*. London: Ithaca Press, 1976.

Sluglett, Peter and Marion Farouk-Sluglett. *Iraq Since 1958*. London: I. B. Tauris, 1990.

Thomas, Gordon. *Gideon's Spies*. New York: Thomas Dunne, 1999.

Timmerman, Kenneth. *The Death Lobby*. New York: Bantam Books, 1992.

Tripp, Charles. *A History of Iraq*. Cambridge, U.K.: Cambridge University Press, 2000.

Unger, Craig. *House of Bush, House of Saud*. New York: Scribner, 2004.

U.S. News. *Triumph Without Victory*. New York: Random House, 1992.

Viorst, Milton. *Sandcastles*. Syracuse: Syracuse University Press, 1994.

Whitney, Craig. *The WMD Mirage*. New York: Public Affairs, 2005.
Woodward, Bob. *Veil: The Secret War of the CIA, 1981–1987*. New York: Simon & Schuster, 1987.
Woodward, Bob. *The Commanders*. New York: Simon & Schuster, 2002.
Woodward, Bob. *Bush at War*. New York: Simon & Schuster, 2003.
Woodward, Bob. *Plan of Attack*. New York: Simon & Schuster, 2004.

Articles and Web Sites

Abd al-Jabba, Faleh. "Why the Uprisings?" *Middle East Report*, May–June 1992.
Amnesty International. "Iraq: Human Rights Violations Since the Uprising." July 1991. AI Index MDE 05/14/91.
Baker, Russ W. "Iraqgate." *Columbia Journalism Review*, March/April 1993.
Barstow, David. "Security Companies: Shadow Soldiers in Iraq." *New York Times*, April 19, 2004.
Cole, Juan. Informed Comment, via http://www.iuancole.com.
Danner, Mark. "The Secret Way to War." *New York Review of Books*, June 9, 2005.
Despratx, Michel and Barry Lando. "Iraq's Crimes and Collusions." *Le Monde Diplomatique*, November 2004.
Draper, Theodore H. "The True History of the Gulf War." *New York Review of Books*, January 30, 1992.
Emery, Michael. "How the U.S. Avoided Peace." *Village Voice*, March 5, 1991, 22–27.
Fadel, Leila. "Embassy? What Embassy?" *Philadelphia Inquirer*, May 21, 2006.
Fallows, James. "Blind into Baghdad." *The Atlantic*, January/February 2004.
Frontline, "The War We Left Behind." WGBH, October 29, 1991.
Frontline, "The Gulf War-Oral History," via www.pbs.org.
Fukuyama, Francis. "Neoconservatism has evolved into something I can no longer support." *The Guardian*, February 22, 2006.
Gettleman, Jeffrey. "Shiite Vigilantes in Baghdad Beat and Kill 4 Men Accused of Attacks." *New York Times*, March 13, 2006.
Glanz, James. "Rebuilding of Iraqi Pipeline as Disaster Waiting to Happen." *New York Times*, April 25, 2006, A1.
Gordon, Joy. "Cool War." *Harper's* magazine, November 2002, via http://www.gulflink.osd.mil/declassdocs/dia/19950901/950901_511rept_91.html+&hl=en.
Gordon, Joy. "Iraq: The Real Sanctions Scandal." *Le Monde Diplomatique*, February 2005.

Hamza, Khidhir. "Inside Saddam's Secret Nuclear Program." *Bulletin of the Atomic Scientists*, September/October 1998, 26–33.

Hersh, Seymour M. "A Case Not Closed." *The New Yorker*, November 1, 1993.

Hoakina, Eric. "The Truth Behind Economic Sanctions: A Report on the Embargo of Food and Medicines to Iraq." In *War Crimes: A Report on United States War Crimes Against Iraq*, edited by Ramsey Clark, et al., 165ff. Washington, DC: Maisonneuve Press, 1992.

Human Rights Watch. "Annual Report for 1988," via hrw.org.

Iraq Index, Saban Centre for Middle East Policy. The Brookings Institute, via http://www.brookings.edu/iraqindex.

Judis, John B. and Spencer Ackerman. "The Selling of the Iraq War: The First Casualty." *The New Republic*, June 30, 2003.

Juhasz, Antonia. "Bush's Economic Invasion of Iraq." *Los Angeles Times*, August 14, 2005.

Knickmeyer, Ellen. "In Haditha, Memories of a Massacre." *Washington Post*, May 27, 2006, A1.

Lando, Barry. "Imagining Saddam's Trial." Salon.com, December 16, 2003.

Lando, Barry. "A Biased Trial." *Le Monde*, October 17, 2005.

Lewis, Neil A. "Judge Scoffs at Defense of Bush on Iraq." *New York Times*, August 24, 1993.

Massing, Michael. "Now They Tell Us." *The New York Review of Books*, February 26, 2004.

McGrory, Daniel. "Baghdad Anger at Bush's Undiplomatic Palace." *The Times of London*, May 4, 2006.

Morgan, Dan and David B. Ottaway. "U.S. Drillers Eye Huge Petroleum Pool." *Washington Post*, September 12, 2002, A1.

Morris, Roger. "A Tyrant 40 Years in the Making." *New York Times* Op-Ed, March 14, 2003.

Moss, Michael and David Rohde. "Misjudgments Marred U.S. Plans for Iraqi Police." *New York Times*, May 21, 2006, A1.

Nagy, Thomas. "The Secret Behind the Sanctions." *The Progressive*, September 2001, via http://www.progressive.org/0801issue/nagy0901.html.

National Security Archives. "The Saddam Hussein Source Book, via http://www.gwu.edu/~nsarchiv/special/iraq/index.htm.

Opell, Richard A., Jr. "Iraq Assails U.S. for Strikes on Civilians." *New York Times*, June 2, 2006, A1.

Parry, Robert. "The Peace Feeler That Was." *The Nation*, April 15, 1991, 480–482.

Priest, Dana. "Report Says CIA Distorted Iraq Data." *Washington Post*, July 12, 2004, A1.

Quandt, William. "Lebanon, 1958, and Jordan, 1970." In *Force Without War*, edited by Barry Blechman and Stephen Kaplan. (Brookings Institution, 1978), 238.

Satia, Priya. "The Defense of Inhumanity: Air Control and the British Idea of Arabia." *The American Historical Review*, vol. III, no. 1, February 2006.

Schuler, Henry. "Congress Must Take a Hard Look at Iraq's Charges against Kuwait." *Los Angeles Times*, December 2, 1990.

Spiegel, Peter. "Bush's Requests for Iraqi Base Funding Make Some Wary of Extended Stay." *Los Angeles Times*, March 24, 2006.

Tolchin, Martin. "U.S. Is Criticized on Iraq Loan Case." *York Yimes*, October 6, 1992.

Viorst, Milton. "A Reporter At Large: After the Liberation." *The New Yorker*, September 30, 1991, 66ff.

Waas, Murray. "Who Lost Kuwait? How the Bush Administration Bungled Its Way to War in the Gulf." *The Village Voice*, January 22, 1991.

Waas, Murray and Craig Unger. "In the Loop: Bush's Secret Mission." *The New Yorker*, November 2, 1992.

Wong, Edward. "Iraq Leader Warns U.S. to Stop Interfering." *New York Times*, March 30, 2006, A1.

Wong, Edward and Sabrina Tavernise. "Sectarian Bloodshed Reveals Strength of Iraq Militias." *New York Times*, February 24, 2006, A1.

Woodward, Bob. "CIA Aiding Iraq in Gulf War." *The Washington Post*. December 15, 1986, 1.

Yaphet, Judith S. "The View from Basra." In Simon Tejirian, *The Creation of Iraq*. New York: Columbia University Press, 2003, 19–35.

Interviews (by author except where indicated)

Abramowitz, Morton. Washington, DC, May 15, 2004.

Aikens, James. Bowie, Maryland, May 13, 2004.

al-Suwaij, Zainab. Boston, May 5, 2004.

Arriaga, Alexandra. Washington, DC, May 5, 2004.

Bani Sadr, Abol Hassan. Paris, April 16, 2004.

Bassiouni, Cherif. Benton Harbour, Michigan, May 8, 2004.

Chalabi, Salem. Baghdad, May 25, 2004 (interviewed by Michel Despratx; transcript provided to the author).

Chevenement, Jean Pierre. Paris, April 18, 2004.

Dickey, Chris. Paris, January 15, 2006.

Dumas, Roland. Paris, April 20, 2004.

Eagleton, William. Paris, January 9, 2006.

Francona, Rick. Secaucus, New Jersey, May 17, 2004.

Galbraith, Peter. Washington, DC, May 16, 2004.

Gonzalez, Rocky. Sierra Vista, Arizona, May 10, 2004.

Gordon, Michael. Washington, DC, May 13, 2004.

Halliday, Denis. Brussels, March 17, 2004.

Hamilton, Lee. Washington, DC, May 13, 2004.

Hatef, Abdallah. Baghdad, May 25, 2005 (interviewed by Michel Despratx; transcript provided to the author).

Heller, Jean. By phone, April 12, 2004.

Howell, Nathaniel. By phone, January 9, 2006.

Kwiatkowski, Lt. Col. Karen. By phone, April 16, 2004.

Mack, David. By phone, May 11, 2004.

McGovern, Ray. By phone, April 14, 2004.

Milhollin, Gary. Washington, DC, May 14, 2004.

Pickering, Thomas. Roslyn, Virginia, May 12, 2004.

Pope, Larry. Paris, November 20, 2005.

Ritter, Scott. By phone, April 12, 2004.

Rouleau, Eric. Paris, April 12, 2004.

Sale, Richard. Stamford, Connecticut, May 16, 2004.

Sick, Gary. By phone, April 10, 2004.

Sluglett, Peter. By phone and e-mail, May–June, 2006.

Trento, Joe. Washington, DC, May 12, 2004.

Von Sponeck, Hans. Brussels, March 17, 2004.

Zimmerman, Peter. By phone, April 12, 2004.

INDEX